THE ELECTRICAL MANUFACTURERS

1875-1900

STUDIES IN ENTREPRENEURIAL HISTORY

Published in coöperation with the
Research Center in Entrepreneurial History
Harvard University

The Electrical Manufacturers

1875-1900

A Study in Competition, Entrepreneurship, Technical Change, and Economic Growth

By HAROLD C. PASSER

HARVARD UNIVERSITY PRESS · CAMBRIDGE · 1953

Distributed in Great Britain by
Geoffrey Cumberlege
Oxford University Press
London

Library of Congress Catalog Card Number 52–10754

Printed in the United States of America

To My Loved Ones

Foreword

UNHAPPILY, Professor Joseph A. Schumpeter did not live to see this volume and — as I had hoped — to write this foreword. He would have enjoyed every page of this study, and he would have given here an interpretation such as he alone could compound. As a senior member of the Research Center in Entrepreneurial History, he urged our attention upon the process of innovation, upon the "creative response" of entrepreneurs to the situations with which they found themselves confronted. And the potency of Professor Schumpeter's influence is reflected in the title of the Center's first publication, *Change and the Entrepreneur.*

Here in his examination of the burgeoning electrical manufacturing industry, Professor Passer is engaged in a study of "change and the entrepreneur." And his "entrepreneurs" represent important typical figures in the "change" in American economic life — the extraordinary industrial expansion in the United States over the past century and a half. These enterprisers were concerned with a novel development in our industrial life and with one in which technological knowledge played an outstanding role.

Sizable new industries have mushroomed on the American economic scene at intervals over the past hundred and fifty years. Yet we have known altogether too little about their advents: what were the opportunities and the alternative possibilities of response; what sorts of men were the innovators; how did they go about introducing the novel products or services; what permanent impress have their actions and their modes of thought imparted upon the industries in which they were active; and the like. Too often economists and even economic historians have written as if industries arose like trees in a virgin forest; too often they have neglected the choices that had to be made and seen how these choices were conditioned by the surrounding economy and society.

Again, economists such as Professors Schumpeter, A. P. Usher, and W. R. Maclaurin have been interested in the process by which inventions and scientific knowledge became embodied in business operations. Here, in the case of the electrical manufacturing industry, Professor Passer has been able to record the various steps almost from the start: how technological competence was mingled with entrepreneurial ability, how courage and flexibility reaped rewards, even how training merely in business practices could gain a place equal with that based upon technological superiority. In many instances, new American industries have drawn heavily upon practices that had been initiated abroad. In this case, with minor qualifications, it appears that Europe's major contribution was limited to basic research. Electricity became business in this country, with American entrepreneurs leading the way.

Professor Passer was unusually well equipped to deal with this study. Trained both in economics and in the physics of his subject, and interested in the entrepreneurial point of view, he has been able to give a fresh cast to an important segment of industrial history. We are asked to consider personality, company, and market factors as well as technology; we are encouraged to note the significance of cumulative decision-making upon the evolution of the new industry; and, before the end, we are directed to observe the influence of entrepreneurial rivalry upon company policy. Professor Passer has done well in elaborating the history of a dynamic, major American industry and examining the part played by entrepreneurs in that history during its formative years.

Arthur H. Cole

Preface

THE late Professor Joseph A. Schumpeter had a particular interest in forces that brought major changes in the economy and an interest in the manner whereby technological innovations became effective in business. Among such forces and innovations he frequently cited the electrical industry as provoking change in the late nineteenth and the twentieth centuries. Then in World War II, electronics came to the fore, and many young men were given instruction in that area of physics that embraces electricity.

These two factors account in large measure for the ensuing study. As a student at Harvard, I was fortunate to have had frequent contacts with Professor Schumpeter; and, as an electronics specialist in the United States Navy, I was able to add to my knowledge of electricity.

This study is not a technical history nor is it an economic history in the traditional sense. Technical descriptions are, of course, included because they are essential to an understanding of the industry. Similarly, the sequence of events and the passage of time is not lost sight of. But the study is made primarily from the analytical point of view. Four problems serve to focus the material and have received major attention: entrepreneurship, competition, technical change, and economic growth.

The term "electrical manufacturing industry," as used in this study, applies only to the manufacture of electrical apparatus for lighting and power purposes. The telegraph, the telephone, electric signaling devices, and the phonograph are not discussed. Electric heating and electrochemical apparatus are not entirely omitted, but they receive neither a systematic nor a complete treatment.

The period covered is the two and a half decades from 1875, when important activity in arc lighting was first beginning, to 1900, arbitrarily chosen as a terminal date because, by that time, the pattern of development in the industry had been pretty well determined. The number of large, full-line producers, the kinds of products, the interfirm relations, and the character of technical change were not altered appreciably in the following decades. Perhaps the rise of Allis-Chalmers, the expansion into home appliances, and the decline of street railways could not have been foreseen. But in general it is true that the industry grew and developed in the twentieth century mainly in directions which could have been predicted in 1900.

A further consideration fixing the terminal date was the matter of company records. The reluctance of the two leading firms in the industry to release current material, for competitive and other reasons, meant that, if internal documents were to be used, a relatively early period had to be chosen. The existence in the General Electric historical files of a considerable amount of correspondence, circular letters, reports, and price data relating to the 1890's was decisive in the final choice. Study of such source material is imperative if economists are to increase their knowledge of business practices and policies beyond that based on the information made public by infrequent and isolated antitrust suits and the activities of the Federal Trade Commission. Undoubtedly economics has made less progress in the past seventy years than, say, electrical engineering, and one of the reasons has been the lack of contact between economists and business firms. One way to improve that contact, and one objective of this study, is to analyze business records in the light of current economic doctrines.

The area covered has been restricted to the United States, because the American electrical manufacturing industry was in advance of that of any other nation in the world except Germany. Most of the important electrical firms in England, for example, were founded by American or German companies. The development of the industry in Germany roughly paralleled that in the United States, although in particular products one led the other. Primarily because of the vast home market, the American industry did not engage in an appreciable export trade until after 1900. Some American firms, however, established branch plants abroad quite early. Almost no electrical apparatus was imported, because only Germany was able to compete in the market and because the tariff on machinery was high. The German firm Siemens and Halske established a branch plant in Chicago in 1892, with a German staff and working force. This plant was the only foreign one of any importance before 1900 and, for a time, achieved success in the sale of lighting equipment to breweries and other firms operated by German-born businessmen. It later went into power equipment, but was purchased in 1900 by General Electric. Contacts with other nations were thus not completely lacking in the American electrical manufacturing industry, but these foreign relationships can be safely neglected because their influence on American development was small.

The order of the material in each of the three parts of this study — arc lighting, incandescent lighting, and electric power — is similar. Each part begins with a brief description of the technical development of the equipment and the potential market for it that existed at the time of its commercial introduction. Then the various engineer-entrepreneurs and their activities are discussed. Where possible, entrepreneurs who failed, as well as those who succeeded, are included. Next, the growth and expansion of the firms which these entrepreneurs founded is outlined. From the individual firms, the transition is made to relations between firms, including competition, patents, and the resulting mergers and consolidations. The conclusion, which follows the three main parts, summarizes the study and states the findings.

The material on which this study is based derives from a number of sources. One major source has been the two leading firms in the industry, General Electric and Westinghouse. Each company maintains historical files (General Electric in Schenectady, New York; Westinghouse in East Pittsburgh, Pennsylvania) which contain company documents, correspondence, contracts, publications, and so forth. This material was made freely available to me. A second major source was the general literature of the industry. I chose the *Electrical World* as the most accurate, most complete, and most authentic periodical of those which were exclusively devoted to the electrical industry. Consequently, I read it completely, every issue of every volume, from the first volume in 1883 until after 1900. Numerous other engineering and scientific journals were consulted in Harvard's Widener Library and in Princeton's Firestone Library. Other libraries which furnished material for this study are Baker Library of the Harvard Graduate School of Business Administration, Houghton Library of Harvard University, the Engineering Societies Library of New York City, and the New York Public Library.

My greatest debt is due Professor Arthur H. Cole. He has read the several drafts with great care; he has contributed numerous suggestions; and he has helped most generously at every stage in the preparation, writing, and publication of this volume. My participation in Harvard University's Research Center in Entrepreneurial History, which Professor Cole has directed since its formation in 1948, was also extremely valuable. The Center's first two years were the period when my ideas on the electrical industry were taking shape.

I also wish to acknowledge a heavy debt to Dr. Philip D. Bradley, Jr., of Washington, D.C. First as my tutor in Harvard College and later as a colleague in the Harvard Economics Department and a fellow associate of Leverett House, he advised me and aided me in ways too numerous to mention. His stimulating ideas and his penetrating and original approach to economic problems are reflected throughout this entire volume.

I also wish to thank Professor E. C. Kirkland of Bowdoin College and Professor L. H. Jenks of Wellesley College for reading an earlier draft very carefully and for making many helpful comments. Professor E. S. Mason, who directed the dissertation which underlies this study, Professor J. K. Galbraith, and Professor A. P. Usher, all of Harvard, also suggested improvements. Dr. Nancy Norton of the Harvard Graduate School of Business Administraiton called my attention to Charles Flint and his promotional activities in the electrical industry.

I have enjoyed financial support from a number of sources. I was awarded an Economic History Fellowship for the years 1948–1950 by the Committee on Economic History of the Social Science Research Council. Princeton University granted funds for typing the final manuscript. The Research Center in Entrepreneurial History has made publication possible.

I wish to thank Mr. W. W. Trench and Mr. Guy Bartlett of General Electric and Mr. J. A. Baubie and Miss Mildred McDonald of Westinghouse for complete and cordial coöperation. To Mr. Charles Edison, executor of the estate of Thomas A. Edison, I am indebted for permission to use quotations from certain of his father's documents now in the Henry Villard collection at Houghton Library, Harvard University. I also am grateful for generous assistance from the staff of the Harvard University Press. Miss Elizabeth Treeman and Mr. J. D. Elder were especially helpful. Thanks are due Miss Florence Armstrong of the Electrical Engineering Department of Princeton University who typed the final manuscript with unusual skill and accuracy.

Finally, let me express a deep appreciation for the part played by my wife. She encouraged me during the long and tedious months that I spent in research and writing. She further helped by preparing much of the statistical material and by suggesting improvements in a number of the chapters.

Harold C. Passer

Princeton, New Jersey
June 1952

CONTENTS

Introduction 1
THE AMERICAN ECONOMY, 1875–1900

Part I. Arc Lighting

I. The Setting 11
II. The Rise of Leading Firms 14
THE BRUSH ELECTRIC COMPANY · THE THOMSON-HOUSTON ELECTRIC COMPANY · THE WESTON ELECTRIC LIGHT COMPANY · THE AMERICAN ELECTRIC AND ILLUMINATING COMPANY
III. Interfirm Relations 41
PATENTS · COMPETITION IN THE ARC-LIGHTING-EQUIPMENT INDUSTRY · THE EXPANSION OF THE THOMSON-HOUSTON ELECTRIC COMPANY
IV. The Arc-Carbon Industry 58
V. The Dynamics of the Industry 63
TECHNICAL CHANGE IN ARC-LIGHTING EQUIPMENT · ENTREPRENEURSHIP IN THE MANUFACTURE OF ARC-LIGHTING EQUIPMENT · THE GROWTH OF ARC LIGHTING, 1880–1900

Part II. Incandescent Lighting

VI. The Setting 75
VII. The Edison System 78
VIII. Marketing the Edison System 105
THE INCANDESCENT LAMP · ISOLATED-LIGHTING PLANTS · CENTRAL STATIONS · MARKET CONDITIONS AND MARKETING POLICIES
IX. The Westinghouse Electric Company 129
THE WESTINGHOUSE SYSTEM OF INCANDESCENT-ELECTRIC LIGHTING · THE EXPANSION OF WESTINGHOUSE

X. Interfirm Relations 151
PATENTS · ALTERNATING CURRENT VS. DIRECT CURRENT

XI. Entrepreneurship 176
THE FIRST PIONEER INNOVATOR · THE SECOND PIONEER INNOVATOR · THE IMITATIVE ENTREPRENEURS · PERSONAL QUALITIES OF THE ENTREPRENEUR

XII. The Impact on the Gas Industry 195

XIII. The Dynamics of the Industry 204
TECHNICAL CHANGE IN INCANDESCENT-LIGHTING EQUIPMENT · THE GROWTH OF INCANDESCENT LIGHTING, 1880–1900

Part III. Electric Power

XIV. The Setting 211

XV. Electric Traction 216
THE PROBLEM OF ELECTRIC TRACTION · UNSUCCESSFUL ENTREPRENEURS IN ELECTRIC TRACTION: THOMAS A. EDISON; E. JULIEN; BENTLEY AND KNIGHT; CHARLES J. VAN DEPOELE

XVI. The Pioneer Innovators in Electric Traction 237
FRANK JULIAN SPRAGUE · THE THOMSON-HOUSTON ELECTRIC COMPANY

XVII. The Electric-Railway-Equipment Business 256
WESTINGHOUSE ENTERS THE FIELD · COMPETITION IN RAILWAY MOTORS · ELECTRIFICATION OF THE ELEVATED RAILWAYS

XVIII. Alternating Current 276
THE EARLY WORK OF WESTINGHOUSE · ELECTRIC POWER AT NIAGARA FALLS

XIX. The Alternating-Current-Equipment Business 296
APPLICATIONS OF POLYPHASE POWER · THE TRANSMISSION OF POLYPHASE POWER · THE GENERATION OF POLYPHASE POWER · STANDARDIZATION OF THE A.C.-SYSTEM CONSTANTS · PRODUCT COMPETITION AND THE PERFECTION OF KNOWLEDGE

XX. Interfirm Relations 321
THE FORMATION OF GENERAL ELECTRIC · PATENTS

XXI. The Dynamics of the Industry 335

TECHNICAL CHANGE IN ELECTRIC-POWER EQUIPMENT · ENTREPRENEURSHIP IN THE MANUFACTURE OF ELECTRIC-POWER EQUIPMENT · THE GROWTH OF ELECTRIC POWER, 1880–1900

Conclusion 349

COMPETITION · ENTREPRENEURSHIP · TECHNICAL CHANGE · ECONOMIC GROWTH · SUGGESTIONS FOR PUBLIC POLICY

NOTES 369

BIBLIOGRAPHY 391

INDEX 401

TABLES

1. Growth of the Thomson-Houston Electric Company 30
2. Efficiency of the Weston and Thomson-Houston arc-lighting systems 33
3. Asset data of the American Electric and Illuminating Company 35
4. Comparison of American and Thomson-Houston (1886 data) 39
5. Street lighting: the gas light vs. the arc light 49
6. Financial data on Thomson-Houston acquisitions, 1888–1889 55
7. Arc-carbon consumption and arc lights in service, 1886–1902 65
8. Price trends in arc-lighting equipment, 1878–1900 67
9. Arc lights in service in the United States, 1881–1902 70
10. Financial data of the Edison Electric Light Company, October 15, 1878 — September 30, 1886 87
11. Edison Lamp Company: cost and revenue data 95
12. Formation of the Edison General Electric Company 103
13. Results of the 1885 incandescent-lamp tests conducted by the Franklin Institute 111
14. Edison isolated-plant installations, May 1880 — September 1885 114
15. Growth in Edison isolated plants, 1881–1888 117
16. Growth in Edison central stations, 1884–1888 121
17. Growth of Westinghouse, 1886–1899 149
18. Growth of Westinghouse central stations, 1886–1893 149
19. Comparison of the three leading firms in the electrical manufacturing industry, 1891 150
20. Price of gas in American cities, 1878–1888 197
21. Manufactured gas in the United States, 1880–1931 199
22. Growth of the manufactured-gas industry in the United States, 1849–1909 202
23. Summary of four early attempts to develop an electric railway 235
24. Griffin's street-railway data, 1888 254
25. Electric streetcars in the United States, 1888–1892 254

26. Sales of GE-800 motors, 1893–1900 265
27. General Electric railway motors 268
28. Effect of the Sprague electrification on the earnings of the South Side Elevated Railway 274
29. Speed, frequency, and field-pole relations in alternating-current generators and motors 280
30. Induction-motor prices, August 24, 1897 300
31. Polyphase-generator sales, 1893–1897 307
32. Comparison of engine-type and turbine-type alternating-current generators 312
33. Induction-motor speeds 317
34. Previous affiliation and status of the directors, officers, and executives of General Electric 323
35. Street railways in the United States, 1880–1902 341
36. Motive power of street railways in the United States, 1890–1902 342
37. Determinants of competition in the electrical manufacturing industry 350

TABLES IN NOTES

A. The electric-lights industry (as reported in the 1880 census) 371
B. Comparison of 1880 data on the electric-lights industry with other census data. 372

Diagrams

1. Series and parallel lighting circuits 81
2. The transformer network 134
3. The dynamo-lamp network 179

Illustrations

1. Brush single-carbon arc lamp, 1882 (from James Dredge, ed., *Electric Illumination*, 2 vols., New York, 1882, I, 423) 18

2. Brush double-carbon arc lamp, with glass globe removed, 1882 (from Dredge, I, 423) 18

3. Brush arc-lighting dynamo, 1882 (from Dredge, I, 206) 18

4. Edison incandescent-lighting dynamo, 1881 (from Silvanus P. Thompson, *Dynamo-Electric Machinery*, 4th ed., New York, 1892, p. 514) 19

5. Edison incandescent lamp, 1881 (from *Electrical World*, XXI, 315, April 29, 1893) 19

6. Edison chemical meter, with lamp to keep electrolytic solution from freezing, 1882 (from Dredge, I, 619) 19

7. Westinghouse alternator, 1888 (from Thompson, p. 658) 140

8. Shallenberger a.c. meter, cover removed, 1888 (from *Electrical World*, XII, 149, September 15, 1888) 140

9. Tesla a.c. motor, 1888 (courtesy of the Westinghouse Electric Corporation, Pittsburgh, Pennsylvania) 141

10. Westinghouse induction motor, Type C, 1897 (courtesy of the Westinghouse Electric Corporation) 141

11. Westinghouse railway motor, No. 12, 1893 (courtesy of the Westinghouse Electric Corporation) 141

INTRODUCTION

Introduction

THE modern electrical manufacturing industry was born in the late 1870's. Its first product was arc-lighting equipment. A few years later incandescent-lighting equipment was added, and by 1890 a third product, electric-power apparatus, had begun to be important. The development of the industry thus proceeded in three stages. The arc-lighting systems were simple and elementary, the incandescent-lighting systems were more complicated, and the electric-power systems were the most complex of all. Because the firms in the industry tended to expand their product lines in this same sequence, the growth of individual firms also followed the threefold pattern.

An underlying assumption of this study is that the electrical manufacturing industry is like many others in that it was based on inventions and scientific advance and grew rapidly. The process of its development may thus be taken as representative of a pattern which has been repeated again and again as new industries, founded on new technologies, have come to be important in the economy.

A key person in this process is the engineer-entrepreneur, the person with technical training who can see commercial possibilities in the application of scientific principles and who labors to perfect usable products and techniques. This kind of entrepreneurship has become increasingly important as the advance of science has made available new knowledge, new products, new production methods, and new resources. For in the long view, the most significant manner in which to increase economic welfare is not through better administration of existing resources or change in the distribution of income but through applications of science which increase the national income.

The process of technical change — changes in products and productive methods — is itself worth examining. In this study, the emphasis is on the change which occurs as a result of market forces after the product or technique has reached the commercial stage. The technical developments immediately preceding commercialization and the contributions of the engineer-entrepreneur are of particular significance. Such contributions are the difference between invention and innovation. And technical change after the initial innovation must be analyzed if the development of the industry is to be understood. This technical change is clearly affected by market forces and cannot be taken as a datum by the economist.

The industry which is based on a new technology, which is founded by engineer-entrepreneurs, and which is affected in its development by continuing technical change is likely to be an industry where the competition between firms is different from that of other industries. This difference is caused by the technical complexity of the product and the fact that the product is continually changing. Product change then becomes the most important aspect of competition. The interaction between technical change in the product and market forces creates a new kind of competition which has not yet received much attention from economists. The theory of monopolistic competition includes product variation, and some additional theoretical work on that subject has been done. But a thorough empirical study of product competition has not been made, primarily because such a study of necessity must be based on contemporary, internal records of at least two firms. Although it is now accepted that the most usual industrial case, from a numbers standpoint, is oligopoly, it is not generally recognized that in these oligopolies, product competition may be more significant than price competition. Furthermore, where product competition is present, the nature of the price competition may be completely altered. The electrical industry is highly technical and oligopolistic in character. By an analysis of that industry, a better understanding may be reached of the segment of our economy which is characterized by product competition.

This emphasis on analysis does not mean that the process of evolution, which may be called nonrepetitive change, is lost sight of. For evolution is evident in the growth of the industry, the expansion of individual firms, and the product changes which took place. Nevertheless, it should be clear that evolution of the industry is only part of this study. The competition between General Electric and Westinghouse, for example, is analyzed in the expectation of contributing to an understanding of product competition as it exists today. Similarly, an analysis of innovation and the engineer-entrepreneur can result in propositions which are useful in studying current innovations. The analytical point of view thus assumes that, in some respects, patterns of change in the electrical industry are repetitive. If the basic forces producing these patterns can be segregated and identified, principles of general validity can be stated.

The distinction between repetition and evolution can be illustrated by an example chosen from outside the electrical industry. Consider the problem of postwar inflations. In the United States, two recent wars — the Civil War and World War I — were financed partly by inflationary means and were followed by inflation. This is a record of economic history. World War II was also partly financed by inflationary methods. A study of the two earlier wars, made on an analytical, nonevolutionary basis, would lead to the conclusion that an inflation after World War II was likely. Such a study would have proved valuable to those economists who attempted to predict, for purposes of public policy, whether World War II would be followed by severe unemployment or inflation and prosperity. Too much stress on the evolution of the economy and its institutions since 1865 and since 1918 obscured the basic forces operating in all three postwar periods. Similarly, an analysis of competition between General Electric and Westinghouse, even though this competition took place in the 1890's, can reveal the basic forces operating in duopolistic product competition. Where those forces are present today, the same kind of competition may result. It is clear that this conclusion has important implications for antitrust policy and other governmental policies concerning industrial markets.

The process of economic growth also deserves treatment in a study of industry of this kind. The chief emphasis is on the patterns of growth and the impact of the growth of the industry on the economy. The latter is of particular interest because commercial applications of electricity have brought about major changes in production, in transport, in the location of industry, in the size and composition of cities, and in the daily life of consumers. In addition, the very rapid development of the industry suggests that an important problem is to analyze the *rate* of growth. If the conditions that seem to govern this rate can be ascertained, it is possible that growth rates in other industries, also highly technical, can be better understood.

THE AMERICAN ECONOMY, 1875–1900

It may be worth while to treat very briefly the American economy of 1875 and its growth during the succeeding twenty-five years. As Professor E. C. Kirkland has pointed out, the half century between the Civil War and World War I has not yet received the complete and systematic treatment by economic historians that it deserves.[1]

The American economy in the period 1875–1900 provided an environment which was extremely favorable to the development of manufacturing enterprise. The limitations of the colonial period — a small market, a severe scarcity of labor and capital, and a hostile government — had largely disappeared. The transition from an economy unfavorable to manufacturing to one very favorable to it occurred during the first half of the nineteenth century. By 1875, the rapid growth of manufacturing had already begun.

The expansion of manufacturing depended, first of all, on a wide and growing market. Such a market existed, partly because of the rapidly increasing population. From four million in 1790, the population increased to forty million in 1870 and by 1900 had reached seventy-six million. The location of this population was also important. It was becoming increasingly concentrated in cities. In 1790, only 3 per cent of the population lived in the 6 cities of 8,000 and more inhabitants; by 1870, 21 per cent lived in the 226 cities of that size. The corresponding figures for 1900 are 33 per cent and 547 cities. The concentration of the population in the very large cities was even more striking. In 1790, there were no cities with 100,000 or even 50,000 inhabitants. In 1870, 10 per cent of the people lived in the 14 cities of 100,000 and more; by 1900, this percentage had doubled and the number of cities of that size had nearly tripled.

The urban, concentrated character of the population helped to produce similarities in tastes and living habits. Another force operating in the same direction was the democratic and egalitarian nature of the society. It is true that approximately 10 per cent of the population were foreign-born and that another 10 per cent were non-white. Nevertheless, localism in attitudes and habits was not strong, and the population of the United States as a whole was reasonably homogeneous.

Homogeneity in the population was increased by the good transportation and communication facilities. At the same time, these facilities made it possible for a manufacturer to view the United States, or large areas of it, as one market. By 1875, there were 75,000 miles of railroad in operation. Most of these were in the region north of the Potomac and the Ohio and east of the Mississippi. Freight rates had fallen to about one cent per mile; they fell further to one-half cent by 1900. Railroad construction continued at a rapid pace. The turn of the century saw nearly 200,000 miles in operation. Communication facilities were also well developed by 1875. There were 200,000 miles of telegraph wire in use, and by 1900 this figure had increased to over 1,000,000. The postal service expanded with the railroads. In the sixties, such major advances as the railroad post office, money orders, and free mail delivery were instituted. By 1900, rural free delivery had been added. An entirely new communication device, the telephone, came into use in the decades prior to 1900. By the latter date, 500,000 telephones and 300,000 miles of telephone wire were in operation.

If a wide market was the first requisite for the development of manufacturing, the second was an adequate supply of labor. Population growth was as fundamental to the latter as to the former. Natural increase and immigration combined to provide workers who were tractable and amenable to the tasks and discipline of factory production. The agricultural lands of the frontier (by now beyond the Mississippi) failed to attract an appreciable proportion of this labor force from the urban areas. Lack of interest in farming and frontier life, lack of capital, and lack of adequate transportation facilities to the lands west of the Mississippi kept many persons, immigrants and native-born alike, in the cities. Supporting evidence for this assertion can be found in the fact that settlement of the Great Plains area, the frontier of the 1870's and 1880's, was carried out mainly by midwestern farmers in a series of relatively short moves.

Although the labor force was largely unskilled, it was at least partially educated. In 1870, the illiteracy rate was 20 per cent, a figure which fell to 11 per cent by 1900. In 1880, two-thirds of those in the population aged 5 to 17 years were enrolled in school. By 1900, this proportion had climbed to three-fourths. Education at higher levels, especially in technical subjects, was also significant. In the years after 1860 such famous institutes of technology as Case, Stevens, and Massachusetts were founded. Numerous state-supported engineering schools were established as a result of the Morrill Act of 1862.

A third requisite for manufacturing was raw materials, of which America possessed abundant supply. The dollar value of mineral output (fuels and metals) tripled in the two decades before 1900. In the same period, the value of agricultural output doubled. The significance of the latter statistic is that the agricultural sector of the economy proved to be productive enough to supply not only some of the needed raw materials but also foodstuffs for the increasing proportion of the work force employed in manufacturing.

A fourth requisite for the formation and growth of manufacturing enterprise was capital funds. While far from plentiful, such funds were present in adequate amounts. In many instances, they were furnished by individuals who previously had invested in merchandising activities. Commercial banks were another important source of funds for new enterprises. Once firms had been established, their capital needs were usually met through reinvested profits. This independence of external sources was more a result of necessity than of choice. In the 1870's and 1880's, the investment bankers were mainly interested in railroad financing. Their best customers, the foreign investors, had no interest in industrial securities. It was only when domestic investors became more important in the organized securities markets that industrials could begin to challenge the leading position of rails.

A fifth requisite for industrial development is an environment free of social and political barriers to enterprise. There can be little doubt that such an environment existed in the United States in the last quarter of the nineteenth century. Governments (federal, state, and local) were reluctant to interfere with business activities. The public-utility concept had not yet been developed. A firm that found it necessary to use the public thoroughfares (such as a street railway or a gas company) required a municipal franchise, but this was freely granted. Such a franchise was often not an exclusive one. The "natural monopoly" aspect of the local water, gas, and transportation companies was not yet universally recognized.

The federal government imposed few restraints on business. Its first attempts at control (the Interstate Commerce Commission, 1887; the Sherman Antitrust Act, 1890) were almost completely nullified by adverse court rulings until after 1900. The federal income and inheritance taxes, created to help finance the Civil War, were abolished before 1875. The import duties, which protected manufacturers from foreign competition, were, however, largely retained. The state governments were in most instances an important aid to enterprise. Incorporation was simple and inexpensive, and the corporate charters contained few restrictions. The lack of interstate barriers helped to convert the entire United States into a single, large, free-trade area.

Labor unions were neither strong enough nor common enough to constitute a barrier to the formation and operation of industrial enterprises. The depression of the 1870's destroyed many of the national unions which had been formed after 1850. The union movement later regained strength, but its emphasis on social and political reform weakened it as a force in labor markets. Only in a few highly skilled crafts was a union able to display enough power to merit the attention of employers. In the decades before 1900, the employer, not the union, most often held the initiative. Union-management relations were typically characterized by the blacklist, the yellow-dog contract, and Pinkerton detectives rather than by the closed shop, the industry-wide strike, and hard bargaining over rates of pay, work loads, and technological changes.

The attitudes of the majority of Americans toward business were basically favorable. The belief was common that business offered equal opportunities for all Americans and that each individual was therefore entitled to keep what he could earn. Although there was a revolt against business, mainly agrarian, those who dissented from *laissez faire* were in the minority. Entrepreneurs could be reasonably confident that the voices raised against business were so few and so weak that they could be safely ignored.

It is thus possible to make a strong case for the view that the period from 1875 to 1900 was one very favorable to manufacturing enterprise.[2] All data on the growth of manufacturing during this period bear out this view. The number of manufacturing establishments doubled, workers doubled, value of products more than tripled, physical output nearly quadrupled, and the value of manufacturing output per capita nearly doubled.

A number of conditions present in these years specifically favored *electrical* manufacturing. One such condition, increasing urbanization, has already been discussed. The central stations which supplied electric lighting (and later, power) for streets, offices, homes, and factories were strictly an urban phenomenon. The same is true of the electric-traction companies. These two types of enterprise were the most important customers of the early electrical manufacturing industry, and the best and biggest of them were in the largest cities.

A second favorable condition was the growth of manufacturing and the increasing use of mechanical power. In the large and numerous factories, electric-power devices found a ready market. The increasing standard of living (real income per capita nearly doubled between 1869 and 1899) also favored the electrical industry. Central-station lighting of homes was at first quite costly and could be correctly labeled a luxury. Such a product secures a wider market as living standards rise.

The declining price level in this period also favored electrical manufacturing. The secular trend of prices was clearly downward. Furthermore, in the three business cycles (which averaged ten years in length) of 1870–1900, prices fell during much more than half of each cycle. The nearly continuous price declines meant prosperity for the lighting and traction companies. Their costs decreased steadily and appreciably. Their prices, sometimes specified in the franchise granted by the municipality, declined very little or not at all. The resulting high profits made them good customers for electrical equipment because they had both an optimistic outlook and the necessary funds.

The declining price level which favored the best customers of the electrical manufacturers was not a seriously inhibiting influence on the manufacturers themselves. As Professor Schumpeter has emphasized, innovations do not require a constant or rising price level to appear profitable. New enterprises, based on innovations, will be formed even when secular price declines are anticipated.[3] The short-term decreases in prices, purchasing power, and output that characterize the usual business depression may, however, impede the formation or growth of such new enterprises. The depressions in the 1875–1900 period were thus not without effect on the electrical manufacturing industry, but that effect was not great. The severe depression which ended in 1877 preceded the first electrical firms. The crisis of 1884 was principally a monetary panic and had little effect on industrial activity. The 1893 depression was long and severe. But by this time the pioneering period of the electrical manufacturing industry was over. The principal firms had been established, and the principal innovations had been made. The main effect of the 1893 depression was to prevent further growth of these companies for a period of about four years.

It is important to note that the 1893 depression, severe as it was, did not dampen the enthusiasm of many entrepreneurs in the electrical industry; they continued to believe that rapid growth of the industry would soon begin again. With such a viewpoint, an entrepreneur can take advantage of a general business depression to prepare for future expansion. Westinghouse did just that in consolidating his manufacturing activities in a very large and modern factory at East Pittsburgh. Low construction costs in 1893 and 1894 made this an extremely attractive investment.

In summary, the period 1875–1900 was one favorable to manufacturing generally and to the electrical manufacturing industry in particular. The spectacular development of the latter is the subject of this volume.

PART I

Arc Lighting

I

The Setting

THE first electric lighting to be of commercial importance was arc lighting. Like all other methods of artificial illumination then in common use, the arc lamp produced light by the consumption of a carbonaceous substance. Unlike the other methods, the light came not from a flame but from an electric arc formed by current between the ends of two pencil-like pieces of carbon. The source of the current was a dynamo.

The initiation of the arc-lighting industry was possible because of two separate streams of development — one scientific and technical, the other commercial. The manufacturer had to know how to construct arc-lighting equipment, and there had to be a market for that equipment, derived from the market for arc lighting.

The arc light first became known to science in 1808 when Sir Humphrey Davy, a leading English scientific figure, gave a public demonstration of his newly discovered electric light. The lighting elements were pieces of charcoal, and current was supplied from a battery of two thousand cells. Davy touched the pieces of charcoal together and then drew them apart, thereby forming an electric arc which gave off intense light. During the following fifty years, hundreds of scientists and inventors tried to improve Davy's arc light. They sought to make carbons which would burn a considerable period and give a steady light and to design a mechanism which would keep the two carbons the correct distance apart as they were consumed. But the arc light was to remain a laboratory instrument and scientific curiosity as long as batteries were the source of current. The cost of current supplied by batteries was too high to permit commercial use of the arc light.

The principle underlying a much cheaper current source, the dynamo, was discovered in 1831 by the English scientist, Michael Faraday. He learned that current is generated in an electrical conductor that is part of a closed circuit when it is moved in the area between the poles of a magnet. In succeeding years, the elements of the practical dynamo were developed. In 1832, Hippolyte Pixii in Paris described a method whereby the moving conductor (called the armature) could be used to obtain a steady current. The current from a battery is in one direction only (direct current), while the current in the armature of a dynamo alternates its direction (alternating current). Pixii's device, a commutator, changed the armature alternating current into direct current at the terminals of the dynamo. Later improvements included better armature designs and the substitution of electromagnets for permanent magnets. By 1870, a number of reliable and reasonably efficient dynamos had been built.

During the years that the two basic components of an arc-lighting system had been evolving, a potential market for arc lighting had come into existence. The growth of American cities in the eighteenth and nineteenth centuries created a demand for street lighting which was originally met by candles and oil lamps. At first individual citizens were required to place lights outside their residences, but by 1800 some city governments were assuming responsibility for lighting the streets. A new illuminant for that purpose, gas, came into use during the early years of the nineteenth century. The first gas company in America was organized in 1816 in Baltimore, and others were formed in Boston, New York, Brooklyn, and New Orleans by 1835. They commonly supplied street, commercial, and industrial lighting, and lighting for private residences. Gas illumination was a major innovation, both technically and commercially. It meant more light and better light, and it was supplied from a central source. The latter implied a business firm whose product was light, rather than light-producing materials. By 1875, there were over four hundred gas companies in the United States. Most of these were located in the larger cities, however, and central-station gas lighting was far from universal. In smaller cities, business firms which wanted gas illumination had to operate their own gas plants, and the streets were lighted, if at all, by kerosene lamps.

The potential market for arc lighting was thus well developed by 1875. Lighting of city streets, especially on moonless or cloudy nights, had become customary. The light was usually supplied by a business firm under contract from the city government. This firm operated a gas plant from which it distributed gas to street lights throughout the city. Industrial and commercial establishments could be lighted by gas from that same central station or from a gas plant of their own. Almost all the buyers of gas plants, therefore, were business firms. This characteristic of the potential market for arc-lighting apparatus meant that cost considerations were to be very important. Arc-lighting equipment would have to be capable of producing light at a total cost, including the cost of the equipment and all operating costs, approximately equal to the cost of producing light by gas.

The technical characteristics of an arc-lighting system that would be able to meet the requirements of this potential market involved a number of improvements in the dynamo and arc light as known in 1875. The dynamo had to generate a quantity of current which was the same regardless of how many lights or other devices might be connected to the dynamo. This was necessary for two reasons. In an arc light there is continual danger that the two carbons may touch and produce a short circuit. Unless the dynamo current were constant, a short circuit would result in a very heavy current with attendant danger of fire and damage to the dynamo. The second reason grew out of the peculiar nature of the arc lamp as an electrical device. The resistance presented by an arc lamp to the electric current is inversely proportional to the current. This characteristic can lead to unstable operation. If, for example, the arc-light resistance should happen to decrease slightly, the current would increase, the resistance would decrease more, and so forth. The current would then be very heavy unless the dynamo were of the constant-current type.

Another technical requirement for a commercially feasible arc-lighting system was a simple mechanism in the arc lamp for feeding the carbons as they burned in order to avoid continual adjustment by hand. Moreover, the entire arc-lighting system had to be reliable and simple to operate. The absolute minimum of accessories and complicating devices was the goal to be sought. An elaborate system would place too high a demand on technical operating ability to be usable at a time when so little was known about electricity by most of the population. The nature of the technical development which was required in arc-lighting apparatus to bring it up to the level of innovation can be summarized in the statement that it had to be simple, reliable, and dependable, and capable of producing light which was equal, if not superior, to gas for about the same cost.

II

The Rise of Leading Firms

THE BRUSH ELECTRIC COMPANY

Charles Francis Brush, the pioneer innovator in arc lighting, received his bachelor's degree in chemistry from the University of Michigan in 1869 at the age of twenty. He then opened a consulting office in Cleveland and worked for several years as a chemist. In his spare time, he studied electricity. Through experimental work and study, he came to believe that arc lighting would be commercially successful if dynamos and arc lights could be improved. His first project was to build a dynamo. This he completed in 1875.

Brush's next problem was to secure financial backing in order to complete experimental work and begin the production of arc-lighting apparatus for market. He turned to his friend, George W. Stockley, vice-president of the Cleveland Telegraph Supply Company. That company had been formed in 1872, and by 1875 it was doing an annual business of $50,000 and employing about twenty-five men. Its products were various items of telegraphic apparatus and equipment.

Stockley agreed to permit Brush to use the foundry, shops, and working force of the Telegraph company; and Brush constructed another dynamo and designed a simplified arc lamp. It had a simple magnetic feed mechanism in contrast to the very elaborate and expensive clockworks usual in the arc lamps of that period. The demonstration of this small dynamo and the single lamp to Stockley in the fall of 1876 convinced him that in backing Brush he had been prescient. Brush and the Telegraph Supply Company entered into an agreement at that time which stated that the company would make and sell Brush dynamos, arc lamps, and whatever else Brush should invent.[1]

During 1877, while Brush was trying to perfect his arc-lighting system, the Franklin Institute of Philadelphia had become interested in the generation of electricity. In February, the Institute secured a Wallace-Farmer dynamo.[2] The Secretary reported that this machine "loaned by the builders to the Committee on Instruction for use in lectures, was in operation on the stage and its power was shown by vaporizing metals, etc. and its construction and action explained at some length by the President."[3] The interest shown by the members of the Institute in dynamos and arc lights led to the decision, announced in the September issue of the Institute's *Journal*, to purchase a dynamo.

> The Institute has decided to purchase, for experimental purposes, a Dynamo-Electric Machine capable of producing not less than 1200 candles' light. In order to decide what kind of machine to select, it has been determined to invite all builders of such machines to send one of their make to be submitted to a comparative trial.
>
> The trial will be conducted by a committee of scientific men, well qualified to judge such apparatus. It is expected that their report will embody a description of each machine, a statement of its performance, including the amount of light produced, power required to drive it, and its capability of long continued work without undue heating or derangement.
>
> It is proposed to make these tests early in October, but it is desirable to know at as early a day as possible what machines will compete. Those entering their machines for this test, will be expected to send them at their own risk and cost, but no expense will accrue in making the tests. It is believed that such a comparative test as is proposed, and the report thereon will be of great benefit by increasing the already great interest felt in this country in the introduction of such machines for producing light and for other industrial purposes.[4]

This announcement also appeared in other scientific periodicals and in newspapers. Direct requests for machines were sent to M. Breguet, of Paris, France, maker of the Gramme machine; Messrs. Siemens Brothers, of London, England, manufacturers of the Siemens machine; Messrs. Condit, Hanson, and Van Winkle, of Newark, New Jersey, who turned out the Weston machine; Messrs. Wallace and Sons, of Ansonia, Connecticut, makers of the Wallace-Farmer machines; and the Telegraph Supply Company, of Cleveland, Ohio, which was now ready to produce the Brush machine. Only the last two firms actually supplied apparatus, but the Institute was able to obtain a Gramme machine from Purdue University.[5]

There existed no precedent for a test of electrical machinery, and the Institute committee had to devise its own methods and procedures. A Brush arc lamp was used in testing all machines. The testing took several months and was carefully done. In the end, the Institute could report that the Brush machine was the most desirable of those submitted. The reasons were: "1. It is admirably adapted to the production of currents of widely varying electromotive force, and produces a good light. 2. From the mechanical details of its construction, especially at the commutators, it possesses great ease of repair to the parts subject to wear."[6]

The Institute's inquiry benefited Brush in several ways. The very careful tests were reported with complete data and analysis, which enabled Brush to improve the design of his dynamo. The publicity attendant upon being selected by an organization of high scientific standing as maker of the best dynamo gave him a competitive advantage over other dynamo manufacturers. The Wallace-Farmer dynamo fared so badly in the tests that shortly afterward it was removed from the market.

The first buyer of a Brush dynamo and arc lights was a Cincinnati doctor who used the apparatus to light the porch and yard of his residence. The Franklin Institute purchased a dynamo in the spring of 1878 upon completion of the tests; and shortly afterwards, John Wanamaker, the Philadelphia store owner, purchased five 4-light dynamos with necessary arc lights.

In October 1878, Brush exhibited his arc-lighting system at the Mechanics Fair in Boston. Wallace and Sons, of Ansonia, Connecticut, also set up an arc-lighting display at the fair. In this second meeting with his competitor, Brush again won. At the close of the fair, the Wallace-Farmer machine was taken back to Connecticut, but Brush sold his machine to a Boston merchandising firm, the Continental Clothing House, which was located at the corner of Howard and Washington Streets. This store, like Wanamaker's in Philadelphia, was interested in better interior illumination and also recognized the advertising value of something as new and noticeable as the arc light. Brush personally supervised the installation of the plant and explained to the store engineer how it should be adjusted and operated for best performance. The arc lamps were first lighted on November 9, 1878, and attracted large crowds.[7]

The dynamos and arc lamps sold by Brush in the first years were built into simple arc-lighting systems. The dynamos were made only in 2-light and 4-light sizes. In both cases, each light was connected on a separate circuit from the dynamo and was independent of the other lights. That arrangement meant that there was no need to regulate the output of the dynamo in accordance with the number of lights in use and that no mechanism to short-circuit a burned-out light was necessary. Brush's success in making the first sales was primarily due to the simplicity and reliability of his equipment. As already intimated, in a time when very few people knew anything about electricity, a system that in its operation required almost no electrical knowledge was essential before arc lighting could be widely used.

But Brush envisaged a market much wider than a few public buildings, stores, and factories. He wanted his light used in street lighting, other outdoor lighting, and in large halls and buildings. To achieve such a goal, he knew that he had to improve his arc-lighting system. The dynamo cost, the copper cost,[8] and the operating cost per lamp would have to be reduced considerably. The way to do this was to run a number of lamps on one circuit from one dynamo. The technical requirements for such a system differed considerably from those of the 2-light or 4-light dynamos and lamps. Moreover, if the arc light were going to displace gas in general outdoor illumination, it was essential to find a way to design a lamp so that it could burn more than eight hours before the carbons had to be changed. The labor cost of frequent carbon changing was a serious handicap to arc lighting.

The transition from a light of only occasional use in odd places to one used nearly everywhere in large-space lighting required, therefore, major technological changes. Brush set out to improve his arc-lighting system, and, by the spring of 1879, he had made considerable progress. His new dynamo produced a more nearly constant current and generated a high voltage. The latter permitted up to sixteen lamps on one circuit. The operation of more than one lamp on one circuit was possible because his new arc lamp had an ingenious but simple mechanism which automatically short-circuited the lamp when it failed and so maintained the current path to the other lamps.

Brush also made major improvements in the carbons. During the period when the arc light was only a laboratory device, the carbons were made of powdered wood charcoal. This was mixed with tar, molded into shape under pressure, and baked in a crucible in a hot fire. After the arc light entered the commercial stage, the increased demand for arc carbons led to the use of a more abundant carbon source, the coke which was produced in the manufacture of illuminating gas. The major disadvantages of gas coke were its refractory nature, which made it difficult to work with, and the impurities it contained. The arc carbons made from gas coke were crooked and soft and burned out rapidly. The impurities (ash content was 3–5 per cent) caused them to flicker considerably. The result was a light low in quality and, with carbons priced at 25 cents each, high in cost.

Brush reasoned that the principal difficulty was the gas coke. He searched for another source of carbon and found what he wanted within a mile of the Brush plant in Cleveland. The Standard Oil Company usually burned the last product of the distillation of crude oil, formed at the bottom of its paraffin stills. This residue was shoveled from the stills in large lumps. It was cheap, easy to pulverize, and very low in ash content (0.02–0.03 per cent).[9]

Brush found that petroleum coke was a nonconductor in the raw state but that it became a conductor after being heated. He carried on experiments to determine the grain size best adapted for burning in the electric arc. He discovered that the best adhesive was coal-tar pitch.

In addition to improving the composition of the carbons, Brush changed their form. He noticed that the tips of the rectangular, blunt-end carbons tended to shape themselves like pencils before burning quietly. He also noticed that round carbons cast less of a shadow. On the basis of these observations, he began to make cylindrical, sharpened carbons.[10]

Brush undertook the manufacture of the carbons he had designed in the Cleveland plant. At first he charged $24 per hundred, but he soon decreased the price to $15 per hundred. He claims to have lowered the price as quickly as costs would allow in order to widen the market for his arc lights.[11]

The first arc-lighting plants using the improved Brush equipment were installed in 1879 and worked very well. By the end of that year, Brush had succeeded in making three more technical changes of great importance. He invented a double-carbon arc lamp which could give light for sixteen hours before needing any attention. He devised an automatic regulator for his dynamo which kept the current almost exactly constant no matter what number of lights were in use. And he copper-plated the arc carbons, which gave good electrical contact and decreased the resistance between the carbon and the carbon holder. The result was that the automatic carbon-feed mechanism could work as well with full-length as with partially burned carbons. The copper-plating also served to slow down consumption of the carbons. These three changes made by Brush marked the end of major technical progress in arc lighting until the 1890's. The technical basis for this innovation had been laid by 1880.

While Brush was solving the technical problems, he also gave attention to the problem of finding a market for his product. His technical work was oriented toward an arc-lighting system principally intended for street lighting. The problem was how to break into this market with a new kind of light produced by new and strange equipment. Some of the 1879 Brush equipments were sold to buyers of the 1878 equipments — for example, the Boston clothing store — who were induced to purchase by the improvements in the new apparatus. But scattered and isolated sales like these did not satisfy Brush's desire to develop the street-lighting market.

His first attempt in the latter direction was in Cleveland. He secured the permission of the city council there to erect high poles on which he placed a total of twelve arc lights. These were first operated in a public

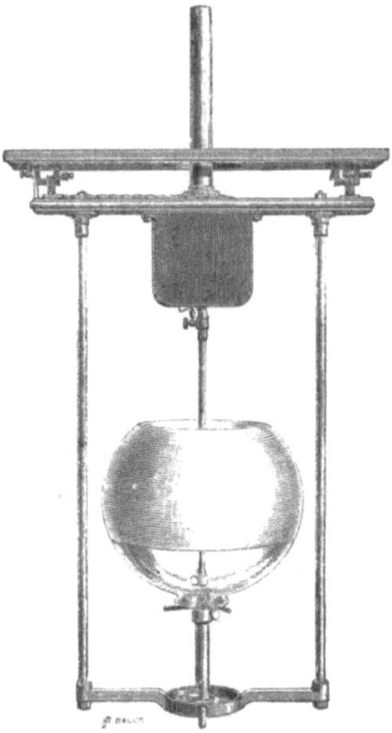

1. Brush single-carbon arc lamp, 1882

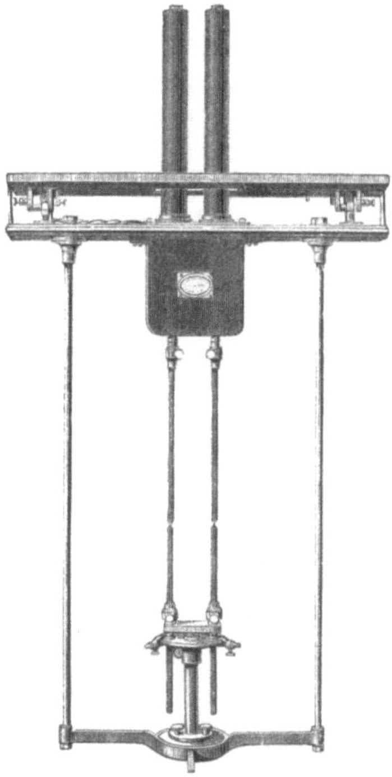

2. Brush double-carbon arc lamp, glass globe removed, 1882

3. Brush arc-lighting dynamo, 1882

4. Edison incandescent-lighting dynamo, 1881

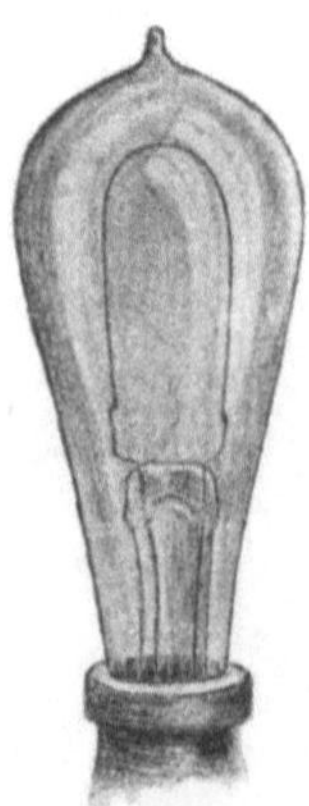

5. **Edison** incandescent lamp, 1881

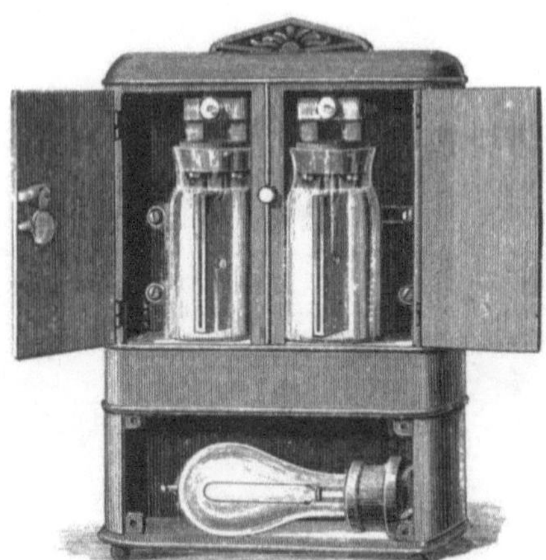

6. Edison chemical meter, with lamp to keep electrolytic solution from freezing, 1882

square in April 1879. This demonstration showed Brush that the cost of replacing carbons during the night was considerable. Soon afterward, he invented the double-carbon lamp.

The Cleveland experiment had no immediate results there in terms of the formation of an arc-lighting company or a contract with the city to light the streets. But, by June, Brush was able to promote formation of the California Electric Light Company of San Francisco. This firm began operations in the summer of 1879 and was the first electric central station in the world. It had two Brush dynamos, supplying a total of twenty-two arc lamps for which a price of $10 per lamp per week was charged. At first its customers were private parties, but soon it was providing light on a number of streets under a city contract. The station was financially successful, and within six months — with additional equipment — it was supplying over fifty arc lights.[12]

During the remainder of 1879 and 1880, Brush central stations were established in a number of American cities, including New York, Boston, and Philadelphia. The usual procedure was for a Brush representative to enlist capital in the city to form a local arc-lighting company. An agreement would then be made between this company and the Brush enterprise, giving the lighting company the right to sell, use, or rent all Brush equipment. If a business firm in that territory installed a Brush arc-lighting plant for its own use (an isolated plant), the local company was to receive a 5 per cent commission on the purchase price of the apparatus. In return for this exclusive license on Brush equipment, the local company was required to turn over to the Brush company anywhere from 32 to 48 per cent of its capital stock, such stock to be fully paid up and non-assessable. Most of these contracts ran until April 24, 1894 — seventeen years from the date of issue of the first important Brush patent. The Brush company was very careful to insert in the agreement clauses which protected its interest in the local company. One such clause read as follows:

> It is also agreed that accurate books of account shall be kept, exhibiting in a clear manner all the business transactions of the lighting company, keeping separately the items of construction or cost of plant and the items of running expenses to which the parent company or its representatives may have access at any time. Quarterly statements from the books of the lighting company shall be furnished regularly to the parent company and 32 per cent of the net earnings shall be paid in dividends on said 32 per cent of stock belonging to the parent company or its assigns and no portion of said 32 per cent of its earnings shall be used by the lighting company for construction account or for extension of the business.[13]

The local lighting companies almost always tried to secure municipal street-lighting contracts. They sometimes offered to light the same streets as the gas company at a 15–25 per cent reduction in cost. In many cases, the company had to provide a free demonstration of its lighting system over a period of months before the city council could be convinced of the reliability and practicability of arc lighting. The Brush Electric Light Company of New York, for example, furnished twenty-two arc lights on Broadway from Fourteenth Street to Thirty-Fourth Street for the six-month period, December 1880 to June 1881, before a contract was signed by the city. These twenty-two lamps displaced five hundred gas lamps, and the price paid by the city was 20 per cent less.[14]

The marketing policy of the Brush Electric Company was based on the premise that the arc lamp, because it produced a high-quality light at low cost, could displace gas from all large-space lighting. A company publication in 1881 stated that "gas will probably continue to hold its own as the light for domestic and small uses in cities and towns and oil will keep the field in similar situations in villages and hamlets."[15] Brush sales literature emphasized the superiority of the arc light over gas for street lighting. It was alleged, for example, that the increased illumination provided by the arc light was of great worth in reducing crime and lessening the need for policemen. For a number of years the Brush company published the *Brush Electric Light*, a newspaper-like publication which contained items on Brush lights and arc lighting in general. Particular effort was made to overcome prejudice against the arc light because of fear of the high voltage of the circuits or of possible ill effects on the eyes or general health from the intense light emitted by the electric arc.

Brush's innovation was a success. By the end of 1880, over 5,000 Brush arc lights and dynamos were in operation.[16] This is more than 80 per cent of the arc lights in use at that time. The Brush company underwent several organizational changes to meet the need for larger and larger rates of production. In 1880, the name of the company was changed from the Telegraph Supply Company to the Brush Electric Company, and the authorized capital stock was increased from $200,000 to $3,000,000.[17] The census of 1880 includes data for the Brush company and gives its annual output (for 1879) at $300,000 and its average employment at 150 workers.[18] Brush continued his arrangement with the Brush Electric Company whereby it had the exclusive license to manufacture under his patents and he received a 20 per cent royalty.

In the decade 1880–1890, the Brush company continued to expand its production of arc-light apparatus and began producing other electrical goods. Brush made 5,000,000 carbons in 1883 and over 20,000,000 annually by 1890.[19] The capacity of the Brush plant increased from about 250 arc lamps and associated equipment per month in 1880 to 1,500 per month in 1885.[20] In 1883, the Brush company brought out a 1200-candle-power arc light, two-thirds the size of the one standard up to that time, in an effort to fit arc lighting into smaller spaces.[21] About that same time, the American rights to an English incandescent lamp were purchased, and Brush was soon marketing an incandescent-light system. In 1882, Brush invented an improved storage battery which was added to the list of products. In 1886, Brush made a number of very large dynamos for the Cowles Electric Smelting and Aluminum Company, of Lockport, New York. In 1889, Brush brought out an alternating-current system. Thus diversification arose out of the signal first success — the design, manufacture, and sale of an economical and practical arc-lighting system.

THE THOMSON-HOUSTON ELECTRIC COMPANY

Brush was the pioneer innovator in arc lighting. He showed what technical features a practical arc-lighting system had to have, and he proved that arc-lighting equipment could be made and sold at a profit. Among the dozens of inventors, scientists, and engineers attracted to arc lighting by Brush's success was Elihu Thomson. The firm that was formed on the basis of his inventions was destined to become a leader in the electrical manufacturing industry.

Born in Manchester, England, in 1853, Elihu Thomson accompanied his parents to the United States in 1858. The family settled in Philadelphia, where young Thomson received his education. After graduation from Central High School in 1870, he was asked to teach there, and by 1876 he had been appointed "professor" of chemistry. The title is somewhat misleading. He was a high-school teacher, not a college teacher, and his main interest was electricity, not chemistry. He and Professor E. J. Houston, an older colleague, conducted experiments in 1875 which disproved Edison's theory of etheric force. Edison had not recognized the electrical nature of what is now known as electromagnetic-wave propagation and thought he had discovered a new force. About this same time, Thomson constructed several dynamos and began to study dynamo design. His published papers on electricity came to the attention of the Franklin Institute, and, in the fall of 1876, the Institute invited him to give five lectures on the subject. The following year, when the Institute decided to buy an arc-light dynamo, Thomson was one of nine people chosen as the committee to test the dynamos and select the one to purchase.[22]

Thomson and Houston constituted a subcommittee on electrical measurements, and their particular responsibility was to test the electrical performance of the dynamos. Such testing was exceedingly difficult with the crude instruments then available. Much ingenuity was required. The current in the circuit was computed by an elaborate, indirect method based on the heat loss in a resistance. Voltages were also obtained indirectly from current and resistance values. The final report submitted by Thomson and Houston showed a clear understanding of the important electrical principles that underlie good dynamo design.

Thomson's interest in arc lighting had been aroused by the testing that he did for the Institute and by the contact he had had with Brush during the course of the tests. A trip to Europe in the summer of 1878 gave him the chance to see more arc lighting and aroused his interest still further. At the mechanical arts exhibition in Paris, he saw a number of arc lights on display. In a Paris railroad station, he saw an arc-lighting system operating on a commercial basis. He soon became enthusiastic about the possibilities of arc lighting and decided to work out his own system on his return to the United States.[23]

Back in Philadelphia, Thomson sought the collaboration of Professor Houston, and together they worked out the technical details of an arc-lighting system. A Philadelphia manufacturer, George S. Garrett, heard of this work and asked Thomson to construct a 4-light dynamo, such as Brush was making in Cleveland. Garrett offered to finance the building of this machine. Thomson accepted the offer, and, by the spring of 1879, he had designed and built a dynamo which could light nine arc lights. This first dynamo was sold to a Philadelphia bakery.[24]

A lawyer from New Britain, Connecticut, Frederick H. Churchill, came to Philadelphia early in 1880 and asked Thomson to become the electrician (that is, the electrical engineer) of a new electrical manufacturing company that was being organized in New Britain. Because Garrett was willing to accept Pennsylvania and several nearby states as his territory for selling Thomson-Houston arc-lighting equipment, Thomson went to New Britain to obtain more information on Churchill's proposal. On his arrival, he suggested that an arc-lighting exhibition be held in order to promote the sale of stock in the new enterprise. A 10-light machine was sent up from the Garrett factory and, on March 29, 1880, the exhibition was opened. In addition to showing arc lights, Thomson connected up a second dynamo as an electric motor and used it to drive a wood saw.

A group of six New Britain businessmen who were attracted by the exhibit formed a committee to investigate thoroughly the Thomson-Houston arc-lighting system and its commercial possibilities. This committee made its first report on April 13 as follows:

> We, the undersigned, appointed a committee to examine the merits of the electric light enterprise that it proposes to organize in this city, based upon the patents of Edwin J. Houston and Elihu Thomson, would respectfully report:
>
> I. That in our judgment the electric generators of said Houston and Thomson are superior machines in economy of power, simplicity of construction,

efficiency, and durability; and we believe after investigation that they are superior to any other electric generators now sold in this country.

II. That their automatic adjuster of the commutator brushes by proportioning the amount of power expended to the quantity of illumination required, constitutes a very valuable adjunct to the generator, and is a decided improvement in the art of electric lighting over any system now known.

III. That their lamps are to work as satisfactorily as those of any other system, including the Brush, of which we have any knowledge, and in simplicity and reliability possess a number of points of superiority.

IV. That we believe the method of transmitting power by means of electricity, as accomplished by Professors Houston and Thomson through the use of their electric generators and motors, will find in the immediate future many useful applications and can be made to form a large and valuable branch of the business of the proposed company.

V. That after an examination of the patents that it proposes to convey to the company, we would state that the new company will possess a remarkably clear field in which to operate, that the validity of the patents cannot be successfully attacked, and that they do not infringe the rights of other inventors.

VI. That we consider Professors Houston and Thomson to possess a remarkable degree of proficiency in electric lighting, and the electric transmission of power, and we believe them to possess the practical ability that will enable them to keep in advance of the times in perfecting the art of electric lighting.

VII. That we would recommend the acceptance of the terms proposed in the agreement between the said Houston and Thomson, and F. H. Churchill, dated January 16, 1880, as the basis for the formation of a joint stock company; except that we recommend that the amount of the capital stock be one hundred and twenty-five thousand dollars ($125,000), three-tenths of which shall be apportioned to the patents; and that the amount of cash to be paid to the patentees upon the assignment of the patents to the company should be the sum of six thousand dollars ($6,000).

VIII. That the rights and privileges claimed by George S. Garrett in his memorandum of agreement dated January 15, 1880, modified by memorandum of April 20, 1880, be conceded to him.

IX. That on the above terms we recommend this enterprise to our capitalists, believing that it contains the elements, which under proper management will soon develop into a large, safe, and profitable business.[25]

The report clearly shows what factors were considered important and what kind of judgments were involved in the decision to form a new firm to make and sell a new technical product. Sections I, II, and III are evaluations of the technical quality of the components of the Thomson-Houston arc-lighting system. Section IV is a judgment on the possible commercial success of electric power, an application of electricity which had not yet matured to the status of innovation. No such judgment was required on arc lighting, because Brush had already proved it to be a commercial success. Sections V and VI evaluate the patents and the technical competence of the man to be the electrical engineer for the new enterprise. The decision to establish a firm to manufacture Thomson-Houston equipment thus was based on the four factors outlined in the report.

After the committee had made its first report, Thomson constructed an improved dynamo which he exhibited to the committee on April 24, 1880. This machine could supply eight arc lamps. It was much smaller in size than his previous dynamo of that capacity and was better constructed. Subsequent to witnessing the operation of the new generator, the committee made a second report, stating that "it embraces several distinctly new methods of construction that have never before been employed in any existing form of electric generator: whereby the weight, quantity of copper wire used, and cost of construction, are reduced far below what exists in any other electric generator hitherto constructed." And the report concludes with a warm expression of faith: "From our examination of this matter, it is our belief that this is an invention that will have the effect to reduce in a marked degree the cost of electricity, and thus to greatly diminish the expense of the electric light as well as to impart a decided impetus to the introduction of the transmission of electric power. We therefore renew with increased confidence and emphasis the recommendations of our original report."[26]

These favorable reports suggest the willingness of the New Britain businessmen to invest in the new enterprise. The American Electric Company was organized on July 16, 1880, with a capital stock of $125,000. Seventy per cent of this stock was sold for cash ($87,500), and the remaining 30 per cent was paid to Thomson and Houston for the use of their patents. In addition, Thomson and Houston together received $6,000 in cash.[27]

The contract between Thomson and Houston and the American Electric Company contained two clauses which were to have much importance later. They indicate that Thomson was not willing to commit himself irrevocably to American Electric, possibly because he feared that the original interest and enthusiasm evidenced by Churchill and the committee of six might not be sustained. Clauses five and six read as follows:

> Fifth, that the said company shall forthwith after its organization proceed with all reasonable diligence to develop and manufacture the improvements protected by said Letters Patent of the said Houston and Thomson . . . and to put the machines, lamps . . . into public use and to extend their manufacture and sale by diligent and continuous attention, effort, and expenditure in all reasonable and advisable ways.
>
> Sixth . . . In case of a failure on the part of said company to comply with

the terms of this agreement and also in case the company shall not proceed with reasonable diligence in the manufacture of the articles . . . the patents shall, if the said Houston and Thomson so elect, revert to the patentees.[28]

In the fall of 1880, the American Electric Company began manufacturing operations in a small two-story wooden building, producing at the rate of about three dynamos and fifty lamps per week. Thomson had general charge of production and testing, and continued to work out new designs. His basic problem was to produce an arc-lighting system better than those of his competitors—of whom the most important was the Brush company. The automatic current regulator, mentioned in Section II of the April 13 report, was one step toward the solution of that problem. This regulator kept the dynamo current constant regardless of the number of arc lamps on the circuit. The regulator was superior to the Brush regulator in two respects. It kept the current more nearly constant, and it consumed less electric energy in the course of its operation.

Another step toward an arc-lighting system which could outsell competitive systems was a larger dynamo. Thomson knew that if he could build dynamos of greater capacity, purchasers of the Thomson-Houston system would be able to provide lighting at a lower cost than with other brands of equipment. The limit on the number of arc lamps fed by one dynamo was the voltage they required. The potential difference across one arc lamp was about 50 volts. In a series connection (that is, with the same current through all arc lamps), the arc-lamp voltages are additive. Forty arc lamps would require a 2000-volt dynamo. Commutation (that is, the conversion of the alternating current from the armature coils of the dynamo into direct current for the external circuit) was almost impossible at such a high voltage. Thomson devised an air-blast technique whereby a layer of air was used for insulation on the commutator. This worked very well and raised the voltage limit considerably.[29]

Thomson felt that another direction in which to advance was to provide lightning protection for his system. This was an entirely new electrical problem, not met in telegraphy or telephony because of the small voltages involved. The essence of the lightning problem was to provide a path for the lightning to discharge to the ground but at the same time prevent the high-voltage arc-light current from doing the same thing. Thomson looked for some way to interrupt the arc of the lightning discharge. Reasoning on basic scientific principles, he considered the effect of a magnetic field on an electric current. He finally devised a lightning arrester which consisted of a spark gap and a permanent magnet. The magnet was used to drive the short-circuit arc out of the gap and so to extinguish it. This lightning arrester, using the so-called magnetic blowout principle, worked very well.[30]

By the end of 1881, Thomson felt that he had an arc-lighting system which was technically superior to any other on the market. The efficient and compact dynamo, the automatic current regulator, the air-blast non-sparking commutator, and the lightning arrester added up to a reliable system with low operating and upkeep costs. But the marketing problem was far from solved. There were no sales offices at any place except the factory itself. An agent in Boston, E. H. Goff, was selling Thomson-Houston arc-lighting equipment, but he called it the American system and tried to conceal the name of the manufacturer. To add to these difficulties, Churchill, the promoter of American Electric and Thomson's most enthusiastic backer, committed suicide. At this juncture, discouraged by the failure of American Electric to exploit his patents adequately, Thomson decided to use the "reasonable diligence" clause in his contract in order to withdraw his patents and services from the company and begin again.

Before Thomson acted, the United States Electric Lighting Company, producer of the Weston arc-lighting system,[31] took steps to buy American Electric. When the United States officials learned of the contract that Thomson had made with the latter, however, they declined to complete the purchase. G. W. Stockley, a Brush official, had the same intention as the United States company, and in April 1882 he purchased a majority of the American Electric stock. Only after the sale had been completed did he learn of the "reasonable diligence" clause in Thomson's contract.

Meanwhile, two Lynn, Massachusetts, businessmen, Silas Barton and Henry Pevear, had decided to buy an arc-lighting plant for the Lynn Grand Army Post. They went to Boston and investigated the lighting system on sale by Goff. Impressed by the excellent performance of the equipment, they decided to deal directly with the maker and went to New Britain. Talks with Thomson began there and continued in Lynn. As a result, a group of Lynn businessmen, including C. A. Coffin, formed a syndicate to buy American Electric. Stockley was willing to sell because Thomson threatened to withdraw his patents and himself, leaving American Electric with little of value. The sale to the Lynn group was completed about the middle of 1882.

The Connecticut legislature was petitioned for the right to change the name of the company, to increase its capital stock, and to carry on manufacturing operations outside of Connecticut. The new incorporation statute, which changed the name to the Thomson-Houston Electric Company, was passed on April 17, 1883. Permission was granted to increase the capital stock to $1,000,000 when and if desired.[32] In the fall of 1883, the Thomson-Houston Electric Company established its manufacturing plant in Lynn.

C. A. Coffin took charge of the new company. He had been the principal salesman for a Lynn shoe-manufacturing firm and had traveled extensively throughout the East and the Midwest, calling on jobbers.[33] He knew almost nothing about electricity and depended on Thomson for technical advice. The team of Coffin and Thomson — the one a good salesman and organizer, the other a keen scientist, a man of sound technical judgment, and an ingenious inventor — was to lead the firm of Thomson-Houston to outstanding success in the arc-lighting field.

Although changes and improvements in the apparatus were to be continued, Coffin and Thomson decided to concentrate on marketing, in view of the technical excellence of the Thomson-Houston arc-lighting system. One problem was to gain some kind of objective scientific appraisal of their product, akin to the stamp of approval given to the Brush system by the Franklin Institute in 1878. The opportunity arose in the spring of 1883, when the city of Cincinnati announced that its annual industrial exposition would feature electric lighting. Only three companies submitted apparatus — Edison, Thomson-Houston, and the United States Electric Lighting Company.[34] The jury of awards, headed by a professor of physics at Ohio State University, was composed of competent scientists. They gave Thomson a top award for his arc light and dynamo. The Thomson-Houston system thus received official scientific recognition in an area far from New England.

The Thomson-Houston policy of taking advantage of opportunities to obtain an objective scientific test of its products was continued in later years. In 1885, Thomson-Houston submitted its arc-lighting system to tests at the London (England) Inventions Exhibition. In a very severe and very long competition with leading European and American arc-lighting systems, it received the only gold medal awarded. The tests given the apparatus included short-circuiting the generator, turning out twenty to thirty lamps at once, pouring oil on the commutator, and running the entire system for ninety days without stopping. In this last phase of the tests, the Thomson-Houston equipment gave no trouble whatsoever — a remarkable record. The automatic regulator enabled the dynamo to stand the short-circuit and change-of-load tests, and the air blast protected the commutator from damage by the oil.[35] Winning the London medal was extremely important to Thomson-Houston in selling in the foreign market. Only the year before an English visitor to the United States had remarked that the Thomson-Houston system was unknown in England.[36] In 1891, the Thomson a.c.-d.c. wattmeter divided first prize with a French meter at a Paris contest. Fifty-one meters from many countries were entered in the competition.[37]

A second problem was to organize a sales staff and develop proper marketing policies. Prospective customers for arc lights could be divided into those who purchased isolated plants to light their own premises—factories, yards, railroad stations, public halls, and so forth—and those who intended to operate central stations to sell light to business firms and to cities for street illumination. Coffin decided that the second type of customer would prove to be the more profitable. Later he reported:

> While some electric manufacturing companies have confined their operations to the "isolated" business . . . which is of inferior value and importance, nearly 90 per cent of the business of your company has been in the sale of its apparatus to corporations organized to furnish light and power from central lighting and power stations. The business of these corporations is profitable and constantly increasing, and the orders received from them for increased plant and for renewal apparatus and supplies are secured with comparatively little solicitation expense, and are chiefly for cash.[38]

Thomson-Houston developed the market for its arc-lighting apparatus by promoting local arc-lighting companies. This technique did not originate with the Thomson-Houston company. It was used by Brush, the United States company, and Goff in arc lighting and by Edison in incandescent lighting. The arc-lighting salesmen of the time were, in effect, promoters. They secured local capital, obtained a franchise from the local city council, drew up contracts for equipment, and helped to organize the operating company. Thomson-Houston would usually place clauses in its contract with the licensee company to insure that the latter would continue to purchase its supplies from Thomson-Houston. The contract between Thomson-Houston and the Jamestown (New York) Electric Light and Power Company, dated August 9, 1887, gave the Jamestown company the right to use the dynamos and the lamps for the purpose of furnishing light in Jamestown but in no other place. The local company further agreed

> that it will not use the apparatus for electric lighting acquired by it under the terms of this instrument, or allow the same to be used, except in the territory hereinbefore specified, and for the purpose of renting electric lights only, and that no portion of said apparatus shall be used in connection with any other apparatus or any part thereof not acquired from or with the consent of the licensor. Said licensee agrees that it will hereafter purchase and use in connection with any apparatus bought of said licensor only such carbons as said licensor may from time to time designate, and that it will use all reasonable efforts to extend its business and increase the demand for such apparatus for electric lighting within said territory.[39]

The policy of requiring licensee companies to use only Thomson-Houston accessories and supplies in connection with its equipment was still in effect in 1891.[40]

Like the other electrical manufacturing companies, Thomson-Houston accepted securities from the local companies in part payment for equipment. This fact, coupled with the rapid growth of the business in 1883 and 1884, created an urgent need for more capital. To meet this need, a number of trusts were formed (in 1885, 1886, and 1889) to purchase for cash from Thomson-Houston certain stocks, bonds, and accounts of local lighting companies. The Thomson-Houston stockholders were permitted to buy stock in these trusts, which eventually were able to dispose of the securities and divide the proceeds among the trust shareholders. This system acted to separate security holding from the manufacturing business and segregated assets of high face-value as an inducement to Thomson-Houston stockholders to invest more in the Thomson-Houston company. The trusts finally paid off, on dissolution, about two dollars for each dollar invested.[41]

Thomson-Houston did considerable advertising in the electrical journals, stressing the reliability, self-regulation, efficiency, and economy of its system. Advertising of other kinds was also carried on. In 1884, Thomson-Houston offered to light the new Rush Street bridge in Chicago with one six-light dynamo and six arc lights. The equipment was to be given to the city free of charge if the Thomson-Houston name were placed in a conspicuous place on the bridge. The city of Chicago accepted this offer.[42]

By building its own sales force, Thomson-Houston eliminated the need for sales agents like Goff, who were selling the Thomson-Houston system under their own names. These independent sales agents were gradually dropped, and, by 1886, all salesmen were directly under supervision of the company. Thereafter, all Thomson-Houston equipment was sold only under the Thomson-Houston name.

No major technical improvements were made after 1883 in arc-lighting apparatus by Thomson-Houston except the 60-light dynamo which was put out in 1884. But Thomson-Houston, like the Brush company, soon expanded into other lines. In 1884, Thomson-Houston began to make incandescent lamps for use on arc-light circuits. By 1885, the company was making a complete incandescent system, including dynamos, and had developed a new filament-treating process which made the Thomson-Houston incandescent lamps superior to the Edison. A line of d.c. motors was added in 1886, while the production of railway motors and a.c. components (transformers, generators) was begun in 1887. In 1888, Thomson-

TABLE 1

Growth of the Thomson-Houston Electric Company

Year	*Employees* [a]	*Output: arc lights (and associated equipment)*	*Sales (all types of apparatus)*	*Profits retained from each year's earnings*	*Local lighting companies using T-H system* [a]	*Arc lights in use by local lighting companies* [a]
1883	45	3,000	$ 426,987.97	$ 93,696.74	5	365
1884	145	...	700,470.47	96,187.10	31	2,478
1885	160	...	983,996.85	106,687.50	59	5,867
1886	335	12,000	1,485,041.74	123,006.05	100	13,227
1887	571	17,949	2,235,594.80	313,596.67	171	21,840
1888	888	19,436	4,435,982.23	660,828.82	303	36,936
1889	1,225	24,031	8,222,789.12	1,309,175.19	419	51,621
1890	2,328	...	10,617,661.67	4,337,117.79	587	68,203
1891	2,422	...	10,304,580.17	1,524,414.25	755	87,131
1892	3,492	...	...	...	873	100,292

Sources: Various documents and publications of the Thomson-Houston Electric Company.
[a] On January 1.

Houston started to make a complete electric-railway system. A carbon plant was built that same year. Thus, by 1890, Thomson-Houston was producing every important item of the electrical industry.

THE WESTON ELECTRIC LIGHT COMPANY

Edward Weston was born in the English Midlands, near Wolverhampton. He early showed an interest in chemistry and electricity, but his parents wanted him to become a physician. After several years of medical study, he decided that a career in the physical sciences would be more to his liking. He searched for an opportunity to work or study in those fields but was unsuccessful. In 1870, at the age of twenty, having decided that a more promising future awaited him in the United States, he came to New York City. His first job was with a firm which manufactured photographic chemicals. A little later he worked as a chemist for an electroplating company. As he learned more about electroplating, he became interested in the possibility of using a dynamo instead of a battery as the source of current, and in 1872 he constructed an electric generator for that purpose.

During the next few years, he built a number of electroplating dynamos. By 1875, he had shifted his location from New York City to Newark and was giving full time to dynamo construction and other electrical activities. The latter included the development of an electric-arc furnace for industrial heating. With technical experience in both generators and carbon arcs, he next undertook to combine the two in arc lighting. He completed his arc-lighting system early in 1877 and placed it on public demonstration in a Newark street.

The commercial possibilities of Weston's work were sufficient to warrant formation of the Weston Dynamo Electric Machine Company in June 1877. The authorized capital was $200,000. This company was to manufacture Weston electroplating dynamos and the Weston arc-lighting system. At first, electroplating dynamos were nearly the entire output, but in 1878 and 1879 Weston sold a number of arc-lighting systems, principally to amusement parks such as Coney Island.[43] In 1879 the name of the firm was changed to the Weston Electric Light Company.

The number of arc lights and lighting dynamos sold by Weston in the early years is not known. It is probable that he made nearly all of the thousand arc lights (and associated equipment) which were in use by the end of 1880 and which are not attributed to Brush. Census data for 1879 show for what probably was Weston's firm that it employed about 75 workers and had an annual output of $150,000.[44] When these figures are compared to the Brush figures for the same period (Brush employment was 150 and output $300,000), it should be noted that Weston was mainly a producer of electroplating dynamos and only secondarily a producer of arc-lighting equipment. His leading position in electroplating was recognized in the following statement which appeared in an English technical journal in 1881: "The name of Mr. Weston has long been before the public as the inventor of one of the most successful dynamo-electric machines that has ever been introduced for electro-plating, and we believe at the present time the greater bulk of the largely increasing industry of nickel-plating is performed by Mr. Weston's machines."[45]

The Weston company was purchased by the United States Electric Lighting Company in 1882. The latter had been incorporated in June 1878 after several years of preliminary experimenting by Hiram Maxim and William Sawyer. Their work convinced S. D. Schuyler and the Equitable Life Assurance Company that the manufacture of electric-lighting equipment would be profitable. Nothing resulted, however, during the first few years. The firm's technical men, who included Maxim, Sawyer, and Moses G. Farmer, were unable to develop a practical lighting system of either the arc or incandescent type. By the end of 1880, Maxim had produced an incandescent lamp that was workable but of little value without the other components (dynamo, switches, and so forth) of a complete system. Charles R. Flint, one of the vice-presidents of the United States company, believed that the company should purchase a manufacturer of arc-lighting equipment to get a marketable system. Flint tried to effect a consolidation with the Brush company but was unsuccessful. He then contacted Weston and arranged for the purchase of the Weston Electric Light Company.[46]

The United States company produced and marketed the Weston arc-lighting system and electroplating dynamos. The Maxim incandescent lamp was combined with a Weston dynamo to form an incandescent-lighting system. Weston served as chief electrical engineer of the United States company until 1886. During those years he made a number of outstanding improvements in dynamos, incandescent lamps, and techniques of electrical manufacturing. After 1886, Weston carried on his own inventing and research. In 1888, he formed the Weston Electrical Instrument Company, which rapidly became very successful and made the name of Weston synonymous with electrical measuring instruments.

It is not possible to say exactly why Weston, in spite of unusual technical skill and inventive ability, did not match the achievement of Brush in arc lighting. Weston began to make arc-lighting equipment about the same time as Brush, but it was Brush, not Weston, who was the pioneer innovator in arc lighting.

One reason for Weston's lack of success in arc lighting was that he had no clear conception of the market he was trying to serve. Some of his arc lights were used in street lighting, but most saw only a more limited application, such as in amusement parks. He did not design his system with any particular use in mind. His technical abilities thus lacked orientation and direction. In contrast, his electroplating dynamos were very successful because he thoroughly understood the characteristics that a dynamo had to have before the manager of an electroplating shop would prefer it to batteries.

Weston's arc-lighting system was technically inferior to the Brush system in two important respects. The Weston arc light was a complicated and somewhat unreliable device in contrast to the simple and almost foolproof Brush light. Furthermore, Weston chose a current of 20 amperes for his arc light, about twice as great as either Brush or Thomson-Houston.[47] The result was an arc light which was very inefficient. Efficiency was relatively unimportant in the first years, but as the use of arc lighting spread and knowledge of electrical engineering became more common, it proved to be a ruling consideration. Table 2 compares the Weston arc-lighting system with the Thomson-Houston system in light production and efficiency.

TABLE 2

Efficiency of the Weston and Thomson-Houston Arc-Lighting Systems

System	*Candle power per arc light*	*Watts per arc light*	*Candle power per watt*
Thomson-Houston	2034	490	4.15
Weston	1316	709	1.86

Source: Thomson-Houston Electric Company, Circular Letter to Agents No. 5, May 8, 1890, (GE Files).

The contrast between Weston and the two very successful arc-lighting entrepreneurs, Brush and Thomson, should not obscure the fact that Weston was responsible for major technical advances. Weston was the first American dynamo maker to use a laminated armature. This feature, which increases efficiency considerably, was not adopted by Brush until 1884. Like Brush, Weston carried out considerable work on carbon improvement. Independently of Brush, Weston developed copper-plated carbons. Brush himself is supposed to have referred to Weston's as an example of a good system in 1881.[48] Sir William Preece, the outstanding English electrical engineer of the 1880's, visited America in 1884 and, after a careful examination of all arc-lighting systems, decided that the Weston system was mechanically the best in the United States. His description of the electrical features seems also to indicate that he held a high opinion of the electrical characteristics of the system.[49]

It is perhaps significant that Weston's greatest contribution to the electrical manufacturing industry in the United States lay in a product where technical excellence alone was of crucial importance. Weston set out to design electrical measuring instruments for laboratory, testing, and central-station purposes which would be accurate. He realized this goal, and to this day the Weston Electrical Instrument Company is the leading firm in its field. In electrical instruments, Weston understood the market and the exacting requirements for product success. He could focus his abilities on developing such products, and he thereby achieved the position of pioneer innovator.

THE AMERICAN ELECTRIC AND ILLUMINATING COMPANY

E. H. Goff entered the arc-lighting business as a sales agent for the American Electric Company in 1881. Very shortly thereafter, he organized his own firm, the American Electric and Illuminating Company, to handle his marketing activities. He located in Boston. Late in 1881, he placed some arc lights in a store on Tremont Street and tried to sell stock to the crowds that were attracted.[50] Goff marketed the Thomson-Houston equipment under the name of his firm, calling it the American system. At this time Goff was not interested in the manufacture of the apparatus and made no attempt to buy the American Electric Company. Evidently he believed that it would be more profitable to concentrate on marketing.

After American Electric was purchased by the Lynn capitalists, Goff's firm continued to serve as sales agent for Thomson-Houston arc-lighting equipment. By an agreement made in the spring of 1884, the American Electric and Illuminating Company became the sales agent for all territory east of the Mississippi River, except Illinois, Louisiana, Pennsylvania, Delaware, and New Jersey. In Illinois and Louisiana, the Thomson-Houston company and the American Electric and Illuminating Company were to operate jointly.[51]

During the time that Goff's firm was sales agent for the Thomson-Houston company, Goff marketed about 20 per cent of its output.[52] Of the 100 local arc-lighting companies that were using Thomson-Houston equipment by January 1, 1886, Goff had organized and sold the equipment to at least 15. Of the 1885 Thomson-Houston output, Goff sold about one-eighth.[53] He handled a higher proportion of the output in the early years than later. In the year between July 1883 and July 1884, his firm sold 3,280 arc lights and the dynamos to operate them.[54] This is probably 50 per cent of the Thomson-Houston output during that period. As the Thomson-Houston company built up its own organization, Goff's firm became less and less important to it as a sales outlet.

Goff's method of finding a market for the arc-lighting equipment differed from that of other arc-lighting salesmen of the period. He did not try to interest local capital in the local company until it was on a paying basis. This meant that Goff's firm would hold the stock in the operating company for from two to three years before selling out to local capitalists. This method assured a well-run firm and saved the effort required in trying to secure local backing before the enterprise had shown its profit-earning ability. But large amounts of capital were tied up for relatively long periods. The problem of securing financial backing was simply transferred from the level of the local operating company to that of sales agent.

The data in Table 3 show that capital invested in local companies (the first four items, approximately) was about 95 per cent of total assets. Goff's big problem was to raise the funds for the local operating companies in

TABLE 3

Asset Data of the American Electric and Illuminating Company

	April 30, 1884 [a]	*February 1885* [b]
Stock in subcompanies	$248,277.37	$419,857.27
Cash due from subcompanies	154,645.09	98,115.61
Bills and accounts receivable	29,564.84	8,609.61
Real estate and mortgages	13,941.00	38,498.09
Merchandise	15,921.22	15,000.00
Cash	5,128.40	4,182.04
Other	4,971.60	3,000.00
TOTAL ASSETS	$472,449.52	$587,262.62

[a] *EW*, III (May 31, 1884), 179.
[b] *EW*, V (February 21, 1885), 77.

order that the Thomson-Houston company could receive payment for the equipment purchased by Goff and sold to the sub-companies. Goff's Tremont Street display in Boston in 1881, it will be remembered, was not to sell apparatus but to sell stock. In an advertisement which appeared in July 1884, the American Electric and Illuminating Company announced that it was offering for sale 10,000 shares of preferred stock at $10 per share.[55] During 1884, a total of nearly $200,000 was raised by the sale of preferred stock to the public. Goff kept up regular and liberal dividend payments in order to create the necessary market for this stock. For a short period, the preferred stock was earning 12 per cent, and by February 1885 a total of over $100,000 had been paid out in dividends since the company's founding.[56]

The continual drain of cash into supplies for the subcompanies and the liberal dividends created cash shortages a number of times. As the asset figures in Table 3 indicate, cash on hand was not very large, and on some occasions, such as on March 1, 1885, the quarterly dividend was actually paid in scrip redeemable some months later.

By 1885, Goff was becoming dissatisfied with his position as merely a sales agent for Thomson-Houston. In his report to the board of directors of the American company, dated February 16, 1885, Goff mentioned the high prices charged for dynamos and lamps and indicated that arc carbons, which sold for about $50 a thousand, cost only $25 a thousand to manufacture.[57] Goff apparently believed that in acting as only a sales agent he was losing considerable manufacturing profit. At the same time, Coffin was building up the Thomson-Houston sales organization and reducing his need for independent sales agents. In these circumstances, Goff had either to think seriously of entering the manufacturing field or face gradual extinction. He chose the first alternative and purchased an interest in the Boulton Carbon Company of Cleveland, a firm engaged in the manufacture of arc-lighting carbons, in January 1885. Goff was particularly anxious to secure carbons at a lower price because his firm owned 24 arc-lighting companies at that time. In March, Goff formed the American Electric Manufacturing Company, which combined his old firm and the carbon company. The capital stock of this new company was $3 million — 30,000 $100 shares. In September, Goff made arrangements to lease the patents, factory, and other property of the Fuller-Wood Company, manufacturers of the Wood system of arc lighting,[58] and thereby became a manufacturer of arc-lighting apparatus. Goff moved his headquarters from Boston to New York, and by the end of 1885 the American Electric Manufacturing Company was making and selling the American (Wood) system of arc lighting. Goff's connection with Thomson-Houston was severed when he gave up the agency in September.

Goff began his career as a manufacturer with $200,000 worth of orders on hand. As before, he organized local companies to buy his apparatus. In January 1886, he filed for incorporation of ten local illuminating companies in New York State. This, in turn, necessitated the issue of 6 per cent twenty-year debenture bonds a few weeks later.[59] The New York factory proved inadequate for the increasing sales. A $200,000 factory at New Haven, Connecticut, was put into operation early in 1887. It could produce arc-lighting equipment of 500-light capacity per week and was financed by the sale of treasury stock.[60]

In April 1887, Goff's firm purchased outright the Fuller-Wood Company, whose patents and factory it had been leasing.[61] Orders were secured at a satisfactory rate during that year, and by October the company could announce that over 10,000 American (Wood) arc lights were in operation and that the output during 1887 would be equipment for more than 15,000 arc lights.[62]

In marketing, Goff pioneered in several innovations. His system of organizing local companies and keeping control of them until they were on a sound financial basis has already been mentioned. This technique was widely used later by the Westinghouse Electric Company. The chief drawback to Goff's method was the fact that it tied up capital for long periods. Goff was thus continually pressed to raise additional funds. That he got these local companies well started and that he could sell them to capable capitalists is shown by a study of one of the early ones.

Goff founded the Hartford Electric Light Company, Hartford, Connecticut, in 1881. By 1884, it was well established and was sold to a group of Connecticut capitalists headed by A. C. Dunham. This light company proved to be one of the most progressive in the United States. It was the first to operate a high-voltage transmission line, a modern alternating-current motor, enclosed-arc street lamps, aluminum conductors, a steam turbine, a mercury turbine, and many other technical advances.[63] While this company is only one example, it shows that Goff was capable of organizing a local arc-lighting company, getting it in operation, and selling to capitalists competent to manage it.

Goff was also at the forefront in his early recognition of the gas companies as possible customers for arc lighting. In November 1886, he claimed that for years he had been stressing the fact that the gas companies should engage in the provision of electric-arc lighting. At that time, two large gas companies — one in St. Paul and one in Jacksonville — were acting as agents for the sale of the American apparatus.[64] Goff's idea evidently was that a gas company could sell to other gas companies more easily than a maker of electric equipment could. Goff was not the only, or the first, arc-lighting salesman to think of the gas companies as customers. Brush also sold to them, and the Thomson-Houston company could boast, by October 1, 1888, that 58 gas companies in the United States were using Thomson-Houston apparatus.[65] But Goff was foremost in the trend that led to the supply of electricity and gas by the same company — a product combination that eventually was to be commonplace.

Another avenue followed out by Goff in his search for markets was his alliance with the Edison interests. In the early part of 1885, Goff made a contract with the Edison Company for Isolated Lighting whereby his firm was to have the exclusive right to use the Edison system of isolated lighting in connection with all its arc-light central stations and isolated plants in New England. In turn, the Boston agent of the Edison Electric Light Company agreed that if an arc-lighting system were needed (for, say, street lighting) when an Edison central station was organized, the

American system (that is, Thomson-Houston) would be chosen.[66] As an example of the coöperation that existed under the Edison-Goff contract, the Consolidated Electric Light Company of Portland, Maine, may be mentioned. This was a Goff subcompany, and Goff made the arrangements for it to install the Edison municipal system of incandescent lighting in September 1885.[67]

The relationship with Edison was no doubt of help to Goff in the selling of arc-lighting apparatus. Association with the strongest incandescent-light company of that period is evidence of Goff's business standing and his ability to seek out new markets. But Goff's ultimate benefit from this was less than it might have been had the Edison people been more interested in arc lighting. The Edison company was the only one to manufacture incandescent-lighting apparatus alone.[68] All the others of any size — Westinghouse, the United States company, Thomson-Houston, Brush — made both arc- and incandescent-lighting equipment.

Goff's advertising and publicity activities showed imagination and the ability to sense opportunities for getting the name of his product before the public. In 1886, a movement was started to light the Statue of Liberty with arc lights. The *Electrical World* attempted to raise funds for this purpose but had little success. Goff stepped in and donated the necessary lighting apparatus — one dynamo and fifteen arc lights — and the money that had been raised was used to provide the steam plant to drive the dynamo. An advertising booklet, published by the American Electric Manufacturing Company in 1887, contained a picture of the Statue of Liberty and the statement that the statue was lighted by the American (Wood) system.[69]

Another publicity technique used by Goff was the competitive challenge. On October 1, 1886, shortly after the Wood patents had been leased, the American Electric Manufacturing Company issued a statement challenging "any and all manufacturers of electric arc light apparatus in this country to meet in a thirty days' competitive test, in all points of superiority claimed for the American (Wood) Dynamo Machine and Lamp." Each company entering the test was to pay $1,000 to defray test expenses, the balance going to the winner, who immediately would donate it to charity. The statement ended as follows: "This challenge is made to all Manufacturing or Parent Companies of Electric Arc Light Apparatus in the United States but is made with especial reference to the Thomson-Houston Electric Company of Boston, Mass." [70] That no company accepted the challenge is hardly surprising, and it is doubtful that Goff really expected any company to do so. He did use the lack of acceptance as a proof of the superiority of the American (Wood) system.

The position of the American Electric Manufacturing Company in relation to the Thomson-Houston Electric Company during 1886 is shown in Table 4. These data indicate that Goff's firm was doing well. If Goff had maintained his 1886 position, he could conceivably have become as important a figure in the electrical manufacturing industry as Coffin, Westinghouse, Brush, or Edison.

But the success of 1886 and 1887 was not permanent. The first sign of trouble was a movement, in May 1887, among the stockholders of the American Electric Manufacturing Company to force Goff from the presidency.[71] The reasons for this attempt are not known. By virtue of his holding proxies for 75 per cent of the stock, Goff was able to keep his position. In April of the following year, Goff sent a circular to the stockholders indicating that money was needed for expansion. He wrote, "I have previously asked you for the increased capital . . . without a satisfactory response." [72] He was asking Boston capital to come in, therefore, and he requested the stockholders to place their stock in trust under a Dr. Amory of Boston. Goff concluded the circular with the statement that his ill health would require a six-months' rest and that he would resign. A few weeks later, he resigned from the presidency, and a Mr. H. C. Adams, who had been treasurer and factory manager, became president. In July, Roland N. Hazard, president of the American Loan and Trust Company of New York, the Gramme Electrical Company, and the Bentley-Knight Railway Company,[73] was elected to the presidency. Goff was relegated to the board of directors.

TABLE 4

Comparison of American and Thomson-Houston (1886 data)

	American	*Thomson-Houston*
Output of apparatus (measured in arc lights)	7,200	12,000
Sales	$864,400	$1,485,000 [a]
Profits	$112,700	$123,000 [b]

Sources: For Thomson-Houston data, see Table 1; American output and sales, *EW*, X (September 3, 1887), 133; American profits, *EW*, IX (June 25, 1887), 307.

[a] Includes some incandescent equipment.

[b] This figure is profits retained, but because Thomson-Houston paid almost no dividends in its first years, retained profits nearly equaled total profits.

On August 14, 1888, a decision was handed down in the United States Circuit Court, District of Massachusetts, upholding the contention of the Thomson-Houston Electric Company that a Goff subcompany which was using the American (Wood) system of arc lighting was infringing a Thomson-Houston patent.[74] This was the current-regulator patent and covered the device which was attached to the dynamo and which kept the arc lights burning at the correct brightness even when one or more were taken out of the circuit.

During this same month, either by coincidence or as a result of the unfavorable prospects for the company in view of the Massachusetts patent decision, two large creditors forced a temporary suspension of manufacturing operations.[75] Then, in September, the Thomson-Houston company secured an injunction from the United States Circuit Court in New York City restraining the American company from selling, delivering, or shipping dynamos with the current regulator. At the same time, Thomson-Houston served notice on all users of the American (Wood) system that they would be sued for damages unless satisfactory settlement were made.[76]

The American Electric Manufacturing Company began operations again on October 1, but shortly thereafter failed and went out of business. The Wood patents and the services of James J. Wood, who had been chief electrical engineer for the American company, were purchased by Thomson-Houston, and, by the spring of 1889, Wood was manufacturing his apparatus in a factory in Brooklyn. Goff played no further part in the electrical manufacturing industry. He died of Bright's disease in 1891 and left his family almost penniless.

III

Interfirm Relations

PATENTS

THE most significant aspect of patents in arc lighting is that neither of the basic elements of an arc-lighting system — the dynamo and the arc light — was patentable. Two attempts were made to monopolize the arc-lighting-equipment industry by means of patents on these basic elements, but both failed. In April 1881, the Brush, Fuller-Wood, and United States companies formed the Gramme Electrical Company, which then purchased the American rights to a dynamo patent granted to Z. T. Gramme in 1871. It was expected that this patent would give absolute control of all dynamo manufacture in the United States and that arc-lighting dynamos could be made only under license from the Gramme company. A patent-infringement suit was instituted in August 1883 against the Arnoux and Hochhausen Electrical Company, a small New York firm. The suit was heard before the United States Circuit Court in Newport, Rhode Island. In a decision rendered within a few weeks, the court declared that the Gramme patent had expired December 30, 1880.[1] The grounds for this decision was the fact that a prior Austrian patent covering the same invention had expired on that date. The effect of the decision was to free the dynamo from threat of patent control. Anybody could manufacture it. It was only minor details in dynamo design and construction — such as particular coil windings or commutators — which were patentable.

The Brush Electric Company was also involved in the other attempt to obtain a monopoly by means of a patent. Brush hoped to secure an absolute control of arc-light manufacture. In 1880, Brush brought suit against a user of Weston arc-lighting apparatus for infringement of the Brush arc-light patent. The case lasted four years, and over 2,000 pages of testimony were taken. The United States Electric Lighting Company, which conducted the defense after 1881, introduced as evidence an arc lamp that had been invented in 1876 by a man named Haynes. This lamp had been a failure, and the Brush company argued that it should be considered an abandoned experiment rather than an invention. But the judge decided that the Brush arc-lamp patent was invalid.[2]

Because there were no basic patents in arc lighting, the patents of significance concerned improvement and detail. These were of minor importance until the industry had been in existence for nearly ten years. The only two arc-lighting patents which had been upheld by 1890 were the Thomson-Houston automatic-current-regulator patent, upheld in 1888, and the Brush double-carbon arc-lamp patent, upheld in 1890.

For both these patents, considerable time elapsed between the date of issue and the establishment of their validity by the courts. The regulator patent was issued in 1881. Seven years passed before it was upheld. The double-carbon arc-lamp patent was issued in 1879. Eleven years passed before it was upheld. Thus, there were no improvement patents which had been proved to be valid in the first decade of arc lighting. Patents were consequently not a handicap to entry into the industry. Firm after firm was organized to manufacture its own arc-lighting system. At one time, nearly fifty different firms were making arc-lighting equipment.

An important question arises. Why was there such a long delay before the two improvement patents received the court certification of their validity that made them effective competitive weapons? The answer to this question seems to lie in several factors. In the early years of arc lighting, the arc-lighting-equipment companies were competing more with gas than with each other. The market was so wide that the firms could grow rapidly and still not have to compete with each other for business. At the same time, the knowledge of electrical equipment was severely limited, and the competitive advantage of a patented improvement was not nearly so great as in later years. Only when arc-lighting systems were better understood and when the buyers of these systems realized the significance of operating costs, maintenance costs, reliability, and the other relevant factors did small improvements give a substantial competitive advantage.

The arc-lighting industry seems to indicate that there are two critical patent periods in the development of a technical industry. In the very beginning, if valid patents are issued which cover the basic components of the new product, the industry will be likely to develop as a monopoly. The telephone and the aluminum industries are examples. If, as in the case of arc lighting, there are no valid basic patents, the critical patent period is delayed until the industry and its buyers have matured to the point where patents on improvements are of great competitive importance. At this time, the various companies take steps to determine the validity of their improvement patents and prevent infringement.

The position of the Thomson-Houston company in improvement patents was particularly strong. Its automatic current regulator played an important part in the excellent reputation of the Thomson-Houston arc-lighting system. When this patent was upheld in 1888, the way was opened to purchase the Wood patents and, in the next year, the Brush company. Other Thomson-Houston patents were also important, especially the air-blast commutator and the lightning arrester. When the Brush double-carbon patent was upheld in 1890, the Brush company was controlled by Thomson-Houston. That patent, too, helped Thomson-Houston achieve a dominant position in the manufacture of arc-lighting equipment.

COMPETITION IN THE ARC-LIGHTING-EQUIPMENT INDUSTRY

Arc-lighting equipment was a capital good. It was sold either to arc-lighting companies who produced light for municipalities, business firms, and, occasionally, for households, or directly to business firms who made for themselves the light that they needed in the conduct of their business. The final product was light, and the cost of producing that light could not be measured by the price of arc-lighting apparatus alone. The operating and maintenance costs of the entire system had to be included. Such costs always involve complex calculations and are hard to estimate with certainty. The efficiency of a dynamo as a converter of mechanical to electrical energy, for example, is a function of the efficiency of the dynamo under all the varying conditions of load which it will meet. The labor costs in operating an arc-lighting system are a function of the amount of attention the generator needs, the frequency with which the carbons require replacement, and the general ability of the apparatus to continue to operate under adverse conditions such as widely fluctuating loads or electrical storms.

The quality of light was another factor which made it impossible to choose arc-lighting equipment on the basis of price alone. Quality included color, intensity, noise, steadiness, and reliability of the service, and these characteristics varied appreciably among the different makes of apparatus. The importance of light quality was determined by the light consumers, who gave consideration, in selecting arc lighting over gas lighting or arc lighting from one company over another company, to quality as well as to price. Price and quality were, of course, interrelated, in that higher quality could usually be secured only at a higher price. What the lighting company wanted was equipment that could produce light of such a quality and at such a cost that maximum profits could be attained. Comparing profit possibilities of different apparatus required separate demand and cost estimates for each. Separate demand estimates were necessary because each brand of equipment produced a different product (that is, light of a different quality). The original, operating, and maintenance costs for each brand were also different.

Arc-lighting equipment was thus a heterogeneous capital good which produced a heterogeneous product. In these circumstances, price competition was not the most significant aspect of competition. A manufacturer who made an arc-lighting system which produced high-quality light at low operating and upkeep costs could charge a relatively high price for his equipment. In 1886, for example, Hannibal, Missouri, decided to install a municipal arc-lighting plant and called for bids. Eight were submitted. The highest was the Thomson-Houston Electric Company bid of $25,000. The lowest was a Brooklyn firm's bid of $12,700. The contract was awarded to the Fort Wayne Electric Light Company, which had bid $16,485.[3] The high bid is interesting in view of the fact that at this time Thomson-Houston was already the largest producer of arc-lighting apparatus. It is possible that the Thomson-Houston bid was actually the low bid, measured in light-production costs.

The uncertainty and inexactness involved in a comparison between the cost of light production using one arc-lighting system as against another was very great. Consider trying to compare the Thomson-Houston system which has an automatic current regulator with a system which does not. Which system is cheaper depends on how the lighting load will fluctuate. An even harder comparison would be between the Thomson-Houston system with its regulator which consumes no energy itself and permits the generator to run at high efficiency at all loads and the Brush system which had a regulator which consumed energy at less than full load. A feature such as a lightning arrester is also difficult to translate into cost terms. The frequency of need for it cannot be foreseen, nor will it always work when it is supposed to.

The complex nature of an arc-lighting system and the key importance of two factors, the quality of the light produced and the over-all efficiency of the system in manufacturing that light, pushed competition into the areas of product improvement and new-product development. One such area was the size of the dynamo. For technical reasons, a large dynamo is cheaper to build and to operate, per unit of light produced, than a small dynamo. Before large machines could be manufactured, considerable experimental work and inventive ingenuity were required to solve voltage and commutation difficulties. And when one manufacturer succeeded in building a large dynamo, the others had to follow or lose many of their sales. One objective and quantitative measure of competitive strength in this instance is the capacity in arc lights of the largest dynamo that each manufacturer produced. By 1885, for example, Thomson-Houston was making a 60-light dynamo and Brush a 65-light machine.[4] At that time, no other arc-lighting manufacturer was making a dynamo larger than the 30-light size.

Where competition takes the form of product improvement, each manufacturer would like to keep his competitors from duplicating improvements that he develops. In some products, such as chemicals, secrecy in the process of production may be sufficient to give protection. In most electrical devices, however, the nature of the improvement can easily be deduced from examination of the final product. To get protection, the manufacturer has to resort to patents. In encouraging product improvement, patents can serve as an important stimulus to technological progress.

In arc-lighting equipment, the complex nature of the product and the continual competitive pressure to effect improvements made virtually impossible any price-fixing agreements. As already intimated, the complexity and uncertainty and the different possible conditions of operation did not permit the calculation of the price of one arc-lighting system in order to equate it in production cost to another arc-lighting system. Even if such a calculation could be made, it is doubtful whether a manufacturer with a competent technical staff would be willing to accept a share of the market given him by agreement. He might reasonably hope to improve his product from time to time and perhaps in patentable ways. If this hope were realized, he would gain a competitive advantage which could increase his sales and profits substantially.

One of the marketing dilemmas in an industry where the product is continually improving over time arises because the customer may decide to wait for more improvements before purchasing. The manufacturer has to convince the prospective buyer that no major improvements are in the offing. At the same time, the manufacturer must continue to improve his product to maintain his competitive position and to force existing products into obsolescence. This dilemma is referred to in an 1889 Thomson-Houston booklet: "There is often much hesitation on the part of intended purchasers of electric lighting apparatus because of an apprehension that some 'cheap system' may in the future be introduced in competition by which lights may be furnished at much lower prices than can be afforded with a good, though higher priced, system."[5]

Other marketing problems resulted from the fact that arc-lighting equipment was based on scientific principles unfamiliar to most people. The usual buyer was not competent to judge the merits of arc-lighting systems. He tended to rely on the judgment of technical experts instead. The Franklin Institute report which rated the Brush dynamo the best one available was an important factor in the early success of the Brush company. The Thomson-Houston company found it desirable to secure impartial scientific appraisals of its dynamo, arc lamp, arc-lighting system as a whole, and watt-hour meter.

The buyer's ignorance of the product meant that he had to be instructed in its operation. He was usually educated by the salesman who had been trained at the factory. What the manufacturer wanted to avoid was the poor operation or failure of his equipment because of lack of technical knowledge on the part of the operating company. In 1885, a Brush official complained that some of the users of Brush equipment were loading the dynamo with more than the designed number of lamps.[6] As a result, the lamps were dim and flickering, and the Brush equipment seemed inferior. Such incidents could not be ignored, since the average buyer, forced by his ignorance to accept expert judgment on technical characteristics, would often give considerable weight in choosing arc-lighting equipment to the quality of light produced by that equipment in commercial use. The Thomson-Houston company was aware of that problem, too. Advertising literature and sales agents' circulars frequently contained information on the poor operation of rival systems. In the early 1890's, Thomson-Houston sales agents were told that a Westinghouse arc-light installation at Susquehanna, Pennsylvania, was not working satisfactorily, that an Edison arc-light installation at Franklin, Pennsylvania, had suffered four burned-out armatures, and that a central station in Chicago had been requested by nine of its customers to change over to the Thomson-Houston system.[7] A sales pamphlet published in 1889 listed twenty-one places where a rival system had been displaced by the Thomson-Houston system, and boasted that the Thomson-Houston system had never been displaced although it had been on the market for nearly a decade.

The potential buyers of arc lighting, as well as the potential buyers of arc-lighting equipment, knew very little, if anything, about this new method of illumination. This fact made necessary the offers of free lighting tendered from time to time by manufacturers and local arc-lighting companies. The offer of the Thomson-Houston company to furnish free of charge the arc-lighting equipment to light a Chicago bridge has already been mentioned. The case of the New York Brush Electric Light Company lighting Broadway free of charge for over six months before securing a municipal contract is paralleled by the experience of the Philadelphia arc-lighting company which volunteered to light three public squares with seventeen lights each for over three months in the hopes of getting a city contract.[8]

The patentable nature of some features of an arc-lighting system enabled the manufacturer to tie purchasers to him permanently. He licensed each purchaser to use the equipment and often to sell it. In return for protection against infringement suits, the purchaser admitted the validity of all the manufacturer's patents and frequently agreed to buy all his supplies and accessories from the manufacturer. Patents also enabled the manufacturer to sell his arc-lighting system as a system and to compete on a system basis with his rivals. The buyer, in choosing among arc-lighting systems, was faced with an all-or-nothing choice and could not combine the best elements of a number of systems. The following quotation from Thomson-Houston literature shows this system conception of competition.

> You are probably well aware, as are all our competitors, that all practicable and operative forms of lightning arresters are covered by patents owned by this company. Our lightning arrester thus becomes a very valuable part of our system and would, could it be applied to other systems, make them of much more value than at present.
>
> We would desire then that this valuable accessory of our system be considered as a part to be used exclusively in connection with our apparatus and not to be sold for use upon other systems.[9]

The patent license held by the local operating company was paid for separately from the equipment in most instances. The means of payment commonly was stock in the newly formed company. This exchange of one intangible for another was a method whereby the manufacturer was paid for the patent license only if, in fact, the patent were worth paying for. If the patented arc-lighting system lived up to the manufacturer's claims, the operating company could prosper and its stock would then possess value.

To describe a product is to imply the description of the market. To label arc-lighting equipment as a capital good is equivalent to saying that the buyers of this equipment were businessmen. But usually a market has characteristics other than those that can be inferred from the product. In arc-lighting equipment, most of the buyers in the years before 1890 were new firms, organized to make and sell light. The gas companies were also in the illumination business, but originally showed no interest in arc lighting. Not until the arc light had proved to be technically and commercially a success did gas companies enter the field. The salesman of arc-lighting equipment, as was said above, was in the first instance a promoter and often organized the companies that were his customers. He then secured local financial backing, tried to interest the city authorities in a street-lighting contract, helped in the organization of the new company, wrote the sales contracts for equipment, and served as a general consultant to the new firm on technical and commercial problems.

The fact that the market was mainly composed of new firms had consequences beyond defining the scope of the salesmen's activities. The manufacturer was often forced to take stocks or bonds of the new firm in part payment for equipment. The severity of the competitive pressure was reflected in the amount of securities that the manufacturer had to accept to make the sale. To take such securities was not sound financial practice, and the frequent reorganizations and failures among manufacturers of arc-lighting equipment can be attributed to it. Goff was the only manufacturer actually to own the local companies until they became established and could be sold to local capitalists. But Goff's procedure was an even more severe drain on financial resources and led to his failure.

Another important aspect of the market for arc-lighting equipment was the relationship between arc and gas lighting. Gas street lamps of the 1880's were generally of 16 candle power and were placed relatively close together along a street. In contrast, arc lights could not be made in small sizes (the most common size was 2000 candle power) and were therefore placed farther apart. Unfortunately for arc lighting, it was not simply a question of providing the same total light as gas by fewer, stronger lights spaced at greater intervals. The basic laws of illumination state that to light a street evenly by means of strong light sources requires a greater total amount of light than to light that same street by means of weak light sources. In other words, because the electric arc gave off so much light, and because illumination decreases in proportion to the square of the distance from the light source, arc lighting could not avoid providing more light than gas lighting. To have used a number of arc lights such that their total candle power equaled the total candle power provided by the gas lamps would have spaced the arc lights so far apart that there would have been extensive dark areas between lights.

A numerical example will illustrate how the inverse-square law works to the disadvantage of a strong light source. The so-called 2000-c.p. arc lamp was actually not that bright a light. To take a figure closer to reality, and to simplify computation, assume the arc lamp emitted 1500 c.p. The usual gas jet emitted about 15 c.p. Therefore, the arc lamp was 100 times as bright as the gas lamp. If total candle power were kept the same, one arc lamp could displace 100 gas lamps. In that case, with the distance between arc lamps 100 times as great as the distance between gas lamps, and assuming both the gas lamp and the arc lamp are point sources of light and are placed along a straight line, the light intensity at the darkest point, midway between arc lamps, would be only 1 per cent as great as it had been between the gas lamps.[10] If sufficient arc lamps were installed so that the light intensity between them were equal to the light intensity between gas lamps, one arc lamp would displace 10 gas lamps. Then the total candle power supplied by the arc lamps would be 10 times that of the gas lamps.

The relationships discussed in the previous paragraph are illustrated in Table 5. The first column of figures is based on an early installation in New York City by which 22 arc lights displaced 500 gas street lamps.[11] Here the arc lamps were so far apart that the light intensity midway between lamps was only about one-fifth of what it was with gas lamps. The

TABLE 5

Street Lighting: The Gas Light vs. the Arc Light

	New York City		*San Francisco*
	1881	*1885*	*1883*
Number of gas lights displaced by arc lights	500	3,000	1700
Number of arc lights	22	650	210
Ratio: arc lights to gas lights	1:22.7	1:4.6	1:8.1
Total c.p. of gas lights [a]	7,500	45,000	25,500
Total c.p. of arc lights [b]	33,000	975,000	315,000
Ratio: arc c.p. to gas c.p.	4.4:1	21.6:1	12.4:1
Minimum intensity between arc lights [c]	1/5 as great as between gas lights	4 times as great as between gas lights	about the same as between gas lights
Total cost gas lights per annum	$8,875	$53,000	$77,350
Total cost arc lights per annum	$7,400	$165,000	$65,520
Annual cost per gas light	$18	$18	$45
Annual cost per arc light	$336	$254	$312
Cost per c.p. of gas light	$1.18	$1.18	$3.04
Cost per c.p. of arc light	$0.22	$0.17	$0.21

Sources: New York City 1881 data from Report of the Superintendent of Lamps and Gas of New York City for 1881 (GE Files); New York City 1885 data from *EW*, V (May 2, 1885), 175; San Francisco data from *EW*, I (May 19, 1883), 312.

[a] Assumes gas light of 15 candle power.

[b] Assumes arc light of 1500 candle power.

[c] Based on computation technique explained in Chapter III, note 10.

arc-lighting company was able to charge about 15 per cent less than the gas company for this installation, even though the latter had supplied only one-fourth as much light. The dark areas between the arc lamps were clearly undesirable, however. The second column in Table 5 shows that the arc lights were much closer together in 1885. At that time, 650 arc lights were in use as street lights, costing the city $165,000 per year. They displaced 3,000 gas lamps for which the annual charge had been $53,000. In this case, the cost of arc lighting was three times the cost of gas instead of 15 per cent less, as it had been in 1880. This was true in spite of the fact that the cost per arc lamp was less than in 1880. The reason for the higher cost of arc lighting was that one arc lamp displaced less than five gas lamps. The dark areas were thereby eliminated. The light intensity between lamps was over four times as great as with gas. And the total candle power supplied was over twenty times as great.

The first two columns of Table 5 show that the arc-lighting companies were forced to supply much more candle power than the gas companies to light a street. Only if there were dark areas between the arc lights would their cost be equal to or less than the cost of gas. Conversely, if there were to be no areas between arc lights darker than the minimum intensity between gas lights, the total cost of arc lighting would have to be much greater than gas lighting. The exception to this rule was that, in a city where the cost of gas was unusually high, an arc-lighting company could eliminate the dark areas between lights and yet not charge more than a gas company. The third column of Table 5 is an illustration of this exception. In San Francisco, gas was selling for over $4 per thousand cubic feet, more than twice the price that prevailed in New York City. This meant that the annual charge for a gas street light was about $45, and for 1700 lamps, $77,350. The 210 arc lights were sufficient to provide a minimum intensity between lamps about the same as that of the gas lamps. But the total cost of the arc lamps was about 15 per cent less than the cost of the gas lamps. The relative cost was the same as in 1881 in New York. The difference was that there were no dark areas between the arc lights in San Francisco.

In most cities in the United States, the price of gas was sufficiently low so that the arc-lighting companies could not expect to light the streets more cheaply than the gas companies if there were to be no dark areas. The arc-lighting companies were thus under the disadvantage of having to supply much more light than the gas companies. Another factor working to the disadvantage of arc-lighting firms was the small scale on which most of them operated. The usual arc-lighting company could not enjoy either the technical economies of a large-scale plant or the technical and organizational economies of a large-scale firm. The basic productive unit — the dynamo — was not made in sizes larger than 40 lights until 1884; the number of these units in a single central station was at first small, and seldom did one firm own more than one central station.

It was thus primarily on the basis of increased illumination that municipal authorities had to be convinced of the desirability of arc lighting, although arc lights also had other, minor advantages. They could all be turned on at once from the central station, in contrast to gas lamps, which had to be lighted one by one. At a time when street lights were used only on nights without moonlight, a sudden darkening of the moon by clouds or a rainstorm created an unexpected need for artificial lighting. This illumination could be supplied quickly and easily by the throwing of a switch if the streets were lighted by arc lights. But the main consideration was the extra light provided by arc lighting. It was a question of whether the extra light was worth the extra cost. The surest way to demonstrate the desirability of more light was to light the streets for three or six months and let the people see the results. The psychological effect of this kind of demonstration was very great. People cannot imagine that they want more light until they have experienced it. Once they know what good lighting is, they are very reluctant to go back to the conditions which had once satisfied them.[12] Sir William Preece illustrates this point very clearly: "I know nothing more dismal than to be transplanted from the brilliantly illuminated avenues of New York to the dull and dark streets of London. . . After so much brilliance in these cities (Montreal, Philadelphia, Buffalo, Cleveland, Chicago, St. Louis, Indianapolis, Boston, New York), the return to dull gas has a most depressing influence." [13]

The arc-lighting companies tried to show that city streets were much safer when lighted by arc lamps, that hoodlumism and crime decreased, and that fewer policemen were required. In 1887, the Brush Electric Company published a booklet listing the testimony of fifty-six policemen on the value of the arc light to the performance of their duties.[14] When the arc lights on the Boston Common were replaced by gas in 1884, the *Electrical World* carried accounts of increased crime and unrest.[15] Such arguments as these were used by the arc-lighting companies in their efforts to convince city authorities and residents that the higher level of illumination provided by arc lighting was more than worth the extra cost.

THE EXPANSION OF THE THOMSON-HOUSTON ELECTRIC COMPANY

The spectacular success of Brush not only taught the existing arc-lighting-equipment manufacturers what type of system would be successful but also attracted new firms to the industry. The threat of these newcomers to Brush and the other early firms led to the attempts, already discussed, to establish patent-based monopolies. Contemporary with these schemes was the plan of Charles Flint, a vice-president of the United States company, to form an electrical "trust." In a period when trusts were being organized in a number of important industries, Flint hoped to negotiate a merger of the leaders and potential leaders in the electrical manufacturing industry. After extended discussions with the firms separately, Flint succeeded in getting around one table in his office Charles Brush, Elihu Thomson, and Edward Weston.[16] The date of this meeting was probably early in 1883. No agreement to combine could be reached, however, and the effort to form an electrical trust was abandoned.

Flint, who later promoted the United States Rubber Company, blamed his failure on the fact that there was no neutral negotiator.[17] As representative of the United States Electric Lighting Company, he was an interested party, and he felt that he was for that reason unable to gain the confidence of the other men. While this interpretation may be partially valid, it is also true that the industry was too young to make such a combination appealing to the leading firms. The market was seemingly unlimited, and a man like Elihu Thomson was confident that his arc-lighting system could capture a large part of that market. Only when the firms had experienced severe competition would combination be preferable to individual action, and only when the various equipment designs had been tested in the market place would there exist an objective basis for negotiations.

A monopoly measure short of combination would have been an agreement fixing prices, sharing the market, or placing restraints on product improvement. The presence of a vigorous product competition made agreements unlikely, however, and there is no evidence that any were entered into. The path to orderly market conditions was to be combination, after all, but some years later than Flint had expected. Product competition was also the source of other forces leading to consolidation and merger. The position of a firm in the race for product improvement was largely dependent on the quality of its technical personnel. One way to increase that quality was to acquire proven talent from other firms. Another reason for combination was present when product improvements could be patented. A firm could increase its competitive position substantially by purchasing competitors who owned patents on key product features.

Charles Coffin was the entrepreneur in the arc-lighting equipment industry who understood the importance of acquiring other firms and who had the necessary financial resources. In 1888, the Thomson-Houston Electric Company initiated a policy of buying out other manufacturers of arc-lighting apparatus when the opportunity arose. In the fall of 1888, the Wood patents were purchased from the American Electric Manufacturing Company, which was soon to fail; and the services of their chief electrical engineer, James Wood, were acquired.[18] In January 1889, Thomson-Houston bought a controlling interest in the Schuyler Electric Company, located in Connecticut.[19] That company had been formed in 1882 by S. D. Schuyler when he left the United States Electric Lighting Company, which he had helped to promote in 1878. Schuyler's was a small company with assets of about $500,000, and it had been in financial difficulty several times. In

April, nearly half the stock of the Fort Wayne (Indiana) Electric Company was purchased by Thomson-Houston for $380,000.[20] The Fort Wayne company had been organized in 1881 by R. T. McDonald, a Fort Wayne clothing manufacturer, to produce the arc-lighting system invented by Charles and James Jenney. The company had been quite successful, and the Jenney system ranked after Thomson-Houston and Brush in number of plants installed. The Van Depoele Electric Manufacturing Company of Chicago sold all its patents, machinery, merchandise, and other assets to Thomson-Houston in July 1889.[21] The Van Depoele firm had been formed in 1881 to manufacture the arc-lighting system of Charles Van Depoele, a Detroit furniture manufacturer who began experimenting with electrical devices in 1877. He later became one of the pioneers in electric railways.[22] In October 1889, Thomson-Houston bought a controlling interest in the Brush Electric Company.[23] Sometime in 1888 or 1889, two other companies, each with assets of less than $100,000, the Excelsior Electric Company of New York and the Indianapolis Jenney Company, were secured.

The Indianapolis Jenney Company and the Van Depoele firm were closed down completely. The Fort Wayne plant was switched from the production of Jenney apparatus to the Wood system. The other companies — Brush, Excelsior, Schuyler — were permitted to operate as before. Early in 1890, a standardizing bureau was formed to coördinate the production of these various companies. The bureau held a meeting at Lynn in February 1891 at which representatives of Brush, Fort Wayne, Schuyler, Excelsior, and Thomson-Houston were present. The Thomson-Houston arc-light switchboard and lightning arrester were adopted as standard. Since all the companies except Fort Wayne were producing arc-lighting systems with 50-volt arcs, Fort Wayne was requested to consider giving up its 30-volt arc. The possibility of standardizing the currents of all the arc systems was discussed as well. Excelsior was directed to make plans for the production of street fixtures for incandescent lighting, and Thomson-Houston announced that it alone would continue the manufacture of naval searchlights. The question of electrical measuring instruments was not settled definitely. The committee voted to contact the Weston Electrical Instrument Company to inquire whether arrangements could be made for buying instruments.[24] The standardizing bureau became a permanent committee and continued to function for a number of years. By 1900, Thomson-Houston was producing only three arc-lighting systems — Thomson-Houston, Brush, and Wood.

The merger movement which has been described needs to be analyzed. Why were the various companies willing to sell out to Thomson-Houston?

Why did Thomson-Houston want to buy them? Where did Thomson-Houston get the necessary funds?

The first question has several answers. Some of the companies were willing to sell their assets or their stock to Thomson-Houston because of financial difficulties they were having. The Schuyler company went into receivership in November 1886 and was reorganized. The American Electric Manufacturing Company was under pressure from its creditors in 1888 when it sold the Wood patents. In November 1888, the Fort Wayne company experienced a severe fire which was only about 75 per cent covered by insurance.[25] Rebuilding was not begun until after Thomson-Houston had purchased an interest in the company. The Thomson-Houston automatic-regulator patent, which was upheld in August 1888, is a second reason why companies were willing to sell out. The decision of Goff to dispose of the Wood patents was probably partly due to the fact that the Wood regulator infringed the Thomson-Houston regulator patent. The Fort Wayne company was also embarrassed by the decision which upheld the regulator patent.[26] There is no evidence that the Brush company was infringing this patent, but the Thomson-Houston regulator was much superior to the Brush. The Brush company may have felt that it would be unable to compete in the future without a better regulator.

Thomson-Houston purchased the various companies primarily to eliminate them as rivals. In the Thomson-Houston annual report for the year ending February 1, 1891, the following paragraph appeared in explanation of the merger policy.

> From 1882 until 1888 active competition was experienced from numerous manufacturing companies of more or less strength, which was so severe as to seriously affect the profits of the business as well as to render it necessary to take a considerable amount of the securities of local companies in payment for apparatus. Since 1887, however, alliances have been made with most of the manufacturing companies controlling important patent systems which have resulted in increasing the profits of your company by checking the competition which existed prior thereto. . . All of these companies, and the able management by which they are represented, instead of being in active and bitter competition and legal contention with the Thomson-Houston Electric Company, are now working in harmony with its interests.[27]

Elimination of rivals to increase profits, securing the services of highly skilled technical personnel (such as James Wood and Charles Van Depoele), and obtaining key patents (such as the Brush double-carbon arc-lamp patent) were the principal strategic reasons for the merger policy of Thomson-Houston. In addition, the acquisitions enabled Thomson-Houston to add to its productive facilities. During the years 1888 and 1889, its output of arc-lighting equipment expanded rapidly. Measured in arc-lights capacity, the annual output increased from 18,000 in 1887 to 24,000 in 1889. The need for additional productive facilities was urgent, and it was much quicker to buy existing plants than to construct them. The purchase of the Brush company, for example, came at a time when the Thomson-Houston plant at Lynn was in operation twenty-four hours a day. The Brush Cleveland plant was then running only part time.[28]

TABLE 6

Financial Data on Thomson-Houston Acquisitions, 1888–1889

Funds Required[a]	
Stock Purchases	
Brush Electric	$3,300,000
Fort Wayne Electric	380,000
Schuyler	200,000
Excelsior	50,000
Asset Purchases	
Wood	70,000
Van Depoele	50,000
Indianapolis Jenney	50,000
TOTAL	$4,100,000
Sources of Funds[b]	
Stock Sales	
March 1888	$ 500,000
April 1889	2,000,000
October 1889	1,500,000
Security Trust	
January 1889 (Trust C)	400,000
TOTAL	$4,400,000

[a] Sources: Fort Wayne data from *EW*, XIII (April 6, 1889), 211; Schuyler data from *EW*, XIII (January 19, 1889), 38; the figures on the other firms are estimates based on data in GE Files.
[b] Sources: Thomson-Houston *Annual Reports*.

Exactly how much money was needed by Thomson-Houston for its merger policy cannot be determined on the basis of available data. Nor can the sources for this money be ascertained accurately. Rough estimates, however, can be made. As shown in Table 6, the total needed for the seven acquisitions was approximately $4,000,000. A check on this total is provided by the Thomson-Houston annual statement of January 31, 1891. The balance sheet listed stock of manufacturing companies at cost, $3,820,000. The total amount paid for the patents and other assets of Wood, Van

Depoele, and Indianapolis Jenney was about $170,000 and surely not over $200,000. The figure, $4,000,000, therefore, is probably correct.

The two principal sources of funds were stock sales and security trusts. As shown in Table 6, stock sales brought in $4,000,000 during 1888 and 1889. The first two security trusts were formed in 1885 and 1886 and preceded the merger period. The last one issued its shares as a stock dividend on Thomson-Houston common stock and provided no cash for the company. But the third one, Trust C of January 1889, raised $400,000 in cash by the issue of trust shares, and this money was turned over to Thomson-Houston in exchange for stocks and bonds of local operating companies. These securities had been accepted by Thomson-Houston as payment for large amounts of arc-lighting equipment. It is for this reason that the retained earnings, which in 1888 and 1889 totaled about $2,000,000, cannot be considered a source of cash for expansion purposes.

A comparison of the funds required and the sources of funds reveals that there were more than adequate funds for the merger policy. The funds were supplied by investors who purchased newly issued stock and trust certificates. The merger policy thus had a sound financial basis. It did not require that Thomson-Houston borrow funds, nor was any stock issued in exchange for assets or stock of the acquired companies. The danger of diluting the equity of the regular Thomson-Houston stockholders was avoided. Some of the funds not needed for the purchase of arc-lighting firms were used to acquire patents and companies in other lines of electrical equipment. Examples are the purchase of the Van Depoele railway patents, the Bentley-Knight Railway Company, and a Cleveland carbon firm.[29]

Through the success of its arc-lighting system and its merger policy, Thomson-Houston became the dominant firm in the industry by 1890. Of the 6,000 arc lights in use at the beginning of 1881, 5,000 were made by Brush and most of the remainder by Weston.[30] Of the 96,000 in use by 1885, 30,000 were Brush and 8,000 were Thomson-Houston. Weston (the United States Electric Lighting Company) and Fort Wayne Electric probably accounted for about 5,000 each, and the remaining 48,000 were the product of approximately twenty smaller manufacturers, most of whom had installed from 2,000 to 3,000 arc lights. By 1890, Thomson-Houston had produced the equipment for over one-third of the 235,000 arc lights in service, and when to this figure are added the arc-lighting equipments of manufacturers purchased or controlled by Thomson-Houston (Brush, Fort Wayne, and so forth), the Thomson-Houston figure is over two-thirds. By 1897, when about 325,000 arc lights were in service, General Electric (the successor to Thomson-Houston) accounted for about 300,000. The only one of the early arc-lighting manufacturers of any significance that was not absorbed in General Electric was Weston. This firm eventually became part of Westinghouse.

The emergence of Thomson-Houston as the dominant firm in arc lighting can be attributed to a number of factors. The technical excellence of the Thomson-Houston arc-lighting system was of great importance. The improvements that could be patented (dynamo-current regulator, air-blast commutator, lightning arrester) were especially significant. The man responsible for the technical superiority of the Thomson-Houston system was, of course, Elihu Thomson. The contrast between Thomson's technical achievements in arc lighting and those of his competitors, Brush and Weston, is relevant. After developing a workable system, Brush turned to other fields of interest and took out no arc-lighting patents after 1880. The Brush system of 1890 was essentially the one he had designed ten years before. Weston also turned to other matters and did almost nothing in arc lighting after 1880. But Elihu Thomson continued to improve and perfect his system all through the 1880's and the 1890's. He thus helped his company to secure and maintain its dominant position in arc-lighting equipment.

A second factor was the strong financial support provided by F. L. Ames, T. J. Coolidge, Jr., H. L. Higginson, and other Boston capitalists. These men were interested in the long-term success of the company and were willing to reinvest the profits and to supply additional funds as they were needed. Money was thus available for the merger policy, and this was the path to market dominance.

Still another factor was the skillful and aggressive leadership of Coffin. He realized the competitive significance of technical personnel, and he tried to bring the outstanding electrical engineers of the arc-lighting industry into the Thomson-Houston organization. Furthermore, he sought the profitable central-station business and left most of the isolated lighting to the small companies. On the formation of General Electric in 1892, Coffin was chosen to be its head, a position that was to reveal even more fully his leadership qualities.

IV

The Arc-Carbon Industry

THE growth of arc lighting increased the demand for the carbons used as electrodes in arc lamps. Prior to 1879, the manufacture of arc-light carbons in the United States was almost negligible. A few small producers, using coal coke and hand methods, made carbons of poor quality and at high cost for the few arc lights in use.

The work of Brush in improving the composition and shape of arc carbons has already been described. In 1879, he established a factory in Cleveland to make carbons for his arc-lighting-equipment customers. At approximately the same time, Weston began production of arc carbons in Newark after several years of experimental work. These steps by Brush and Weston can be taken as the beginning of the carbon industry. Other factories were soon set up by carbon firms which quickly came into existence. The processes of arc-carbon manufacture and the new designs were in general not patentable. The main raw material — petroleum coke — was readily available. Capital requirements were not large. A reasonably efficient plant could be established for less than $50,000. Entry to the industry was thus unrestricted on the production side — as shown by the low capital requirements and the availability of technical knowledge and raw materials. In regard to markets, Brush and Weston were the only arc-lighting-equipment manufacturers who also produced arc carbons in the early years of the industry.[1] By 1883, when a number of new arc-lighting-equipment manufacturers — such as Thomson-Houston and Fort Wayne — were in production, numerous arc-lighting firms were a potential market for any seller of arc carbons. Even many of the Brush and Weston arc-lighting companies purchased their carbons from independent carbon producers.

Arc carbons of the various makers were very similar. Their shape, composition, and electrical characteristics had to permit of satisfactory use in the various arc-lighting systems. While all arc carbons were not identical in quality, differences were small. With a homogeneous product and with entry free, the arc-carbon industry assumed the characteristics of pure competition. There were usually at least fifteen firms, competition was on a price basis, prices were driven down to production costs, and the exit of old firms and the entry of new firms was fairly frequent. Brush was able to charge $250 per thousand for his first carbons, but by 1882 the price had dropped to $63. By 1886 the price was $10. The effect of this price competition on the quality of the carbons is difficult to determine. The arc-lighting companies seem to have given price first consideration in deciding where to buy carbons. In an 1885 editorial, the *Electrical World*, fearing deterioration of quality, expressed concern over the price cutting in arc carbons. "The importance of purity and density in the carbons cannot too strongly be pointed out. No mechanism however delicate has been or ever will be devised to produce a steady light where imperfect carbons are employed. Our earnest advice to electric light companies is that they should be ready to pay a fair price for carbons."[2]

The apparent willingness of the lighting companies to accept inferior carbons at low prices was paralleled by their willingness to overload their arc-lighting circuits. In both cases, the quality of the light was worsened. Their main interest was in maximum short-run profits, and they gave little weight to the long-run effects of quality deterioration on the market for arc lighting.

It was the carbon manufacturers themselves who took action to eliminate the severe price competition. While some producers may have been primarily interested in making carbons of better quality, most of them were undoubtedly seeking to increase their profits. The number of arc carbons sold did not depend appreciably on the price. A high price would not choke off demand, nor would a low price expand it. This lack of response to price changes had several causes. The carbon cost is a small part of the total cost of producing arc lighting, and many arc-lighting companies had long-term contracts for street lighting. The effect of a price change on profits depends, of course, on the cost curve as well as the demand curve. From the fact that many carbon firms were small, the inference can be drawn that the cost curve was not sharply decreasing. The existence of some large firms is good evidence that the cost curve was not sharply increasing. The conclusion can be drawn that the cost curve of the usual carbon firm was fairly horizontal. Where the industry demand curve is inelastic, and where the firms are operating under conditions close to constant cost, an increase in the price of the product will increase profits.

Some of the manufacturers held a conference in Cleveland late in 1885, but no agreement could be reached. A year later another meeting was held to try to increase the "ruinously low price for electric carbons."[3] This second meeting had concrete results. Six large producers — Brush was not among them — concluded a price agreement. The following circular was issued:

> With a view of improving the quality of the products shipped and preventing the shipment of lower grade and inferior goods, with the consequent variation of prices and uncertainties of results, the undersigned carbon manufacturers in convention have considered these questions. The result of their deliberations was that a uniform scale of moderate prices would be of benefit both to the consumer and the manufacturer and they have agreed upon the following schedule.[4]

The circular then listed prices for carbons of all sizes, with the price for the 7/16-by-12-inch carbon, plain or copper-coated, set at $12 per thousand. Prices were f.o.b. factory. Uniform terms and discounts were also listed.

While the success of this price agreement cannot be accurately ascertained, the six firms seem to have maintained the announced prices in the following months. The next step was to attempt to include more producers and to establish a permanent organization. E. C. Hawks, works manager of the Buffalo Electric Company, one of the carbon producers not in the December agreement, took the initiative. He became agent for the carbon producers and began to lease carbon plants. Some he could not lease. He made arrangements with these to take their entire output at a fixed price. He then entered the petroleum-coke market with the objective of becoming the only source of coke for the carbon producers. His over-all plan thus included the control of existing productive facilities and, further, the control of the key raw material to prevent entry into the industry. The lighting companies were instructed to order carbons only from Hawks's Cleveland office, which would then allocate the orders among the various plants. The producers who made up the Hawks combine included the original six and four in addition. These ten probably accounted for over three-fourths of the carbon capacity in the United States. The Brush company, while a member of the combine, did not participate in the orders pool.[5] A possible explanation is that Brush supplied the licensee users of its own arc-lighting equipment.

The price set by the combine for 7/16-by-12-inch carbons was $20 per thousand. It became effective April 15, 1887. The price increase from $10 per thousand (and even less on large orders) in 1886 to twice that in 1887 aroused the opposition of the lighting companies. Particularly strong objections were made by those companies that had signed long-term lighting contracts but had not covered themselves with future delivery contracts for carbons. Through their own group, the National Electric Light Association, the local lighting companies began to take steps to establish their own carbon plant on a coöperative basis. Hawks had evidently not succeeded in cornering the petroleum-coke supply.

Some lighting companies tried to secure carbons from Europe. There is no evidence that these efforts were successful. Several new carbon firms entered the industry and remained outside the combine. Thomson-Houston, anxious to protect its customers, announced in July that it intended to start its own carbon factory at Fostoria, Ohio.[6] Toward the end of July, the combine began to lose its unity. Several of the largest firms accepted orders at below the established prices. On July 26, the formal dissolution of the combine was reported.[7]

There are several reasons for the failure of this attempt to monopolize arc-carbon production. Most important was that the combine never secured control of the supply of petroleum coke. The firms outside the combine could continue to produce and new firms could enter the industry. The identification of interest between the arc-lighting-equipment manufacturers and the lighting companies also was important. The Brush company was a member of the combine and ostensibly agreed to its prices. But it probably continued to supply users of its equipment at prices below those set by the combine. Thomson-Houston, which up to 1887 had never felt it desirable to produce arc carbons, decided to begin carbon production to supply its customers. It was willing to become a carbon producer to prevent the profitability of the local lighting companies from being endangered. The interest of Thomson-Houston in lighting-company profits is not difficult to explain. Thomson-Houston held large amounts of lighting-company securities and therefore participated directly in their prosperity. Even more important, the market for arc-lighting apparatus depended on the earnings of the local lighting companies. Unless they were profitable, neither expansion of existing companies nor formation of new ones would occur.

In retrospect, it seems clear that the combine set the carbon price too high. The threat to the profits of the lighting companies was so serious and immediate that they resisted with all their strength. And they were aided by Thomson-Houston, and perhaps Brush, who became alarmed over the effects of the high carbon price on the market for arc-lighting apparatus.

Although the combine failed, it had permanent effects on the arc-carbon industry. One has already been mentioned. Thomson-Houston entered the industry and built a plant at Fostoria, Ohio. When Thomson-Houston secured control of Brush in 1889, it gained further productive capacity in carbons. Shortly thereafter, it was also in control of the National Carbon Company, another large carbon firm in Cleveland.

The second and more important effect was the transformation of the industry from one that strongly resembled the economist's conception of pure competition into an oligopoly. Before the combine, there were seventeen carbon firms. Afterward, there were eight. The smaller number resulted from two causes. The combine had leased or purchased a number of plants which were shut down and never produced again. And three of the large Cleveland firms — Boulton, Crystal, and Cleveland — merged and formed the Standard Carbon Company.

Patents were never of much importance in arc carbons. Brush's attempt to establish the validity of his patent on copper-coated carbons in 1887 failed. Lacking patent protection, manufacturers were very secret about their methods and processes in carbon production. But the efficacy of secrecy was limited by the tendency of key personnel to leave and found firms of their own. For example, one of the leading carbon producers, Boulton, had originally worked for Brush.

By 1890, Thomson-Houston, through growth and merger, was by far the most important producer of arc-lighting equipment and accounted for over half the annual production. The proportion of the carbon output it controlled was probably as great. One writer estimated that, by 1895, five firms produced 90 per cent of the arc carbons.[8] This concentration of production, together with the "lessons" of the competitive era, was sufficient to stabilize the industry after 1890. Details are lacking, but the general appearance is that of mature oligopoly. Just exactly what kept new firms out of the industry is not known. A change in production methods, necessitating factories equipped with much machinery, may have so increased the economical plant size that capital requirements were much higher than before. Or Thomson-Houston's control over the market for arc-lighting equipment may have given it control of most of the arc-carbon market. In spite of the lack of vigorous competition after 1890, prices continued to fall and by 1900 had reached $7 per thousand. Competition from incandescent lighting partly accounts for this decline.

V

The Dynamics of the Industry

TECHNICAL CHANGE IN ARC-LIGHTING EQUIPMENT

THE general pattern of technical change in arc-lighting equipment can be most easily understood in terms of the marketing problems faced by the manufacturer of this equipment. The basic problem, the one that Brush was the first to conceive and solve, was to design an arc-lighting system that could be used in street lighting. From his four-light, separate-circuit machines and poor carbons, Brush had to advance to larger generators, higher-quality carbons, and an arc light which would be short-circuited automatically on failure so that a number could be operated on one circuit. At this point, Brush had an operative street-lighting system.

There were major faults in that system, however, and these faults held back the growth of arc lighting because they meant high equipment and operating costs. The carbons had to be replaced every eight hours or so, and the replacement cost was appreciable. The generators could not adjust to less than full load. Arc lights had to be kept in the station to be turned on when circuit arc lights were turned off. Fuel costs were high because generator efficiencies were relatively low. Generator cost per arc light was high because the maximum number of lights per machine was about sixteen and because armature winding was a costly, laborious process.

The next series of technical changes was intended to meet these drawbacks and produce an arc-lighting system of lower first cost and lower operating cost. Copper-plated carbons and the double-carbon arc lamp reduced carbon costs and the labor costs of replacing burned-out carbons. The dynamo-current regulators permitted large changes in the number of arc lamps on a circuit with no damage to the lamps or the dynamo. Armature design began to be better understood, and laminated armatures were introduced, reducing internal losses. Voltage and commutation problems were partially solved, and generators of larger capacity were built. The 6-light dynamo of 1878 was followed by the 16-light machine in 1880 and the 40-light machine in 1882. Dynamo capacity further increased to 65 arc lights in 1884, 80 in 1890, and 125 in 1894. The larger dynamos, together with improved techniques of armature winding, considerably reduced the dynamo cost per lamp.

By 1885, the victory over gas in street lighting was reasonably complete. The arc-lighting systems had proved to be reliable and could produce light at such a cost that consumers were willing to buy it. The problems now became those that arose because the arc-lighting central stations had grown large and in many cases were supplying miles of circuits and hundreds of lamps. One such problem was the need for switchboards and switching devices. As these were developed, measuring instruments such as ammeters and voltmeters were added. Another problem, the lack of protection against lightning, was solved by the invention of the lightning arrester.

By 1890, the arc lamp was experiencing competition from two new light sources. The late 1880's saw the development of large incandescent electric lamps which were suitable for large-space lighting (including street lighting). About the same time the incandescent gas lamp was invented. This gave a bright, good-quality light and also was well suited to large-space lighting. Against these two very good lamps, the faults of the arc lamp seemed glaring indeed. The open arc produced a harsh, flickering light and deep shadows. Furthermore, the color content of the light was so different from daylight that very few objects looked their usual color. Most of these objectionable characteristics were eliminated in the enclosed arc lamp which was developed by Professor L. S. Marks of Harvard in 1893. Marks enclosed the arc in a glass globe. This softened the light and made it comparable in quality to incandescent light.

The high quality of Mark's light was accompanied by a loss in efficiency because some of the light was absorbed by the glass. But the lowered efficiency was more than outweighed by the increased life of the carbons. In contrast to the open-arc carbon, which lasted about eight hours, a carbon in an enclosed lamp could burn for over a hundred hours. The result was an annual saving in carbons and labor of about $15 per lamp. The enclosed arc lamp thus produced better light at lower cost, and it is not surprising that it came into widespread use very rapidly. Of 386,000 arc lamps in service by 1902, over 200,000 were enclosed.[1] Of 160,000 arc lamps manufactured in 1899, 135,000 were enclosed.[2]

Table 7 shows the quantities of arc-light carbons consumed and the arc lights in service for three different years. The increase in annual carbon consumption per lamp from 1886 to 1895 reflects the increase in hours of

TABLE 7

Arc-Carbon Consumption and Arc Lights in Service, 1886–1902

Year	*Arc-carbon consumption*	*Arc lights in service*	*Annual carbon consumption per arc light*
1886	55,000,000	140,000	392
1895	200,000,000	300,000	667
1902	173,000,000	386,000	448

Sources: Data on arc carbons for 1886, estimate based on *EW*, IX (March 19, 1887), 147, and IX (June 25, 1887), 306; for 1895, *EW*, XXV (January 5, 1895), 8; for 1902, *Manufactures: Twelfth Census*, X, 170. Arc-light data for 1886, *EW*, IX (January 29, 1887), 50; for 1895, from GE Files; for 1902, *Abstract of the Twelfth Census*, p. 407.

use of the arc lights in street lighting during the period. In the first years of arc lighting, the lights were turned on only on dark nights and often not after midnight. By 1895, all-night lighting every night had become common. The decrease in annual carbon consumption per lamp from 1895 to 1902 reflects the appearance of the enclosed arc lamp. A continuing trend of increasing use prevented the decrease from being as great as the enclosed arc lamp alone would have caused.

Most of the remaining technical changes in arc lighting which occurred before 1900 were designed to make the arc lamp usable on any kind of electric circuit, direct or alternating current, series or parallel. One step toward such an arc lamp was taken about 1890 with the invention of an arc lamp for parallel circuits. This lamp could be used on the ordinary direct-current incandescent-lighting circuits. Within a few years, an arc lamp for alternating-current circuits had been developed. General Electric had such a lamp in production in 1893.[3] The one fault of these lamps for parallel circuits (both a.c. and d.c.) was that they were less efficient than the series arc lamp. Where a number of arc lamps were used, it still was economical to have a special arc-lighting dynamo supplying a special series circuit which contained only arc lights.

The step which eliminated the need for special arc-lighting dynamos was taken in 1897 by Elihu Thomson when he invented the constant-current transformer. This permitted arc lights to operate efficiently on current taken from ordinary a.c. supply circuits. Through use of Thomson's transformer, the arc lamp could be treated like any other electrical device and supplied by the regular central stations. The device which launched the electrical manufacturing industry in the United States thus finally became integrated into the complex central-station networks which had grown up to supply incandescent lighting and electric power.

In summary, technical change in arc-lighting apparatus took place in four stages which were defined by the marketing problem of the manufacturer. The first stage saw the development of a reliable, practical arc-lighting system that could technically and commercially replace gas in street lighting. The second stage saw the efforts to lower the cost of arc lighting to enable it to compete better with gas. The third stage was characterized by certain problems attendant upon the growth of large arc-lighting circuits. The fourth stage involved changes to meet the competition of incandescent lighting (electric and gas) and to make the arc light flexible enough to be useful anywhere that electric current was available.

Table 8 gives price data on the main components of an arc-lighting system for the period 1878–1900. The data are very incomplete, but they indicate in a rough way the price declines which accompanied the technical changes which have been described. The sharp drop in prices in the 1890's, however, was not mainly the result of technical change. The depressed conditions in the electrical manufacturing industry and the competition from incandescent electric light were responsible.

ENTREPRENEURSHIP IN THE MANUFACTURE OF ARC-LIGHTING EQUIPMENT

Entrepreneurship in a new and highly technical industry involves both commercial and technical innovation. The process of innovation requires a technical understanding of the product and the related problems of making and using it. Moreover, the innovator must possess the ability to envision the place that the product can occupy in the economy and the ability to solve the technical problems incident to creating that product.

The beginning of the arc-lighting industry can be divided into three stages. In the first stage, many inventors were working on arc-lighting apparatus and trying to develop a practical system. Some of them thought they had designed equipment which would be commercially successful and organized firms to manufacture and sell it. Edward Weston was one of these first-stage engineer-entrepreneurs. He was a competent inventor and electrical engineer, but he was not the pioneer innovator in arc lighting. He cannot be credited with starting the industry. He failed to envision exactly what the market for arc lighting was going to be, and, lacking that vision, he could not carry out the technical developments that were necessary before arc lighting could become of commercial significance. In one sense, Weston was not at all important to arc lighting. He represents dozens of men who worked in arc lighting but did not succeed in converting it into an innovation.

In the second stage, one of the many engineer-entrepreneurs carried out the act of innovation that founded the arc-lighting-equipment industry.

TABLE 8

Price Trends in Arc-Lighting Equipment, 1878–1900

Year	*Generator cost per 2000-c.p. arc lamp for the largest-size generator*	*Price per single-carbon arc lamp of 2000 c.p.*	*Price per 1000 carbons*
1878	..	..	$250
1880	..	..	$150
1882	$65	$65	$63
1884	..	..	$27
1886	..	..	$10
1888	..	..	$20
1890	$50	..	
1892	..	$50	..
1894	$40	..	..
1896	..	$40	..
1898	$20	..	..
1900	..	$15	$7

Sources: Price statistics in GE Files, mainly Brush and Thomson-Houston. The prices in the table are actual prices, not list prices.

That entrepreneur, the pioneer innovator, was Charles Brush. He combined in one person the commercial ability to envision where arc lighting could be used successfully and the technical ability to invent an arc-lighting system that fitted his commercial vision. Brush was aware that most cities of any size were buying light for their streets from gas companies. Here was a market for light that the arc lamp could secure if an arc-lighting system of certain technical and economic characteristics could be designed. With this commercial vision before him, Brush solved the technical problems. The result was the spectacular success of the Brush Electric Company.

In the third stage, engineer-entrepreneurs entered arc lighting after Brush had shown that it could be commercially successful. One of these imitative or follower entrepreneurs was Elihu Thomson. There was no need for him to envision a place in the economy for arc lighting. Brush had already done that and more. He had proved that firms in two new industries — arc-lighting equipment and arc lighting — could sell their products at prices which were greater than cost. Thomson's vision could therefore be quite narrow. He thought that he could design an arc-lighting system which was technically superior to any system then on the market. The improvements he made in arc lighting were major contributions to the art. The Thomson-Houston system was probably the best one of that time — best in the sense of most reliable and lowest in operating cost.

Entrepreneurship in the early years of the arc-lighting industry thus required a high degree of technical ability. The designs and patents of an inventor were the basis of the usual firm engaged in manufacturing arc-lighting equipment. The inventor's services were essential to the firm, for he acted as designer, supervisor of production, and test engineer. He also trained men to install and operate the equipment. The fact that the firms were not large made it possible for one man, who had the title of electrician, to perform a number of functions. In these conditions of a new technology and a small-scale business, the electrician was a key person without whom the firm could scarcely have continued to operate. The other executive personnel — the man in charge of sales, the president of the company, and so forth — and the investors who supplied the capital were relegated to subsidiary roles.

When the arc-lighting industry had been in existence four or five years, the importance of the electrician declined in relation to others in the firm who shared the entrepreneurial function. As knowledge of how to design, build, and install arc-lighting equipment became widespread, it was much easier to find personnel to carry out these functions. The emphasis shifted to marketing and then, as the firms grew in size, to the problems of administration, organization, and financing. The key men in the firm were the men who could solve these problems satisfactorily.

Coffin and Goff illustrate how entrepreneurship had changed by 1884. Both these men were leaders, organizers, administrators, financiers, and salesmen. Neither was a technician. Coffin depended, of course, on Thomson for advice on all decisions where technical knowledge was essential. Whether Goff had a technical adviser is not known, but he seemed to possess good technical judgment on broad issues in spite of his lack of engineering training. Of the three arc-lighting systems which survived into the twentieth century — Brush, Thomson-Houston, and Wood — Goff was associated with two. Coffin had the same ability to make broad technical judgments. When he saw the Thomson-Houston equipment on display in Boston, for example, he was much impressed and took steps to investigate the equipment further.

Goff entered the industry as a salesman and a financier. He organized local lighting companies which he kept ownership of until they had shown the ability to earn profits. He raised money for this work by selling the stock of his own company to the general public. His marketing policy, therefore, involved selling equipment only to central stations and organizing and owning those central stations. His financial policy was to sell stock to the general public. This required that his own firm pay regular and liberal dividends. When he undertook manufacturing, he continued these sales and financial policies as before. His eventual failure resulted chiefly from the problems of raising capital which his sales policy created.

Like Goff, Coffin concentrated on sales to central stations. But his sales policy did not involve ownership of the local companies by Thomson-Houston. Local capital was always secured. In accepting securities as part payment for equipment, Thomson-Houston played a part in the financing of the local companies, but a small part compared to Goff. Coffin's financial policy was also different from Goff's. The stock in Thomson-Houston was more closely held than in the American company, and Coffin was not forced to pay heavy dividends to be sure of a future market for stock. Coffin was able to raise additional funds as he needed them. Among his financial innovations were the trusts which he formed from time to time to hold the securities of local companies. This device appealed to the investors and enabled Thomson-Houston to convert the securities into cash.

In business administration, Coffin made several innovations. In the early 1880's, manufacturing was not organized along functional lines. Coffin was one of the first businessmen to see the need for that kind of organization. About 1885, he set up a number of departments, such as production, purchasing, accounting, sales, and so forth, and placed a manager in charge of each department. A more rational system of cost accounting was also developed. Its main improvement over existing methods was in the allocation of overhead among different products.

The entrepreneurship of Goff and Coffin emphasized marketing, financing, and business organization. Freed from a narrow technical outlook, both Goff and Coffin were interested in building large, profitable companies and in reaching a position of leadership in the industry. The technical work of designing and manufacturing the product were still essential, but with the growth and expansion of the industry, the entrepreneurship also had to expand. The original technical innovations were followed by innovations in marketing, finance, and business administration. The most successful innovator in these latter fields, Coffin, was the leader of the industry by 1890.

THE GROWTH OF ARC LIGHTING, 1880–1900

Table 9 shows arc lights in service for selected years from 1880 to 1902. Arc lights were laboratory instruments and scientific curiosities in 1877. Twenty-five years later there were nearly 400,000 in everyday use. The rapid growth of arc lighting can be partly attributed to the fact that the

TABLE 9

Arc Lights in Service in the United States, 1881–1902

Year	*Arc lights in service*
1881	6,000
1883	75,000
1885	96,000
1886	140,000
1890	235,000
1895	300,000
1902	386,000

Sources: For 1886, 1895, 1902, see Table 7, p. 65; data for 1881 and 1886 from *EW*, IX (January 29, 1887), 50; statistic for 1883 from *EW*, I (May 12, 1883), 297; statistic for 1890 from *EW*, XV (April 5, 1890), 236. These data are in most cases for January 1 or very early in the year.

demand for street lighting and other large-space lighting was well established. The gas companies had spent over fifty years developing the market for illumination before arc lighting was introduced. Once people realized that they wanted more light, which the arc light could easily provide, there was no serious obstacle to the growth of arc lighting. The arc-lighting companies did not have to convince city residents that the streets should be lighted or that the lighting cost should be paid from public funds. They only had to convince the people that city streets should have more light than gas could give.

The initiative taken by the manufacturers in promoting arc-lighting companies is another reason for the rapid growth. They literally created a market for their product by creating the firms who were their most important customers. In view of the almost total ignorance of electric lighting among the general public, it was the task of manufacturers to show light consumers that the arc light was a better source of illumination than their existing sources and to convince businessmen and capitalists that the production and sale of arc lighting could be a permanent and profitable business.

Arc-lighting systems were relatively simple to install and operate. Almost no accessories or extras, like fuses, meters, switches, switchboards, and so forth, were required in the first systems. All that was needed were the dynamo, the arc lamps, copper wire to connect the lamps to the dynamo, and a prime mover to drive the dynamo. The series system with no individual control of the arc lamps was well suited to street lighting. The high voltage made even long street-light circuits económical. Arc-lighting systems were simple and uncomplicated, and their technical faults were not important in street lighting. Under such conditions, rapid growth was possible.

PART II

Incandescent Lighting

VI

The Setting

PART I told the story of arc lighting in the United States. The arc light was an electric light and therefore revolutionary. But it was also traditional because it produced light by burning a substance composed primarily of carbon. Like other illuminants, the arc light was restricted to uses where an open flame was permissible. The arc light had the further limitation of being a bright light which could not be reduced in intensity. It was consequently not suitable for most interior illumination. These defects of the arc light left a gap which was destined to be filled by a second electric light, the incandescent light.

The scientific groundwork for incandescent lighting was laid by the same scientist who discovered the principle of the electric arc. In 1802, Sir Humphrey Davy carried on experiments in heating materials to a state of incandescence by means of the battery he had constructed. Although he did not make an incandescent electric light, he concluded from his tests of various materials that carbon rods and platinum wires could probably be used in such a light. Many years were to elapse between these first experiments by Davy and the construction of a successful incandescent electric light. The numerous inventors who worked in incandescent lighting in the years after Davy were handicapped by an expensive source of current, the battery, and by the lack of a method of producing and maintaining a vacuum. The cost of battery current was so high that even had a successful lamp been invented, its use would have been very restricted.

The vacuum problem was solved in 1865 with the invention of the mercury vacuum pump by Herman Sprengel. The development of a practical dynamo by Gramme in the early 1870's provided a relatively cheap source of current. With the vacuum pump and the dynamo available and the principle of incandescence widely known, technological advance had proceeded to the point where the development of a commercially feasible incandescent-electric-lighting system was possible. This possibility could not be realized, however, unless the inventor had a good understanding of the basic laws of electricity and used them to direct the design of the electric-lighting system toward lowest lighting costs. What was needed was a lamp which was not only workable but also durable, efficient, and of high resistance. Its resistance had to be high in order to reduce the current and therefore the amount of copper required to connect the dynamo and the lamp. The dynamo had to be very efficient, and here, too, a genuine understanding of electricity was necessary. The internal resistance of the dynamo would have to be as low as possible, not equal to the load resistance as it was in the Gramme dynamo. The distribution network which connected the lamps to the dynamo would have to permit individual control of the lamps and yet have a copper cost per lamp which was not too high. The commercially successful incandescent-electric-lighting system would have to be made up of components — dynamo, conductor network, and lamp — whose original cost and operating cost would be low enough to make the cost of electric lighting not substantially greater than the other methods of illumination available.

The really intensive efforts to invent an incandescent light began after the arc light was fairly well known but not yet extensively used. It was generally conceded that, while the arc light was suitable for large-space lighting, it was too intense for ordinary home or office use. The recognized problem was to make a smaller electric light, and most of the experimenters working with incandescent lights had this objective in mind. The potential market for such a light consisted of homes, offices, apartment houses, hotels, institutions (hospitals, prisons, and so forth), and some factories. The 400 gas companies of the United States had shown that a demand for light in these places existed and that the buyers were willing to pay as much as 1.25 cents for a 16-candle-power light for each hour of use. Certain light users were firms or institutions which consumed light in their ordinary operations. For these users, the electric light would have to be directly cheaper than other available methods of illumination or it would have to possess advantages over the other methods which would result in a lower production cost per unit of output. The second class of users were dwellers in ordinary residences, and here the quality of the electric light, as well as its cost, would be important. If the consumer would show a marked preference for the electric light over other illuminants, its cost could be somewhat higher than those illuminants and it still would become widely used.

The most significant fact about the potential market for the incandescent light, like the arc light, was that the demand for light was known to exist and was being supplied by various illuminants at prices and in ways that could be easily determined. The prices and methods in use could serve as general guides to the incandescent-light inventor and to the capitalist in back of the inventor. All other illuminants had disadvantages which a successful electric light would probably not possess. These illuminants were open flames which produced soot, dirt, and heat, consumed oxygen, and presented a continuous fire danger. Matches were needed to light them, and they would burn only under special atmospheric conditions and in certain positions.

The use of gas, oil, kerosene, and candles showed the character of the market for light, but there were many places where no open-flame illuminant could be used at all. In certain chemical plants and furniture factories, the fire danger was so great that daylight illumination alone was employed. Similarly, some special-function buildings such as Gore Hall, the main library of Harvard College, were not lighted artificially because of the fire risk. Thus, both the quality and cost characteristics of an incandescent-lighting system would play a part in its commercial success. The main problem was to design a system which could effectively displace other forms of artificial illumination, but the extension of light into places never before lighted would also be important.

VII

The Edison System

THOMAS ALVA EDISON, born in 1847 at Milan, Ohio, received almost no formal education of any kind. His knowledge of science, and of electricity in particular, was gained from reading and experimenting which he began as a small boy. In his teens, he learned to operate the telegraph and entered that well-paid, skilled work which kept him in close contact with the only electrical device then in common use. As a telegrapher, he took jobs at many widely scattered places. In 1868, he went to Boston. There he bought a set of Faraday's works which he studied with great care. He began to invent shortly afterward. His first inventions were a vote recorder, a stock ticker, and an alphabetical dial telegraphic device — all instruments based on the principle of the telegraph. None of these netted Edison any financial gain, however, and in 1869, at the age of twenty-two, he went to New York to better his prospects.

In New York, Edison worked as a repairman for the Gold and Stock Telegraph Company, a firm which supplied gold and stock quotations by means of a stock ticker to brokers in the Wall Street district. He soon invented an improved stock ticker, for which the company paid him $40,000. Edison used this money to establish himself in Newark as a manufacturer of stock tickers and other telegraphic devices. He continued to invent and did consulting work on telegraphic problems. By 1876, he had accumulated enough money to cease manufacturing and devote all his time to experimenting and inventing. He purchased some land in the small hamlet of Menlo Park, a few miles from Newark, and set up a well-equipped laboratory with a permanent staff. Most of the staff members were men who had worked for Edison in Newark. One of the Newark employees who did not go to Menlo Park, Johann Sigmund Bergmann, went to New York, where he continued the manufacture of Edison's inventions and other electrical devices. Edison's inventive activities at Menlo Park during the first years were very fruitful. He sold at least three of his inventions for large sums of money. The carbon telephone transmitter and the nonmagnetic telegraph sounder were sold to the Western Union Telegraph Company for $100,000 each. A nonmagnetic telephone receiver was sold to the English Bell company for £30,000.

The experiences of Edison before he took up the electric light were excellent preparation for his activities in that field. His work in telegraphy had given him practical experience in electrical circuits and electromagnets. His financial success in inventing and manufacturing had enabled him to organize a laboratory well equipped for electrical inventing and manned by trained workers. The manufacturing in Newark also gave Edison practical experience that was to prove very valuable when he began to manufacture the components of the Edison electric-lighting system. The telegraph is thus to be credited with playing an important part in preparing Edison for his work on the electric light. And the influence of the telegraph extended beyond the period of preparation to the work itself. Edison's financial backing in the electric-light experiments came from men who had known him as a telegraph engineer and inventor. It is more than coincidence that Edison, the pioneer innovator in incandescent lighting, should receive his first financial support from telegraph men, just as Brush, the pioneer innovator in arc lighting, received his original financial support from a firm connected with the telegraph industry. Electricity was new and little understood in 1877. It is logical that persons connected with one electrical device, the telegraph, should have been among the first to see the commercial possibilities in another electrical device, the electric light.

In the fall of 1877, Edison began experimenting with incandescent lights. There is no evidence which explains why he turned to the incandescent light at that time. There were many inventors working on arc lights and incandescent lights, and presumably Edison was curious about the possibilities in electric lighting. His invention of the phonograph interrupted his experimental work early in 1878, and he did not return to electric lighting until late the following summer. By that time, his plans for work in that field had begun to crystallize.

The plan he evolved was striking in its breadth and originality.[1] He decided, first of all, that he was not interested in arc lighting. The nature of the arc light limited it to street lighting and other large-space lighting. Edison knew that over 90 per cent of the revenues of the gas companies came from home and office illumination. Here the arc light could not be used. Edison had sufficient inventive and manufacturing experience in electricity to give him confidence in his ability to solve the harder problem of inventing an electric light which could eventually displace gas entirely.

In rejecting the arc light, Edison was refusing to follow a path which looked very promising. Even after Edison had invented a successful incandescent lamp late in 1879, arc lighting still seemed to be the only feasible commercial form of electric lighting to as competent an electrical engineer as Elihu Thomson. He visited Menlo Park, saw the Edison light, and decided that the incandescent light had a very small chance of becoming profitable.[2] Compared to the arc light, it was inefficient in its conversion of electric energy into light, and transmission losses were much higher. Similarly, a very competent German electrical engineer, Werner Siemens, declined to accept a license from Edison in 1881 to manufacture the Edison lamp. Siemens thought the arc light would force it off the market within a short time.[3]

In choosing the incandescent light over the arc light, Edison was putting aside the technical advance that had brought the arc light to the commercial stage. Very little of that technical advance could be applied to incandescent lighting. Instead of using it as a foundation on which to build, Edison would have to achieve comparable technical advance in a separate field. To develop an electric light for use in homes, he could not merely replace the lighting element in the arc-lighting system. He would need to design a new dynamo, one with high efficiency to compensate for the low efficiency of the incandescent light and with a constant-potential characteristic. The arc-lighting dynamo had a constant-current characteristic — the current output tended to be the same regardless of the number of lamps connected to the dynamo — which was suitable for a series but not for a parallel system. Edison wanted to use the parallel system because it permitted each user to operate any light independently of the others (see Diagram 1). The series system, where all lights are turned on and off at once, was satisfactory for street lighting but not for home lighting. Protection against short circuits, not needed in a constant-current system, and sockets and switches would also be required. The introduction of the electric circuit into homes instead of confining it to the streets meant that the voltages used would have to be much lower than those permissible with the arc light. Low voltages raised problems of energy loss in transmission. These led to the complicated transmission networks which were quite foreign to the simple series circuits of arc lighting.

If arc lighting, the one electric-lighting system known in 1878, could

Diagram 1

SERIES AND PARALLEL LIGHTING CIRCUITS

ARC LIGHTING: SERIES CIRCUIT

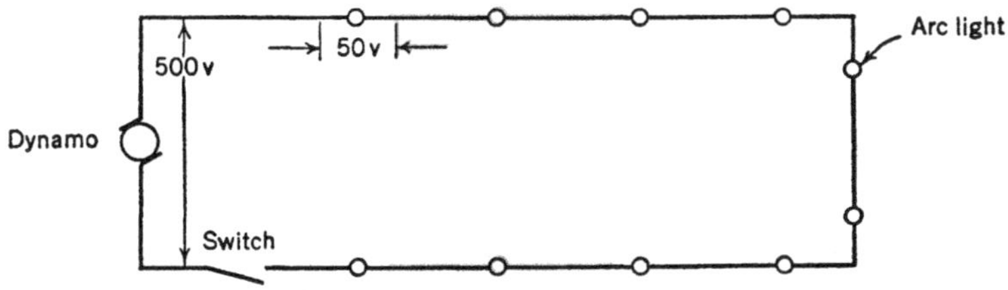

High-voltage, constant-current dynamo. Current is 10 amperes. Voltage is dependent on number of arc lights in circuit (50 volts per light). Same current through all lights. Closing one switch turns on all lights.

INCANDESCENT LIGHTING: PARALLEL CIRCUIT

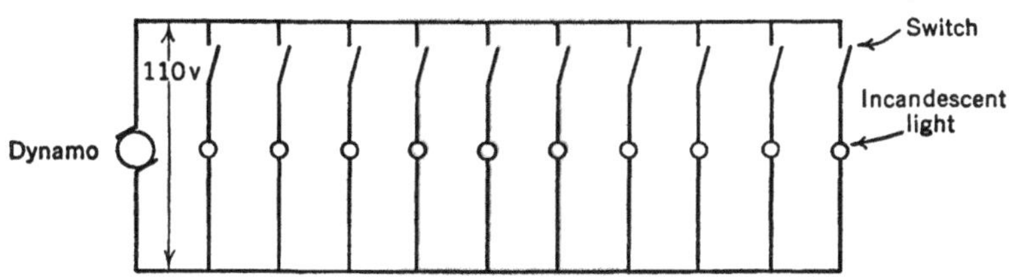

Low-voltage, constant-voltage dynamo. Potential difference is 110 volts. Current is dependent on number of incandescent lights in circuit (1.1 amperes per 100-ohm light). Closing any one switch turns on only one light.

not serve as a technical basis for Edison's work, neither could it serve as a commercial basis. The markets were quite different, overlapping only in the area of industrial users. In arc lighting, the typical sale of light was to a municipality at a fixed yearly sum. There was no measurement problem and no need to deal with thousands of small consumers. In Edison's system, a meter to measure each consumer's use of light would be needed, and Edison would have to devise techniques to estimate the demand for light and to maintain contact with many small users.

With arc lighting offering almost no precedents to Edison, either technically or commercially, he turned to the system of gas illumination for guidance. In the summer of 1878, he began a very careful study of the gas industry. In referring to that study, Edison said: "I started my usual course of collecting every kind of data about gas; bought all the transactions of the gas engineering societies, etc., all the back volumes of the gas journals. Having obtained all the data and investigated gas-jet distribution in New York by actual observations, I made up my mind that the problem of the subdivision of electric current could be solved and made commercial." [4]

Edison's conception of the problem before him is shown by entries he made in one of his notebooks about this same time. "Object, Edison to effect exact imitation of all done by gas so as to replace lighting by gas by lighting by electricity . . . Edison's great effort not to make a large light or a blinding light but a small light having the mildness of gas." [5]

Edison's basic plan, as suggested in the above quotations, was to imitate the gas system of illumination as closely as possible. He believed that the devices, methods, and practices which had gained wide consumer acceptance in the sale of gas should be used in his electric-lighting system whereever possible. His goal was to develop a system of light supply which would differ from gas only in providing a superior and more desirable light.

In deciding to try to invent an incandescent light, Edison was attempting to solve a problem which many scientists thought to be insoluble. It was believed that the subdivision of the electric light was theoretically impossible in the same sense that the construction of a perpetual-motion machine is theoretically impossible. An English electrical expert, in a work published in 1879, declared that the subdivision of the electric current (as a step to subdivision of the electric light) is "incompatible with the well-proven law of conservation of energy." [6] Another English scientist, Professor Sylvanus Thompson, in lecturing on the problem of the subdivision of the electric light in 1878 stated that "any system depending on incandescence will fail." [7] Sir William Preece lectured before the Royal United Service Institution on February 15, 1879, where he said:

It is, however, easily shown (and that is by the application of perfectly definite and well-known scientific laws) that in a circuit where the electromotive force is constant, and we insert additional lamps, then when these lamps are joined up in one circuit, i.e., in series, the light varies inversely as the square of the number of the lamps in the circuit and that joined up in multiple arc, the light diminishes as the cube of the number inserted. Hence a subdivision of the electric light is an absolute *ignis fatuus*.[8]

The modern electrical engineer can explain why these early scientists were wrong. They were thinking of a fixed amount of current which would be divided among a number of lamps. Edison saw that it was possible to increase the amount of current and solve the problem. His boldness in undertaking the impossible was based on his own profound understanding of fundamental electrical laws and his ability to apply these laws to a practical problem. He knew he wanted a small light which could be independently controlled. Independent control implied a parallel circuit where, with a constant-voltage generator, the current units could be multiplied as desired. But the increase in current could mean either heavy energy loss in transmission or excessive copper cost. To avoid these, the light would have to be of high resistance. That conclusion is easily reached by an elementary application of Ohm's law. But in Edison's time, it was an important achievement which placed Edison far ahead of the other incandescent-light inventors and scientists and led him to develop a commercially successful electric-lighting system. The concept of the high-resistance lamp is a perfect illustration of that blend of technical and economic reasoning which underlay the successful innovation in the first years of the electrical manufacturing industry.

From the economist's viewpoint, the most significant aspect of Edison's activities in electric lighting was his concern at every step with economic factors. There may be some question about his motivation in inventing. The lure of financial reward was probably not all-important. He wanted to be the first to invent a successful lighting system to prove his superiority over other inventors and to demonstrate that he was a better scientist than the university-trained ones who treated him with contempt. But there can be no question whatsoever about the economic orientation of his efforts to develop an electric-lighting system. To him, the successful system was the one which could produce light for the home at a price lower than gas. Nearly all his inventive activities were directed toward making his system as efficient as possible. If his system were to be successful in the sense of coming into common use, it would have to survive the market test that every product in a free economic system has to meet. It would have to produce light of such a quality that it could be sold to consumers exercising free choice, at a price equal to the cost of the productive factors used in making that light. In deciding to invent a high-resistance lamp, in deciding to design an entire system rather than the lamp alone, and in deciding to direct his efforts toward developing a system which could produce light at low cost, Edison was organizing his technical activities in such a way as to make a high contribution to the real national income of the American people.

When Edison had evolved his basic plan, there remained the numerous problems incidental to carrying it out. The first of these was financial backing. The scope of the plan and the difficulties he had experienced in his first incandescent-lamp experiments led Edison to believe that his own resources were not sufficient. In spite of the fact that the first years of the Menlo Park laboratory had been financially successful, and in spite of that fact that he had a trained staff, a well-equipped laboratory, a carpenter shop, and a carbon shed, Edison was unwilling to attempt as large a task as the development of an incandescent-lighting system without more facilities and strong financial backing. He needed at least two more buildings — a machine shop and an office-library — as well as additional equipment and a larger staff. To design a satisfactory dynamo, for example, he required the facilities to construct dynamos and a power source for testing them. Furthermore, he needed assurance of funds sufficient to cover labor and material costs during a period long enough to permit the development of all the components of a lighting system.

Although only thirty-one years of age in 1878, Edison already was one of the most famous inventors in the United States. His work had given him personal contact with a number of prominent businessmen, and he was in a position to secure unusually good financial support. His plan for a lighting system and his need for funds were known to Grosvenor P. Lowrey, general counsel of the Western Union Telegraph Company. Lowrey had become acquainted with Edison in the course of the latter's transactions with Western Union. The two men had worked together on a number of infringement suits involving the patents Edison had sold to Western Union. In the course of working with Edison, Lowrey came to think very highly of his inventive ability and shared with him a strong belief in the commercial possibilities of electric lighting. Lowrey proposed that a corporation be formed to finance Edison's development of an incandescent-lighting system. The patents on that system were to be the property of the projected corporation.

Lowrey interested about a dozen men in his plan. Included in this initial group of Edison backers were three of Lowrey's law partners, George W. Soren, Charles F. Stone, and George S. Hamlin; the president of Western Union, Dr. Norvin Green; a prominent Western Union stockholder, James H. Banker; a leading Gold and Stock Telegraph Company stockholder, Tracy R. Edson; and a J. P. Morgan partner, Egisto P. Fabbri.[9] On October 15, 1878, these men, with Edison, incorporated the Edison Electric Light Company. The authorized capital stock was $300,000. The importance of Edison's work in telegraphy to the financing of his work on electric lights can be seen in the fact that eight of his twelve supporters had had contact with the telegraph industry in operation, financing, or legal counseling.

While Lowrey can be correctly considered the founder of the Edison Electric Light Company and chiefly responsible for securing the participation of the men who originally invested in it, the support of the Morgan partner, Egisto P. Fabbri, was of more long-run significance to the enterprise. Fabbri, a partner in Drexel, Morgan, and Company since January 1, 1876, was a close personal friend of Lowrey, and this friendship probably accounts for Fabbri's interest in the Edison firm.[10] Lowrey's law offices were on the third floor of the Drexel Building on Wall Street, where Drexel, Morgan, and Company occupied the first floor. Physical proximity combined with a personal relationship to place Lowrey in a position where he could successfully solicit the support of Fabbri and the Morgan firm.

The importance of Morgan support to Edison's electric-lighting project can hardly be overemphasized. The failure of Jay Cooke in 1873 had left Drexel, Morgan, and Company the unquestioned leader among the New York investment-banking firms. The participation of the Morgan firm in a project's financing was a stamp of approval that gave it a privileged position in the New York capital market. This was particularly true where, as in the Edison Electric Light Company, the interest of the Morgan firm increased with the passage of time.

Fabbri took an active part in the Edison firm. He served as director, treasurer, and a member of the five-man executive committee from the firm's founding until 1883, when ill health forced him to curtail his business activities.[11] Other Morgan partners who were associated with Edison's lighting work were C. H. Coster, J. Hood Wright, and George S. Bowdoin. J. Pierpont Morgan himself was not a director or official of the Edison firm, but his personal interest in the project is shown by the fact that he was one of the financiers who visited Menlo Park in the spring of 1879 to learn at first hand of Edison's progress.[12] Morgan was also one of the first New York residents to have his home supplied by its own electric-lighting plant. During the 1880's, he became a heavy investor in Edison lighting companies in New York, Brooklyn, and Boston. By 1892, he was in a position to play a leading part in the formation of the General Electric Company, on whose board he served until his death in 1913.

Another financier who supported the Edison firm and one whose reputation on Wall Street (at least for a brief period around 1880) was exceeded only by that of J. P. Morgan was Henry Villard. Villard's successes in railroad reorganization and financing in the years 1875–1882 gave him great personal prestige. This reached its height in the so-called "blind pool" of 1881, when he received pledges for $8,000,000 for a project unrevealed to those who pledged.[13] Villard was not one of the original Edison incorporators, but by 1880 he was on both the board of directors and the executive committee of the Edison Electric Light Company. It is probable that he came to be associated with Edison through acquaintanceship with Lowrey, who did legal work for him, and with the Morgan firm, which backed Villard in various railroad financial transactions. Villard's interest in Edison's work, like Morgan's, included the applications of the Edison electric light. Villard was able to give Edison his first order for an electric-lighting plant to be used commercially. This plant was installed in May 1880 on the *Columbia*, a steamship of the Oregon Railway and Navigation Company (of which Villard was president).

Financial support from Villard and the Morgan firm was strong support indeed. It should be emphasized that this support was not for the purpose of financing the production and sale of an existing product but rather to enable Edison to invent a complete system of incandescent electric lighting. This purpose is clearly and completely stated in a contract, dated November 15, 1878, between the Edison Electric Light Company and Edison.

> The company has been organized with the view of becoming the owner of and making, using and vending and licensing others to make, use and vend within the United States and other countries or colonies hereinafter mentioned all the inventions, discoveries, improvements and devices of said Edison, made or to be made in or pertaining to Electric Lighting, or relating in any way to the use of electricity for the purposes of power or of illumination or heating, or relating to improvements in Electric Engines or to the developing of electric currents by machines or otherwise, for any use or purpose except electric telegraphy.[14]

Edison agreed to assign to the company all his inventions and improvements in the specified electrical fields for a five-year period. In payment, he received 2,500 of the 3,000 shares of the company and $30,000 in cash. Twenty-five thousand dollars of this cash was to be used in conducting experiments. The company agreed that after it had earned $50,000 it would pay him a lump sum of $100,000 and royalties on the electric lamps sold, if net income were sufficiently high.[15]

Financial data pertaining to the first years of the Edison Electric Light Company are given in Table 10. The data show how much money Edison required to develop his lighting system and how the funds were obtained.

From October 15, 1878, until September 30, 1881, a total of approximately $150,000 was spent on experimental work. This figure included $7,700 for a machine shop and steam plant, $3,200 for an office-library, $2,400 for dynamos, $1,400 for a chemical laboratory, and $500 for books. The rest

TABLE 10

Financial Data of the Edison Electric Light Company
October 15, 1878 — September 30, 1886

	Sources of Funds		*Uses of Funds*		
Period	*Sale of stock*	*Loans from stockholders*	*Experimental work*	*Patent expenses*	*General overhead*
Oct. 15, 1878 to Jan. 20, 1879	$ 40,000	...	$ 23,914.22	...	$ 3,047.98
Jan. 21, 1879 to Nov. 11, 1879	10,000	...	18,954.99	$2,409.20	1,497.06
Nov. 12, 1879 to Nov. 11, 1880	...	$78,225	57,568.33	6,277.15	7,882.08
Nov. 12, 1880 to Sept. 30, 1881	129,600	...	52,011.54	[a]	61,846.04
Oct. 1, 1881 to Sept. 30, 1884	240,000	...	120,967.55	[a]	144,676.69
Oct. 1, 1884 to Sept. 30, 1886	360,000	...	[b]	[a]	145,869.06
Totals	$779,600	$78,225	$273,416,63	$8,686.35	$364,818.91
TOTAL SOURCES [c]	$779,600		TOTAL USES	$646,921.89	

Source: Edison Electric Light Company, *Annual Statements* (GE Files).
[a] After November 11, 1880, the patent expenses are included in general overhead.
[b] Data not available.
[c] The stockholder loans were repaid before the end of the period covered by the table and therefore are not a source of funds for the period as a whole.

was spent on labor and materials. The trial central stations at Menlo Park which demonstrated the Edison system to the public in December 1879 and again a year later accounted for much of the expenditure.

From October 1, 1881, until September 30, 1884, experimental expenses totaled $120,000. Since very little was done at Menlo Park after the spring of 1881, this figure represents the development work which was continued in New York City. Administrative expenses amounted to about $220,000 in the 1878–1884 period. Experimental expenses over the same six-year period totaled about $270,000.

These data reveal that to bring the Edison lighting system to the commercial stage required nearly half a million dollars. This sum was unquestionably much higher than Edison or his backers had anticipated. The 500 shares issued for cash were fully paid up by June 1, 1879, but the $50,000 they provided scarcely lasted for one year. During the next year, approximately $80,000 was borrowed from stockholders to meet the increasing expenses. On October 27, 1880, two years after the company's founding, a circular letter was sent to the stockholders by Calvin Goddard, secretary of the company, in which he said: "The investigations and experiments conducted by Mr. Edison at Menlo Park, in connection with the use of electricity for light and power, have covered a much wider range than was expected at the outset, and at a consequent largely increased expenditure." [16]

To meet this increased expenditure, the capital stock was increased to $480,000 on November 30, 1880. Of the 1800 additional shares, 504 were issued to Edison in return for an enlargement and extension of the 1878 patent agreement. The remaining 1296 shares were sold for cash. The resulting funds were used to repay the stockholder loans and meet experimental and administrative expenses. Further increases in the authorized capital stock of the Edison Electric Light Company were as follows: January 31, 1882, $720,000; September 24, 1883, $1,080,000; late 1886 or early 1887, $1,500,000.

With his capital needs provided for, Edison turned in the fall of 1878 to the task of inventing the components of his lighting system. Because of his ability to organize a research laboratory and direct the work of his assistants on problems that he posed, he was able to carry on the invention of various components simultaneously. As the work progressed, he found it necessary to add to the research staff a number of trained men, including a chemist, a glass blower, a mathematician, and machinists. The lamp and the dynamo were worked on first, although the meter, the fuse, the lamp socket, and other accessories were taken up early. On October 21, 1879, the first successful incandescent electric light was made and tested. On December 31 of that same year, Edison held the first public demonstration of his lighting system at Menlo Park. He lighted the laboratory, the office, the streets of Menlo Park, and some adjoining houses with over fifty lamps. Hundreds of people from New York and elsewhere traveled via the Pennsylvania Railroad to witness the demonstration.

The completion of the basic inventions permitted emphasis on further development and improvement. When the first central station was projected, the principal technical characteristics of the system had to be chosen. What were to be the values of the electrical constants in the commercial lighting system? The problem here was to decide on the lamp resistance, the circuit voltage, the conductor sizes, and the energy loss to be permitted. In view of the difficulties of making high-resistance lamps and the dangers of high voltage in the home, Edison decided to use 100-ohm lamps and 110-volt circuits. The transmission energy loss was to be about 10 per cent, a figure which permitted a reasonably small copper investment at 110 volts. These decisions implied the economical size for a district served by one central station — about one square mile.

Edison's clear understanding of Ohm's law and its application to the problem of economizing copper costs and transmission losses led him to choose correct values of voltage, lamp resistance, and conductor size. Edison himself did not carry out the lengthy calculations involved in making these choices. He had neither adequate mathematical training nor sufficient time. The calculating was turned over to Edison's mathematician, F. R. Upton, who was able to apply mathematical techniques in solving the problems. Because Upton's education reflected the state of scientific knowledge, Edison had to reëducate him to a true understanding of electrical laws. At first Upton could not understand why Edison wanted a lamp of high resistance. Years later Upton commented: "I cannot imagine why I could not see the elementary facts in 1878 and 1879 more clearly than I did. I came to Mr. Edison a trained man, a postgraduate at Princeton; with a year's experience in Helmholz's laboratory; with a working knowledge of calculus and a mathematical turn of mind." [17]

When Upton had learned Edison's use of Ohm's law, he could compute the most economical conductor sizes by taking account of copper costs, energy costs, and interest costs. Here he applied calculus to an ordinary minimization problem and worked out a number of solutions depending on various assumed conditions. Upton's work, under Edison's guidance, is further evidence of the inventor's talents. Edison was always aware of the economic implications of technical work, and he had the ability to conceive and understand problems which he did not have the mathematical training to solve.

With his technical problems on the way to solution, Edison could turn to his marketing problem. He decided to solve this in the most direct way possible — by establishing a central station in New York City to demonstrate the economic worth of his lighting system. The erection and operation of this station originally was to be handled by the Edison Electric Light Company, but use of the streets for laying the underground wires could be obtained only by a corporation organized under the gas statutes. A separate illuminating company was therefore required.

The Edison Electric Illuminating Company of New York was

incorporated on December 17, 1880, by six men, of whom five, including Lowrey and Fabbri, had been incorporators of the Edison Electric Light Company two years before. The directors and officers of the two firms were, with one or two exceptions, the same men — a result of the fact that the purpose of the Illuminating company was not to attract additional capitalists but simply to gain the right to use the streets. The Illuminating company's authorized capital stock was $1,000,000. $250,000 of this was issued to the Edison Electric Light Company in return for a license permitting the Illuminating company to use Edison's patented inventions. The remaining $750,000 of stock was offered to the Edison company stockholders in proportion to their Edison holdings.[18] The Illuminating company also paid the Edison company a cash sum equal to 10 per cent of the Illuminating company's stock. In April 1881, the City of New York granted a franchise to the Illuminating company, giving it the authority to lay its wires in New York streets.

Edison chose to place his first commercial central station on Pearl Street in lower Manhattan. This location brought the Wall Street financial district within the area to be served by the station. Edison wanted to prove to the financial community that his lighting system was practical, economical, and much superior to gas.

In the fall of 1881, the installation of equipment in a building on Pearl Street, the laying of conductors in the streets, and the wiring of buildings for the electric lights were begun. These tasks were nearly finished by the following July, and after several months of testing, the central station was officially placed in operation on September 4, 1882. Edison himself turned on the lights at the offices of Drexel, Morgan, and Company in the presence of J. P. Morgan and the directors of the Illuminating company.

The design of the Pearl Street central station was based on lessons learned in the operation of Edison's experimental central stations. The 1879–80 public demonstrations of the Edison light at Menlo Park had required the hasty construction of a central-station system which was small and employed overhead wires, carbonized-paper-filament lamps, and crude sockets. For the 1880–81 demonstrations, the central station was rebuilt and enlarged. It used ten generators, underground wires, bamboo-filament lamps, and screw sockets. A third central station was constructed the following year in London, England, by Edison engineers. This station, which began operation in the spring of 1882, tested the entire Edison central-station system under commercial conditions. Of particular interest was the performance of the "Jumbo" dynamos. The Jumbos were designed especially for central-station use and were an innovation in two respects. They were made in capacities of about twelve hundred lights, over four times the size of the largest incandescent-lighting generators previously made, and they were directly coupled to a steam engine which was mounted on the same foundation. Satisfactory operation of the Jumbos in England led to their installation in the Pearl Street station.

The size of the Pearl Street station, that is, its generating capacity measured by the number of lights it could serve, was determined on the basis of data obtained by Edison's men. They canvassed the district thoroughly to learn the number of gas jets burning at each hour up to 3:00 A.M. A house-to-house survey was made later which provided information on the number of gas jets in each building. The data obtained in these surveys also helped in planning the transmission network. A miniature network of conductors was constructed with a battery serving for the central station and with resistors for the lights. Careful studies were made of the voltage conditions in the model network, using various sizes and arrangements of the conductors.[19]

Edison planned to set the price of electric energy equivalent to the price of gas. He apparently reached this decision after one of his surveys in which the gas consumers were asked whether or not they would take the electric light if its price were the same as gas. Users of all but 850 of the 16,000 gas jets in the Pearl Street district answered in the affirmative.[20] There remained the question of exactly how much these consumers had paid for gas light with the price of gas at $2.25 per thousand cubic feet. To answer this question, Edison collected twenty-four books of gas bills paid by consumers in the district.

Expected revenues of the Pearl Street station were computed. The price assumed was 1.2 cents per lamp-hour, the price equivalent to gas, and the quantity assumed was based on the number of gas jets of the consumers who would switch to electric lighting.[21] To determine the profitableness of the station, it was also necessary to estimate costs. The expected costs were computed on the basis of economy tests made at Menlo Park and in London. The Menlo Park test, run in January 1881, gave costs low enough to result in the moving of Edison's headquarters from Menlo Park to New York City and the termination of Menlo Park experimental work. The London test provided data on the Jumbo dynamos, which were used in central-station work there for the first time.

Edison took three steps to ease the introduction of his innovation, the electric light, into the consumer's household. He first obtained a statement in writing from the New York Board of Fire Underwriters concerning insurance rates on a building wired for Edison lights. The Board said that the insurance rates would be unaffected if a Board inspector examined the wiring before connection was made to the street main.[22] Late in July 1882, the Illuminating company sent a circular to every household in the district which stated that the company would bear the expense of making the connection between the street main and the house wiring and the expense incurred in wiring the building until the consumer had decided whether or not he wanted the electric light permanently. Any consumer who, after a period of trial, decided not to adopt the Edison light would not be charged for the wiring or the connection.[23] The charges for the electric current did not begin until December, although the station began operation on September 4. The company wanted to make certain that it could provide reliable and satisfactory lighting service before making any charge.

The Edison light was 16 candle power, the same as the ordinary gas jet. The consumers were thereby given the light intensity that they had been accustomed to use. The business methods adopted by the Illuminating company also strongly resembled those of the gas companies. Monthly bills were rendered, and the Edison lights were usually referred to as burners. The customer was billed for light-hours instead of for electric energy to avoid confusing him with mysterious terminology and to stress the fact that he was in reality buying an old, familiar product — light — and not a new, unfamiliar product — electricity.

When Edison had invented his electric-lighting system and when he had laid his plans for marketing it, there still remained an important set of problems. He had to make arrangements for the manufacture of the system components. Because the Edison Electric Light Company did not desire to enter the manufacturing field, Edison was faced with the choice of finding someone to carry on the necessary manufacturing or of becoming a manufacturer himself.

In lamps, the experimental work involved manufacture on a small scale and, through this, Edison gradually became a full-fledged lamp manufacturer. The production of lamps for other than purely experimental work began in the late fall of 1879, when a number were made at the Menlo Park laboratory for the December 31 demonstration. It soon became clear that separate provision for this activity was needed. The manufacture of lamps was segregated from the experimental work for accounting purposes in April 1880, but was still carried on in the laboratory. That summer Edison purchased a nearby wooden building which was vacant and repaired it. He then worked out lamp-manufacturing methods for factory production and by early autumn was ready to install equipment. Electric power as well as electric lighting was used throughout the factory. Current was supplied from the dynamos in the Menlo Park machine shop until March 1881. At that time a separate steam-power plant was built for the lamp factory. This steam plant was used for heating the factory and for driving six Edison dynamos. Electricity was employed in the lamp factory for lighting the building and for testing the completed lamps. It was also used for "flashing" the lamps, a process of applying current to the filaments while the exhaustion of the bulbs was being completed. This drove off the occluded gases, and a much better vacuum resulted. The electricity also operated four motors employed in the production process. One drove a bamboo saw, another rotated the glass annealers, a third operated the blowers for glass blowing and the carbonizing furnace, and the fourth rotated an Archimedes screw which served as a mercury pump. The mercury was used in the 200 Sprengel pumps which exhausted the lamp bulbs. In addition to its own steam plant and electric plant, the factory also had its own gas plant. The gas was used in glass blowing and the carbonizing furnaces.[24]

Edison and three of his key employees — Charles Batchelor, Francis Upton, and Edward Johnson — formed the Edison Lamp Company, a partnership, on October 1, 1880.[25] Edison supplied over 80 per cent of the capital. This he probably obtained by selling some of his Edison company stock. The period from October 1 until November 11 was spent in training labor and making other final preparations. On November 11, production was begun.

Edison's lamp-manufacturing firm was formally recognized by the Edison company in an agreement concluded in March 1881. Edison was given the exclusive right to make, within the United States for consumption there, the Edison incandescent lamp. The patents on this lamp were, of course, the property of the Edison company, and the manufacture of the lamp could not be carried on without the company's permission. In return for this license to manufacture the lamp, Edison agreed to supply all demands of the users of the Edison lighting system within the United States and to invest at least $50,000 in manufacturing facilities.

Edison was to furnish the lamps to the Edison company at a price not to exceed 35 cents per lamp, including packing and delivery to the railway station. The Edison company would then sell the lamps to users of the Edison system. Edison was to attempt to cut production costs, and if the cost went below 32 cents per lamp, the additional profit was to be divided with the Edison company. The lamp contract was to continue during the life of the incandescent-lamp patents. Edison was given the right to make, without royalty, lamps for export to foreign countries (except North and South America).[26]

The Menlo Park lamp factory was operated until April 1, 1882, with a labor force which fluctuated between 100 and 135 workers. A total of 130,000 lamps were made in the period from November 11, 1880, to April 1, 1882. Of these, 80,000 were shipped and 50,000 were in stock on April 1. The factory was moved to East Newark (now Harrison), New Jersey, between April 1 and June 1. The principal reason for moving was the lack of sufficient labor in the Menlo Park area. The initial working force at East Newark was 150, and the capacity of the plant was 1,200 lamps per day.[27]

Cost-reducing changes were continually made in the lamp and in the methods of manufacture. The time for air exhaustion was shortened, a cheaper way to fasten the filament to the lead-in wires was devised, cutting and carbonizing the bamboo for the filament were simplified, and the design of the lamp base was changed to lessen breakage. The cost reductions which resulted from these technical changes and from the reorganization of production made possible by the expansion in the rate of output are shown in Table 11. Comparison with the revenue figures shows that cost did not go below average revenue until 1883. The fluctuation in the average revenue figure is probably caused by varying proportions of home and foreign sales. The contract with the Edison company, setting the lamp price at 35 cents, applied only to home sales. Edison was free to sell in the foreign market as he desired.

For the smaller components and accessories of the Edison system, Edison relied on S. J. Bergmann, who had been manufacturing various Edison inventions since 1876. Early in 1881, Bergmann and Edward Johnson, a partner in Edison's lamp company, formed Bergmann and Company. Shortly afterward, Edison was taken in as a third partner although he made no capital investment. Bergmann undertook to supply Edison with lamp bases, lamp sockets, switches, fuses, fuse blocks, electric-light fixtures, drop cords, chemical meters, voltage regulators, electrical instruments, and numerous additional items. Bergmann met Edison's needs ably and became a successful manufacturer. In the summer of 1882, Bergmann and Company purchased a large factory of the United States Electric Lighting Company which had been equipped to make Maxim lamps and dynamos. Within a few months, over 300 men were employed in that factory. In 1889, after the merger of his company with the Edison General Electric Company, Bergmann returned to Germany, where he founded an electrical manufacturing firm which grew to employ over 30,000 men.[28]

In dynamos, as in lamps, Edison had to establish his own manufacturing firm. He purchased a vacant ironworks in March 1881 and formed the Edison Machine Works. This plant was located on Goerck Street in New York City. Edison moved the tools and machinery from the Menlo Park machine shop after the Edison company agreed to purchase all Edison-system dynamos from him.[29] Production of dynamos was begun very soon, and by August 14, 1882, 800 men were on the payroll. Up to that time, two "Jumbo" dynamos and 355 smaller dynamos had been built and work was under way on twelve additional "Jumbos."[30] A testing department and an installation training school were established in con-

TABLE 11

Edison Lamp Company

Cost Data

Year[a]	Number of lamps produced	Total cost of lamps produced	Average cost per lamp
1881	50,000	$35,000.00	70.0¢
1882	68,488	36,243.00	52.9
	147,511	74,199.00	50.3
1883	229,532	73,141.59	31.9
	170,420	50,065.00	29.4
1884	196,337	58,238.29	29.7
	198,961	60,910.44	30.6
1885	244,098	...	...
	189,987	...	...
1886	337,202	...	...
	367,431	...	...

Revenue Data

Year[a]	Number of lamps sold	Total revenue from lamps sold	Average revenue per lamp
1881	34,597	$ 13,175.00	38.1¢
1882	60,292	33,576.00	55.7
	141,264	67,064.00	47.5
1883	155,278	80,491.82	51.8
	164,905	75,836.00	46.0
1884	174,166	74,468.54	42.7
	195,907	87,898.64	44.9
1885	180,641	78,304.07	43.3
	251,640	104,766.06	41.6
1886	272,123	113,948.10	41.9
	351,352	144,861.03	41.2

Source: GE Files.

[a] Except for 1881, figures are given for the first six months (January–June) and the second six months (July–December) of the year.

junction with the factory. In January 1884, the Edison Machine Works was incorporated with an authorized capital stock of $200,000.

To make underground conductors (that is, the street mains), Edison founded the Electrical Tube Company in February 1881. Like the dynamo works, the tube works was located in New York City. The techniques developed for the second Menlo Park demonstration were employed in tube manufacture. The copper conductors were placed in wrought-iron pipes twenty feet in length. A tarlike substance insulated the copper from the iron. After several years of operation, the tube works was absorbed by the Edison Machine Works and operated as a department of the latter firm.

Edison assumed the responsibility for the operation of his manufacturing enterprises — the lamp works, the dynamo works, and the tube works — and personally directed their activities. But of necessity he was forced to rely on works managers for continuous day-to-day supervision of the work in progress. He picked these managers from his Menlo Park staff — from the men who had worked with him in the development of his lighting system and had demonstrated technical proficiency, managerial ability, and unquestioned loyalty.

Edison's chief assistant and most trusted lieutenant at Menlo Park was Charles Batchelor. An Englishman by birth, he had been sent to the United States in the early 1870's by a British engineering firm to help install machinery at the Clark Sewing Thread Mills in Newark. After completing that job, he obtained employment in Edison's shop there. When Edison moved to Menlo Park, Batchelor accompanied him. He worked closely with Edison in the various experiments and soon became his principal assistant. When the Edison Lamp Company was formed, Batchelor was one of the partners. He managed the lamp works until early in 1881. In the spring of that year, he assisted Edison in starting the dynamo and tube factories, and in July, Edison sent him to France to install and take charge of the Edison exhibit at the International Electrical Exhibition in Paris. Remaining in France for two years, Batchelor started an Edison lamp factory and a dynamo works and placed both in operation. He returned to the United States in the fall of 1883 and became manager of the Edison Machine Works in New York City.

Francis R. Upton was also an important Edison assistant. He was educated at Andover, Bowdoin, Princeton, Johns Hopkins, and in Germany under Helmholz. His graduate training was in physics and mathematics. He came to Menlo Park in November 1878, on Lowrey's recommendation, to become Edison's mathematician and physicist. His principal duties were to keep Edison informed on the existing state of scientific knowledge relative to problems which arose, to advise him on theoretical questions, especially those involving advanced mathematics, and to prepare technical and scientific papers on Edison's work. As the Menlo Park activities expanded, Upton was led into managerial work. His first important assignment of that kind was supervision of the installation of the lighting system on the *Columbia*. Like Batchelor, Upton was one of Edison's partners in the lamp company. He became manager of the lamp factory in January 1881 and continued in that position for over a decade.

A third man who assumed positions of responsibility under Edison was John Kruesi. Swiss born, he had worked as machinist for Edison in Newark and, after the move to Menlo Park, took charge of the laboratory machine shop. He left Menlo Park in February 1881 to become manager of the tube works. The street mains for the Pearl Street station were laid under his direction, and, in 1883, he became assistant manager of the machine works, a position he held until about 1890 when he became manager of the works, then located at Schenectady.

When the Edison system of electric lighting had been developed and when the lamp factory was in satisfactory operation, Edison found it advisable to move from Menlo Park to New York City, where the machine works, the tube works, Bergmann's electrical-accessories factory, and installation of the Pearl Street station engaged his attention. The second Menlo Park public demonstration (December 1880) marked the end of important development work in electric lighting there. In January 1881, a careful and complete test of the Menlo Park installation led to the conclusion that the system was ready for commercial use. Edison moved, with his family, to New York, and his chief assistants, with the exception of Upton who remained to manage the lamp factory in East Newark, accompanied him. Edison's move to New York coincided with the establishment of the Edison company headquarters at 65 Fifth Avenue, a brownstone building that had formerly been a residence. The company had been largely a "paper" organization previous to 1881 and had not needed separate office space of any magnitude.

One reason the Edison company had begun a more active existence was that there was now an opportunity to sell Edison lighting equipment to individuals who desired to use the Edison light in their places of business or their homes. The sale of these so-called "isolated" plants (as distinguished from central stations) became an important source of revenue sooner than Edison had expected. This business was first handled by a Bureau of Isolated Light in the Edison company, but later, in November 1881, a subsidiary, the Edison Company for Isolated Lighting, was formed to take over the isolated-lighting market.

Sixty-five Fifth Avenue was also used to display the Edison system of incandescent lighting. Interested individuals could see the Edison light in everyday use. Special exhibits, such as a printing shop, were set up to demonstrate how the Edison light could meet the lighting needs of various kinds of business enterprises. Edison spent many hours at 65 Fifth Avenue, explaining his system to important visitors and offering suggestions on possible uses of his light.

The years 1881–1884 were extremely busy ones for Edison. Directing the operations of his three manufacturing firms, the installation and operation of the Pearl Street station, Bergmann's manufacturing operations, and the development of improved components for his system — these were his principal activities. In spite of his delegation of authority to Batchelor, Upton, and Kruesi, Edison had to keep in personal touch with all operations in order to coördinate them. As Samuel Insull, Edison's secretary, wrote in May 1881, "So you can imagine what Mr. Edison has to do as he is the mainspring and ruling spirit of everything." [31]

Although Edison was working energetically to place his lighting system in widespread use, the ultimate control over the system lay not in him but in the patents. The system could not be made, sold, or used unless the owner of the patents gave permission. That owner was the Edison Electric Light Company. Originally Edison had held five-sixths of the stock and was therefore in control, but when his financial backers refused to supply money for the manufacturing activities, Edison was forced to sell most of his stock to obtain funds. This enabled him to establish the lamp works, the machine works, and the tube works. Only the electrical-accessories factory, for which Bergmann supplied most of the necessary capital, was set up without Edison's funds.

Losing control of the Edison company eventually led to serious problems for Edison. The fundamental difficulty was that the men in control were excessively cautious and unwilling to invest enough additional money or take vigorous action in marketing the Edison system. Their caution was probably rooted in a lack of understanding of the system and a failure to appreciate its commercial possibilities. They did not share Edison's optimism and confidence in the ultimate success of his system. The difference in the points of view of Edison and his backers was commented on by Edison in 1883: "I have come to the conclusion that my system of lighting having been perfected, should be promoted, and I could take hold and push the system better than anyone else. It is so complicated that I do not like trusting it to new and untried hands, because science and dollars are so mixed up in it." [32]

The main policy of the Edison company, and the one that forced Edison to take the initiative in setting up manufacturing units, was enunciated in the 1882 annual report: "The policy of our company . . . had always been . . . that of merely paying the expenses of experiments and of taking out and holding patents and not of investing capital in the actual business of lighting." [33]

The organization of the central stations in the larger cities (New York, Boston, Chicago, Philadelphia, and so forth) did not involve any capital investment by the Edison company. When a local company had been organized, it would receive a license from the parent company and then would order the equipment it needed from the Edison manufacturing companies. The isolated-plant business, however, required the maintenance of sales offices throughout the country. Sizable inventories of dynamos, lamps, and the other components had to be carried in these sales offices. Capital investment in the marketing organization was therefore needed, and the Edison Company for Isolated Lighting was formed. It received a license to sell Edison equipment outside of cities served by gas companies. In return for this license, it issued $255,000 of its $500,000 capital stock to the Edison company.

The Isolated company sold electric-lighting plants to business firms and private persons and also to central-station companies in the smaller cities and towns. Sales efforts in promoting the latter kind of business were not nearly so vigorous as Edison desired. When he had invented the three-wire system of distribution, he felt that copper costs were low enough to permit his system to operate on a commercial basis in small villages and hamlets where the houses were far apart and the load density low.[34] To stimulate the sale of equipment in such places, Edison wanted to set up central stations in a number of villages and bring them into profitable operation. Only then would local capitalists be asked to invest. Neither the Edison company nor the Isolated company was willing to participate in that plan, however. Edison was forced to act by himself and with his own funds. In 1883, he formed the Thomas A. Edison Construction Department and proceeded to install a small central station at Sunbury, Pennsylvania. By the fall of 1884, when his new venture was merged with the Isolated company, he had installed central stations in nearly twenty towns.

Edison's dissatisfaction with the Edison company management was not confined to the sales policies of the Isolated company. He was also dissatisfied with the conservatism and caution exhibited by the management, particularly in regard to patent suits. The patent policy grew partly out of the circumstances of the time, but the Edison company management could also be held responsible for it. The root of the difficulty lay in the fact that the complete technical details of the Edison system were published in a newspaper article in December 1879, some time before Edison had intended it to appear.[35] He was not then ready to market his lighting system, and he would not be ready for several years. When Edison's solution to the incandescent-lighting problem was completely described in print, the other inventors working on the incandescent light were given the opportunity to work out their own systems while Edison was completing his. Normally, vigorous enforcement of Edison's patent rights could have prevented wholesale usurpation of his inventions. But because infringement suits would have required Edison's personal attention and perhaps his testimony, nothing was done. The Pearl Street installation, the manufacturing activities, the continuing development work, and the demonstrations at 65 Fifth Avenue simply left Edison no time for patent suits, and none were initiated. The 1881 annual report of the Edison company stated that the patent-infringement suits were being postponed until Edison had time to give his attention to them. The 1883 report included the information that notices of infringement had been served but that no suits had yet been instituted because nobody had injured the company sufficiently to make it worth while. "The business ascendancy which we have acquired is of itself sufficient, certainly for the present, to give us a practical monopoly."[36] The no-suit policy was thus partly due to the unavailability of Edison and the lack of serious competition. It surely expressed, in addition, the timidity and caution of the Edison company and encouraged infringers to believe that the Edison patents were weak and would not be sustained.[37]

Edison finally decided to effect a change in the Edison company management. The man he chose to head the company and assume the responsibility for carrying out his policies was Edward H. Johnson. Originally a telegrapher in Colorado, Johnson went to New York City in the early 1870's to work on an automatic telegraph system. Edison was called in as a consultant on this project and became acquainted with Johnson. When Edison invented the phonograph some years later (1877), he hired Johnson to publicize it. In 1878 Edison sent Johnson to England to aid in establishing the Edison telephone company there. Johnson returned in 1879 but was soon sent to England again, this time to form the English Edison Electric Light Company and to demonstrate the Edison light to the British people. He directed the installation of the trial central station in London and took charge of the Edison display at the Crystal Palace Exhibition in London in 1882.

In the fall of 1882, Johnson returned to the United States in time for the opening of the Pearl Street station. Already a partner in the Edison Lamp Company and Bergmann and Company, he was elected vice-president and a director of the Edison Electric Light Company on October 24, 1882. He was reëlected to both positions at the 1883 annual meeting. During these years, he was also a director of the Isolated company.

Although Edison owned only a small amount of Edison company stock, he secured the support of some of the large stockholders (including, apparently, the Morgan partners) and appealed to others for proxies. At the October 28, 1884, annual meeting, Edison was able to elect a board of directors and officers who were sympathetic to his views on company policies.

The retiring president and member of the board of directors, S. B. Eaton, explained Edison's efforts to reorient the company policies as follows: "Mr. Edison has been for some time dissatisfied with the direction and executive management of the company. He wished to make use of money to push the enterprise, but some of the directors, including myself, were opposed to employing it on the terms offered, deeming it unadvisable on account of the dullness in business everywhere." [38]

Of the thirteen directors, eight were replaced in the 1884 election. Most of these had been prominent in the founding and operation of the company. Lowrey and the men who had become associated with the company on his suggestion gave way to Edison. The replaced directors included, in addition to Lowrey, Dr. Norvin Green, president of Western Union, 1878–1893, and president of the Edison company, 1878–1882; S. B. Eaton, president of the company, 1882–1884; W. H. Meadowcroft, Eaton's secretary; Calvin Goddard, secretary of the company, 1878–1883; and José de Navarro, New York banker and a director since 1880. Villard was also replaced, but it is doubtful that his retirement was desired by Edison. Villard had lost control of the Northern Pacific in 1883, and much of his personal fortune was lost as well. It is probable that he was forced to sell his Edison stock in order to meet pressing financial obligations. Even had he remained on the Edison board, he would not have been able to take an active interest in the company, because he left for Europe in the summer of 1884 and remained there for two years.

Of Edison's three most important financial supporters — Lowrey, Villard, and J. P. Morgan — the first two were thus not of major importance after 1884. To fill this gap, the Morgan firm increased its interest in the Edison company. Morgan had one director on the board from the very beginning, Egisto Fabbri, and upon his retirement in 1883, J. Hood Wright, also a Morgan partner, was elected to the board. The 1884 meeting brought the reëlection of Wright and the election of C. H. Coster, one of Morgan's most trusted partners. Either Wright or Coster served on the executive committee every year, with the exception of 1886, from 1884 to 1889.

Newly elected directors in 1884 included, in addition to Coster, Charles Batchelor and Francis Upton. Johnson, already a director and vice-president, was reëlected to both positions and with Batchelor was placed on the executive committee. The new president was Eugene Crowell, an elderly man who did not take an active part in the operation of the company. Consequently, Johnson assumed the responsibilities and duties of the chief executive.

Edison wanted a more vigorous promotion of his lighting system. With the election of directors, officers, and an executive committee who shared this viewpoint, the policies of the Edison company were radically altered. The first patent suits were initiated in the spring of 1885. Johnson pushed these suits with great vigor and publicly warned infringers that trouble was ahead for them. He also effected a change in the patent-licensing system. Instead of selling large territorial rights for the Edison system to sales agents and promoters, Johnson initiated the policy of selling only local rights. The Edison company could thus have a more direct hand in central-station development. Another of Johnson's activities was to encourage the expansion of Edison central stations in New York and Boston, and he was instrumental in securing J. P. Morgan's support for these expansions. By the end of 1886, the new Johnson policies seemed to be bearing fruit. The 1886 earnings of the Edison company exceeded the total of all its earnings prior to 1886.[39]

With Johnson in charge of the Edison company, Batchelor and Kruesi in charge of the machine works (now combined with the tube works), and Upton in charge of the lamp works, Edison was ready, by 1886, to withdraw again to his laboratory. After leaving Menlo Park, he had maintained a small laboratory at the plant of Bergmann and Company in New York City. In 1885, he shifted his laboratory to the lamp works at Harrison, and in 1886, he moved to West Orange, where he built an extensive, modern laboratory and purchased a large home. His first wife died in August 1884, and he married again in February 1886. His move to West Orange thus marked the resumption of family life, a return to the laboratory, and a retirement from the electrical industry which he had created. He continued to serve the Edison manufacturing companies and central stations as a consultant on technical problems, but most of his time in the laboratory was spent in exploring completely new fields.

The principal development in the organization of the various Edison companies during 1886 and 1887 was the emergence of the parent Edison company as a firm whose sole activity was the holding and licensing of the Edison electrical patents. The company offices were moved to Wall Street, and the selling and promotional activities were taken over by the newly formed United Edison Manufacturing Company, which moved into 65 Fifth Avenue. United was wholly owned by the three firms which manufactured the Edison system components (the Edison Lamp Company, the Edison Machine Works, and Bergmann and Company) and acted as their agent in the sale and installation of the Edison lighting system.

The amalgamation of the three manufacturing companies and the patent-holding company into one firm was effected by Henry Villard in 1889. He had returned to the United States in the fall of 1886 and had rapidly regained an important position among New York financiers. His principal activity was dealing in railroad securities for German clients. His interests extended to the electrical manufacturing industry, which he had become acquainted with through his early participation in the Edison

Electric Light Company. He thought that the parent company and the three manufacturing companies should all be one firm in order to achieve effective coördination of manufacturing, selling, and installation. His German clients, particularly the Deutsche Bank of Berlin, showed interest in such a consolidation. Villard was also able to secure the financial support of C. H. Coster.

TABLE 12

Formation of the Edison General Electric Company

Consolidating Companies	*Payment in EGE Stock (at par value)*
Edison Electric Light Company	$3,500,000
Edison Lamp Company Edison Machine Works Bergmann and Company	2,158,333[a]
Sprague Electric Railway and Motor Company[b]	750,000[c]
United Edison Manufacturing Company Canadian Edison Manufacturing Company Leonard and Izard Company[d]	200,000[c]
Total stock issued to stockholders of consolidating companies	$6,608,333
Stock issued for cash[e]	2,250,000
Stock issued to Villard in payment for promotion fee	175,000
Total stock issued in consolidation	$9,033,333

Sources: Henry Villard Papers (Houghton Library, Harvard University); data in GE Files; Edison General Electric Company, *Annual Report* (January 2, 1890).

[a] In addition to the stock, a cash payment of $1,166,667 was made.

[b] For 5,200 of 14,000 shares.

[c] Estimated.

[d] A small construction company which installed some Edison equipment.

[e] Issued to the syndicate, which included Drexel, Morgan, and Company; Kuhn, Loeb, and Company; and the Berlin Deutsche Bank.

Villard called the new firm the Edison General Electric Company. It was incorporated in New Jersey in January 1889 and had an authorized capital stock of $12,000,000. Financial data of the consolidation plan, which was worked out by Villard and Coster, are shown in Table 12. The Edison Electric Light Company had almost no physical assets. The $3,500,000 of Edison General Electric stock was a payment for the Edison patents on the components of the lighting system and for stocks and bonds in central-station companies. These stocks and bonds had been received in part payment for patent licenses to operate the Edison equipment. The securities were carried on the company balance sheet at $1,500,000. The patents alone were therefore considered worth about $2,000,000.

The price for the three manufacturing companies was based on their earning power. Their annual earnings totaled about $700,000. The $3,300,000 total of cash and stock indicates that 20 per cent was approximately the rate of return used in computing the worth of the three firms.

The other companies in the consolidation accounted for about $1,000,000 of Edison General Electric stock.[40] Stock of par value $2,250,000 was issued in exchange for $1,750,000 in cash to a syndicate headed by Morgan, the Berlin Deutsche Bank, and Kuhn, Loeb. A total of about $9,000,000 of Edison stock was thus issued. For his part in the promotion, Villard received $175,000 in stock.

The individual companies continued to maintain their own identities until August 1, 1890. At that time, the operations of the manufacturing companies (excepting the Canadian company) were merged into one organization, and seven district offices were established to handle all sales.[41] The salesmen were shifted from commissions to salaries, and efforts were made to weld them into a more coherent organization. Villard became president of the new firm. Johnson and Edison were on the board, but neither took an active interest in the company. Johnson had purchased a large Connecticut country estate in 1887, and thereafter he devoted less and less time to business.[42]

At the formation of Edison General Electric, Edison withdrew almost completely from the electrical manufacturing industry. After 1886, he had not actively directed the operation of the machine works and the lamp works, but he had kept his controlling interest in both firms. He gave his reasons for selling his electrical manufacturing enterprises in a letter which he wrote to Villard in 1890. "I have been under a desperate strain for money for twenty-two years, and when I sold out, one of the greatest inducements was the sum of cash received, which I thought I could always have on hand, so as to free my mind from financial stress, and thus enable me to go ahead in the technical field."[43] Edison went on to say that he was no longer interested in electric lighting and that "working day and night to advance efficiency from 80 to 85 per cent is an absurdity."

Thus, by 1890, Edison was ready to turn to new fields of endeavor. He had achieved the goal he set for himself in 1878 — to develop an incandescent-electric-lighting system — and he had seen that system attain widespread use. With the manufacture of incandescent-lighting equipment and the operation of the central stations both firmly established as profitable activities, he could leave their administration and the promotion of further growth and development to others.

VIII

Marketing the Edison System

THE INCANDESCENT LAMP

Edison's monumental contribution to the incandescent lamp was the high-resistance filament. Edison was the first inventor to understand and apply the fundamental electrical laws governing the relations among voltage, resistance, current, and energy loss to the problem of an incandescent-lighting system. He determined the one characteristic that an incandescent lamp had to possess before it could be commercially successful and demonstrated that he had the technical competence and inventive ingenuity to construct a lamp with that characteristic.

When Edison had conceived of the high-resistance lamp and had learned how to make a high-resistance filament, he had to decide how large that resistance should be. From the standpoint of energy lost in transmission and interest cost on the investment in copper conductors, the higher the lamp resistance, the more economical the lighting system. A high lamp resistance meant that a high voltage and low current could be used to deliver energy to the lamp filament. Since the energy lost in transmission is a function of the current and the size of the conductor, a low current meant either a small energy loss (for a given conductor) or a small conductor (for a given energy loss).

There were disadvantages, however, to a high lamp resistance. As the resistance increased, it became more difficult to make a lamp filament of high efficiency and good durability. A high filament resistance thus meant heavy current consumption, excessive lamp consumption, or expensive lamps. The high voltage which a high lamp resistance permitted was also not without disadvantages. More and better insulation was necessary. And even with adequate insulation, the danger of shock and fire was increased when higher voltages were brought into offices and residences. Here, then, was a situation where the choice of the lamp resistance had to be based on a compromise of conflicting factors: transmission energy loss; conductor cost; lamp cost, efficiency, and durability; insulation cost; and safety. Edison decided on 110 volts and a filament resistance of about 100 ohms.

Constructing a 100-ohm filament which would endure for several hundred hours was at first so difficult that little attention could be paid to the relation between lamp life and efficiency. This relation became important, however, as knowledge of incandescent lamps increased. The life and the efficiency of a lamp are both functions of its candle power. If a lamp is operated to produce a high candle power, it will have a high efficiency and a short life. If the same lamp is operated at a low candle power (by the application of a lower voltage), it will have a lower efficiency and a longer life. Edison saw that the problem in designing a 16-candle-power lamp, for use on 110-volt circuits, was to choose the combination of efficiency and life that would minimize lighting costs. He decided that an electric-energy cost of 1 cent per 16-candle-power hour and a lamp cost of $1.00 called for a lamp which would consume about 75 watts and have an average life of about 600 hours. This optimum lamp had a filament resistance of about 160 ohms, a figure considerably higher than that of the first Edison lamps. The higher resistance was feasible because of the substantial advance in the technique of lamp manufacture.

The 75-watt, 600-hour lamp gave minimum lighting costs only where the lamp and energy costs which were assumed in its design actually prevailed. Because some central stations had lower energy costs, a lamp of lower efficiency and longer life was also manufactured. This lamp consumed 5.8 watts per candle power, instead of 4.6 watts, but lasted over 1000 hours.[1]

The production of lamps of different efficiency to meet better the needs of consumers with widely different energy costs required a close coördination between manufacturing and marketing. The same kind of problem arose years later. It was learned through experience that high-efficiency lamps were very susceptible to voltage variations. If a high-efficiency lamp were operated at voltage other than the designated one, its life would be materially shortened. The increased cost for lamp replacement in such a case would more than offset the saving in electric energy resulting from the high efficiency. A low-efficiency lamp, which would not be affected appreciably by voltage variations, was consequently a more economical lamp to use where the operating voltage was subject to considerable variation. To meet this problem of voltage variation, Edison incandescent lamps were made in the 1890's in three efficiencies. The most efficient, which consumed 3.1 watts per candle power, were designed for use where voltage regulation was nearly perfect. The central stations in the large cities met that standard of voltage regulation. The next most efficient, 3.5 watts per candle power, were designed for use where the voltage varied not more than 4 per cent. Smaller central stations fell within that class. The least efficient, 4 watts per candle power, were designed for use in isolated plants where wide variations in operating voltages were common.[2]

The fact that lamp buyers varied in their electric-energy costs and in the voltage regulation of their lighting systems made the production of lamps of different efficiencies desirable. But coördination between marketing and production was not solely for the purpose of adjusting production to market conditions. Another objective was to adjust the market to production. When a lamp had been made, its proper operating voltage was determined by a photometer. If the lamp were designed to emit 16 candle power, it would be placed on a test circuit and the operating voltage would be adjusted until the lamp produced its rated candle power. This voltage would then be marked on the lamp. Only a small fraction (about one-fourth) of the lamps in any one lot would come out at the intended voltage. The market, therefore, had to be arranged to consume the pattern of lamps manufactured.

Individual determination of lamp voltages, with the resulting variation in these voltages, was necessary until the advent of the ductile tungsten filament in 1911. The reason for the variation in voltage required was that it was impossible to make the filament to the exact dimensions desired. In the period 1881–1886, the filaments (bamboo) had large ends in order to radiate sufficient heat to prevent melting of the copper-plated connection with the lead-in wire. The large ends prevented any adjustment in filament length once the filament had been cut and carbonized. The result was that the required filament voltages varied as much as 20 per cent. Beginning in 1886, carbon paste was used to make the connection between the lead-in wire and the filament. Enlarged ends were no longer needed, and the length of the filament could be adjusted after carbonization. The variation in filament voltages was reduced but still of importance. Carbonized filaments were employed exclusively until about 1900, when various metallic filaments came into use. In all these filaments, voltage variations could not be avoided.

Various Edison-lighting-system installations, both central stations and isolated plants, were adjusted to operate at different voltages. The equipment salesmen were informed from time to time of the voltages at which new installations should operate. The manager of the Eastern Sales District of the General Electric Company was requested in 1894 to install new incandescent-lighting plants at varying voltages.[3] On June 13, 1895, S. D. Greene, manager of the General Electric lighting department, spoke before a meeting of lighting-equipment salesmen. He requested that lighting plants be installed at voltages other than 110 volts in order that the lamps of 112 volts, 113 volts, and so forth, could be used.[4] In 1897, Greene sent a circular letter to all local sales-office managers in which he stated that, in the future, incandescent-lighting plants should be sold for voltages other than 110. He went on to say: "So many plants have been sold within the last year or two for this voltage that our Lamp Works find it difficult to meet the demand for lamps without accumulating too large a stock in neighboring voltages."[5] He then listed the specific voltages and efficiencies in which the stock was too large. When these efforts to coördinate plant installations with lamp voltages were unsuccessful, the excess lamps were sold at exceedingly low prices. One dealer offered 16-candle-power lamps for operation on 100–105 volts at 12 cents each.[6] Regular Edison lamps were selling for about 25 cents at that time.

The marketing policies of the Edison Lamp Works were further complicated by the distinction between licensee customers and ordinary customers. The licensee customers were the central-station companies who held the exclusive sales agency for Edison lamps and other parts of the Edison system in their territories. They were given substantial reductions from regular prices. Up to about 1890, when the price to ordinary buyers was $1.00 per lamp, the licensee companies paid $0.40. In the mid-nineties, when the regular price had fallen to about $0.45, the licensees paid $0.25. Another segment of the market, the foreign buyers, were apparently treated like the ordinary home buyers until 1893. At that time Edison, as a member of the General Electric board of directors, suggested that the lamps be sold abroad at cost to permit a larger scale of production, which would lower manufacturing costs. The Sales Committee considered this suggestion on December 12, 1893, and decided to accept it in a modified form. Lamps were to be sold at $0.25 each, f.o.b. foreign ports. That figure was not as low as cost, but was equal to the price then being charged the home licensees.[7]

Edison's suggestion on foreign sales was one marketing policy designed to reduce production costs. It depended on the economies of a larger rate of production. Another sales technique with the same purpose was the future-delivery contract. Beginning about 1893, General Electric entered into ten-year contracts for 16-candle-power incandescent lamps. At a time when the lamp price to ordinary customers was $0.50, the following prices were quoted for future delivery: 1893, $0.475; 1894, $0.475; 1895, $0.45; 1896, $0.40. The price for the balance of the ten years covered by the contract was to be the same as to other customers of the same classification.[8]

The future-delivery plan reduced production costs primarily because it permitted better production scheduling. Production for inventory was possible at no risk, and the costs in changing from one rate of production to another or from one kind of lamp to another could be lessened. S. D. Greene reported in 1895:

> It is essential in order to make lamps at a minimum cost that the factory should be run constantly at as uniform an output as possible. Our future delivery plan in lamps has been very successful. Up to date we have secured future delivery orders for about three million lamps, of which we have shipped about one-half. . . It is very expensive work changing from one rate of production to another in factories. . . The benefit of the future delivery plan is apparent since we can manufacture to stock knowing that all the stock is to be taken within a certain time.[9]

In the first years of production, the Edison lamps were sold only to users of Edison apparatus. This policy was enunciated by the board of directors of the Edison Electric Light Company on May 16, 1882.[10] The Edison lamp was the best lamp obtainable at that time, and the purpose of the policy was to stimulate sales of the Edison system through the reputation of the lamp. Because the Edison lamps were not available through regular channels to owners of other makes of lighting equipment, these users were forced to pay more than the regular price. Edison lamps were advertised for sale at $3.00 each in the latter part of 1883.[11] When good-quality incandescent lamps became available from other makers, there was no longer any reason to restrict the sales of Edison lamps to users of Edison apparatus. This restriction was consequently removed in the late 1880's. By 1893, Edison lamps were being sold to almost everyone who would buy. The General Electric Sales Committee received a report from the assistant manager of the Edison Lamp Works on October 20, 1893, which stated that during the period from July 1, 1892, to June 30, 1893, 1,605,000 lamps were shipped to licensee companies, 424,000 to non-licensee companies, and 149,000 to opposition plants.[12]

The Edison company, like the Brush and the Thomson-Houston companies, realized that objective evaluation of its products by scientific experts could provide convincing sales arguments. The Edison company had its lamp tested at the 1881 International Electrical Exhibition held in Paris. Three other lamps were in the competition, the Maxim lamp and two English lamps. The Maxim lamp was made by the United States Electric Lighting Company and was sold in connection with its lighting system.

A commission of the Paris Exhibition measured a number of the technical characteristics of the four kinds of lamps. The efficiency data were as follows: Edison, 12.73 lamps per horsepower; Maxim, 9.48 lamps per horsepower; Swan, 10.71 lamps per horsepower; Lane-Fox, 10.61 lamps per horsepower.[13] The Edison lamp thus was more efficient than any of the others. But the specification of efficiency without lamp life is incomplete. The Edison company had an opportunity to secure life tests of its lamps by competent, unbiased engineers in 1885. In the fall of 1884, the Franklin Institute sponsored an electrical exhibition in Philadelphia. Several committees were appointed to examine the electrical exhibits carefully and scientifically. One of these committees conducted life and efficiency tests of incandescent lamps. The tests were conducted in April and May 1885 after elaborate preparations to ensure accuracy and fair treatment. Dr. Weston, chief electrical engineer of the United States company, and Upton and Howell of the Edison Lamp Works checked the testing procedures and agreed that they were fair and reliable. Before the tests were begun, however, Weston requested that the United States lamps be withdrawn. He stated that they were an inferior batch. The committee agreed to let him submit a second batch, but he never did. The first batch was therefore tested as originally planned.[14]

Of the lamps tested by the Institute committee, only the Edison and United States (Weston) lamps were entered by the manufacturer. The Institute purchased the other lamps from dealers. The results of the tests are shown in Table 13. The life test was a conclusive victory for Edison. The efficiency test, however, showed that to gain its longer life the Edison lamp had sacrificed efficiency. The lower efficiency was partly the result of the preference for a longer life. It was also partly due to the fact that the Edison filament was the only one not treated by a hydrocarbon. It should be noticed that the lamp of highest efficiency was the Westinghouse 44-volt lamp. This illustrates the fact that the lower the lamp voltage and resistance, the higher the efficiency that could be attained. It will be seen later that the Westinghouse system, which employed high voltages (1000 or 2000) for transmission, used only 50 volts in the local circuits. More efficient lamps were therefore feasible.

The Edison lamps and other components were entered into contests at a number of other exhibitions. At the 1883 Cincinnati Exhibition, where the Thomson-Houston system received the top awards in arc lighting, the Edison equipment received the top awards in incandescent lighting. The United States company was also in the incandescent-lighting competition at Cincinnati. The Edison victory here, as in the life tests in Philadelphia in 1885, was particularly useful to the Edison company because the United States company was its only important rival until about 1885. Edison also received all the first prizes for incandescent systems at the Southern Exposition, held at Louisville, Kentucky, in 1884.

TABLE 13

Results of the 1885 Incandescent-Lamp Tests Conducted by the Franklin Institute

Make of lamp	*Number that failed in 1065 hours*[a]	*Watts per candle power*	*Lamp voltage*
Edison	1 out of 21	4.46	100
United States (Weston)	17 out of 24	4.51	70[b]
		3.71	110[c]
Westinghouse (Stanley)	19 out of 22	4.04	96
		3.54	44
Woodhouse and Rawson[d]	11 out of 11	3.60	55

Source: "Report on the Efficiency and Duration of Incandescent Lamps," published as a supplement to the *Journal of the Franklin Institute*, CXX (September 1885).

[a] The figures in this column do not separate lamps of different voltages by one maker. Both United States and Westinghouse submitted lamps of two different voltages, as is indicated in the last column of the table.

[b] A lamp with a carbonized-paper filament.

[c] A lamp with a tamidine-carbon filament, an invention of Weston's.

[d] An English make of lamp.

The excellent reputation of the Edison lamp reflected the careful production and testing techniques employed by the Edison Lamp Works. The goal was a lamp of uniformly high quality. The individual photometering of each lamp to determine the voltage at which it would emit 16 candle power has already been mentioned. Samples of the output were tested periodically to insure that the claimed efficiency was being met. Continual research was carried on to learn how to improve the lamps. The Edison policy of stressing quality in lamp manufacture was clearly expressed by the General Electric executive committee in 1893. The statement was for internal administrative use only and did not appear in any publicity or advertising material.

Resolved, that it is the sense of this committee that it is very short-sighted policy to make poor lamps (in hopes of profit from more frequent renewals or to save some trifling cost of manufacture) and that no effort should be spared to make the *very best possible* commercial lamps consistent with reasonable cost; and that, failing to do this, we shall lose our lamp business, notwithstanding the reduction of prices.[15]

ISOLATED-LIGHTING PLANTS

The Edison electric-lighting system was sold to two kinds of users, the firms and private persons who desired to produce light for their own use and the central stations who were in the business of producing and selling light. The plants installed for the first kind of customer were referred to as isolated plants and preceded the central stations by several years. The first commercial installation of the Edison lighting system, it will be recalled, was on the steamship *Columbia* of the Oregon Railway and Navigation Company in the spring of 1880. The dynamos and lamps were constructed in the Menlo Park laboratory. Four 6-kilowatt (60-lamp) dynamos — one to act as a source of field current for the other three — and 115 lights comprised the installation. The plant gave very satisfactory service and was in use more than fifteen years. The next isolated installation was in the shops of a New York lithographing firm, Hinds, Ketchum, and Company.

The customers for isolated systems were mainly business firms. Textile mills, for example, commonly needed artificial illumination during the early morning and late afternoon hours, particularly during the short days of winter. In other industries, the physical conditions of production made the use of daylight very difficult. Artificial illumination was necessary, for instance, in cleaning the vats in a brewery and in mining operations. Before the incandescent light, these firms used arc lights or gas or a non-system form of illumination, such as kerosene lamps. Many firms, of course, were unable to use any artificial illumination when only open-flame light sources were available. Selling isolated plants to firms that needed artificial light to carry out their productive process was mainly a problem of convincing them that their total production costs would be reduced.

Many of the first firms to adopt incandescent lighting required a light which would permit discernment of colors. Printing shops, like Hinds, Ketchum, textile mills, and furniture factories found that the incandescent light was superior to both the arc light and the gas light in this respect. It enabled workmen to distinguish colors in inks, fabrics, and woods. Other firms used a productive process that rendered any open-flame light very dangerous. Flour mills and chemical factories realized early that incandescent electric lighting was the only system of artificial illumination which did not employ a combustible material, consumed by a flame in the open air.

In many cases, the isolated-plant salesman could argue for an incandescent installation on the basis of cost alone. In contrast to arc lighting, incandescent lighting permitted placing a small light by each machine or workman. In contrast to gas lighting, a small light near the workman did not cause discomfort and inefficiency because of heat or fumes. Many factories reported substantial increases in output per worker after incandescent lighting had been installed. Another way in which incandescent lighting reduced production costs was to lower the fire-insurance rates. The rate for incandescent lighting was lower than the arc-light or gaslight rate. One mill owner reported that the difference in insurance premiums was sufficient to pay for the isolated plant in two years.[16] The initial cost of the plant and the operating costs had to be part of the calculation to determine whether total costs would be reduced. Operating an isolated-lighting plant was very inexpensive for any factory equipped with a steam boiler for general heating and power purposes. The extra steam needed to drive the dynamo was usually so small in comparison to the total amount of steam generated that fuel and water consumption were not noticeably affected. Maintenance costs were also low, because the men who tended the boiler and the steam engines could take care of the engine and dynamo of the isolated plant as well.

Some of the buyers of isolated plants were firms which supplied light as a part of the product sold to the consumer. These included hotels, apartment houses, stores, theaters, steamships, and office buildings. The sales arguments to these buyers were based largely on the quality advantages that the incandescent lamp possesses compared to other forms of artificial illumination. No matches were needed, the lights could be turned on from a remote place, the air was not vitiated or heated, the light was steady and even, and, in general, the light users enjoyed safety, comfort, and convenience. If the hotel, apartment house, theater, and so forth had its own steam boiler for heating purposes, the cost of running an incandescent-lighting plant was small. In many cases, incandescent lighting was secured at a cost below the amount paid for gas. The Boston Post Office Building, for example, was lighted by an Edison plant at an annual cost of $6,000 as against $12,000 for gas.[17]

The Edison isolated-plant installations through September 1885 are classified according to the analysis in Table 14. The threefold classification is only approximate and should be interpreted with care. The basis of the classification is not an installation-by-installation examination of why that installation was made but rather a deduction from the physical characteristics of the factory or other building where the lights were installed. It should be noted that the plants installed in sugar refineries and textile mills were, on the average, much larger than in other industrial establish-

TABLE 14

Edison Isolated-Plant Installations, May 1880–September 1885

Probable reason for installation	*Establishments*	*Number of isolated plants*	*Number of lamps*	*Average number of lamps per installation*
Increased worker productivity could be expected because of better light distribution, better color discernment, or better working conditions	Cotton, woolen, textile fabric mills	81	25,898	320
	Ironworks, car, and machine shops	40	7,828	196
	Newspapers and printing offices	30	6,521	217
	Furniture, piano, woodworking factories	15	2,360	157
	Other manufacturing	39	5,088	130
	TOTALS	205	47,695	232
Percentage of total Edison Isolated-Plant Installations		*42*	*38*	
Safety of the incandescent lamp compared to any open-flame lamp	Flour mills and grain elevators	26	1,934	74
	Oil refineries, chemical works, etc.	29	3,392	117
	Sugar refineries	11	4,864	443
	Pulp and paper mills	30	3,318	111
	TOTALS	96	13,508	141
Percentage of total Edison Isolated-Plant Installations		*19*	*11*	
Consumer comfort	Banks, office buildings, stores, residences	73	23,757	325
	Theaters, other places of amusement	20	14,033	702
	Hotels, apartment houses, club rooms	23	11,035	480
	Steamships, yachts	51	8,092	158
	Hospitals, educational institutions, etc.	26	7,173	276
	TOTALS	193	64,090	332
Percentage of total Edison Isolated-Plant Installations		*39*	*51*	
Total Edison Isolated-Plant Installations		494	125,293	254

Source: *EW*, VI (October 3, 1885), 143.

ments. In commercial establishments, the theater installations were by far the largest.

The competitors of the Edison Company for Isolated Lighting ranged from producers of nonelectric illuminants, such as gas and kerosene, to the arc-lighting-equipment producers and the other producers of incandescent isolated plants. The chief competitor in incandescent lighting was the United States Electric Lighting Company. The *American Electrical Directory* for 1885 listed a total of 449 isolated incandescent plants in the United States, of which 368 were Edison, 80 were United States Electric Lighting Company, and one was Brush-Swan.[18] These figures are probably incomplete in that there were undoubtedly installations by other manufacturers. But the fact that the United States company was Edison's only important competitor is substantiated by other evidence. The sales literature of the Edison company scarcely ever mentioned any competitor except the United States company. The *Bulletins* of the Edison Electric Light Company published during the years 1882–1884 and the *Bulletins for Agents* of the Edison Company for Isolated Lighting published during 1885 and 1886 contained numerous references to United States company installations which were unsatisfactory and had to be replaced by Edison plants. Detailed information was given on the exact faults in the United States system in order to provide the Edison sales agents with convincing talking points. On one occasion, after eighteen months of service, an Edison plant was replaced by a United States plant of larger capacity. The local Edison sales agent investigated and learned that the user, the Palmer House in Chicago, had decided to increase the capacity of its plant. The United States company had offered a larger dynamo at an exceedingly low price. The manager of the Palmer House wrote the Edison agent that the Edison plant had never given any trouble and that "the light was absolutely steady and satisfactory, and fully up to your representations in every respect." [19] One motive behind the United States company's action was to refute the Edison claim that none of their plants had ever been replaced by that of another manufacturer. Thereafter, the Edison company was forced to add to its claim the qualifying phrase "for reasons of unsatisfactory operation."

When the Isolated company was formed at the end of 1881, the Edison Machine Works was making only the 60-lamp dynamo for isolated lighting. Not more than eight isolated plants had been sold up to that time. Additional dynamo sizes and a satisfactory steam engine for driving the dynamos were needed. During 1882, the Isolated company arranged with the Edison Machine Works for the production of three additional dynamo sizes — the 15-lamp size, the 150-lamp size, and the 250-lamp size. A large number of steam engines were given careful consideration. Finally, the

Armington and Sims engine was selected as the one which operated an Edison dynamo most satisfactorily.

Attention was next focused on the marketing problem. The selling was done by local agents who were paid on a commission basis. The agent received anywhere from 11 per cent on small plants to nearly 20 per cent on large plants. The most significant aspect of the marketing policy is the liberal guarantees the Isolated company was willing to give. The lamps, which sold for $1.00 each, were guaranteed to last for 600 hours, on the average. The dynamo brushes, which cost $10 a set, were guaranteed for 200 hours of service, and the commutator, which cost $50 to renew, was guaranteed for 1500 hours.[20] Later, lamp efficiency and dynamo efficiency were also guaranteed. These guarantees made it possible to compute the maximum cost per lamp of operating an Edison isolated plant when the costs of steam power and labor were known. The guarantees were an effective competitive weapon because no other manufacturer could make comparable ones. At the same time, there was little if any risk on the part of the Edison company because the durability and efficiency of guaranteed components were safely above the minimum guarantees.

In pricing, the Isolated company adhered to what it called a one-price policy. Prices were not reduced to particular buyers to secure sales. The published prices were maintained at all times. The early annual reports of the Isolated company stated that the one-price policy was followed without exception. The 1886 report of the Edison Electric Light Company, however, commented on the severity of competition in isolated lighting and stated that many sales had been made at less than cost. Whether the list prices supposedly adhered to before 1886 were high or low compared with those of competitors cannot be accurately ascertained. In 1883, a 200-lamp installation of Fuller equipment cost about $3,000. In 1885, an Edison installation of that same capacity cost only $2,200. But a report from Des Moines, Iowa, in 1885 stated that the price of an Edison plant was much higher than that of a United States plant of the same size.[21] The price of the isolated incandescent-lighting plant, like the price of the arc-lighting plant as was discussed above, was not important by itself. What was important was the cost of producing light.

The operating and maintenance costs, as well as the initial cost, had to be taken into account. The Isolated company emphasized the fact that total costs should be considered when it made performance guarantees and supplied sales agents with data on operating costs. The total cost calculations made comparisons between different makes of isolated incandescent systems easier. Such calculations also could serve as a basis for comparisons with lighting methods other than incandescent — arc lighting, gas lighting, or kerosene lamps — where a component-by-component price comparison was not possible.

The marketing policies and problems of the Isolated company are summarized in the following list of sales "pointers," prepared by Paine and Stickney, Edison sales agents in New England, for the use of other Edison agents.[22]

1. The Edison company has installed over 145,000 lamps in the United States and thus has wide experience.

2. Prices are as low as may be consistent with thorough workmanship and proper construction.

TABLE 15

Growth in Edison Isolated Plants, 1881–1888

Date	*Number of isolated plants in operation*	*Number of lamps in use*	*Average number of lamps per installation*
November 1881	8	. . .	. . .
December 1, 1882	153	29,192	191
October 1, 1883	221	53,071	240
October 1884	368	74,432	202
October 1, 1885	520	132,875	255
October 1886	702	181,463	258
May 1, 1887	891	230,674	259
October 23, 1888	1291	343,654	266

Sources: Various documents and publications of the Edison Electric Light Company and its affiliates.

3. In numerous cases the Edison company has been called upon to replace plants of competitors bought at a lower price. In no case has the Edison system been replaced by another on account of unsatisfactory operation of the former.

4. The Edison company is ready to submit to tests to see if guarantees make good before plants are accepted.

5. Patents have been established as valid against Swan and others in Germany. Suits will be vigorously prosecuted in the United States.

6. Lamps are superior in life to any other make.

7. Lamps of 10, 16, 20, 24, 32, 50, 100 candle power are made.

8. If automatic regulation is desired, the Edison company uses an automatic regulator, outside of and entirely distinct from the dynamo. Regulates for changes in speed of motive power or changes in load, while the regulators of other companies regulate for changes in load only.

The growth in the number of Edison isolated plants in use is shown in Table 15. The data refer to the total number of plants in operation, not the new installations each year. The steady rise in the size of installation (as measured in lamps) from 1882 to 1888, with the exception of 1884, should be noted. A comparison of Table 15 with Table 16 will show that until 1887 the isolated plants in operation accounted for more lamps than the Edison central stations. It can also be seen that the central stations averaged about ten times the size of the isolated plants.

CENTRAL STATIONS

The Edison central-station companies were new firms organized for the purpose of supplying light to homes, offices, and wherever else it was desired. The Edison Electric Light Company promoted the central stations in the large gas-using cities. In smaller cities and villages, the central stations were organized under the direction of the Isolated company, which sold them the equipment they needed on a cash basis. The dividing line between gas and non-gas cities was set at the 10,000 population mark as of the 1880 census.

The central stations in the non-gas cities paid for their equipment and license in cash. The license gave them only the exclusive right to operate the patented Edison equipment for central-station purposes in the city in which they were located. In a city using gas, a central station received a license from the Edison company separate from the equipment. The central-station company paid for this license by issuing from 25 to 30 per cent of its capital stock in fully paid-up shares to the Edison company and paying, in addition, a cash sum equal to 5 per cent of its capitalization. The license was exclusive for a specified territory — usually a city or a county — and included the right to operate an Edison central station, to sell isolated plants, and to supply them with renewal lamps and repair parts. The local licensee company thus possessed the exclusive rights to operate a central station in its territory, to sell all Edison lighting equipment in its territory, and to sell Edison lamps. The local company agreed to prosecute diligently and to extend its business of central-station lighting, to use only Edison apparatus, and to keep suitable records and books of accounts to which the Edison company could have free access.

The first Edison central-station company, the Edison Electric Illuminating Company of New York, was formed by almost the same men who organized the Edison Electric Light Company. The Illuminating company was incorporated on December 17, 1880, with a capital stock of $1,000,000. The agreement between the Edison company and the Illuminating company, dated March 23, 1881, gave the latter exclusive use and sales rights of the Edison system in two New York City districts. The Illuminating company agreed to issue $250,000 of its stock to the Edison company as well as to make a cash payment of $100,000. The Edison company agreed to supply lamps to the Illuminating company at thirty-five cents each or at cost, whichever was higher. Two clauses of the agreement expressed opinions about the future. Clause four said that the Illuminating company was to receive exclusive license rights for the remainder of New York City only if it would occupy and equip each of four such districts with a central-station plant annually, beginning in September 1881. Clause eight stated that the central station to be erected in the first district was expected to cost $250,000.[23]

The contract between the Illuminating company and the Edison company cannot be considered as typical of the licensee contracts. The Illuminating company was separate from the Edison company only because no corporation, unless it were formed under the gas statutes, could use the streets. Nevertheless, the contract contained provisions which were common to all or nearly all of the central-station licensee contracts. All licensee stations were given an exclusive license, all paid for the license in stock and cash, all could buy lamps at much below the market price, and all agreed to permit the Edison company to examine their books and accounts.

The first permanent, commercial Edison central station, erected on Pearl Street in New York City by the Illuminating company, should be viewed as the final step in the development of the original Edison lighting system. It was a model station, designed to bring the Edison system out of the Menlo Park experimental stage into the commercial stage. When the timetable of New York central stations is compared to the expectations of the March 1881 agreement, it is clear that the model station presented more difficulties and problems than had been anticipated. The Pearl Street station was not put into operation until September 4, 1882. The first annual report of the Illuminating company, dated December 13, 1881, stated:

> Your Board has confidently expected that the installation of the Pearl Street district would have been completed by this annual meeting and the district lighted. But events entirely beyond their control has [*sic*] prevented it. Had the contracts made by the company for supplies been filled, the district would have been lighted by this time. But the impossibility of securing fulfillment of contracts on the part of manufacturers, have caused delay. . . Our principal delay arises at present from inability to get street mains.[24]

The expected cost of the Pearl Street station, like the expected date of completion, was incorrect. The station cost nearly $600,000 instead of the estimated $250,000. The increased cost was mainly due to unforeseen difficulties in installation and operation. The extra costs and delays in the construction of the Pearl Street station and the experience of operating it led the Illuminating company to adopt a policy of caution. The third annual report, dated December 11, 1883, stated: "Our policy has been to postpone the question of installing other central stations until the one now running shall have been in operation long enough to completely demonstrate the commercial possibilities of the business." [25]

The postponement policy is in sharp contrast to the four new stations annually which were originally contemplated. The Pearl Street station was the only Edison central station in New York until 1886, when a small 2000-light station was installed as an annex to the Pearl Street station. No uptown station was erected until 1888. The Twenty-Sixth Street station began operations in December of that year, and the Thirty-Ninth Street station began operations the following January. No downtown station operated outside the first district until 1891.

The construction delay and the higher cost should not be taken as evidence of failure or incompetence on Edison's part. The erection of a central station, complete with boilers, steam engines, dynamos, and underground conductors, was a very difficult undertaking. Edison directed both the manufacture of the equipment and its installation in the Pearl Street station. He literally worked night and day for over a year in endeavoring to bring the station to completion. Testing began in June 1882, and enough difficulties were ironed out by September so that regular operation could begin. The principal difficulty which appeared after the commencement of operations was a hunting or oscillation which occurred when two dynamos, each driven by its own steam engine, were connected in parallel to supply the main circuit. The steam engines came up to full speed and then the governor cut them to zero speed. They thus alternated between standstill and maximum speed. Only one dynamo was used until the trouble was corrected. Edison devised a complicated rod-lever arrangement which tied the governors of the various steam engines together. This overcame the difficulty, but eventually these engines, which had gravity-operated governors, were replaced by steam engines of another make, which had centrifugal governors. The vibration of the structure on which the engines were mounted was sufficient to upset the operation of the gravity governors.

The price of light was set at 1.2 cents per 16-candle-power hour and was equivalent to the price of gas in New York City, $2.25 per thousand cubic feet. By 1885, the gas rate had been reduced to $1.50 for large customers and $1.75 for small customers, but the Illuminating company left its rate unchanged until 1890, when it was reduced to 1 cent. The business of the company grew steadily from 59 customers and 1,284 lamps in October 1882 to 472 customers and 8,573 lamps in October 1883, and to 600 customers and 13,000 lamps in June 1885. By 1890, the Illuminating company was serving over 95,000 incandescent lamps. The demand for light exceeded the station capacity as early as April 1883. The company thereafter picked its customers very carefully, taking only those who were heavy users of light. The company showed losses in 1882 and 1883, but earned $33,000 in 1884. The following year saw the beginning of quarterly dividends, equal in amount to 1 per cent of the face value of the capital stock.

On the basis of the technical and commercial lessons learned in the installation and operation of the Pearl Street station, the Edison company promoted licensee central stations in most of the large cities of the United States, and the Isolated company promoted cash stations in the smaller

TABLE 16

Growth in Edison Central Stations, 1884–1888

Date	*Number of central stations*	*Number of lamps in use*	*Average number of lamps per station*
October 28, 1884	18	34,000	1,890
October 27, 1885	31	63,480	2,040
August 1, 1886	58	149,900	2,580
May 1, 1887	102	290,300	2,840
October 1887	121	328,080	2,710
October 23, 1888[a]	185	385,840	2,080
Cash stations	117	87,640	750
Stock stations	68	298,200	4,390

Sources: Various documents and publications of the Edison Electric Light Company and its affiliates.
[a] This is the only date for which figures for both types of stations are available.

cities. Table 16 illustrates the growth in Edison central stations. Only the 1888 data separate the licensee (stock) stations from the cash stations. The contrast in the size of the stock and cash stations should be noted. The Edison central stations which operated 10,000 lights or more on October 23, 1888, were all stock stations. These were: New York, 41,000 lamps; Chicago, 15,000; Boston, 14,000; Brooklyn, 10,000; and Detroit, New Orleans, Philadelphia, and St. Paul, each 10,000. These eight stations accounted for 120,000 lamps or about one-third of all central-station lamps in use.[26]

The common practice, especially among the large central stations, was for the station to provide lamps to the customer as part of the price of electric lighting. Because these large stations were licensee stations, they were the sole source of supply in their territory for Edison lamps. Their problem was whether to sell the lamps to the customers separately or to include them as part of one charge for current, meter reading, and lamps. The reason for choosing the latter was probably in most cases that given by the New York Edison Illuminating Company in 1893. It reported that its practice was to "give them [the customers] such supply of lamps . . . as they call for, rather than possibly to check the development of the business." [27]

It was also the larger stations which adopted the meter rather than the contract system. Of the twenty-nine stations, with a total lamp capacity of 145,567, which were using meters in February 1889, the eight largest stations accounted for nearly 85 per cent of the lamps. Most of the smaller stations used a monthly charge system until the 1890's. Since few were operating on a 24-hour basis, a contract system was workable and provided steady and certain revenues. At the same time, the extra investment and operating expense of the meter system was avoided.

The Edison company was interested in the Edison central stations as its principal customers whom it hoped would prosper and, in the case of the licensee stations, as investments which it wanted to be profitable. If the central stations were successful, promotion of additional central stations would proceed faster, widening the market for Edison equipment. To improve the management of the central stations and to bring them into closer contact with the Edison manufacturing companies, the Association of Edison Illuminating Companies was formed in April 1885.[28] The actual formation was carried out by four small licensee central stations, but the presence of officials of the Edison Electric Light Company, the Edison United Manufacturing Company, and the Edison Lamp Works at the organizational meeting indicates that the Edison officials probably were responsible for the formation of the association. The purpose of the association was declared to be the improvement of station management through exchange of views and through advice offered by the men from the Edison manufacturing companies.

At first, meetings were held twice each year. At these early meetings, a wide range of problems in the operation of central stations was discussed. At the second meeting, for example, the following subjects were debated: methods of street lighting by incandescent lamps, the meter system vs. the flat-rate system, engines and boilers, and high-speed vs. low-speed engines. A representative of the Edison Lamp Works explained how to reduce lamp breakage.[29]

While the association benefited both the central stations and the Edison company in improving station operation, it also served as a vehicle through which the central stations could criticize products and policies of the parent Edison company and the manufacturing companies. At the June 1886 meeting, the Lamp Works was asked to produce lamps which did not blacken, to make the globes of the lamps uniform in size, and to make a 250-candle-power, 210-volt lamp for use in competing against arc lamps.[30] At the August 1888 meeting, several delegates brought up the question of a fire in the Edison Lamp Works, which they claimed would force a shutdown of all central stations within sixty days. They requested the Lamp Works to maintain an inventory of 50,000 lamps. The manager of the Lamp Works, Francis Upton, replied at length, stating that the risk of fire was very small because of a sprinkler system with 60 pounds pressure. He revealed that most of the important lamp-making tools were stored in a fireproof safe.[31] At the meeting a year later, a resolution was passed to call the attention of the Edison company to the need for (1) an efficient, inexpensive arc-lighting system, (2) an arc lamp which could be operated on the three-wire system, and (3) an economical method to enlarge the territory served by one station (a method which used less copper than the three-wire system).[32]

The licensee relationship with the stock central-station companies was originally established when the parent Edison company was itself doing no manufacturing or selling. The granting to the licensee of the exclusive right to sell Edison lamps and equipment in its territory enabled the parent company to avoid organizing a sales department. When the manufacturing and selling of Edison apparatus were brought under one corporation in 1889, the licensee stood in the way of a rationalized and integrated manufacturing-marketing operation. The practice of giving exclusive sales rights to new licensee stations was consequently terminated about 1890. Moreover, a central-station license-agreement form which was used after 1892 contained a clause which specifically reserved to the licensor (the General Electric Company) the right to sell isolated plants and lighting apparatus for railway companies in the central-station territory.[33]

MARKET CONDITIONS AND MARKETING POLICIES

If a business firm is to formulate marketing policies which will maximize its profits, complete data on market conditions must be available. The sales executives should know the products and prices of their chief competitors, the customer reactions to price and product differences, the marketing areas where new customers can be secured, and the probable market for new products. The information on all these factors must be kept up to date if marketing policies are to reflect changing conditions.

In the first years of the Edison company, the sales organization was small, competitors in incandescent lighting were few and unimportant, and the sales managers of the Edison company could formulate marketing policies on the basis of personal experience in the market. But as the Edison company grew and as important competitors, such as Thomson-Houston and Westinghouse, appeared, formal methods were devised to channel data on market conditions from the salesmen in the field to the officials responsible for marketing policies. The formation of Edison General Electric in 1889 was accompanied by an integration of the marketing activities of all the Edison manufacturing companies. A single sales organization was established, and most of the salesmen were placed on salary instead of commission. The formation of General Electric in 1892 resulted in the merging of the Thomson-Houston and Edison sales organizations.[34] The size of sales organization that resulted, the wide area over which the salesmen were scattered, and the strong competition in incandescent lighting meant that it was essential to set up procedures to place market data before the two General Electric officials in charge of the sales of incandescent-lighting equipment — Eugene Griffin, first vice-president in charge of sales, and S. D. Greene, manager of the lighting department.

District sales offices and sales agents were required to make reports to Schenectady in all cases where business was lost to competitors. The agreement between General Electric and the Grand Rapids Electric Company, dated December 5, 1892, which appointed the latter as General Electric sales representative in twenty-four Michigan counties, contained the following paragraph: "In cases where you lose business to competitors, you are to send us full information in regard to prices made by you, and so far as can be ascertained, the prices obtained by our competitors. This and other information that may be of mutual interest and benefit to be furnished us on our regular printed forms designed for the purpose." [35]

The same kind of report was required from the members of General Electric's own selling organization. An example of such a report is a letter from the manager of the Eastern Sales District to Griffin. The letter concerned a lighting-plant installation at the Buffalo Insane Hospital. The contract had gone to the Western Electric Company, which had bid $14,184. General Electric had bid $19,060. There were six other bidders, all of whom had bid higher than General Electric. The letter concluded with the comment that "General Electric could have met that [Western Electric] bid [only] by giving away the dynamos." [36]

In addition to these routine reports on lost business, the sales managers were requested to make special reports from time to time. On May 11, 1895, S. D. Greene sent a circular letter to the local sales managers, asking for answers to the following questions:

1. In what respects, if any, are our present lines of lighting apparatus incomplete?

2. What complaints, if any, have you had during the past year regarding the operation of our lighting apparatus?

3. Have you any complaints to make about our present prices of lighting apparatus?

4. Have you any suggestions of how we can better meet existing competition on lighting apparatus and secure a larger percentage of the business than we have during the past year in (a) isolated lighting, (b) central-station lighting, (c) municipal plants?

5. Have you been able to secure letters of recommendation?

6. Have you had any suggestions or complaints from your licensee customers?

7. Have you any suggestions on the incandescent-lamp business — as to quality, price, or shipment of lamps?

8. What are the alleged advantages of opposition apparatus over ours?

9. From what manufacturers of lighting apparatus and incandescent lamps do we experience the greatest competition?

10. How can we increase our sales? [37]

To supplement the replies to the above questions and to disseminate the information among the local office managers, a meeting was held in Schenectady in June 1895. A full account of the reports sent in by the various sales offices was presented to the group. Discussion was held and additional information was supplied by many of the sales managers. Prices, products, competitors, and customer relations were the principal topics under consideration.

By 1900, the information that General Electric was obtaining from its salesmen on market conditions included estimates on prospective business as well as data on past business. Vice-president Griffin sent a circular letter to local sales managers in May 1900, asking for early, complete, and systematic reports of all prospective business. He suggested that such information as preferences of the prospective customer, equipment the customer uses, and competition expected would be of great value to the head sales office.[38] These reports were specific elaboration of the kind of *ex ante* data that had been requested before. In 1893, for example, President Coffin asked the district sales managers to supply him with a list of cities in their territory of population 2,500 and over that would be suitable for electric lighting.[39]

The market data furnished by the local and district sales managers were used in the formulation of marketing policies. The depressed business conditions of 1893, 1894, and 1895 were reflected in the severity of the competition experienced in the market for incandescent lamps and lighting equipment. Decided changes in many marketing policies were required, and current market data were urgently needed. The most important problem was to lower prices sufficiently to keep a good volume of business. The Sales Committee, made up of the first vice-president and the four department managers (lighting, railway, power, supply), held a meeting on August 28, 1893, to discuss the problem of selling prices. It was decided that the company was "losing business because of too high prices on stationary motors and light apparatus for isolated plants." [40] Each department manager was to secure from the district managers a list of apparatus considered to be priced too high, with suggestions regarding price.

The general price policy adopted was enunciated in December 1893 in a letter that Griffin sent to all department, district, and local managers. General Electric was very short of liquid funds and could not accept anything but cash business. Prices would be lowered as necessary to secure "all business in sight." Griffin went on to say: "We must not wait until our competitors have obtained a good standing, but must reduce our prices in time to prevent our competitors from securing the business." [41]

The general procedure was to set prices on the basis of information supplied by the local sales managers, and, if sales were still lost, prices were revised downward. The local office managers were not given the power to vary prices, nor were prices changed to secure particular orders. By 1895, however, the local office managers were instructed to contact the Schenectady office on large bids where competition was expected to be sharp. The third vice-president, in charge of manufacturing, was to check over cost figures of the equipment involved to see if he could cut prices.[42] Such a pricing procedure is very close to, if not identical with, the marginal cost pricing pictured in economic theory.

The low-price policy of General Electric did not place its prices below its competitors on most products. A frequent remark at the June 1895 meeting of the lighting-equipment salesmen was that the only advantage of many competitors was in price. In view of their better quality, General Electric products could be priced higher than those of competitors, and General Electric could still secure the bulk of the business. The Eastern Sales District manager reported in 1895 that in his district General Electric got 60 per cent of the business, Siemens and Halske got 15 per cent, Westinghouse got 15 per cent, and the rest went to Western Electric and the smaller companies.[43]

The existence of both high-price, good-quality products and low-price, poor-quality products in the incandescent-lighting-equipment market resulted from the fact that there were two general classes of customers. The large customers — the large central station or the large firm buying an isolated plant — were aware of the fact that what was important was the cost of producing light, not the cost of the equipment alone. They paid attention to life and efficiency guarantees, maintenance costs, voltage regulation, and the other technical features that determine the cost of light. General Electric, Westinghouse, Siemens and Halske, and several other firms produced for this segment of the market. Quality was not sacrificed for price. In contrast to the large buyers, the small customers purchased almost exclusively on the basis of first cost. They had neither the accounting methods nor the engineering staff which could guide them in the direction of considering the total cost of producing light. These small customers were usually supplied a low-quality, low-price product manufactured by a small firm selling only in a regional market. General Electric and the other large manufacturers did not usually attempt to secure the small-customer business.

General Electric's chief competitors for the large-customer business were Westinghouse, Siemens and Halske, and Stanley.[44] Competition took place in price, terms of payment, product, and guarantees. The sales manager of the Eastern District reported on competition in his district in 1894. His comments reveal the kind of competition General Electric was meeting. On direct-connected d.c. generators, the principal competitor was Siemens and Halske, whose apparatus was 15 per cent lower in price and "well built, highly finished, and in every way satisfactory." On transformers, the principal competitor was Stanley. General Electric prices were about 10 per cent higher, but the price differential was unimportant. What made Stanley a serious competitor was that "they make better guarantees as to regulation and against damage." On other alternating-current apparatus, Westinghouse was the chief competitor. "In addition to price being low their claim for superior armature construction [is] very effective."[45]

In most items of electrical equipment, General Electric's price was slightly higher than its major competitors and much higher than its small competitors. The case of direct-current incandescent-lighting equipment may be taken as typical. Here the General Electric price was 15 per cent above Siemens and Halske and 30 per cent above a small maker, Waddell-Entz. In alternating-current apparatus, the price pattern was similar. But in some products, General Electric was as low in price as any of the small firms. The Edison bi-polar dynamo is an example. In some other products, every competitor was 30 per cent below General Electric's price. In arc-lighting equipment, for instance, the Westinghouse prices were as low as the small firms.

General Electric's high-price, high-quality policy is explained only in part by the existence of large, economically rational buyers. The licensee stations, it will be recalled, were required to buy their lamps, supplies, and equipment from General Electric. The presence of these buyers, insulated from other sellers, enabled General Electric to ignore the price cuts of competitors. The fact that General Electric owned substantial blocks of stock in these licensee companies was in itself an incentive to manufacture lighting equipment which could produce light at the lowest possible cost. If that meant a high-quality, high-price line of products, General

Electric would be serving the best interests of its customers by its price and product policies.

While the licensee companies provided an insulated market for lighting equipment, the same contract in which they agreed to use only General Electric equipment appointed them as exclusive sales agents for their territory. General Electric had to be careful not to sell lamps or any other products directly to customers in these licensee territories. The General Electric salesmen were instructed in the names and territories of licensee companies in order that there would be no encroachment of licensee rights. The licensee companies thus prevented a thoroughly integrated sales organization and were continually presenting administrative problems. The Westinghouse company often stressed the awkward position of General Electric because of its licensee companies. These companies influenced the 1896 patent agreement between General Electric and Westinghouse, for example, by means of their license rights. Lamp patents had to be completely omitted from the agreement because the licensee companies wanted to keep their local monopolies of Edison lamps.

IX

The Westinghouse Electric Company

THE WESTINGHOUSE SYSTEM OF INCANDESCENT-ELECTRIC LIGHTING

George Westinghouse received no formal education after the age of fourteen except during the three months he attended Union College, Schenectady, New York. His father operated a machine shop in Schenectady, where George worked for a number of years before and after his Civil War service. At the age of 21, in 1867, he invented a device for returning derailed railroad cars to the track and an improved form of railroad frog. With two partners, who each contributed $5,000, he organized a firm to market these inventions. He contracted with steel mills at Troy, New York, and Pompton, New Jersey, to manufacture them, while he acted as the company's salesman and called on railroads throughout the East and Middle West. In 1868, Westinghouse dissolved his Schenectady firm and shifted operations to Pittsburgh. The principal reason for this move was that in Pittsburgh he was able to have his car replacer manufactured more cheaply than before. Westinghouse's contact with the railroads had brought to his attention the need for an automatic power brake for railroad trains. He began work on this problem sometime in 1868, and in the early part of 1869, he invented the air brake. With the financial help of Ralph Baggley, a Pittsburgh foundry manager, Westinghouse constructed a complete air-brake unit and equipped a train for a trial run, which was held in April 1869. The test was a success. In September, the Westinghouse Air Brake Company was organized. Westinghouse became president; Baggley and five others, nearly all railroad men, made up the board of directors. The capitalization of the company was $500,000. Manufacturing operations were started in the factory which Baggley's foundry firm had occupied.

Westinghouse spent much time in England during the decade 1870–1880, selling his air brake to the English railroads and establishing manufacturing plants for the European market. He became interested in English signaling and switching devices, which were considerably in advance of those in use on American railroads, and finally decided to enter the switch and signal business. In 1881, he bought control of two companies, one a Pennsylvania company and the other a Massachusetts company, which he combined to form the Union Switch and Signal Company. The company headquarters and manufacturing plant were established at Pittsburgh. Within a few years, Westinghouse invented a number of automatic switching and signaling devices for his new firm. In these inventions, he combined a force familiar to him, compressed air, with a force new to him, electricity.

The experiences of Westinghouse up to 1881 were good preparation for his entrance into electrical manufacturing. His work in the air brake gave him inventive, manufacturing, and marketing experience. Beyond that, the air brake became the basis of future financial support, both directly from profits and indirectly from the reputation Westinghouse had achieved. The Union Switch and Signal Company, with its engineering staff, manufacturing facilities, and electrical devices, was to be the organization which Westinghouse could use to begin electrical manufacturing.

One other of his many activities played an important part in his preparation for electrical manufacturing. That activity was his work in nattural gas. It was well known that natural gas was plentiful in the Pittsburgh area, but because the gas was under enormous pressure and had no odor, it was difficult and dangerous to handle. Almost no attempt had been made to commercialize it. Westinghouse studied the gas problem and thought he could devise ways to handle it safely and economically. In 1883, he drilled a well on the grounds of his Pittsburgh estate and discovered a large amount of gas under very high pressure. After he had the gas under control, he formed the Philadelphia Company, which distributed gas to factories and residences in the Pittsburgh area for many years.

Westinghouse made many technical contributions to the art of handling gas. Among the most important was his system of conveying gas over relatively long distances. The high pressure at the well could force large quantities of gas through small and inexpensive pipes for distances up to four and five miles. But such a high pressure could not be utilized by the gas consumer. To reduce the pressure to the level which was safe for ordinary use, Westinghouse widened the pipes near the place of gas consumption. The concept of a gas-distribution system which uses high pressure for transmission and has a device to convert this high pressure into usable low pressure for consumption is analogous to the concept of an electrical distribution system which uses high voltage for transmission and has a device to convert this high voltage into usable low voltage for consumption. The pressure-reducing device in the gas system was the large-diameter pipe. The pressure-reducing device in the electrical system was to be the transformer. The success of Westinghouse in developing a high-pressure system of gas distribution gave him confidence in his ability to achieve similar success in developing the alternating-current system of electrical distribution.

When Westinghouse first contemplated entering the electrical industry, he decided to investigate incandescent lighting. He assigned several of the electrical engineers of the Union Switch and Signal Company to the problem and carried on studies of his own. His brother, H. H. Westinghouse, was at that time manufacturing a high-speed steam engine he had invented. The engine was suitable for driving dynamos, and in the course of his business activities, H. H. Westinghouse came into contact with an electrical engineer, William Stanley. Stanley had invented a self-regulating d.c. dynamo and an incandescent lamp with a carbonized-silk filament. In 1884, H. H. Westinghouse introduced Stanley to George Westinghouse, who placed Stanley on the Union Switch and Signal Company staff with the intention of developing a complete incandescent-electric-lighting system based on Stanley's lamp and dynamo patents. These patents had been assigned to the Swan Incandescent Electric Light Company. Westinghouse purchased them for $50,000. Stanley agreed to assign all future inventions to Westinghouse on the condition that Westinghouse make and sell them. Stanley was to receive one-tenth of the profits and a salary of $5,000 per year.[1] Production of the lighting system was begun in 1884 by the Union Switch company. The Stanley lamps were exhibited at the Philadelphia Electric Exhibition in the fall of 1884.[2] A number of lighting plants were installed in 1885 and 1886.[3]

Westinghouse's interest in electric lighting prior to 1885 was not very strong, nor were his ideas unusual. He simply entered a field which he thought might be profitable. In the spring of 1885, however, his attention was drawn to a new method of transmitting electricity — with which he was to revolutionize the electrical industry. He read an article in an English engineering periodical which described an alternating-current system on display at the Inventions Exhibition in London. Gaulard and Gibbs transformers were used to change the voltage from a high transmission value to the low value necessary to operate incandescent lamps. The article described these "secondary generators" in great detail. It was stated that the induction coils had no moving parts, were 90 per cent efficient, and could be used to produce any desired voltage.[4] Westinghouse began to see that alternating current, which could use the transformer, might provide an economical distribution system for electrical energy. One of his employees, Guido Pantaleoni, happened to be in Italy at this time because of the death of his father. Westinghouse cabled Pantaleoni to secure options on the Gaulard and Gibbs patents and to make a thorough investigation of the Gaulard and Gibbs a.c. system. Pantaleoni met Gaulard at Turin and saw a Gaulard-Gibbs installation which transmitted electrical energy from a waterfall ten miles away to light a theater. Because Pantaleoni did not feel fully competent to appraise the Gaulard and Gibbs system, he asked the German electrical manufacturing firm, Siemens and Halske, for advice. Pantaleoni later reported the advice he obtained. "Werner von Siemens, whom I had known, assured me that there was nothing whatsoever in alternating current, that it was pure humbug and his five-wire system had rendered alternating currents useless." [5]

Pantaleoni, however, also secured advice from a Budapest firm, Ganz and Company, who were the European pioneers in alternating current. The Ganz engineers tried to impress him with the possibilities in alternating current. The result was that Pantaleoni strongly recommended to Westinghouse that work in alternating current be taken up.

In the summer of 1885, Westinghouse ordered several Gaulard and Gibbs transformers and a Siemens alternator from London.[6] While awaiting the arrival of this equipment, he assigned Stanley and several other engineers to begin work on alternating-current problems. The decision of Westinghouse to shift to alternating current was not in accord with the advice he received from his engineers and patent lawyers. Pantaleoni gave sole credit to Westinghouse for making the decision. "I investigated and reported on the Gaulard and Gibbs alternating current system . . . but the opposition by ALL the electric part of the Westinghouse organization was such that it was only Mr. George Westinghouse's personal will that put it through." [7] "Generally the opposition was far greater than I had thought possible; George Westinghouse himself was the only man who was determined to go to the bottom of things." [8]

Pantaleoni is probably correct in regard to the taking up of the Gaulard and Gibbs system. There may have been universal opposition in the Westinghouse organization to this step. But on the broader question of alternating current Westinghouse did not stand alone. Stanley was an early and enthusiastic advocate of alternating current, and he urged Westinghouse to finance development work on it. Stanley's opposition to the Gaulard and Gibbs system was apparently based on the correct belief that their technique of connecting the transformers was not workable. Another influential member of the Westinghouse organization and a noted electrical engineer and patent lawyer, Franklin L. Pope, advised against alternating current at first on the grounds that high voltages would be dangerous to life and property.[9] Ironically enough, ten years later, in 1895, Pope was killed by the high voltage of Stanley's first installation at Great Barrington, Massachusetts.[10]

The opposition to alternating current among the electrical staff of the Union Switch company was not surprising in view of the reception that most engineers had given the Gaulard and Gibbs system when it first was introduced in 1883. A British engineer, Rankin Kennedy, experimented with the Gaulard and Gibbs transformers that year and reported the results in a letter to one of the English technical journals. He found that the transformers worked much better when connected in parallel rather than in series. But he did not realize that the significance of the transformer was that it could be used to obtain economical transmission voltages. His letter shows that he contemplated no use for the secondary generators of Gaulard and Gibbs other than to adjust light intensity. If the core of one of these coils were varied in position, the lights could be dimmed as desired.[11] The same issue of the journal which carried Rankin's letter contained an editorial which expressed the general opinion of electrical engineers toward alternating current. The editorial remarked that a number of scientists had worked on alternating current and then said: "We cannot believe that men like Paul Jablockhoff, Professors Houston and Thomson, and Sir Charles Bright — men who are electricians and not visionary enthusiasts — would have allowed this subject to dwindle away to mere nothingness had there been a chance of bringing the matter to a successful issue." [12]

Gaulard and Gibbs made a contribution to the development of the electrical industry by calling attention to alternating current, but they had not grasped its real significance. In their system, shown in Diagram 2, the transformers were wound in a one-to-one ratio and were all connected in series. The high voltage in their system, and the copper saving which resulted, was due to the series connections employed, like an arc-lighting circuit, and not to the transformation of voltages by means of the transformers. The transformer or secondary generator was merely a device to insulate the high-voltage transmission circuit from the consumption circuit and to permit parallel connection and therefore individual

Diagram 2
THE TRANSFORMER NETWORK

THE GAULARD AND GIBBS SYSTEM

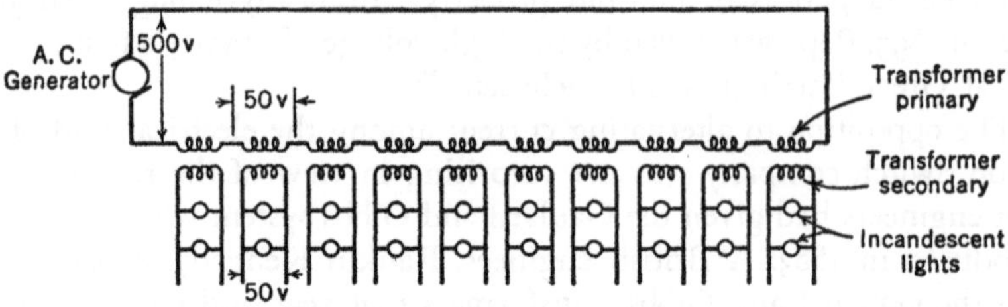

Transformer primaries connected in series; 50 volts across each. No voltage transformation in transformers; 50 volts across each secondary.

THE WESTINGHOUSE SYSTEM

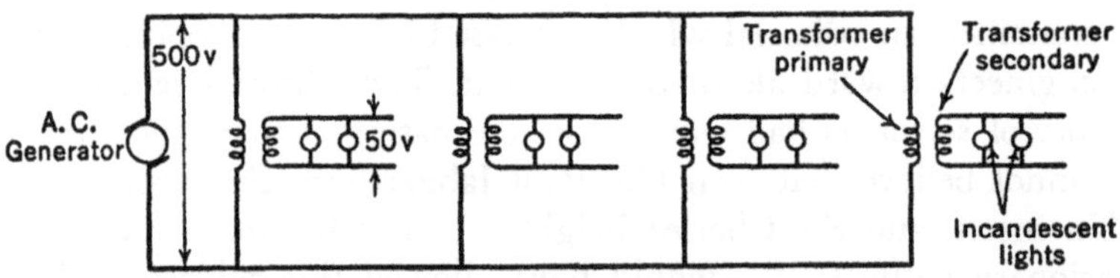

Transformer primaries connected in parallel; 500 volts across each. Voltage transformation of 10:1 in transformer; 50 volts across each secondary.

control of the lights in the various consumption or secondary circuits. Diagram 2 also shows the Westinghouse system, which used the transformers in parallel. Here it was understood that the key function of the transformer is to change voltage values between transmission and consumption circuits. That this function was not generally understood in 1885 is indicated by an *Electrical World* editorial of that year. In comparing the series and parallel systems of connecting transformers, the editorial concluded that the parallel system used more copper and was therefore less efficient.[13] By 1885, Ganz and Company had produced an a.c. system using transformers in parallel and for the purpose of voltage transformation. This was the modern a.c. system, but the importance of it was not well understood in Europe and was unknown in the United States. It remained for Westinghouse, like Edison, to perceive the economic significance of a technical concept and to have enough faith and conviction to try to translate that concept into reality. The fact that most well-known electrical engineers discounted alternating current did not deter Westinghouse. He was positive that it could provide an economical distribution system, and he was willing to spend the money necessary to develop an efficient, practical transformer and an efficient a.c. generator.

The transformers and alternator from London arrived in Pittsburgh in November 1885.[14] An English electrician, Reginald Belfield, who had been in charge of the Gaulard and Gibbs installation at the London Inventions Exhibition, accompanied the equipment to the United States and entered the employ of Westinghouse. Stanley, Belfield, and several other engineers of the Union Switch company staff worked very intensively to develop a commercial transformer. In this effort, Westinghouse himself played a leading role. The objective was an efficient and reliable transformer which would be capable of economical production on a commercial scale. The Gaulard and Gibbs transformer with its copper discs and iron-wire core was found to be unsuitable for commercial work. In a period of a few weeks, Westinghouse and his engineers developed the modern transformer. The core was built up from iron plates, not from iron wire, and the coils were constructed from copper wire, not from copper plates. The coils could be machine wound and the plates machine stamped.

After a practical transformer had been developed, the next step was to design a network to connect the generator and the transformer. It will be recalled that Gaulard and Gibbs employed the series system in order to be able to use high voltages in transmission. They did not view the transformer as a voltage-changing device. When it became understood that the transformer was a very efficient and convenient voltage-changing device, there still remained the question of whether a series or parallel circuit should be used. As shown in Diagram 2, Westinghouse connected the transformers in parallel. This choice was made because the series connection had two serious faults. If one transformer primary were to fail, the circuit would be opened, putting all the transformers out of service. Even more important, there was no way for the secondary circuits to draw more energy from the primary circuit when needed. If the number of lights on one secondary circuit were to be increased, all would dim slightly. Rankin Kennedy noticed the good self-regulation of the transformer secondaries under a parallel system, but did not realize its significance. In 1885, Stanley perceived the advantages of parallel-transformer operation. Belfield had the same idea after his experiences with the Gaulard and Gibbs system in London. In Budapest, Ganz and Company were manufacturing the parallel system. Thus it is not possible to attribute the idea of parallel transformers to any one man. What is significant, however, is that the Westinghouse system employed the parallel-connection method.

The initial development work was so promising that the electrical department of the Union Switch and Signal Company was incorporated as a separate company. The Westinghouse Electric Company was formed on January 8, 1886, with a capital stock of $1,000,000. Westinghouse was elected president. Of the 20,000 shares of stock, Westinghouse originally held 18,000, which he received for various inventions made by Stanley and himself which he turned over to the new company. Two thousand shares were sold to seven of his business associates for $100,000 in cash. To provide more cash for the company, Westinghouse later turned back some of his shares, which were then sold. By September 1886, Westinghouse held only 9,605 shares.[15]

At about the same time that the electric company was being formed, Westinghouse reached a new agreement with Stanley, who had been forced to leave Pittsburgh in the fall of 1885 because of his health. He had gone to Great Barrington, Massachusetts, where he had established a laboratory and carried on work in transformer development. Westinghouse agreed to give Stanley one-tenth of the stock in the new company to be formed. In return, Stanley was to maintain the Great Barrington laboratory and to assign all his inventions to the company. Besides the stock, Stanley was to receive $600 per month for laboratory expenses and an annual salary of $4,000.[16]

One of the first acts of the new company was to send Pope and Pantaleoni to Europe to buy the American rights to the Gaulard and Gibbs patents, on which Westinghouse had held an option since the previous summer. The two agents paid $50,000. The reason the Gaulard and Gibbs rights were purchased was not to enable Westinghouse to make and sell their transformer. A much better transformer had already been designed. Westinghouse thought the Gaulard and Gibbs patents would protect him in his exploitation of alternating current in the United States. He had a similar objective in mind in 1887 when he purchased the incandescent-lighting patents of Phillip Diehl, an American inventor who used induction coils to operate incandescent lamps. No lead-in wires were necessary because one induction coil was placed inside the glass globe. It is probable that Westinghouse never planned to produce the Diehl system, but wanted the patents because they covered general a.c. principles. After the Gaulard and Gibbs patents proved to be of almost no value because they applied only to the use of transformers in series, Westinghouse tried to purchase a patent covering the use of transformers in parallel. In 1889, he bought the parallel-transformer patent of Rankin Kennedy, but this patent also proved to be of little worth.

At Great Barrington, Stanley worked on transformer development and then began the installation of an a.c. lighting system. He leased an old rubber mill near the village and installed there the Siemens alternator and a steam engine to drive it. The alternator generated 500 volts; the power was led on copper conductors into the center of the village, a distance of about a mile. Six transformers were placed in the cellars of buildings to be lighted. In March 1886, Stanley got the system into operation. On the 17th, he wrote Westinghouse:

> I am pleased to be able to inform you that the secondary system is being rapidly completed. As I mentioned sometime ago, I believe the true way to study it is to give it a commercial test here in town. I have, therefore, run wires from the laboratory to the village and have placed a converter in my cousin's store in order to test the commercial possibilities. The lamps in the store were running last night. . . All the converters are under lock and key so that no one knows anything about them. . . I might say a great deal about the system, but briefly, it is all right.[17]

On March 20, Stanley held the first public demonstration of the system, and on April 6, a party from Pittsburgh, including Pantaleoni, Pope, and the two Westinghouse brothers, visited Great Barrington and inspected the installation.[18] Westinghouse was pleased with what he saw and became completely convinced that alternating current was satisfactory for the transmission of electric energy. The success of parallel-transformer connection and voltage transformation had been demonstrated.

A more complete test of the a.c. system was made at Pittsburgh in the summer of 1886. The Siemens alternator had shown very poor voltage regulation, that is, the generated voltage had decreased markedly as the number of lights was increased. Stanley designed an alternator with good regulation, and this generator was installed in the plant of the Union Switch company. A line was run to East Liberty, three miles away, and transformers were installed at both ends of the line.[19] Careful measurements were made of the efficiency of the distribution system. The results of testing this installation were so favorable that Westinghouse decided to place the a.c. system on the market.

The first commercial system was manufactured in the fall of 1886. It was tested for two weeks by lighting 400 lamps in Laurenceville, four miles from Pittsburgh. The energy was transmitted at 1000 volts. After testing, the alternator and transformers were shipped to Buffalo, New York, where a local lighting company put them into service. The Buffalo installation was very successful, and, within a few months, orders for twenty-five a.c. plants had been secured. To take care of these orders and future ones, more manufacturing space was needed. Early in December, the Union Switch and Signal Company moved to Swissvale. Their Pittsburgh plant was purchased by the Westinghouse Electric Company and converted to the manufacture of electric apparatus.

The alternating-current incandescent-lighting system that went into commercial use at the end of 1886 was based on the transformer, the alternator, and the parallel connection of transformers — all of which had been developed by the Westinghouse company. The lamp in the Westinghouse system was the Stanley lamp, which Westinghouse had been manufacturing as a component of his d.c. lighting system for several years. The transmission voltage was set at 1000 volts and the consumption voltage at 50 volts, a ratio of twenty to one. The lamp voltage was thus less than half that chosen by Edison. This was possible because the a.c. system permitted widely different voltages for transmission and consumption. More satisfactory values could be chosen for each. In contrast, the transmission voltage in the Edison system could not be much different from the consumption voltage. Through use of the feeder-main and three-wire principles, Edison tried to achieve a transmission voltage that was higher than the consumption voltage, but the ratio was less than three to one.[20] The voltage selected for the lamps thus severely limited the maximum transmission voltage which was feasible, and the lamp voltage itself had to be a compromise between a transmission voltage and a consumption voltage.

The major fault of the a.c. system as first marketed by Westinghouse was that it had no meter. The Edison meter operated on the principle of electrolysis, which is solely a d.c. phenomenon. Some other meters were in use, but none would operate on alternating current. Westinghouse knew that his system needed a meter if it were to be used in large central-station work. He assigned several engineers to work on the problem of inventing an a.c. meter in 1887. Their efforts were not successful. In the spring of 1888, O. B. Shallenberger, the chief engineer of the company, was conducting experiments on a.c. arc lamps. He accidentally dropped a small spring on a magnet coil which was connected to an a.c. voltage. When he noticed that the spring was slowly revolving, he realized that he had discovered a principle which could serve as the basis for an a.c. meter.[21] Within a month, he had constructed a workable meter. By August, the Westinghouse company had the Shallenberger meter in commercial production.[22] The principle of this meter — that a conductor in a moving magnetic field will revolve — underlay the a.c. motor which was marketed a few years later. Like the Edison meter, the Shallenberger meter measured current and not electric energy. In a constant-voltage circuit with a noninductive (lighting) load, the energy consumed is proportional to the current. No appreciable error results from measuring the current alone.

The main reason for the introduction of the a.c. system was the economy in the transmission of electric energy that it achieved. The Westinghouse a.c. system came into use first in those places where this advantage was the most important. Consequently, it was confined to central stations. In isolated plants, the distance from the dynamo to the lamps was in most cases not more than a few hundred feet. The newly developed Westinghouse system could hardly expect to compete with the well-established d.c. systems where the transmission distance was so small. In the central-station field, the Westinghouse system had the greatest advantage over the d.c. system in areas not densely populated — the outlying districts of large cities or the smaller cities and towns. The first Westinghouse installations were, therefore, relatively small installations. Where population was dense, as in the central areas of large cities, the heavier copper investment of the d.c. system was economical because the copper investment per light was small. Small advantages in operating efficiencies that the d.c. systems possessed because of the many years of experience in their manufacture and operation were enough in such cases to throw the balance in favor of direct current. The main advantage of the a.c. system lay in the economical transmission of electric energy to customers far apart and far from the central station. The copper costs of the d.c. system in areas of low population density were so high that the customers would not have been willing to pay a price for light high enough to cover all costs.

In addition to the transmission advantages, alternating current possessed several minor advantages over direct current. The a.c. system could use 50-volt circuits. The advantages of a lower voltage than the usual d.c. system employed were greater safety and lamps of greater efficiency and durability. Moreover, the shorter lamp filament emitted a more even pattern of light.

The Westinghouse lighting system was first marketed on a cash basis. Although the Westinghouse salesmen often promoted central-station companies, no stocks or bonds were taken in return for the equipment or the patent license to use the equipment. An 1888 license defined the territory of the equipment user and provided that no repair or duplicate parts should be sold by the licensee to other manufacturers of electrical apparatus. The contract contained no other restrictive provisions.[23] In later years, the marketing methods changed considerably. By 1895, it was the practice of the Westinghouse company to enter a city, secure a franchise, establish a central station, and place it in profitable operating condition. The station would then be sold to local capitalists.[24] This same method had been used by Goff in arc lighting and by Edison in the first three-wire central stations a decade earlier. Further evidence that Westinghouse had abandoned its straight cash-sale basis is provided by the arrangement made with the United Electric Light and Power Company of New York in 1895. The Westinghouse company sold to the United company ten 1000-horsepower electric generators and received in payment $1,875,100 in stock and bonds. That same year, $170,000 worth of equipment was sold to the Brush Electric Company of Baltimore, and payment was received in 5 per cent first-mortgage bonds.[25]

The Westinghouse pricing policy recognized four classes of buyers: the general purchaser, the dealer, the central station using Westinghouse equipment, and the central station signing a contract to purchase all of certain kinds of equipment from Westinghouse. The discounts from list price granted these four classes varied from time to time but usually were 20 per cent for the general purchaser, 25 per cent for dealers and Westinghouse central stations, and 33⅓ per cent for contracting central stations. An example of the kind of purchase agreement entered into by the contracting central stations is the agreement between Westinghouse and the Missouri Electric Light and Power Company of St. Louis, made in 1892. "The purchaser will not, during said period, purchase converters of other manufacture; but in case purchaser shall do so, then the purchaser shall pay to the Westinghouse Company upon all converters theretofore purchased under this agreement the difference between the prices given in the list and the prices for the same articles to the general customer."[26]

As far as can be ascertained, the Westinghouse company had no licensee class of customers comparable to the Edison licensee central stations, which were obliged to buy all their equipment from the licensor. The contracting Westinghouse stations were apparently given price concessions in return for agreeing to use certain items of Westinghouse equipment exclusively.

7. Westinghouse alternator, 1888

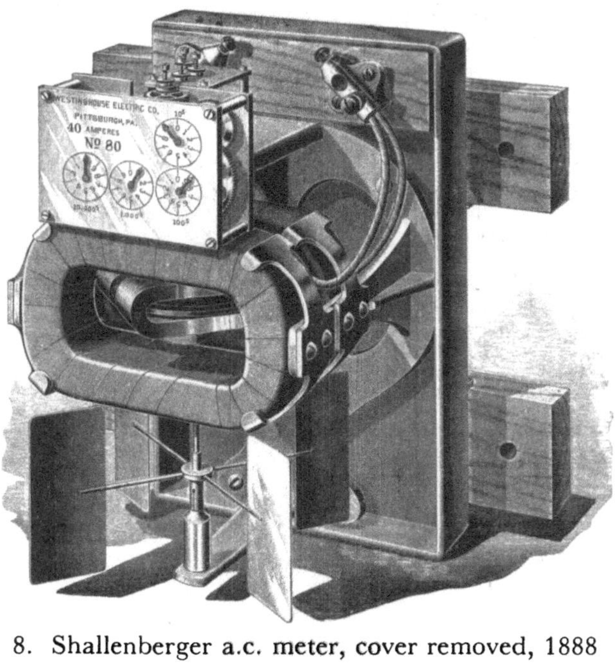

8. Shallenberger a.c. meter, cover removed, 1888

9. Tesla a.c. motor, 1888

10. Westinghouse induction motor, Type C, 1897

11. Westinghouse railway motor, No. 12, 1893

In lamps, Westinghouse prices were about equal to Edison prices. Westinghouse tried to compete in quality instead of price. The fact that the Westinghouse lamp circuits were 50 volts rather than 110 volts meant that a lamp of higher efficiency and longer life could be made. It was also claimed that the shorter, thicker filament of the Westinghouse lamp gave a more even distribution of light.[27] The other fact that the Westinghouse company could use to buttress the argument of superior quality was the existence of the Edison licensee stations. The licensees were a group of specially favored customers who insisted on lamps of high efficiency and who, in many instances, were large enough to establish their own testing facilities to insure that all lamps met their standards. The general purchaser of Edison lamps very likely was offered ones of inferior quality. Because Westinghouse had no licensee customers, the ordinary buyer was alleged to have a much better chance to secure lamps of high quality.[28]

To explain the a.c. incandescent-lighting system to prospective investors in central stations, the Westinghouse company published several pamphlets. A number of rules of thumb were given for guidance in the central-station field. The electric light could supposedly compete with gas so long as the price of coal per ton was not more than twice the price of gas per thousand cubic feet. The size of the station could be estimated by assuming that there should be one light for every eight inhabitants in the area to be served. And it was suggested that the central station bear the cost of wiring the houses and other buildings. "We have observed that where it is attempted to exact the cost of the wiring from the customer, the market is stunted and an antagonism is generated which it is difficult to overcome." [29]

The first Westinghouse central stations were forced to use the contract system of payment because no meters were available. When the Westinghouse company placed Shallenberger meters on the market, it tried to sell them to all Westinghouse central stations. The main sales argument for these meters was their effect on revenues and costs. Cases were cited where, when customers were changed from the flat-rate system to the meter system, their monthly bills had tripled. It was well known that flat rates for many business users and most residences could not be set accurately. The meters demonstrated how far from correct most flat rates were. Increasing revenues was only one effect of meters. A second, and nearly as important, effect was a reduction in total costs. This occurred because customers on meters were usually careful not to have their lights burning unless they were actually in use. Less fuel, labor, and capital investment were required. The Westinghouse company found that a metered station serving the same number of lights as a station without meters needed only 50–70 per cent as much generating capacity.[30]

The meter was a device which demonstrated basic economic principles. It forced the behavior pattern of the individual consumer into conformance with the configuration of resource scarcity. Without a meter, the choices which seemed economic to the consumer were not economic from an over-all point of view. The consumer paid the same bill regardless of the amount of current he used. He would weigh the decision to turn off a light on the basis of lamp consumption and the inconvenience to him of turning lights off and on. Most of the time he did not even think of turning off lights and kept them burning continuously. If he purchased his own lamps, he preferred lamps of the longest life possible, regardless of their efficiency.[31] Because he did not pay for current consumed, a highly efficient but short-lived lamp simply increased his total lighting cost. When electric current was metered, the consumer no longer erroneously treated it as a free good but economized it along with lamps and his own time and energy in turning lights on and off. Resources devoted to electric lighting could then produce greater consumer satisfaction per unit of resource employed.

The essence of the marketing problem is to bring one's product to the attention of potential buyers in such a way that the product is easily seen to be superior to all competing products. The a.c.–d.c. controversy of 1886–1890, which is treated extensively in the following chapter, called attention to the Westinghouse system but not only to its advantages. A much more successful advertisement of the Westinghouse system was the illumination of the Chicago World's Fair in 1893. In the spring of 1892, the Fair directors asked for bids to light the Fair grounds. The Edison lamp-patent suit was coming to a close at that time, and, confident of winning, the Edison company bid very high. No competition was expected because the Edison company anticipated achieving a monopoly of incandescent-lamp manufacture. The Edison bid was over $1,000,000. A Chicago contractor, C. F. Locksteadt, submitted the only other bid, $335,000. Locksteadt's bid was not given serious consideration because of his obvious inability to carry out the contract. Westinghouse became interested, however, and finally convinced the Fair directors that new bids should be submitted. The Westinghouse company bid $399,000 and secured the contract.

The main problem was to fulfill the contract if the appeals court upheld the circuit court decision of July 1891, which had sustained the Edison lamp patent. A decision was not expected from the appeals court until the fall of 1892. Westinghouse assumed that the decision would favor the Edison company and undertook to design a lamp which would circumvent the Edison patent. The features of the Edison lamp that were considered patentable by the lower court were the high-resistance filament and the one-piece glass bulb. The high-resistance filament could be avoided by Westinghouse because the 50-volt circuit permitted a filament of relatively low resistance. The one-piece globe was more difficult. Westinghouse finally made use of patents on a two-piece globe and devised a workable lamp. It had a ground-glass stopper which fitted into the base of the glass globe like a cork into a bottle. Cement was used to provide an air-tight seal. While the vacuum could not be maintained as well as in a hermetically sealed one-piece bulb, the two-piece bulb could serve in an emergency. Westinghouse set up a glass factory in Allegheny, Pennsylvania, and designed machinery to grind the bulb and the stopper. When the decision sustaining the Edison lamp patent was handed down on October 4, 1892, Westinghouse was nearly ready to supply lamps to users of Westinghouse equipment. On October 6, the Westinghouse company issued a circular announcing to all users of incandescent lamps that Westinghouse was making a lamp which did not infringe the Edison patent and which could be supplied in quantity after December 1. The price of the stopper lamp was 30 cents for the 16-candle-power size. A 10 per cent discount was given to central stations.[32] The Edison lamp was selling for about 60 cents to ordinary customers and 25 cents to Edison licensees at this time.

With the lamp problem solved, the Westinghouse company could complete its World's Fair lighting contract on schedule. Generating equipment of over 180,000-lamp capacity was installed, and a circuit of 250,000 lamps was erected. In addition to lighting the Fair grounds and buildings, the Westinghouse company had its own exhibit, where the a.c. system of energy transmission was demonstrated. For the lighting contract and extras, the Westinghouse company received nearly $500,000. The generators were sold to central stations at the conclusion of the Fair. The Westinghouse company computed the net cost of running its exhibit and fulfilling the lighting contract. It was only $16,000.[33] The publicity given to the Westinghouse system and in particular to the non-infringing lamp was unquestionably worth much more than that.

THE EXPANSION OF WESTINGHOUSE

The chief rival of Westinghouse in a.c. incandescent lighting was the Thomson-Houston Electric Company. In its first years, Thomson-Houston produced only arc-lighting equipment in conformity with Thomson's belief, expressed after his visit to Edison's laboratory in 1879, that incandescent electric lighting would not become widely used. This judgment was basically an engineering one. The relative inefficiency of the incandescent system as opposed to the arc system was a handicap that Thomson thought could not be surmounted.

By 1884, it had become evident that Thomson was wrong. Incandescent lighting was commercially successful, and the potential market had hardly been tapped. The profit possibilities appeared to be good. Accordingly, Thomson-Houston decided to undertake production of an incandescent system. It already had engineering talent, manufacturing facilities, and a marketing organization. All of these could be used to advantage. Entry was relatively easy except for one obstacle, patents on the incandescent lamp. To market a complete d.c. incandescent-electric-lighting system, Thomson-Houston either had to invent and patent a basic type of incandescent lamp or secure rights under one of the existing lamp patents. Edison held what was to turn out to be the basic and controlling lamp patent, but in the early eighties the common belief was that a number of other patents were equally strong.

By 1884, intensive experimental work in incandescent lamps had been going on for nearly a decade, and the lamps had been in commercial use for over three years. At such a late date, the possibility that Thomson-Houston could invent and patent an incandescent lamp was exceedingly small. The company consequently decided to secure a license under one of the existing sets of lamp patents, the Sawyer-Man patents.

These patents covered the incandescent-lamp inventions of William E. Sawyer, a telegraph operator turned inventor, who had begun experiments about 1875. Some of his early work formed part of the technical foundation of the United States Electric Lighting Company, organized in June 1878. His connection with this firm was principally on a consulting basis, however, and his main efforts, and the resulting patents, became the property of the Electro-Dynamic Light Company, incorporated in July 1878. Sawyer's backer in this enterprise was Albon Man, a Brooklyn lawyer. Sawyer continued his attempt to achieve a practical incandescent lamp, but his belief that the lamp had to be low in resistance handicapped him.

From 1878 to 1884, the Sawyer-Man lamp patents changed ownership several times. Electro-Dynamic failed, and the patents were sold to the Eastern Electric Manufacturing Company, formed about 1880. This firm had a manufacturing plant at Middletown, Connecticut, and Sawyer became its electrical engineer. In 1882, the newly organized Consolidated Electric Light Company purchased the Sawyer-Man lamp patents from the Eastern Electric company and continued the manufacture of Sawyer-Man lamps.[34] Although the Sawyer-Man patents covered a low-resistance, rod-type carbon filament, the Consolidated company made an Edison-type lamp. It had a thin, high-resistance filament.[35]

Sawyer's lack of commercial success was partly the result of technical difficulties. He did not understand the significance of Edison's filament and continued to try to make a low-resistance lamp. Another factor contributing to Sawyer's failure was his erratic personality. He was difficult to work with and caused dissension in several of the companies with which he was associated. In March 1881, he shot a fellow boarder and was sentenced to four years at hard labor. While his case was being appealed, he was permitted to remain at home because of ill health. He died in the spring of 1883 before serving the sentence.[36]

To secure manufacturing rights under the Sawyer-Man lamp patents, Thomson-Houston purchased control of Consolidated in 1884. The latter then formed the Sawyer-Man Electric Company and gave it an exclusive license to make Sawyer-Man lamps. Thomson-Houston purchased 90 per cent of the Sawyer-Man capital stock, and Consolidated held the remaining 10 per cent.

Thomson-Houston found a ready market for its incandescent-lighting system. In 1886, after Westinghouse had proved the commercial worth of his a.c. system, Thomson-Houston was faced with the problem of deciding whether or not to extend its activities to alternating current. Thomson advised against alternating current on the grounds of safety. He saw that the high-voltage side of a transformer could become "shorted" to the low-voltage side, permitting a dangerously high voltage to enter a building. After nearly a year of work, he found a reliable method of protecting the consumption circuits from high transmission voltages. He grounded the low-voltage side of the transformer. This meant that if the high voltage should become shorted to the low-voltage consumption circuit, the high voltage would pass harmlessly to ground. Now Thomson could advocate alternating current with a clear conscience. In 1887, Thomson-Houston began the production and sale of an a.c. incandescent-lighting system.

George Westinghouse did not welcome a rival in the field in which he had spent large sums of money for patents and experimental work. About the middle of 1887, he instituted suit against Thomson-Houston for infringement of the Gaulard and Gibbs transformer patent. Thomson-Houston consented to a settlement and the suit was dropped. The agreement, dated August 23, 1887, stated that Thomson-Houston recognized the validity of the Gaulard and Gibbs patent. Thomson-Houston was to pay royalties of $2.00 per horsepower of rated capacity for each transformer sold and was licensed to manufacture and sell a.c. apparatus in New England and to Thomson-Houston local lighting companies outside New England. Westinghouse acquired the right to sell the Thomson-Houston arc-lighting system throughout the United States.[37] A supplementary agreement was reached in December. This agreement set minimum prices for the transformers, established penalty royalty rates (about $10 per rated horsepower) for transformers sold in cities of less than 10,000 population, and specified that Westinghouse was to supply Thomson-Houston with certain types of a.c. equipment.[38]

The recognition by Thomson-Houston of the strong position held by Westinghouse in transformer patents was reciprocated by Westinghouse's recognition of the superiority of the Sawyer-Man lamp patents, which were owned, it will be recalled, by Consolidated, a company then under Thomson-Houston control. In the autumn of 1887, Westinghouse sold its Pittsburgh lamp factory to Consolidated and agreed that thereafter the owners of Westinghouse lighting equipment would use Sawyer-Man lamps.[39] This step terminated the manufacture of Stanley lamps by Westinghouse. Consolidated paid for the Westinghouse lamp factory with shares of its capital stock. The following year, Westinghouse sold more lamp-making assets to Consolidated, again taking payment in Consolidated stock, and, in addition, purchased some Consolidated stock on the open market for cash. In December 1888, Thomson-Houston sold its Consolidated stock to Westinghouse. Control of Consolidated passed to Westinghouse at that time. This last step was purely formal, however, for on October 1, 1888, Westinghouse had leased the assets of Consolidated and was again making its own lamps.[40]

This transfer of Consolidated from Thomson-Houston to Westinghouse was accompanied by the sale of the Sawyer-Man Electric Company stock which had been held by Thomson-Houston. The stock was sold to Consolidated, which then held 100 per cent of the Sawyer-Man shares. In order to continue making Sawyer-Man lamps, Thomson-Houston needed a license from Consolidated. This was obtained. Under its terms, Thomson-Houston could make lamps only for use on its own equipment. As late as 1893, this restriction was still in effect.[41]

It is not possible to say exactly why control of Consolidated and the Sawyer-Man lamp patents was relinquished by Thomson-Houston to Westinghouse. It is likely that Thomson-Houston wanted funds to finance its extensive expansion program, which involved merging with arc-lighting competitors and other firms. The benefit which Westinghouse derived from getting control of Consolidated is easier to see. Westinghouse wanted to strengthen its patent position in incandescent lamps in preparation for the coming legal battle over the validity and scope of the Edison lamp patents.

It will be recalled that 1887 marked the first agreements between Westinghouse and Thomson-Houston. At that time, Westinghouse adopted the Sawyer-Man lamp which was controlled by Thomson-Houston. This step was made permanent the next year when Westinghouse purchased control of Consolidated and the Sawyer-Man patents. But the other two major aspects of the 1887 relationship between Westinghouse and Thomson-

Houston were only temporary. In the fall of 1888, Thomson-Houston terminated its license under the Gaulard and Gibbs transformer patent, and Westinghouse stopped selling Thomson-Houston arc-lighting apparatus.[42]

One reason for cancellation of the 1887 agreement was that an infringement suit under the Gaulard-Gibbs patent had been unsuccessful. In May 1887, Westinghouse brought suit against the Sun Electric Company of Boston. In an opinion rendered August 7, 1888, the judge decided in favor of Sun on the grounds that the Gaulard-Gibbs patent covered only the use of transformers in series.[43] With the patent restricted to a method not in commercial use, it is hardly surprising that Thomson-Houston no longer thought it necessary to operate under a license from Westinghouse.

After giving up its agency for Thomson-Houston equipment, Westinghouse decided to manufacture its own arc-lighting system. It made no attempt to develop its own system *ab initio* in an industry nearly ten years old. To purchase an existing system seemed wiser. In the fall of 1888, Westinghouse acquired the entire capital stock of a small arc-lighting manufacturer, the Waterhouse Electric and Manufacturing Company.[44] In January 1889, Westinghouse leased the assets of the United States Electric Lighting Company, makers of the Weston arc-lighting system.[45] The Waterhouse and Weston systems were combined to form the Westinghouse arc-lighting system.

Although leasing of the United States company occurred at a time when Westinghouse was entering the arc-lighting field, acquiring the Weston arc-lighting system was not the main reason for securing that company's assets. The United States company owned incandescent-lighting patents which were comparable in strength and importance to the Sawyer-Man and Edison patents. In securing first the Sawyer-Man patents and then the United States company patents, Westinghouse had purchased nearly all non-Edison patents of any merit. Preparation was thereby completed for the coming patent conflict with the Edison Electric Light Company.

The United States Electric Lighting Company, it will be recalled, was formed in 1878 with the financial support of the Equitable Life Assurance Company. The development work of Hiram Maxim and William Sawyer in electric lighting was the technical foundation of the company. But Sawyer's association with the United States company was only temporary. The sustained attempt to bring both arc- and incandescent-lighting systems to the marketable stage was carried on by Maxim. He appears to have concentrated first on the incandescent lamp. In the fall of 1880, approximately one year after Edison first made a successful lamp, Maxim announced that he had invented a practical incandescent lamp.[46] One of Edison's laboratory assistants who worked at Menlo Park during the incandescent-lamp period has stated that Maxim drew on Edison's work for both ideas and techniques. Maxim visited Menlo Park, where Edison explained his lamp fully. Subsequently, Maxim hired one of Edison's skilled workmen, a glass blower, to supply the details on exactly how the Edison lamps were made.[47] Like the Sawyer-Man lamp, the Maxim lamp was constructed with the thin, high-resistance filament essential to its success only after Edison had led the way.

The United States company made the first commercial installation of its incandescent-lighting system in the fall of 1880, about six months after the first Edison commercial installation on the steamship *Columbia*. The United States company installation was in the vaults of the Mercantile Safe Deposit Company in New York City.[48] This firm was located in the Equitable building at 120 Broadway, where the Equitable Life Assurance Company and the United States company both had offices.

In spite of its early start in the electrical manufacturing industry, the United States Electric Lighting Company was not very successful. Until about 1885, it was Edison's only important competitor, but its share of the incandescent-equipment market was only one-fifth as large as Edison's. Moreover, it was generally believed in the industry that the United States company was not a profitable one.[49] This view is substantiated by an 1889 report by Edison in which he claimed that the United States company had incurred losses of about $1,500,000 in the period 1882–1889.[50]

The relatively poor performance of the United States company can be partly attributed to the fact that its technical personnel, while competent, did not realize the importance of developing an entire incandescent-lighting *system*, rather than certain components. Maxim concentrated on the incandescent lamp and neglected the other components (the dynamo and connecting network). Charles Flint attempted to strengthen the company by hiring technical experts such as Professor Cyrus Fogg Brackett of Princeton and Moses Farmer, a famous electrical inventor. Flint also promoted the merger with the Weston company and encouraged Maxim to sail to Europe so that Weston could become chief engineer. Maxim was lured away by the promise of the French Legion of Honor, to be arranged by Flint, or, failing that, a cash payment of $10,000 from Flint. Maxim went to Europe, received the Legion of Honor, and never returned to the United States company.[51] But even these moves by Flint were not sufficient to improve the position of the company.

Like Thomson-Houston, the United States company began the manufacture of an a.c. incandescent-lighting system in 1887. Aware of the Westinghouse patent claims, the president of the United States company wrote in July 1887 to Westinghouse and stated that the Westinghouse claims would not be respected. The president went on to say: "We also take this occasion to notify you that we are engaged in the manufacture and sale of electric light apparatus in which alternating currents of high tension are converted by inductive action at the points of consumption into currents of low tension for incandescent lighting." [52]

TABLE 17

Growth of Westinghouse, 1886–1899

Date	*Annual sales*	*Authorized capital stock*	*Employment*
1886	$ 180,000	$ 1,000,000	200
1887	800,000	5,000,000	...
1890	4,700,000	10,000,000	1,300
1899	12,000,000	15,000,000	5,000

Sources: Various documents and publications of Westinghouse.

The Westinghouse response to this letter was evidently so convincing that the United States company decided it could not continue to make a.c. apparatus without infringing the Gaulard and Gibbs patent. In 1888, Westinghouse purchased for cash 7,000 of the 15,000 shares of United States stock outstanding. In January 1889, the Westinghouse company leased the plant and equipment of the United States company, which, from that time on, was integrated into the manufacturing and marketing operations of Westinghouse. In succeeding years, Westinghouse purchased additional United States shares, giving Westinghouse stock in payment. In May 1911, the last 16 shares were acquired, and, in May 1912, the United States Electric Lighting Company was dissolved.

TABLE 18

Growth of Westinghouse Central Stations, 1886–1893

Date	*Number of central stations in use and under construction*	*Capacity of the central stations in 16-c.p. lamps*	*Average number of lamps per central station*
January 1886	27	...	...
September 1887	68	134,000	1,970
October 1888	116	196,850	1,700
April 1889	160	300,000	1,875
June 1890	301	554,350	1,840
November 1890	350	700,000	2,000
1893	511	...	...

Sources: Various documents and publications of Westinghouse.

In summary, Westinghouse entered the electrical manufacturing industry in 1884 and produced a d.c. incandescent-lighting system. In 1886, it pioneered the first commercial a.c. incandescent-lighting system. In the years that followed, it merged with Consolidated, United States, and Waterhouse for the double purpose of strengthening its position in incandescent-lamp patents and adding arc-lighting equipment to its line of products.

TABLE 19

Comparison of the Three Leading Firms in the Electrical Manufacturing Industry, 1891

	Westinghouse	*Edison General Electric*	*Thomson-Houston*
Annual sales	$5,000,000	$10,900,000	$10,300,000
Authorized capital stock	$5,000,000	$15,000,000	$10,400,000
Employment	1,300	6,000	4,000
Number of central stations (incandescent only)			
a.c.	350[a]	none	500
d.c.	negligible	400	100
Capacity (in 16-c.p. lights) of central stations			
a.c.	700,000[a]	none	520,000
d.c.	negligible	750,000	82,000

Sources: Company documents and publications in GE Files and WE Files.
[a] Late 1890.

Data showing the growth of Westinghouse are given in Table 17. The success of the company can also be measured by the expansion in the use of its lighting system. Table 18 shows the rapid increase in the number of Westinghouse central stations in the period 1886–1893. The relative position of Westinghouse in the incandescent-lighting-equipment industry is roughly indicated by Table 19. It can be seen that Westinghouse was approximately equal to Edison General Electric and Thomson-Houston in incandescent central-station equipment in service. Both Edison General Electric and Thomson-Houston were much larger firms, however, as the sales and employment data show. They manufactured isolated incandescent plants, electric-railway equipment, and electric-power equipment in larger quantities than Westinghouse. In addition, Thomson-Houston did most of the arc-lighting-equipment business in the United States.

X

Interfirm Relations

PATENTS

THE early patent policy of the Edison company has already been described. It will be recalled that no infringement suits were initiated until 1885. The principal reasons for that delay were that Edison was too busy to give time to patent litigation, the Edison company had nearly the entire incandescent-lighting market, and the Edison directors were very cautious. The paradoxical aspect of the delay in the patent suits is that the Edison company was expressly and solely a company for financing experiments and holding patents on the inventions that resulted. The only important assets of the parent company were the Edison patents and central-station securities which had been taken in exchange for exclusive patent licenses for specific territories.

Edison's success in securing control of the board of directors in 1884 led to the initiation of the first patent suits in 1885. Another event which helps to explain the initiation of suits in 1885 is the victory Edison won in Germany in 1884 in a legal contest with the Swan incandescent-lighting patents.[1] The German decision bolstered the confidence of the Edison directors in the Edison patents. In commenting on that decision Edison said: "The effect of the decision is in the highest degree important, not only there but here and in every other country, for it practically affirms that every other incandescent lamp is an infringement upon the Edison patent."[2]

Patent suits were instituted in May 1885 by the Edison company against the United States Electric Lighting Company, the Consolidated Electric Light Company, and a number of other manufacturers and users of incandescent lights.[3] The Edison company based its suits upon patent No. 223,898, which was applied for on November 4, 1879, and granted to Edison on January 27, 1880. Its claims were for: "(1) An electric lamp for giving light by incandescence consisting of a filament of carbon of high resistance, made as described and secured to metallic wires. (2) The combination of carbon filaments with a receiver made entirely of glass and conductors passing through the glass, and from which receiver the air is exhausted."[4]

Although a number of suits were begun in 1885, the only suit carried through was the one against the United States Electric Lighting Company. The actual hearings in this suit did not begin until 1889. Completion of the suit required two more years, and, because the decision was appealed, still another year passed before the status of the Edison patent was finally determined. In the period from 1885 until 1892, the Edison company attempted to restrain the producers and users of non-Edison lamps by making its intention to enforce its patent rights widely known. On May 23, 1885, the Edison company issued a circular indicating that the patent suits would be prosecuted and that all makers, users, and sellers of non-Edison lamps would be punished.[5] In October 1886, the Edison company published a 25-page booklet on the legal and commercial status of the Edison electric light. The booklet mentioned that a hundred infringement suits involving Edison patents were then pending and went on to say, to users of non-Edison lamps:

> For the purpose of enabling you to estimate your liability in the event of the Edison patents being sustained, we may state that a conservative valuation apportions a damage of $25 for each lamp in an original installation and $2.50 for each renewal lamp, independent of the fact that such decision would necessarily render your plant inoperative. . . You are further reminded of the fact that the delay in reaching a decision does not impair its force when attained, a notable example of which is the Goodyear Rubber Company, whose suits were not *finally settled until after the expiration of the patents,* when large amounts of money were collected in damages.[6]

The booklet then listed the twelve patents used in making the Edison lamp and showed a picture of the lamp with each patented feature labeled. Pictures of the United States company lamp, the Westinghouse lamp, the Sawyer-Man lamp, and the Brush-Swan lamp were also shown with the infringing features of each of these lamps plainly marked. The conclusion was supposed to be that it was impossible to build a commercially successful lamp without infringing the Edison patents.

The efforts of the Edison company to protect its business by threatening the other incandescent-lamp manufacturers and their customers were not very successful. Most lamp manufacturers seriously questioned the validity of the Edison lamp patents. The United States company, for example, considered its patent position much stronger than Edison's because it owned the incandescent-lamp patents of Farmer, Maxim, and Weston. Both Farmer and Maxim had worked in incandescent lighting long before Edison. The Consolidated company was even more confident of its patent position. It initiated infringement suits against several local Edison light companies in 1885, shortly after the Edison company had begun its suits. The basis for the Consolidated suits was a patent issued to Sawyer and Man on May 12, 1885, after a five-year period of interference with an Edison patent application in the Patent Office. The case had gone to the Secretary of the Interior for decision. The main claims of the Sawyer-Man patent were for: "(1) An incandescing conductor for an electric lamp, of carbonized fibrous or textile material and of an arch of horseshoe shape. (2) The incandescing conductor for an electric lamp, formed of carbonized paper." [7]

The Consolidated suits gave the impression that the basic Edison lamp patent had been defeated in the Patent Office proceedings with Sawyer-Man and that the Edison patent would not be sustained in court. That impression was wrong, because the patent serving as the basis for the Edison suits was not the one which had lost to the Sawyer-Man patent. E. H. Johnson, president of the Edison company, issued a statement in 1886 in an attempt to clarify the status of the basic lamp patent. "Mr. Edison's carbon filament patent of 1879 covers broadly the modern incandescent lamp. The claim that this patent has ever been in litigation in the United States Patent Office is absolutely false. In Germany and in England, this fundamental patent has finally prevailed against all infringers, thus establishing the fact that Mr. Edison's great invention has nowhere been anticipated — *ergo*, a like result must follow in the United States." [8]

The strong patent positions of the United States company and the Consolidated company were only partly responsible for the general belief that the Edison patent would not be upheld. Events in Canada threatened for a while to terminate the Edison patent. The life of a United States patent could depend upon the life of a foreign patent for the same invention because of the following clause in the American patent law: "But every patent granted for an invention which has been previously patented in a foreign country shall be so limited as to expire at the same time with the foreign patent, or if there be more than one, at the same time with the one having the shortest term, and in no case shall it be in force more than seventeen years."[9]

The Edison patent had been granted in Canada before it was granted in the United States, and the above clause applied. On February 26, 1889, the Canadian Commissioner of Patents decided that the Edison patent was void because certain regulations regarding manufacture in Canada had not been complied with. This decision caused the expiration of the Edison patent in the United States and resulted in the dismissal of the suit against the United States company. The Canadian Minister of Agriculture later reversed the February decision, and the Edison suit against the United States company was reinstituted.[10]

The widespread distrust of the Edison patent was increased still more by an occurrence in England. In a patent suit there in 1889, the Edison patent had not been sustained because no workman was able to make an incandescent lamp by the process described in the patent. It was quite generally believed that the Edison company would likewise be unable to show that an incandescent lamp could be constructed by following the directions given in the patent.[11] Because one of the purposes of the patent law is to bring new inventions to the attention of the public, any patent which does not give a complete description of the invention and how it is made can be declared void.

The general pattern of events up until about 1889 created reasonable doubt that the basic Edison patent would be sustained. It is probable that few manufacturers and users of incandescent lamps considered it a serious business risk to make and use these lamps without permission from the Edison company. Beginning about the middle of 1889, however, the specific reasons for believing that the Edison patent would not be sustained were gradually eliminated. First, the Canadian decision was reversed. Secondly, a suit against the McKeesport Light Company, an Edison licensee, initiated by the Consolidated company for infringement of the Sawyer-Man patent, was decided in favor of the Edison company. The 1885 Sawyer-Man patent was declared invalid.[12] Thirdly, the belief that the Edison patent description was not complete was upset early in 1890, when the Edison company called upon one of its lamp engineers, John W. Howell, to make lamps by the method outlined in the patent. Howell constructed twenty-seven lamps and tested them. The lamps, the test data, and the tools used were introduced as evidence in the suit against the United States company.[13]

The decision in that suit was rendered on July 14, 1891, in the United States Circuit Court for the Southern District of New York. The Edison patent was sustained. The features of the Edison lamp which were judged to be patentable were the high-resistance filament and the one-piece glass globe. The decision was appealed but upheld in October 1892. The meaning of the decision seemed to be that the Edison patent could be the basis for an absolute monopoly of incandescent-lamp manufacture in the United States. The patent claims which had been made almost from the beginning of the Edison Electric Light Company and which were thought to be extravagant and unfounded were finally realized. The many years during which the Edison patent was not given serious consideration had seen the growth of numerous incandescent-lamp manufacturers and the installation of hundreds of central stations and isolated plants which used non-Edison lights. The problem facing General Electric, which was formed by the consolidation of Edison General Electric and Thomson-Houston in 1892, was to decide what course of action to pursue in view of the monopoly power suddenly gained.

The first question was whether or not to take advantage of the monopoly power and try to profit from it. General Electric could have licensed the existing lamp manufacturers in return for moderate royalty payments. Such a policy would have been popular in the electrical manufacturing industry, because it would have left practically undisturbed the structure of production and marketing which was the result of over twelve years' growth. But General Electric was not inclined to treat its competitors generously, and it is doubtful that a liberal licensing policy received serious consideration.

The decision to seek an absolute monopoly of incandescent-lamp manufacture grew chiefly out of two circumstances. The Edison Electric Light Company had been solely an experimental, patent-holding firm, and it had spent many thousands of dollars in developing the Edison system of electric lighting. After the system had been developed, it had watched other firms which had spent very little, if anything, on research, take away its market by imitating its product. General Electric felt it had a moral right to the profits to which it was legally entitled. It viewed these profits as no more than a fair return on the money invested in developing the electric light. The fact that nearly thirteen of the seventeen years of patent life had elapsed before a monopoly return on the patent could be secured seemed to mean that all possible profit should be obtained in the remaining four years.

The second circumstance pointing toward a strict enforcement of patent rights was the presence of the Edison licensees. These firms insisted upon a monopoly of incandescent-lamp sales and central-station use in their territories. They had paid heavily in stock and cash for the license which promised a monopoly that had not been realized. A liberal licensing policy which would have permitted manufacturers of non-Edison lamps to supply lamps to firms in licensee territory was completely unacceptable to the licensees.

The next problem was to decide how to achieve a monopoly of incandescent lamps. The attitude of the courts was one factor which influenced the policy adopted. While the courts were willing to grant injunctions closing down the lamp factories of competitors, the injunctions required that the Edison company supply lamps to users of non-Edison electric-lighting apparatus if such apparatus were installed before the July 1891 decision. Furthermore, the lamps had to be supplied on fair and reasonable terms. The injunction granted on January 6, 1893, against the Mather Electric Company, a small lamp-manufacturing firm, was typical in the restrictions it imposed on General Electric. Mather was given the right "to move hereafter for the vacation, suspension or modification of the injunction upon proof of specific instances of refusal on part of the complainant . . . to supply the lamps of the patent on reasonable terms under the conditions of the particular case to the owners of electric lighting apparatus made by the Mather Electric Company which were installed before the rendition of the interlocutory decree of the Circuit Court sustaining the validity of the patent."[14] General Electric was thus limited in the prices it could set and the buyers to whom it could refuse to sell. Even more important, the apparent desire of the courts to protect the users of incandescent lamps made the outcome of any suits against infringing users uncertain.

Two additional factors, the nature of incandescent lamps and the relative numbers of users and manufacturers, also influenced the policy adopted. Incandescent lamps usually lasted from 600 to 1000 hours. The frequency of replacement depended upon the amount of use, but, on the average, lamps would last from four to six months. Because this is a relatively short time, the obvious course of action was to proceed first against the lamp manufacturers. If their operations were halted, all users would be forced to buy from the Edison company within a year or so. The quick and sure way to prevent users from infringing was to cut off the source of supply. The several dozen lamp manufacturers as contrasted to the thousands of infringing users was a consideration which led to the same conclusion.

A final factor should also be mentioned. The General Electric Company was aware that it was disliked by a part of the electrical industry which labeled it the "electrical trust." In order not to arouse public opinion against it, and to keep the good will of lamp users who might be induced to purchase Edison lamps, the company decided that the wise procedure would be to act against the lamp manufacturers and not against the lamp users.

In the light of the foregoing conditions, the Edison company decided to exercise its monopoly power by closing down all competing incandescent-lamp factories. This policy was enunciated by S. D. Greene, manager of the lighting department of General Electric: "We are, as you know, concentrating the energies of our entire legal staff in closing up the manufacturing concerns for the very reason that absolute perpetual protection to our licensees cannot be obtained until we cut off the source of opposition supplies." [15]

The first injunction was secured against the United States company, defendant in the infringement suit, on July 23, 1891. This injunction forced Westinghouse to carry on all its lamp-making activities in its other subsidiary, the Sawyer-Man Electric Company. After the decision by the higher court of October 1892, General Electric sought additional injunctions. In November, injunctions were secured against the Sawyer-Man company and the Perkins Electric Lamp Company of Hartford, Connecticut. In January 1893, an injunction was secured against the Mather Electric Company, and, during the succeeding six months, nearly a dozen more injunctions were obtained.

The decision to move first against the lamp manufacturers was not popular with the Edison licensees. They were clearly in accord with the policy of securing an effective monopoly of incandescent lamps, but each licensee wanted immediate action in its own territory. Competing non-Edison central stations had been established in many licensee territories, and the licensees were anxious to close down these stations. They also wanted to sell lamps to all isolated plants in their territory. The licensees were especially dissatisfied because they viewed the patent suits which had begun in 1885 as battles to protect their interests, and they had eagerly watched the progress of the litigation. In 1886, the Association of Edison Illuminating Companies issued the following statement: "The sub-companies give the parent Edison company their hearty cooperation and support in the fight to sustain and enforce the Edison incandescent light patents." [16]

But the years that followed saw more incandescent-lighting competitors rather than less. Thomson-Houston and Westinghouse established hundreds of central stations, and the number of incandescent-lamp manufacturers continued to increase. The Edison licensees became bitter and disgruntled as competition cut into their profits and forced them to struggle for business. The October 1892 decision sustaining the Edison patent merely increased their disappointment. They had hoped, of course, that suits would be undertaken immediately against all infringing users. Instead, Greene advised them that caution and patience were necessary. On December 16, 1892, he sent out a circular letter urging restraint:

We should like to have you send us at an early date, a résumé of the situation in your territory, giving us a list of the infringers, the apparatus used by them, and when it was installed. We hope in a very short time to be able to communicate directly with you, with a view of arranging a definite policy of dealing with the infringers in your territory. In the meanwhile, there are certain other steps to be taken in order to make our victory as complete as possible, and we trust that you will institute no proceedings and commit yourselves to no line of action which may afterward prove to have been unwise in view of the complexities of the situation and the necessity that it should be dealt with intelligently as a whole. . . It is obviously unwise and impolitic to deal harshly with infringing users.[17]

Some licensees were so impatient to begin legal action against infringing users that they violated Greene's instructions and initiated their own suits. The Edison central station in Fall River, Massachusetts, notified Greene in April 1893 that it was about to institute suit against a manufacturing firm which owned and operated an isolated plant using Perkins lamps. The Fall River station expected the Edison company to pay the costs of this suit.[18]

Most of the licensees, however, followed Greene's instructions and refrained from taking action on their own initiative. But many became very impatient when several months had passed and nothing had been done to prevent the sale and use of infringing lamps in particular localities. The St. Paul Edison company wrote to Greene in March 1893:

Some time has now elapsed since the public announcement of the decisions of the courts affirming the validity of the Edison patents on incandescent lamps but as yet we have heard nothing from you in relation to what steps you propose to take, to protect us in the sale of lamps within our territory, and recompense us for the losses we have suffered in the past, through failure of such protection. We think we are entitled to prompt and efficient action on your part to protect and compensate us, and respectfully ask that you will let us know immediately what course you intend to pursue.[19]

A letter sent by the Edison licensee at York, Pennsylvania, reflects the same attitude as the St. Paul letter but in more simple English:

Now what we want is protection and that at once. I learned today that the President of the Westinghouse company of the Westinghouse from Pittsburgh was expected to come today. Now if the decisions of the court mean anything, and we have paid our money for nothing let us know at once and we will order our add [*sic*] out of the papers, if not why does not the Edison General Company take hold of matters and stop them? They are putting in lights daily and getting our customers.

This Company says the General Westinghouse Company are sending money here to fight the case. Where is the Edison Company? Will they not defend us according to our agreement with them, or shall we suffer after they have taken our money? Come to the front gentlemen and show that you will do as you have promised. It has now come to such a point that something must be done and that at once.[20]

The procedure of General Electric in achieving its incandescent-lamp monopoly thus was to proceed not against the users but against the manufacturers. After the latter had been forced out of business, action was to be taken against infringing users where necessary. To prepare for this second step, General Electric requested the licensees to supply data on infringing users, as the above excerpt from Greene's letter of December 1892 shows, and undertook to ascertain the legal position of these infringing users. Legal clarification required the following course of action:

We are . . . bringing in the Circuit Court of New York, and before the same judges who rendered the decision in the Filament case in our favor, and who therefore are most familiar with the subject, test cases against users of infringing lamps in the New York Illuminating Company's territory. These cases will, of course, serve as a precedent for similar cases in other licensee territories, and we thought it much better to bring them right here, where we have not got to go over the whole history of the case and familiarize the judges again with all the technical details. We intend to push these cases with all possible dispatch, and trust we may be able to advise you, as well as all other licensees, of their successful termination.

We believe the licensees will agree with us that it is much better to start with test cases of this kind, rather than to divide our forces by bringing suits in different cases, which would unquestionably have the effect of weakening our case.[21]

The difficulties that General Electric had with its licensees were not confined to those arising out of the delay in legal action against infringing users. When a number of lamp factories had been closed by injunction and the supply of non-Edison lamps thereby reduced, the owners of electric plants who previously had used other lamps began to use Edison lamps. Where these plants had been installed prior to July 14, 1891, the licensees could not legally refuse to supply Edison lamps. Where the plants had been installed after that date, the licensees were under no obligation to furnish lamps and frequently did not. In many of these new installations, however, the operator managed to secure Edison lamps from some other source. Any sale of Edison lamps in the territory of a licensee by someone other than the licensee was in violation of its exclusive license under the Edison patents. When such sales took place, the licensee was quick to inform General Electric, which was, of course, the ultimate source of all Edison lamps.

The St. Paul licensee wrote in April 1893 that Powers Dry Goods Company had installed a Western Electric incandescent plant with 425 16-candle-power Edison lamps. The lamps had not been purchased from the licensee.[22] The Harrisburg licensee wrote that two isolated plants which used Edison lamps had been installed in its territory. The lamps had not come from the licensee, which had lost two large customers by reason of the installation of the two plants.[23] Complaints such as these forced General Electric to adopt the policy of selling lamps to no one except actual users of lamps. But this policy did not eliminate the trouble completely, because licensees would be occasionally deceived into selling for use in their territory lamps which would later get into the territory of other licensees.

The plan to close all competing lamp factories was only partially successful. Many new firms entered the business of lamp making, and one company succeeded in producing a non-infringing lamp. The Columbia Incandescent Lamp Company of St. Louis, Missouri, fought hard against an injunction and convinced the court that inventive activities of Henry Goebel, who claimed to have invented an incandescent lamp in the 1850's, were relevant. The judge refused to grant an injunction. His decision was appealed and was reversed by a higher court. The successful efforts of Westinghouse to produce a non-infringing lamp have already been described. Westinghouse owned both the United States company and the Sawyer-Man company at this time, but injunctions prevented the manufacture of either lamp. Westinghouse took a personal interest in developing the stopper lamp and deserves major credit for its success. It was based on Maxim and Weston patents, owned by the United States company.

The stopper lamp was inferior to the Edison lamp in life and efficiency, but it was priced much lower and gave satisfactory service. It enabled Westinghouse to fulfill the World's Fair contract, to supply the Westinghouse central stations, and to provide lamps for other users. As a demonstration of good faith in compliance with the injunctions against his lamp-making subsidiaries, Westinghouse sent some of the stopper lamps to the Edison company for examination. After the lamps had been received, Greene expressed the view that "we have no confidence whatever in the commercial test of the lamp." [24] To substantiate this view, General Electric sent a lamp engineer, W. S. Howell, to York, Pennsylvania, where the stopper lamp was in use at the Westinghouse central station. Howell reported that the lamps burned out quickly, were dull and not uniform, and had a fine fibrous deposit inside the globe. Howell's conclusion was that the stopper lamp was of no commercial value.[25]

General Electric's complacency about the stopper lamp was not shared by the licensees. The Grand Rapids (Michigan) licensee wrote in February 1893 that "the new Westinghouse lamp is in use here and seems to be giving satisfaction." [26] The opinion of the Edison licensee in York was much stronger:

> It seems very strange to us that we fail utterly, either by letter or by visits to New York to awaken any interest on your part, in the urgency of the situation here. We would like to have some positive information as to what you propose to do regarding the new Westinghouse lamp. . . It is of no use for you people to rest content with the conceited idea that the new lamp is of no commercial value; as it is giving very good satisfaction here, and if, as we said above, they can go ahead with it, it is going to prove a formidable rival.[27]

The Westinghouse central station at York switched to the Buckeye lamp, an infringing brand, in April. This would seem to indicate that the stopper lamp was not completely successful. As late as August 4, 1894, however, a General Electric official thought it worth while to reiterate that "we do not regard the new Westinghouse incandescent lamp as a market success." [28] The fact that such a statement was considered necessary indicates that the stopper lamp had probably achieved widespread use. It surely gave good service in many places. Years later a Westinghouse employee reported that two stopper lamps were used in a Colorado hotel for eighteen years.[29]

General Electric did not have as long as it had planned to achieve a monopoly in incandescent-lamp manufacture. The lamp patent had been granted in January 1880 and normally would have run until 1897. But the Canadian patent expired on November 14, 1894, and the United States patent consequently expired on that same date. For several years afterward, competition in the incandescent-lamp industry was very severe. Relying on its low production costs, General Electric cut prices and tried to secure the bulk of the market by price competition. The other firms also cut prices, and General Electric's proportion of the market remained at about one-half. Two years of severe competition were sufficient to make a price-output stabilization plan look attractive. Such a plan could not be based on the General Electric lamp patents because the Edison licensees insisted that General Electric could not permit others to use these patents without violating the licensee contracts.[30]

Unable to use its patents to buttress stabilization of the industry, General Electric nevertheless succeeded in reaching an agreement in August 1896 with six other lamp producers whereby lamp prices were fixed and business was allotted to each firm. Shortly afterward, ten more lamp manufacturers joined the agreement, which was given a permanent basis several months later.[31] Advantage was taken of the fact that in incandescent-lamp patents, the position of Westinghouse was second only to General Electric. Moreover, several of the Westinghouse improvement patents were essential to the production of lamps of the best quality. These patents were made available to the members of the August agreement in January 1897, when Westinghouse licensed General Electric and the smaller firms to manufacture incandescent lamps under its patents. These firms together produced 95 per cent of the lamps made in the United States.[32] All of the licensees, including General Electric, paid a royalty of one-third of a cent per lamp to Westinghouse. No additional producers were to be licensed unless two-thirds of the licensees requested it.[33] Westinghouse agreed to the following price policy:

> The Westinghouse Company (and its allied Companies) will sell incandescent lamps at the market prices as established by its licensees, except in cases where, owing to local conditions or business reasons connected with the sale of other apparatus, it deems it to its interest to make special prices. If at any time the licensee is not satisfied with the practice of the Westinghouse Company in regard to prices, such licensee may surrender his license, in which case both parties to the license will be restored to their former position.[34]

The above statement seems to imply that Westinghouse was willing to follow the price set by its licensees, which in reality meant the price set by General Electric. This implication is supported by a statement made by a Westinghouse official in regard to a later agreement which licensed General Electric under the Westinghouse patents. "It was verbally understood that in case we found occasion to not maintain the established prices of the General Electric Company we should notify Mr. Jackson." [35]

The fact that Westinghouse was the licensor and General Electric the licensee cannot be interpreted to mean that Westinghouse was dominant in the incandescent-lamp industry. Although the basic Edison-lamp patent had expired in 1894, General Electric had many patents on minor features and improvements. The objections of its licensees prevented General Electric from licensing any other lamp producer under these patents. General Electric was producing 50 per cent of the lamp output, while Westinghouse was producing less than 15 per cent, and about thirty-five firms accounted for the rest. Where one firm produces such a large proportion of the industry output, it can hardly avoid setting the price, because its sales have a sensible effect on price while those of any single small producer may not. The curious position of the dominant firm paying royalties to a lesser company was recognized by George Westinghouse in the letter to Coffin, cited above. Westinghouse was very apologetic over accepting royalties from General Electric and would gladly have had General Electric as a co-licensor. The small firms objected, however, and insisted that

General Electric be treated as any other licensee, that it pay the full royalty, and that none of the royalty be refunded.

The prices established by the General Electric–Westinghouse group were only slightly above the prices in the preceding year and a half of severe competition. One estimate places the lamp price at 20 cents, as compared to the previous prices of from 12 to 18 cents.[36] Such a moderate price increase was probably due in part to the responsibility that both General Electric and Westinghouse felt for central stations using their equipment. Fear that a high price would attract numerous firms into the industry or tempt firms that were participating in the stabilization agreement to break away also kept the price low. The firms in the agreement knew that they could account for 95 per cent of the industry output only so long as the price was kept near the competitive level. Potential competition meant that their *share* of the market did not indicate their *control* of the market. Their power to affect the price of lamps was very small.

George Westinghouse showed his concern over potential competitors in an 1897 letter. "It is to be feared, however, that where so many parties are interested and where there is such keen competition, that the licenses which have been executed will not become permanent and profitable, in fact I have been informed that a number of new concerns have recently started in business." [37]

Although the lamp patents were not the only patents relating to incandescent lighting, patents on various of the other components were much less important to the development of the industry. Dynamos were not patentable, only improvements and variations in the basic design. After Edison had shown how to make an efficient dynamo, any manufacturer was free to produce one. The distribution network (that is, the method of connecting the lamps to the dynamo) was patentable, and attempts were made to establish the validity of some of these patents. Through its ownership of the Gaulard and Gibbs patent, Westinghouse tried to gain control of alternating-current systems in the United States, but failed when the courts interpreted the patent narrowly. When the Edison company attempted to enforce its distribution patents, it also met with little success.

Patents in incandescent lighting were not of great significance in the growth of the industry. The dominant position held by the Edison company up to 1885 cannot be attributed to its patents. The entrance of Thomson-Houston and Westinghouse into incandescent lighting and the emergence of dozens of lamp manufacturers are evidence that patents did not give any one firm a monopoly. Of the three main components of an incandescent-lighting system — the dynamo, the distribution system, and the lamp — only the lamp was covered by a single, basic patent. Even here, the influence of the patent was small, because its status was uncertain for so long, because its life after it had been upheld was only two years, and because during that two years Westinghouse produced a non-infringing lamp. The purchase by Westinghouse of the Consolidated company (Sawyer-Man) and the United States company can be attributed to lamp and a.c. patents. But the merger of Thomson-Houston and Edison General Electric in 1892 to form General Electric and the patent agreement between General Electric and Westinghouse in 1896 were not primarily intended to resolve patent conflicts in incandescent lighting. Lamp patents were, in fact, specifically excluded from the 1896 agreement. Even the part played by patents in the 1896–1897 lamp manufacturers' agreement is uncertain. General Electric could not use its own strong patent position to induce or force other firms into the agreement because of the objections of the licensee companies. The Westinghouse patents seemed to serve as the façade or framework of an agreement not based on patents at all. And additional firms were probably kept from entering the industry by the low level of prices maintained and not by patent control of the lamp or the process of lamp manufacture.

ALTERNATING CURRENT VS. DIRECT CURRENT

Westinghouse designed, produced, and marketed an alternating-current incandescent-lighting system because he believed that alternating current permitted a more economical distribution of electric energy than the direct-current method, which had originated with Edison and had become standard for all systems of incandescent lighting. This substitution of alternating for direct current was the only important dissimilarity between the Westinghouse and Edison systems. Westinghouse employed a lamp no different in essentials from Edison's, a generator which was basically the same except that it had no commutator, and the parallel-distribution network. Prior to the introduction of the Westinghouse system, the competition which Edison had encountered was from systems as nearly like his own as patents allowed or which used direct current in less effective ways. The United States company was the chief competitor of the first kind, and it did not succeed in preventing a practical monopoly by Edison. The Heisler series system, the Bernstein series system, and the Brush battery system represented competition of the second kind and were even less of a threat than the United States company. Unlike these ineffective competitors, the Westinghouse company with its a.c. system offered a threat to the Edison system which could not be ignored.

The reason for this threat was that the Edison d.c. distribution system required a heavy copper investment. This investment was so large that it severely limited the area that one generating station could serve and made it necessary that consumer density in that area be relatively high. The cost of electric lighting was consequently kept high by the cost of the copper needed, the small size of the generating unit, and the location of that unit in the area of consumption. Placing the generating station in the light-using area meant that real-estate costs were high and that transfer costs of fuel and water were also likely to be high. The alternating-current system permitted a substantial lowering of all these costs. An a.c. station could be large, permitting generation economies, and it could be located near facilities for water and fuel transportation in a low-rent area. Furthermore, copper costs were reduced sufficiently so that areas of low consumer density could be profitably served.

There were other factors which added to the economic advantages of alternating current. The commutator of a d.c. generator was always its weakest feature from a technical standpoint. It was likely to give trouble, it had to be repaired frequently, and it severely limited the current and voltage capacity of the generator. Because of the small size of generating units when alternating current first came into use, the commutation advantage was not then of great moment, but its importance increased year by year. Similarly, the greater flexibility of the alternating-current system in producing different voltages for a large number of uses with little extra expense became more important as the utilization of electric energy in transportation and manufacturing increased.

The economic advantages of alternating current were thus those which would become more and more significant as electric-energy consumption increased, as its distribution area widened, and as the number of ways to use it multiplied. Barring the invention of cheap and effective d.c. voltage converters and noncommutating d.c. generators, the inherent advantages of alternating current in the generation and distribution of electric energy would eventually force direct current to give way before it. But the a.c. system of 1886 was not a perfected one. It had several defects which allowed direct current to hold its position of dominance for a number of years. The first Westinghouse a.c. generators were less than 75 per cent efficient in contrast to the 90 per cent efficiency of d.c. generators. Furthermore, it was not possible until the 1890's to operate a.c. generators in parallel, although d.c. generators were so operated by Edison as early as 1882. Parallel operation of generators in a central station permits two or more to supply a single network of conductors and allows flexibility in use that leads to economies in operation and repair. Other disadvantages of alternating current were the difficult insulation problems arising out of the alternating action and the lack of either a meter or a motor. All of these defects turned out to be temporary or of minor importance and were largely eliminated within a decade. It was Westinghouse who saw that they were temporary and minor. His courage to act on that insight lay back of his decision to promote alternating current.

The advantage of alternating current which was most important in the early years was the saving in distribution costs in areas of low consumer density. The economies in the generation of electricity in large plants located near fuel, transport facilities, and water, and in using large generators without commutators were significant only much later. The main disadvantage of alternating current in the first years was the lack of a meter. Motors were not yet in common use, and parallel operation of generators was important only in the central stations in the large cities. The greatest net advantage of alternating over direct current was, therefore, in the smaller cities and towns, where consumer density was low, where the central station would be small enough to preclude the large-scale economies of d.c. operation, where the contract system would be workable because 24-hour service would not be required, and where the motor load would be negligible.

The foregoing deductive reasoning is confirmed by evidence. It will be recalled that the 1887 patent-license agreement between Westinghouse and Thomson-Houston set penalty royalty rates for transformers sold by Thomson-Houston in cities of less than 10,000 population. It seems likely that Westinghouse desired to reserve the smaller cities for its own system in view of the attractiveness of that segment of the market.

The Edison company attempted to meet the competition of alternating current by showing that the Westinghouse system was inefficient, unreliable, and incomplete. The 1887 annual report of the Edison company included a short discussion in which it was pointed out that alternating current is undesirable because of the dangerously high voltage, the inefficiency of the transformers, the heavy lamp breakage, and the inability of the generators to operate in parallel. In a publication issued the following year, it was argued that the cost of the transformers offset any savings of copper which the high transmission voltage permitted. Data were given to prove that an Edison plant of 8,400 lamps installed in Minneapolis was cheaper than an a.c. plant of the same size.[38] At a meeting of the Association of Edison Illuminating Companies held in Chicago in February 1888, the superintendent of the New Orleans Edison central station presented a report on the Westinghouse system. He said that the a.c. system was undesirable because it was not safe or reliable, could not run twelve 16-candle-power lamps per horsepower, could not operate the lamps evenly or make them last a reasonable length of time, could not supply motors, and could not sell by meter. "Let them load up and break down as they did in New Orleans," he said, referring to Westinghouse central stations.[39]

A fully documented report, allegedly proving the inefficiency of the

Westinghouse system, appeared several years later. In April 1889, Harold P. Brown, a consulting electrical engineer with an office in New York City, wrote to Westinghouse asking that a 650-light plant be sent to Johns Hopkins University for an efficiency test. Brown was supposedly seeking to determine whether the claims appearing in the Westinghouse advertisements were correct. He was challenging the following statement: "This Company will guarantee from its apparatus and lamps 50 per cent more light from a given expenditure of power (fuel) than can be obtained from any direct current system."[40]

Brown received no answer from the Westinghouse company, but, in August 1889, Westinghouse gave a lighting plant to the Electrical Testing Bureau of Johns Hopkins for test. The report of this bureau, made public on January 24, 1890, stated that the full-load efficiency of the Westinghouse plant was between 73 and 74 per cent. This efficiency was lower than that of the Edison plant and certainly did not meet the advertised claim. The Johns Hopkins report, along with interpretation and comments by Brown, was published in 1890.[41] It is probable that the Edison company sponsored Brown in this project.

These efforts by the Edison company to prove the technical inferiority of alternating-current lighting systems did not succeed in preventing the growth of a.c. lighting. By 1892, Westinghouse and Thomson-Houston each had over five hundred a.c. central stations in operation. Further evidence of the success of alternating current can be found in the meetings of the Association of Edison Illuminating Companies. In the August 1888 meeting, an Edison company salesman spoke of the competition he was receiving from agents selling a.c. apparatus. He called attention to the demand for long-distance lighting methods in villages and towns and urged the Edison company to manufacture an a.c. system to meet that demand.[42] At the meeting a year later, the following resolution was passed: "Resolved, that the Association respectfully call to the attention of the Edison General Electric Company the difficulties under which the local companies are now laboring in consequence of the lack of . . . a flexible method of enlarging the territory which can be profitably covered from their stations for domestic lighting by higher pressures and consequently less outlay of copper than that involved by the three-wire method."[43]

The Edison central stations were discreet enough not to use the words "alternating current" in their resolution. Nevertheless, a request for a high-voltage system was a tantamount to a request for alternating current, because Edison had no high-voltage d.c. system to offer.

When it became evident that in market competition with a.c. lighting the Edison system was losing its dominant position, the Edison company decided to compete outside the area traditionally identified with commercial rivalry. In that area, the basis of competition is economy in the use of scarce resources as measured by the price system. Outside that area, competition can be based on any of a number of criteria, such as human welfare, national defense, public health, or public safety. These criteria all have one thing in common. The degree to which a particular product satisfies one of them cannot be precisely and accurately measured. There is thus considerable room for speculation and conjecture, which are likely to work to the disadvantage of a new and untried product. The Edison company hoped to capitalize on this disadvantage of alternating current.

As the foundation stone of its extra-market competition with alternating current, the Edison company chose public safety. The Edison viewpoint was that alternating current endangered the lives of all members of a community where it was present. Since resources are employed to satisfy the wants of the people, a method of producing light which is more economical than another method may not be more desirable if the total effect on human welfare is taken into account. The danger to the people which the use of alternating current involved could conceivably more than offset the utility of the extra light it made possible. The strategy of the Edison company was to educate public opinion to the view that alternating current was an intolerable menace to the American people, foisted upon it by a selfish and profit-seeking corporation. With public opinion so formed, laws could be passed which would either prohibit alternating current entirely or regulate it in such a way that its main economic advantage would be removed.

The publicity campaign against alternating current was opened by the publication of a booklet already cited. This pamphlet, entitled *A Warning* and bound in red, appeared in February 1888. It contained many pages which recounted the dangers of alternating current. The appendix listed the names of individuals allegedly killed by it. The next step in the campaign was a series of experiments on the lethal qualities of alternating current. Brown conducted these experiments in July 1888 at the Columbia School of Mines, New York City. His results and his comments were widely quoted by the press. In part, Brown said: "Alternating currents are not safe, and there is no safety device for this system yet provided. These alternating currents are, therefore, a horrible menace to life. What company has ever spent money for the safety of the public until forced to do so?" [44]

Brown also carried on experiments in the Edison laboratory in New Jersey. His professed purpose was to compare the lethal characteristics of alternating and direct current. He claimed to have discovered that 1420 volts d.c. were required to kill a dog, while, with a.c., 160 volts at a frequency of 288 cycles per second were sufficient.[45] Brown later wrote that his experiments in the Edison laboratory proved that "the alternating current would produce instant and painless death at very low pressure."[46]

Brown's experiments and attendant publicity had two objectives. One was to create the general impression that alternating current was much more deadly than direct current. The other was to convince the New York state legislature that electrocution should be the method of capital punishment. The latter was attained in the fall of 1888, when the legislature amended the Code of Criminal Procedure to read: "The punishment of death must in every case be inflicted by causing to pass through the body of the convict a current of electricity of sufficient intensity to cause death, and the application of such current must be continued until such convict be dead."[47]

The New York state authorities requested Brown to select and purchase for them the electrical equipment needed for electrocution. In May 1889, Brown purchased three Westinghouse alternators, one for each of three state prisons. The choice of Westinghouse equipment meant that the voltage used for the electric chair was the same as that in the Westinghouse lighting systems. The identification of the Westinghouse system with death was thus complete and officially sanctioned by the New York state government. Appeals and other legal proceedings delayed the execution of the first criminal by electricity until August 6, 1890. This legal controversy received extensive publicity, and the public was continually reminded of the deadly qualities of alternating current.

The adoption of alternating current for electrocution in New York was an important victory for the Edison company. The ultimate purpose of creating a public opinion unfavorable to alternating current was the enactment of legislation restricting its use. To this end, the attacks continued. In January 1889, Brown challenged Westinghouse to a competition in which Brown would send direct current through his body and Westinghouse alternating current through his. The voltages would be raised by steps until either one offered to quit.[48] This challenge was ignored by Westinghouse. In July 1889, Brown sent a letter to several New York papers in which he condemned the Westinghouse company for promoting alternating current. He listed ten victims of alternating current by name and spoke of there being many others.[49] Brown had additional letters of this nature published from time to time, and finally the Westinghouse company decided to take action. Westinghouse sales agents were instructed to determine whether Brown's allegations were correct. The summary of the agents' findings showed that of the thirty deaths attributed by Brown to alternating current, only one was possibly so caused. One was uncertain (probably drowned). In twelve deaths, there were no Westinghouse plants in the city at the time of the accident; and in sixteen cases, a d.c. system (arc lighting) was the cause of death, or no death occurred. This information was sent to all Westinghouse sales agents.[50]

Brown continued his attack on alternating current in the fall of 1889. In October, he circulated a letter containing his views and stressing the impossibility of satisfactory insulation for a.c. conductors because of the rapid alternations which he claimed broke down the insulation. An article by Brown covering the same material appeared in the November issue of the *North American Review*.[51]

In that same issue, Edison also had an article on alternating current. He emphasized the dangers of any high voltage—a.c. as well as d.c.—and so demonstrated an engineering integrity not shown by Brown. Edison expressed the opinion that all high voltages were dangerous to life and property because there was no way to insulate them adequately. Although Edison said that his "personal desire would be to prohibit entirely the use of alternating currents," his practical recommendation was milder.[52] He wanted legislation passed which would limit voltages to safe values, namely, 600 or 700 volts. The legislation recommended by Edison and toward which the entire campaign against alternating current was directed came before several state legislatures but never was enacted into law in any state. Edison appeared before a committee of the Senate of the State of Virginia in the fall of 1889, testified on the dangers of alternating current, and gave his support to a bill which proposed to limit voltages. A similar bill was before the Ohio legislature about this same time.[53]

As already mentioned, the Westinghouse company at first disregarded the attacks by Brown and the Edison company. There was no scientific evidence that alternating was more dangerous than direct current, and d.c. voltages as high as 3000 volts had been common in city streets after 1880. The years that had elapsed since then had proved that the arc-lighting companies could use these high voltages without jeopardizing the public safety. The Edison company had been in existence from the beginning of arc lighting, but it had never felt compelled to point out the perils of high voltages until the Westinghouse system began to be a serious competitor. The belatedness of the Edison warnings on high voltages was paralleled by considerable inaccuracy in regard to alternating current. The Westinghouse system used at most 2000 volts, this voltage was confined to the streets, and in homes and offices the Westinghouse voltage was only 50 volts, or less than half the Edison voltage.

By the summer of 1888, Westinghouse began to realize that the Edison publicity was convincing to a public which knew little about electricity.

The red-covered *Warning* and other Edison material directed against alternating current and the Westinghouse company aroused the anger of Westinghouse to the point where he contemplated legal action against the Edison company. He wrote in July 1888: "It is a matter worthy of very serious consideration as to whether or not we could not proceed against the directors of the Edison Company, Johnson and others, for conspiracy under the laws of New York; for their recklessness, and you might say, criminal course, should in some manner be brought to an end." [54]

No legal action was initiated, however, and the first steps to meet the attack on alternating current were not taken until the following summer. At that time the evidence was gathered to refute Brown's charges of a.c. deaths. A second move was to publish, in the fall of 1889, a booklet on the safety of alternating current.[55] A number of reasons were given to explain why it is safer than direct current. Alternating currents will not decompose body liquids by electrolysis as do direct currents. The fire risk is less for the reason that an a.c. arc, formed by the opening of a switch or otherwise breaking the circuit, is less than a d.c. arc, because the reversal of the current tends to interrupt the arc. The booklet also emphasized that the high a.c. transmission voltage cannot come into contact with the consumer.

Further statement of the case for alternating current was made by Mr. Westinghouse himself. In the December 1889 issue of the *North American Review*, he wrote a reply to Edison's article.[56] Following the line of argument presented in the October booklet, Westinghouse tried to show that alternating is safer than direct current. He concluded his article with legislative recommendations. These recommendations are interesting because they show how easy it is to phrase legislation, supposedly designed to protect the public, in such a way that the product of your competitor is outlawed. Westinghouse proposed that the voltage in buildings should not be allowed to exceed 100 volts. It will be recalled that Westinghouse was using 50 volts and Edison 110 volts. Westinghouse also proposed that no underground system be placed in direct connection with wires in buildings. The use of a transformer for each consumer (or group of consumers) in the a.c. system meant that there was no direct connection — in the sense of a continuous copper path — between consumers and the transmission network. In an article which appeared several months later, Westinghouse again emphasized the safety of alternating current and the dangers of direct current.[57]

The opposition of the Edison company to alternating current is more complex than it appears to be at first sight. It is true that the Edison company had been successful in marketing its lighting system and that it had a vested interest in the d.c. system of distribution. It had important patents on the d.c. system, and its licensee companies had large investments in it. The Edison company's fight against alternating current can therefore be interpreted as a defense of business property similar to the assault on electric lighting carried on by the gas companies in the early 1880's or the campaign against home permanents initiated by beauty salons in the 1940's. But there were two other courses of action open to the Edison company. Edison agents in Europe called the attention of company officials to the Zipernowsky-Beri-Blathy alternating-current system in 1886. That system was being manufactured by Ganz and Company, of Budapest, and was in successful operation in a number of European cities. The patents on the system covered the use of transformers in parallel, the method initiated by Westinghouse in the fall of 1885. The Edison company purchased the American rights to these Hungarian patents in November 1886 and secured an option to buy the American patents when they should be granted. These patent rights and options gave the Edison company the opportunity to take up alternating current with patent protection so strong that Westinghouse, depending on the Gaulard and Gibbs series patent, might have been forced out completely. If the Edison company had recognized that alternating is superior to direct current, it could have manufactured both systems while gradually displacing the d.c. with a.c. installations.

The president of the Edison company, E. H. Johnson, requested Frank Sprague, a very able electrical engineer who later became famous for his work in electric traction, to prepare a private report on alternating current in 1886.[58] In his report, Sprague strongly urged the Edison company to take up alternating current because of its economy for long-distance transmission. This recommendation was ignored, however, and the option on the Hungarian a.c. patents was allowed to lapse.

Even if the Edison interests were unwilling to develop a complete a.c. system, they could have followed Sprague's advice and tried to use alternating current for transmission, if not for generation or local distribution. The objective would have been to secure some cheap and efficient method to convert direct to alternating current after generation and back to direct before local distribution. In this manner, the experience of the Edison company in the production of efficient and reliable d.c. generators could be used and the investment of the licensee companies in local distribution systems would not be jeopardized. The rotary converter developed by Westinghouse in the early 1890's was a device which would have met this problem. But the Edison company had no a.c.-d.c. converter, and no evidence survives which indicates that an effort was made to develop one.

If the Edison company had chosen to produce a.c. lighting systems, it could have done so with less difficulty than the Westinghouse company, which had to build up a production and marketing organization and which had to avoid Edison and other patents on the various system components. Just why the Edison company preferred not to enter the a.c. field is not easy to understand. The explanation is probably similar to that which reveals why the gas companies at first refused to enter electric lighting, either arc or incandescent, and why the ball-point pen was first produced by a firm outside the regular fountain-pen industry. The firms in an established industry are often unable to see value in a new product which fulfills the same want as their own product. The gas companies could not believe that electric lighting would ever have any significance at all. Similarly, the Edison company could not believe that alternating current was more desirable than the direct current which had served so well in its lighting system.

The attitude of Edison himself was important to the policy adopted by the Edison company. In 1886 and 1887, Edison still played an influential role in the various Edison enterprises. An early associate of his stated that Edison thought of alternating current as something so abnormal as to be impossible of practical use. Edison is supposed to have said, "How can they reverse the direction of the current?" [59] He was unalterably opposed to alternating current and was convinced that the Westinghouse system was so inefficient that it never could be a permanent competitor in large cities against his system.[60] He would not permit the Edison company to introduce an a.c. system, and he threatened to leave the company if it were adopted. His stand on alternating current was given in the article he wrote for the *North American Review*. "The electric-lighting company with which I am connected purchased some time ago the patents for a complete alternating system and my protest against this action can be found upon its minute-book. Up to the present time I have succeeded in inducing them not to offer this system to the public nor will they do so with my consent." [61]

In that article, Edison revealed, in part at least, why he opposed alternating current. He stated that his system of electric lighting was perfectly harmless and perfectly successful and that he could "therefore see no justification for the introduction of a system which has no element of permanency and every element of danger to life and property." [62] Edison recognized that the main reason for the high-voltage a.c. circuits was to reduce investment in copper conductors and real estate, but he rejected this as insufficient. That Edison, a man whose entire inventive effort in developing an electric-lighting system had been directed toward economizing the copper and other resources required, should come to regard a further step in the direction of economy as unnecessary is peculiar indeed. Edison's opposition to alternating current was seemingly based on a failure to understand it and its significance in reducing lighting costs and on a desire to maintain the system which he had spent years of intensive work in perfecting.

Edison's antagonism to alternating current and the Westinghouse system of lighting grew to encompass Westinghouse himself. The bitter feeling of Westinghouse toward the Edison interests, suggested in the letter quoted above, was matched by Edison's bitterness toward Westinghouse. Edison revealed his feeling early in 1889 when E. D. Adams, a partner in the New York investment-banking firm of Winslow, Lanier, and Company, and a close friend of Westinghouse, invited Edison to accompany him to Pittsburgh to visit Westinghouse. Edison refused the invitation and explained his refusal in a brief but pungent communication: "Am very well aware of his resources and plant, and his methods of doing business lately are such that the man has gone crazy over sudden accession of wealth or something unknown to me and is flying a kite that will land him in the mud sooner or later."[63]

The attitude of the Edison company toward alternating current, apart from the views of Edison himself, was disclosed before a meeting of the Association of Edison Illuminating Companies by E. H. Johnson, president of the Edison Electric Light Company. When asked why the Edison company did not produce an a.c. system, Johnson replied that several years' experience had shown that the a.c. system was dangerous and inefficient and would tend to destroy the reputation of the Edison company, which was due to the safety and economy of its d.c. system. He mentioned that the German firm, Siemens and Halske, had decided that the a.c. system was not practical commercially, and he suggested that if a 500-volt three-wire system were used, the cost of apparatus per lamp would be less than in the Westinghouse a.c. system.[64]

In 1879, Edison was a bold and courageous innovator. In 1889, he was a cautious and conservative defender of the *status quo*. This marked change in his position within a decade is an excellent example of the pattern of economic change. In 1879, Edison envisioned a new system of illumination which was to be superior to gas, the best system then known. Scientists said that his ideas were unsound and impractical, and they accused him of following an *ignis fatuus*. The gas companies were not willing to admit that their system of illumination, which was satisfactory and well liked, would be superseded. Similarly, in 1885, Westinghouse envisioned a new system of electrical distribution which was to be much more efficient and flexible than the best system then known. Now it was Edison who said that the idea was impracticable and who refused to admit that his system would be superseded. The 1888 Edison booklet stated that high-voltage alternating current was not destined to assume any permanent position and then went on to speak of it as an *ignis fatuus*, the very phrase used by Edison's opponents ten years before. George Westinghouse was characterized as "the inventor of the vaunted system of distribution which is today recognized by every thoroughly-read electrician as only an *ignis fatuus*, in following which the Pittsburgh company have sunk at every step deeper into the quagmire of disappointment."[65]

The fight against alternating current was against Westinghouse, and the fight for alternating current was by Westinghouse. The Thomson-Houston company took no part in it. Coffin's deliberate policy was to stay out of the controversy and to concentrate on producing and selling as much electrical equipment as possible. The contrast between the pioneer innovator, Westinghouse, and the imitative innovator, Thomson-Houston, is sharp. Thomson-Houston waited before entering the field. When it entered, it avoided patent litigation by taking a license from Westinghouse, and it kept completely out of the a.c.-d.c. controversy.

The outcome of this controversy was a victory for Westinghouse and yet not a defeat for Edison. The Westinghouse company grew and prospered in the business of making and selling a.c. equipment. Eventually, over 95 per cent of the electric energy generated annually in the United States was alternating current. This did not seriously embarrass either the Edison company or the Edison central stations, however. The Edison company consolidated with Thomson-Houston in the formation of General Electric and lost its identity as an opponent of alternating current. The Edison central stations adopted alternating current for generation and transmission and obtained direct current for their local distribution networks by means of rotary-converter substations. They could thus preserve their heavy investments in the d.c. distribution systems and, at the same time, secure the generation and transmission economies of alternating current.

XI

Entrepreneurship

THE FIRST PIONEER INNOVATOR

EDISON was a pioneer innovator whose contribution to economic development has been exceeded by very few persons. His work in mimeographs, telegraphy, stock tickers, phonographs, electrical equipment, telephones, storage batteries, and motion pictures — to mention only the more important fields in which he was an innovator — has been of enormous value to the world. With regard to his activities in the electrical industry, the most significant single statement that can be made is that, whatever his motivation, he set out to invent an electric-lighting system which would be commercially successful. He wanted to produce light with the smallest possible amount of resources. He realized that the meaningful test of inventive activities is economic. Can the product be made and sold at a price which will cover the cost of production? Unless his electric-lighting system passed that test, any claim that he benefited mankind would be open to question. The real meaning of the profit calculus in a market economy with consumers exercising freedom of choice can hardly be overemphasized. The word "profit" has been so frequently associated with income-distribution problems that the logic of profits has received very little attention. *Because* Edison's work was profit-oriented, not in spite of it, he fostered economic development, increased the national income, and raised the standard of living of the mass of the people. If he had refused to submit to the dictates of the profit calculus and market discipline and had acted instead in accord with some pattern of his own choosing, his contribution to human welfare would have been much smaller and perhaps nonexistent. If Edison had been motivated by broadly humanitarian ideals — and possibly he was — he could hardly have acted more effectively than he did.

How the pattern of Edison's activities in electric lighting was influenced by profit considerations can be briefly outlined. He chose electric lighting over other possible areas such as the telegraph, the telephone, and the phonograph because he felt that there were bigger rewards in lighting. In the electrical field, he was not interested in arc lighting or electric power. He believed that their profitability could not approach that of incandescent electric lighting. And in regard to the latter, he decided that he would have to set the price for light equivalent to the price of gas light. With the price thus fixed, the path to greatest profits was to reduce costs as much as possible. To lower costs, he made a series of inventions which were designed to economize the materials used in his incandescent-lighting system.

The economic orientation of Edison's inventive work in electric lighting defined his approach to the problem of subdividing the electric light. His goal was to invent a system which could produce light at the lowest possible cost. And his inventions were inventions primarily because he was looking for a low-cost lighting system. The Edison lamp differed from those that preceded it in the high resistance of its filament. Edison was the first inventor to realize that an incandescent lamp which could operate in a constant-voltage parallel circuit would necessarily have to be of high resistance in order to keep the cost of the copper conductors from being prohibitive. The high lamp resistance permitted a voltage high enough to reduce the copper cost to a reasonable level.

Edison's work in dynamo development was also directed toward reducing costs. His dynamo differed from those that preceded it in its high efficiency. He reduced the energy lost as heat in the dynamo by making the armature resistance as small as possible, by maintaining good contact between the pieces of iron in the magnetic circuit, and by using a very narrow gap between the armature and the pole pieces. Edison also attacked the waste of energy in transmission from the prime mover to the dynamo. His principal contribution here was to substitute a direct mechanical connection for the usual belt-pulley method.

The parallel between Edison's work on the dynamo and on the incandescent light is apparent. In each case, he perceived the function of the component in the system. He then determined the characteristic of that component which would result in a system with the lowest production cost of light. The next step was to apply the electrical principles and to conduct numerous experiments until the desired end was reached.

The transmission network which connected the dynamo and the lamps was a third main component of the Edison lighting system. As in the lamp and the dynamo, Edison's contribution was to invent a cost-reducing component. In his preliminary work on the lighting system, he had thought that an ordinary parallel network, like that shown in Diagram 3, would suffice. In this network, the lamps are of uneven illumination because the voltage is less on the lamps which are farther from the dynamo. One solution would be to construct lamps for operation on different voltages. The impossibility of controlling lamp voltages in manufacture and the complications which would arise in use of lamps of different voltages on a single circuit necessitated a change in the network. The object was to provide a uniform voltage for the lamps whether they were near or far from the dynamo; and the method was to use conductors of large cross-section near the dynamo, tapering off as the distance from the dynamo increased. The large conductors prevented any appreciable voltage drop. The main drawback to this system was that a very large copper investment was required. When Upton had calculated that the amount of copper needed would cost about $25 per lamp, Edison realized that some means had to be found to reduce the copper cost. He finally evolved the feeder-main network which is shown in Diagram 3. The essence of this network was that the voltage drop took place in a feeder conductor. The main conductor could be operated at a nearly constant voltage. The amount of copper in the feeder could be determined with reference to minimizing the total of copper cost and energy loss and did not have to meet the problem of voltage variation at the individual lamps.[1] The feeder system cut copper costs by about 85 per cent. Calculations made at an infringement trial involving the feeder patent showed that it reduced copper investment for an area of nine city blocks containing 8,640 lamps from $200,000 to $30,000 (with copper at $0.25 per pound).[2]

The Pearl Street station in New York City used the two-wire feeder network, but Edison sought to lessen the cost of copper still further. Early in 1883, he invented the three-wire system, shown in Diagram 3. This reduced the copper to approximately what would be required if the potential difference across each light were increased from 110 volts to 220 volts. The outside conductors could consequently be cut to one-fourth their previous size. Because the use of the third, balancing wire added some copper, the net saving over the two-wire system was not 75 per cent but only 63 per cent. The main advantage of the three-wire principle, like the feeder-main principle, was that it saved copper without raising the voltage on the individual lamps. The two inventions together reduced the copper cost per lamp from the original $25 to less than $1.50.

The fourth main component of the Edison lighting system — the meter — was also a cost-reducing invention, but not in the same sense

Diagram 3
THE DYNAMO-LAMP NETWORK

ORDINARY PARALLEL NETWORK

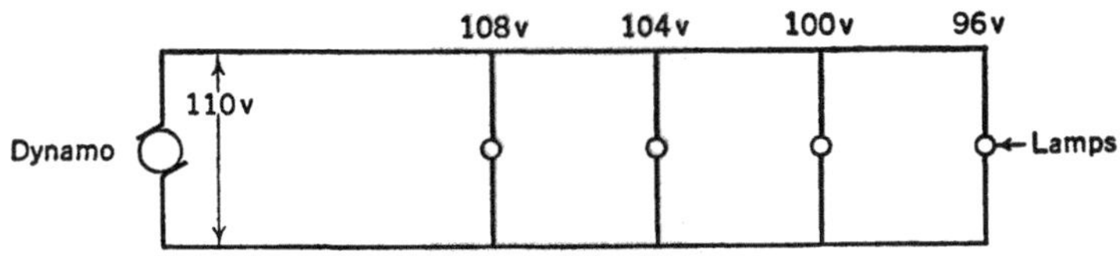

Lamps are of uneven illumination. Voltage is less on lamps farther from the dynamo.

EDISON'S FEEDER-MAIN NETWORK

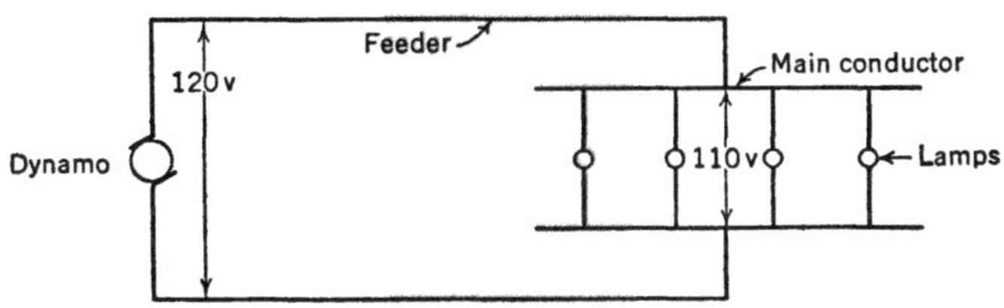

Most of the voltage drop occurs in feeder conductor. Main conductors operate at a nearly constant voltage.

EDISON'S THREE-WIRE FEEDER-MAIN NETWORK

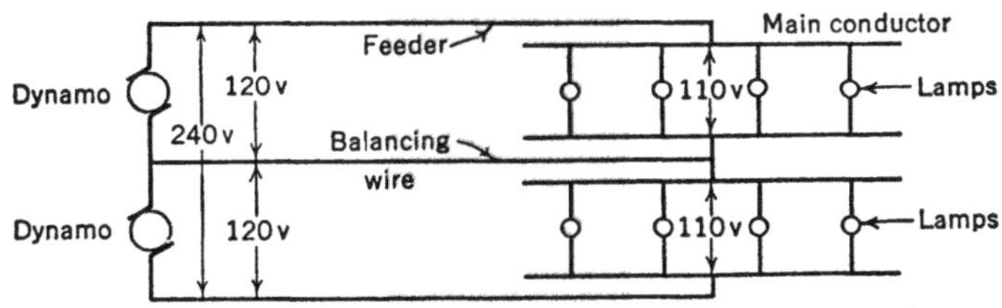

Voltage effectively doubled without increasing voltage at the lamps.

that the other three were. The lamp, the dynamo, and the distribution network were designed to form a lighting system which would, for a given amount of light, use the smallest amount of resources. The meter was designed to inform the light company and the consumer how much light the consumer was using. The light company could thereby charge the consumer in accordance with the cost of producing the light he used. The consumer was encouraged to use light only for those purposes which he felt justified the expenditure. He was given an incentive to economize in the use of light just as he would in the usual economic good. The result was that the same number of customers could be served with lower operating expenses and a smaller investment in generating and transmission equipment than if meters were not used. The cost of light per consumer was therefore less, and, at the same time, the consumers were using light only where its utility to them was great enough to justify its cost. The meter, in short, economized not by reducing the amount of resources needed to produce a given quantity of light—that is, by reducing "waste" in production—but by reducing the amount of light consumed—that is, by reducing "waste" in consumption. If a product is treated by consumers as though it were a free good, the total production costs can conceivably be so high that it is impossible to cover them. Consumption waste can stand in the way of commercial success just as production waste can. Edison's meter was similar to the other three components. It economized the scarce resources of society.

The significance of Edison's work in electric lighting should by now be apparent. It was not his contributions to science, although he understood scientific laws better than many scientists of his day. It was not his inventive work, although he is probably one of the most ingenious, thorough, and painstaking inventors the world has ever known. It was not his engineering work, although he excelled in the design and construction of simple, reliable, and practical lighting systems. Edison's significance is the economic value of his scientific, inventive, and engineering activities. Everything he did was directed by the realization that, in a free economic society, the market test is the sole test of achievement. If the result of a man's work can command the purchasing power of the consumers in a free market, that work is worth doing.

The following statement by Edison summarizes the point of view that is mainly responsible for his achievements:

Clarke, Doctor ——— is a fine fellow. He knows a lot but he doesn't stick to the job. I set him at work developing details of a plan. But when he happens to note some phenomenon new to him, though easily seen to be of no importance in this apparatus, he gets sidetracked, follows it up and loses time. *We can't be spending time that way!* We have got to keep working up things of commercial value — that is what this laboratory is for. We can't be like the old German professor who as long as he can get his black bread and beer is content to spend his whole life studying the fuzz on a bee! [3]

While Edison's success in the development of a lighting system was ultimately due to his orientation toward a low-cost system, the channeling of his efforts in the direction of that goal was provided by his search for an electrical analogue to the gas-lighting system. As has already been mentioned, he refused to follow either the technical or commercial precedents set by arc lighting, the only other electric lighting then known. The widespread acceptance of his lighting system, which is standard today in the United States, is an indication of his wisdom and insight in choosing gas as his guide.

Edison was not simply following the general opinion of his day in searching for an electrical analogue of the gas system. Many inventors and electrical engineers doubted the wisdom of such a plan of action. A Boston inventor, Alexander Bernstein, questioned the gas-system analogy in a statement he made in 1886: "When the parallel system was first developed, the prevailing idea appears to have been to make electric lighting from central stations similar to gas lighting. But the conditions under which electrical energy in its active form is best transmitted are so different from those requisite for the transmission of the potential energy of gas that the desire to imitate the gas system has proved a disadvantage." [4]

The Edison policy of setting the price of electric light equal to the price of gas was criticized in 1885 before a meeting of the American Institute of Electrical Engineers by F. L. Pope, the electrical engineer and patent lawyer who worked with Westinghouse. Pope said: "I think that it is a cardinal mistake that has been made from the beginning in the electric light business, to endeavor to compete with gas in the matter of price when every well-informed electrician has been perfectly well aware from the beginning that in the present state of knowledge it was not possible to do it; and for that reason the attempts which have been made to furnish house to house lighting from central stations have not I think been a commercial success as far as my knowledge extends." [5]

In order to show the high degree of similarity between Edison's system and the gas-lighting system, a detailed comparison will now be made. The similarities between the two systems can be discussed from the technical and the commercial points of view. The technical features common to the two systems stem from Edison's understanding of electrical laws. He was able to make useful comparisons between electrical pressure and gas pressure and between resistance to the flow of electricity and resistance to the flow of gas.

Edison designed his electric light to emit 16 candle power, the same as the standard gas jet of the 1880's. He decided on a system of central supply, with mains (copper conductors) carrying the electricity to the lights in the houses. This is exactly how gas was distributed. The novelty of Edison's approach is emphasized by the opinion of Sir William Preece, the most prominent English electrician of that period, who wrote in 1882 that each house would have its own dynamo driven by a gas motor and that "it is in this direction that the practical illumination of houses will be carried out." [6] That Preece was wrong and Edison right can be attributed to Edison's perception of the gas-system analogy.

Edison decided to put his conductors underground like the gas mains instead of on poles like the telegraph, telephone, arc-light, and fire-alarm circuits of that day. He realized that the similarity between his conductors and the gas mains was far greater than any similarity between his conductors and the common electrical conductors. When questioned about putting his mains underground, Edison replied, "Why, you don't lift water pipes and gas pipes up on stilts." [7] It will be recalled that the decision to put the mains underground necessitated that the Edison Electric Illuminating Company be incorporated under the gas statutes of the State of New York, for only then could the company have the power to break up the streets. Designing and installing the underground mains was a difficult, expensive process, but the essential wisdom of this method is indicated by the fact that within ten years no overhead wires were permitted in New York City.

Gas was distributed under constant pressure, with each jet controlled independently of the others. Likewise, in Edison's system, the electric current was delivered at constant pressure (parallel system), and each light could be controlled independently. This was in sharp contrast to the arc-light systems, which were series systems, which had a different voltage between the terminals of each lamp, and in which the lights were all turned on and off together with no independent control.

The gas consumption of each user was measured by a meter located on his premises. Edison decided that his system also should have a meter. Here is another instance where the extent of the novelty of Edison's idea is hard to imagine. At that time, electricity was a mysterious force which could be measured only crudely and imperfectly in the laboratory. To suggest that this force could be measured in some simple, reliable, and inexpensive way seemed fantastic in the extreme. Yet such measurement was necessary if electric light were to become a commodity.

The gas meters had a dial mechanism whereby pointers indicated the cubic feet of gas consumed. Edison realized the advantages of such a direct-reading type of meter from the consumer's point of view. He tried to perfect an electric meter which was direct-reading and measured electricity used in *cubic feet* (like gas), but failed.[8] The meter he finally worked out fulfilled all the requirements except that it was not direct-reading. It was a chemical device and contained plates which were removed each month and taken to the central station, where they were weighed. The customer could learn nothing about his consumption of electricity from the meter and had to trust the company to be accurate and honest. For this reason, these chemical meters were never completely successful and eventually were replaced by direct-reading, mechanical meters.

The thinking of Edison in developing the technical features of his system is brought out very clearly when his reasons for rejecting the storage battery are examined. It was thought by some electricians that the most practical system of light distribution would involve storage batteries in each house to be charged during the daytime by the central-station dynamo, which could then supply current to other lights — say street lights — at night. This method had the following advantages: (1) while the battery would be discharged at a low voltage suitable for inside a home, it would be charged at a high voltage, thus reducing the energy lost in transmission from the central station; and (2) the central station could have a much steadier load and therefore lower cost per unit of electrical energy.

Edison was interviewed on January 28, 1883, by a newspaper reporter and made the following remarks on the storage battery: "In 1879 I took up that question and devised a system of placing storage batteries in houses connected to mains and charging them in the daytime, to be discharged in the evening and night to run incandescent lamps."[9] Edison went on to say that he found this system unworkable. The reporter next asked, "Then you consider storage batteries wholly impracticable? Is there no hope for their doing good, legitimate work?" Edison replied:

> None whatever. Except in a very limited number of cases, storage of gas could be made analogous to storage of electricity. One of the principal outlays of a gas company is for pipes. The average diameter of their mains is five or six inches. But under pressure greater than they now force the gas through their mains, an inch pipe would answer under the storage principle of having a small gasometer in every house. The difference saved to the company by this arrangement would be about $15 for pipes from house to house, 25 to 30 feet apart. But the gasometer would cost a great deal more in each house than the 25 feet of pipe buried in the street. Besides, gasometers might not be just the thing in the hands of the public; there might be explosions; some of them might

not have room. The gasometer would require some little mechanism to reduce the pressure down to a limit where it could be burnt. Now, these little mechanisms are uncertain.[10]

Edison's reasons for rejecting the battery method, apart from technical difficulties which might have arisen from batteries as such, were based, therefore, on his analysis of why the gas companies had never adopted the corresponding method in gas distribution. Considerations of safety, reliability, and convenience applied equally to the storage of gas and electricity. The reservoir of gas in each home would be a potential source of fire or explosion, just as the battery, especially its high-voltage side, would be a potential cause of fire or personal injury. The gasometers and the batteries were both costly and unreliable to the extent that any savings in cost of gas pipes or electric conductors would be more than offset. If there would be inconvenience to a household in having space occupied by the gas reservoir, there would also be inconvenience in having space occupied by the coffin-sized battery.

With the conception of the electrical analogue to the gas system in his mind, Edison and his associates worked for nearly four years designing the components of his system and perfecting the details. In essence this meant inventing a suitable dynamo; a system of underground mains; switches, sockets, and junction boxes; a fusing device; and, of course, the incandescent lamp itself. What Edison finally achieved was a system of light supply vastly superior to the gas system from a purely technical point of view. The light was of much better quality. It did not flicker or vitiate the atmosphere or give off a noticeable amount of heat. The system was much safer, too, in that there was no open flame, no danger of explosion or suffocation, and almost no chance of personal injury or fire. The Edison meter was extremely accurate and marked a great improvement over the gas meters, which were, at times, notoriously inaccurate.[11]

Commercially, the Edison system showed the same similarity to the gas system that it did technically. It will be remembered that the estimates of the demand for light in the area of New York City chosen for the first central station were based on the number of gas jets in use. And the price of the Edison electric light was set equal to the price of gas light. On the assumption that a 16-candle-power gas jet consumes 5 cubic feet per hour, the price of 16-candle-power hours of light when gas is $2.25 per thousand cubic feet (which was the price for small consumers in New York City in 1882) is 1.125 cents. The price of the light supplied by the Pearl Street station, with the station supplying both the light bulbs and the electric energy, was set at 1.2 cents per 16-candle-power hour.

Edison was aware that if his system were really effective, the gas companies might conceivably reduce the price of gas. In an 1882 interview, he explained that he had calculated that the cost of the gas which sold for $2.25 per thousand cubic feet was $0.90 — of which $0.45 was variable production cost and $0.45 overhead. Even if the price of gas were reduced to $1.00, Edison was confident that he could get one-half of the lighting business in the district by setting the price of electric light equivalent to gas at $1.50. With their volume cut in half, the gas companies would find their cost to be $1.28, and Edison did not consider them strong enough to sell below cost for very long.[12] By the time several years had elapsed, the Edison people became more confident and expressed the belief that the electric-light customer could be held at the existing price no matter what happened to the price of gas. They made the comparison with the success of the gas companies in retaining their customers in the face of lowered kerosene prices some years before.[13]

In the business methods adopted by the Edison Electric Illuminating Company of New York, every effort was made to simulate the practices and terminology of the gas companies. Monthly bills were rendered, and the Edison lights were often referred to as burners. The parent Edison company also based its marketing policies on gas-company experience. Edison did not expect to find a market for central-station lighting in communities too small or too poor to support a gas company. The division between cities chosen for licensee central stations and those for cash central stations was accordingly based on whether or not the city had a gas company. The Edison company thought it worth while to own stock only in stations located in cities where a gas company had been established. Here, as before, Edison hesitated to depart very markedly from the business practices of the gas companies.

Edison's success as the pioneer innovator in incandescent electric lighting was in a large part due to his ability to select from the gas system those elements which could serve his electric system. The gas system had evolved over more than half a century. In this period the gas companies had shown that central-station illumination was a business that could sell its product at a price that justified the use of resources for this purpose. Edison built on the foundations laid by the gas companies and, using a new process of illumination, made a major contribution to economic development.

His original conception of an electrical analogue to gas carried him to exceedingly sound judgments in the design of his electric-lighting system. How sound they were is proven by the test of time. The size of the area he chose to be served by one central station is still used, although now the immediate source of electric energy in each such district is a substation which contains transformers and, in the central areas of some large United States cities, rotary converters which change the alternating to direct current. His choice of voltage (110 volts) and the constant-pressure parallel system are standard throughout the United States. The bamboo filament of the Edison light has been replaced by a metallic filament, and the glass is commonly frosted now, but the physical size of the incandescent light, its electrical characteristics, its life, and other principal features are not radically different from the originals of 1882. Edison's decision to put the conductors underground and his work in the accessories of the system — the fuses, the switches, the underground mains, and the sockets — were also correct anticipations of the future.

The meter, it will be recalled, was satisfactory except that, unlike a gas meter, it was not direct-reading. Later inventions made possible a direct-reading mechanical meter which largely replaced the chemical meters by 1900. The one important respect in which Edison failed to imitate the gas industry turned out to be a source of consumer complaint which was not remedied until a direct-reading meter was developed.

Edison's objective was to develop a low-cost electric-lighting system for homes and offices. His guide in the pursuit of that objective was the gas-lighting system. This choice of objective and guide can be interpreted as resulting from Edison's emphasis on the development of a *successful* lighting system. He believed that he could find a market for home electric lighting if its cost were low and if it were not radically different from an accepted and successful form of illumination. Cost reduction and imitation of the gas system were not the only rules of thumb, however, that led Edison to success. Another rule he employed was that the risks of innovation should be reduced as much as possible. Much of the planning and careful preparation prior to the marketing of his lighting system were deliberately aimed at eliminating the possibility of failure.

The technical risks were minimized by the establishment of trial central stations. Two were installed at Menlo Park. The first was crude, but the second contained many items of equipment in the form in which they were later used in the Pearl Street station. These stations helped to uncover technical difficulties and permitted an economy test of the system. Only small dynamos were used in the Menlo Park stations, and the development of the large, direct-connected Jumbo dynamos necessitated another trial station. This station was located on Holborn Viaduct in London. It began operation in January 1882 with one Jumbo, and, by April, a second was added. The operation of this station provided a practical test of the entire Edison system under commercial conditions. The Jumbo dynamos and the chemical meters in particular were watched closely. It was learned that the Jumbo dynamos could be operated in parallel — a fact which was important to the design of the Pearl Street dynamo circuits and transmission network. Two English electrical engineers, J. A. Fleming and J. Hopkinson, made complete tests of the central-station plant and the entire system and reported the results to the Edison company in New York. Careful records were kept of coal and water consumption in order to determine generation costs. In 1886, after the station was no longer needed for testing purposes, it was dismantled.

The small-scale model of the distribution network served by the Pearl Street station also helped to reduce technical risks. At a time when the characteristics of electrical networks were not very well understood, the surest procedure was to construct the network on a miniature scale. Edison could then ascertain the voltages at various points in the network and decide on the size and arrangement of conductors. He was also able to determine the best location for the central station. The model thus helped to prevent errors which could have been very costly.

On the basis of the testing of individual components which had been done at Menlo Park and at the various Edison manufacturing plants, and on the basis of the system testing which had been done at Menlo Park, in London, and on the model, Edison constructed the Pearl Street station. Before the station was placed in operation, several months were spent in testing items of equipment and segments of the system. Current leakages were discovered and corrected. It was found that many fuses did not function properly. Other small troubles were located and remedied. The testing was completed by the end of August and finally, on September 4, 1882, regular operation of the station began. At first only one dynamo was used. Everything seemed to operate perfectly. Then a second dynamo was started. Immediately a hunting or oscillating of the two steam engines began and could not be stopped. The hunting forced a return to only one dynamo.

The testing which preceded the operation of the Pearl Street station did not prevent a very serious trouble from developing the first day. This trouble was not detected earlier because, in the testing of the Pearl Street station, only one dynamo was operated at a time. When two Jumbo dynamos had operated satisfactorily in the London station, it was assumed that they would also operate satisfactorily in the New York station. This assumption was wrong because the physical structures on which the dynamos were mounted in the two stations were not the same. In London, the dynamos, each connected directly to its own steam engine, were mounted on a solid foundation. In New York, the dynamos were mounted upon long iron beams. At the high speed of 350 revolutions per minute, the engines caused enough vibration in the beams to upset the operation of the engine governors. The iron structure had been carefully tested with a dead-weight load, but it had not been tested for vibration under a live load. Edison temporarily eliminated the difficulty by a complex mechanism which tied the governors of the steam engines together. The permanent remedy was to change to a make of steam engine with a centrifugal instead of a gravity governor.

Edison's careful testing procedures failed to prevent this serious mechanical difficulty, but they did eliminate electrical faults. In spite of this good record, the Pearl Street station cost over two times the original estimate. But it operated satisfactorily and continuously from 1882 until 1890, when a severe fire put it out of service for ten days.

Edison's methods of minimizing marketing risks have already been described. He first made a careful study of the gas companies and adopted business practices as much like theirs as possible. He then surveyed the gas customers in the Pearl Street district in order to have a basis for demand estimates. He wanted to assure himself of a market before establishing the central station.

A third risk that Edison faced was that someone else would begin the production of his system before he did. The obvious way to eliminate this risk was to patent the system and its components. Edison followed this procedure, but the patents were not very effective. Publicity on Edison's system was released long before he had completed the development work. Other inventors, following his lead, were given time to perfect systems of their own, and no efforts were made to prevent patent infringements for many years.

Patents are not the only method of averting manufacture of a product by rivals. If the design and production techniques can be kept secret, no other firm may know how to make the product. The effectiveness of secrecy was recognized by Edison, but only after important information had been secured by competitors. Visitors were freely welcomed at the Menlo Park laboratory during the first public demonstration on December 31, 1879. At that time, a number of persons were caught trying to steal lamps, but the significance of these attempts was not understood. In the weeks that followed, numerous visitors were shown through the laboratory. On several different occasions, minor employees gave visitors very complete explanations of what was being done. Edison finally realized that many visitors to Menlo Park were inventors who were trying to learn his methods. On February 19, 1880, he issued the following order to the Menlo Park employees:

> Employees will treat visitors courteously, but under no circumstances will they leave their work or give any information of any kind to visitors.
>
> No information will be furnished except by myself or Messrs. Batchelor, Upton, Kruesi and Carman.
>
> *You will regard this as a positive order.*
>
> Thomas A. Edison [14]

Edison's first backer, Lowrey, also took precautions to keep the Menlo Park employees from supplying information to competitors. He assigned a man to the laboratory staff whose prime function was to report on which men were loyal to Edison and which were not. When it was discovered that the Menlo Park glass blower, Ludwig Boehm, was in contact with Hiram Maxim, the chief engineer of the United States Electric Lighting Company, Boehm was dismissed. This action came too late, however. It will be recalled that Boehm entered Maxim's employ and supplied enough information to enable Maxim to construct a successful high-resistance lamp.

The secrecy policy applied to published material as well as to information transmitted verbally. The Edison company did not permit publication of Edison's scientific findings until after a considerable time had elapsed. Francis Jehl reported that while in Europe doing installation work for the Edison company, he wrote an article which appeared in a London journal in the fall of 1882.[15] He explained the principles on which Edison had constructed his generators. For publishing this article, Edison severely reprimanded Jehl in a letter which said: "Francis, I don't mind your airing your knowledge but it must not be at our expense. You must not tell them 'why' we do this or that in building our dynamos." [16] This reluctance to publish is further illustrated by the economy test of the Menlo Park central station made in January 1881. The purpose of this test was to secure a preliminary estimate of operating costs of the Edison system. Edison had intended to publish the report, but, at the insistence of Henry Villard, an Edison company director at that time, the report was not made public. Villard wanted to keep the information from possible business rivals.[17]

The innovational work of Edison in electric lighting can be more adequately judged if a comparison is made with his contemporary inventors who failed to innovate. The incandescent-light inventors, with the exception of Edison, either did not envision the place that electric lighting could occupy and therefore could not design a practical system or they lacked the technical ability to invent such a system. All but one of the unsuccessful inventors, as far as can be determined, fall into the former category. These inventors sought a durable lamp of low resistance. Such a lamp could not be part of a commercial system, because if the lamps were connected in parallel, the copper cost would be prohibitive. If they were connected in series, independent control would have been possible only with heavy expense and undue complication. Various of the inventors had one or more of Edison's ideas, but none had them all. Sawyer worked with parallel circuits, but insisted on low-resistance lamps. He believed that resistance was a characteristic to be avoided. Swan, an English inventor and the man whom the English people believe to have invented the incandescent electric light, did excellent work on incandescent materials, but the resistance of his lamps was low and he advocated the series system. Furthermore, he made no attempt to develop the other components needed in a complete lighting system. Maxim produced only low-resistance lamps until after Edison had announced his high-resistance unit. The only inventor who, like Edison, had the concept of a system using high-resistance lamps connected in parallel was an English inventor, Lane-Fox. But he was unable to make a workable high-resistance filament.[18]

Edison's innovational abilities were largely confined to the sphere of technical activity. In business administration and in marketing, he usually employed methods which were already in use. It has been shown that he closely imitated the gas companies in the business practices of his first commercial central station. The forming of that first illuminating company might be labeled an act of innovation, but it will be recalled that Brush promoted arc-lighting central stations as early as 1879. Likewise, Edison's formation of the first three-wire central stations, which were entirely owned by him, followed a precedent set several years earlier by Goff. Edison apparently believed that the marketing methods and the techniques of business organization and administration that had been developed by the gas industry and the arc-lighting industry were adequate for his purposes.

The fact that Edison did not innovate except in technology can also be attributed to the lack of any time for nontechnical innovation. Research, inventing, and manufacturing kept him fully occupied until about 1885. He was ultimately responsible for operation of the Menlo Park laboratory, the various manufacturing companies, and the Pearl Street station. There is little evidence that he succeeded in delegating much of the entrepreneurial function. He had well-trained assistants who were capable and trustworthy, but he alone had the full vision and complete technical understanding of his lighting system, and he had to give continual attention to the activities of his various enterprises. One exception may have been S. J. Bergmann, who operated the accessories-manufacturing plant very ably. He received the least direction from Edison, although the products made had to be capable of use with the Edison system. In the absence of assistants with the initiative and business acumen of Bergmann, Edison was almost solely responsible for the design, manufacture, sale, and installation of his lighting system. When he began to withdraw from his electrical activities, after 1885, the Edison companies suffered from the lack of an imaginative and decisive leader. The difficulty was not corrected until the consolidation with Thomson-Houston in 1892. Coffin then supplied the leadership that was needed.

THE SECOND PIONEER INNOVATOR

After the Edison system had been in operation for several years, it became apparent that the heavy copper investment required by the low-voltage distribution system severely limited the area that one central station could serve. The result was that the cost of electric lighting was high, and none but the upper-income classes could use it freely. Furthermore, electric lighting was restricted to areas of dense population. If a low-cost distribution system were available, the area served by one central station could be increased with resulting generation economies, and it would be economic to serve districts of low consumer density. Many inventors knew that a low-cost distribution system was needed and that high voltages would reduce copper costs substantially. But no one was able to devise a satisfactory high-voltage system. If it were a series system, it brought high voltage into the home and made independent control of lights difficult. If the battery were used as a voltage converter, the system was unreliable and inefficient. Westinghouse was among those who realized that the use of electric lighting was being retarded by high transmission costs. His experience with natural gas had taught him that the solution could be a system which used high voltage for transmission and converted it into low voltage at the point of use. When he heard of the Gaulard and Gibbs transformers, he realized that they might be the conversion device he was looking for. With an able group of engineers, he designed a complete alternating-current system. The main technical contributions of Westinghouse and his staff were the designing of an efficient, inexpensive, and reliable transformer, connecting these transformers in parallel, developing an efficient alternator, and inventing an alternating-current meter. Westinghouse left undisturbed the basic features of the Edison system — the parallel connection of lamps and the central-station method — and improved the major weakness, the high cost of distribution.

THE IMITATIVE ENTREPRENEURS

The principal imitative entrepreneurs in the manufacture of incandescent-lighting equipment before 1885 were Hiram Maxim and Edward Weston. They successively directed the technical activities of the United States Electric Lighting Company. Under Maxim, the company began production of incandescent-lighting plants for isolated use in 1880. Later, under Weston's guidance, the company entered the central-station field. It will be recalled that the United States company was never a very profitable concern. Its lack of success is at least partly attributable to the fact that neither Maxim nor Weston had as clear an idea of the economic place of incandescent lighting as Edison.

The principal imitative entrepreneur after 1885 was Elihu Thomson of the Thomson-Houston Electric Company. Thomson, it will be remembered, was also an imitative entrepreneur in arc-lighting equipment, to which he was attracted by Brush's success. In incandescent-lighting equipment, he was attracted first by the success of Edison and later by that of Westinghouse. Originally, Thomson did not believe that incandescent lighting would be practical. After Edison had proved the economic worth of his system, Thomson-Houston entered the field. Here, as in arc lighting, Thomson's emphasis was on reliable and efficient equipment. When alternating current was developed, Thomson again held back. He advised Coffin that it was too dangerous for commercial use. After Westinghouse had shown that the a.c. system was commercially practical, Thomson-Houston began the manufacture of an alternating-current system. The emphasis was again on the production of high-quality equipment. Patent disputes and the a.c.-d.c. controversy were avoided. The Thomson-Houston company thus proved itself to be very successful in adapting to market conditions. It refused to take up a line of production until some other firm had shown it to be profitable. After a market had been created, Thomson-Houston entered the field. Thomson was an outstanding electrical engineer, and he could usually design equipment superior to that already on the market. Coffin was an exceptionally able salesman and organizer. He provided the administrative and marketing talent that led to success.

PERSONAL QUALITIES OF THE ENTREPRENEUR

The similarity between the two pioneer innovators in incandescent lighting, Edison and Westinghouse, is striking. Both borrowed techniques from the gas industry. Both set out to develop an entire system, and both took a personal interest in the invention of the system components. The impetus behind the principal inventions in each system was to reduce costs. Edison found a parallel in the gas system, which served as his guide. Westinghouse found a parallel in the d.c. incandescent system, which served as his guide. Edison formed a number of firms to manufacture the components of his system. Westinghouse formed a firm to manufacture the components of his system. And both Edison and Westinghouse had become famous as inventors in other fields before turning to the problems of incandescent lighting.

The most important similarity between Edison and Westinghouse is the doggedness, the perseverance, and the faith in his own ideas that each possessed. Thomson and Coffin did not seem to have any of these qualities to the same degree. It is probable that a pioneer innovator must possess these qualities or he never could complete his work. Both Edison and Westinghouse ran into strong resistance when they attempted to carry out their plans.

The official biographers of Edison report that he never saw a statement in a scientific book without involuntarily challenging it and wishing to demonstrate that it was either right or wrong.[19] He was an independent thinker and took nothing on authority. The interesting aspect of such a person is that once he is convinced he is right, he cannot be shaken. This rule applies to cases where Edison, in fact, was right and where, in fact, he was wrong. In his work on lighting, he sought to subdivide the electric light, a goal which many scientists thought impossible. He designed a generator with as low an internal resistance as possible and was labeled by some engineers as incompetent. His plan of a central-station lighting system was believed by many to have no chance of success. In all these things, Edison was right. But in some other projects, he was completely wrong. His opposition to alternating current is a good example. He refused to admit its utility and would not relinquish his belief. Another belief he held was that electricity could be produced directly from coal, just as electricity is produced in a primary battery by the consumption of zinc. He hoped thus to eliminate the 70 per cent energy loss caused by the steam engine. He worked on this problem for many years. In 1884, he announced, "I have got far enough to know the thing is possible. I can get quite a current now directly from the combustion of fuel." [20] He thought that he could achieve his objective in five years. That Edison really considered electricity direct from coal as a probable development is proved by the fact that the patent-license contracts between Edison General Electric and the Edison licensees covered all equipment to be used for the generation of electricity except that which was produced directly from coal.[21] How much money Edison spent on coal research is not known, but it was probably substantial. Edison had other ideas which in the eyes of modern scientists are not worth pursuing. Shortly before his death in 1931, he expressed the belief that an alloy could be found which would insulate from gravity.[22]

Westinghouse was also an independent thinker and had the courage to act on his beliefs no matter how strong the opposition. When he brought out his alternating-current system, he was opposed by Edison, the most famous inventor and electrician of that day, and by Thomson, a highly respected engineer. As the a.c.-d.c. controversy progressed, Westinghouse became subject to more and more violent attacks and abuse. But he held his ground because he believed that he was right, and, before very long, the purchasers of electrical equipment vindicated his viewpoint. Westinghouse was right when he believed alternating current was superior to direct current for the transmission of electrical energy. Westinghouse was also right some years earlier when he proved that a certain accepted law of friction was wrong. In a series of air-brake tests carried out in England in 1878–79, he demonstrated that friction sometimes varies inversely as the velocity and is not always independent of it, as had been stated in a certain "law of nature."

Westinghouse, like Edison, could be wrong, but he, too, refused to accept other peoples' judgments. This was shown when an early paper by Lord Kelvin on thermodynamics came to his attention. The paper stimulated his imagination, and after considerable thought he drew up plans for a device which would use the heat of the atmosphere to generate power. When he submitted these plans to Lord Kelvin, the English physicist told Westinghouse that such a device could not possibly work. Engineers in the Westinghouse organization told him the same thing. But he continued until nearly the end of his life trying to devise an atmospheric engine which was, in reality, a perpetual-motion machine.[23] Westinghouse had known laws of nature and great authorities to be wrong before. He refused to give up his project until convinced by his own experiments.

Thomson, the imitative entrepreneur, contrasts sharply with Edison and Westinghouse. Thomson was a trained scientist and engineer who was formally educated and spent nearly ten years as a teacher. Neither Edison nor Westinghouse had any formal education of importance. Thomson was one of the best electrical engineers of his generation and largely confined himself to electrical work. Edison and Westinghouse invented in many fields besides electric lighting and power. Thomson erred in rejecting incandescent lighting and alternating current when they first appeared. Yet he was never guilty of the gross errors committed by both Edison and Westinghouse. Thomson's scientific training and broad understanding were at once a handicap and an aid. They prevented him from conceiving any major innovations. His thinking was too much along traditional scientific lines. At the same time, his expert engineering knowledge and his inventive ability enabled him to do better technical work than either Edison or Westinghouse, once a path had been broken.

XII

The Impact on the Gas Industry

THE growth of electric lighting had a profound and permanent effect on the gas industry. It lost a few customers when arc lamps began to replace gas lamps in street and other large-space lighting. Within a few years, interior gas lighting was threatened by the appearance of the incandescent electric light. With their principal markets under assault, the gas companies could not ignore electric lighting. They were forced to take positive steps to survive.

The gas industry had met successfully a similar threat which appeared in the 1860's. The beginning of large-scale petroleum production and refining, following E. L. Drake's discovery of oil in Pennsylvania in 1859, together with technical developments in oil illumination, led to a new and economical source of light, the kerosene lamp. This became a serious competitor of gas lighting. Although the gas industry continued to grow, its rate of growth was much less than it had been in the 1850's.

The ability of the gas industry to meet the competition of the kerosene lamp and resume a faster rate of growth in the late 1870's and early 1880's was chiefly the result of a new technique in gas manufacture. In the 1870's, American inventors developed practical processes for making water gas. The advantages of water gas over coal gas were several. Labor and equipment costs were lower. The coke which was a by-product of coal-gas manufacture and of little value could serve as the principal raw material. It was thus advantageous to add water-gas facilities to a coal-gas plant, and production of both types of gas by the same company became common.

In addition to reducing production costs, water gas made possible a substantial increase in illuminating power at small extra expense. Water gas was produced by blowing steam through red-hot coke. Oil vapors could then be added to give the gas a high illuminating power. When enriched water gas was mixed with coal gas, a high-quality, low-cost illuminant resulted. Oil was thus employed to help meet the competitive threat that oil itself had fostered.

Electric lighting first appeared as arc lighting. Since this was confined to large-space use and could not compete with the major portion of a gas company's business, it caused no great concern to the gas industry. A second alleviating factor was that street lighting often was unprofitable for the gas companies. It was undertaken because city councils commonly required it before granting a franchise. In many instances, the gas companies were forced to supply gas for street lighting at rates that could be justified only because they opened the door to the more lucrative private consumers.

Incandescent lighting was something very different. It was closely competitive with interior gas lighting, which accounted for 90 per cent of gas revenues, and it threatened the very foundation of the industry. To meet this threat, the most common defense was to lower prices. Table 20 shows the decline in the price of gas over the ten-year period, 1878–1888. In 1878, arc lighting had yet to make its appearance on a commercial basis. By 1888, incandescent lighting had proved to be a formidable competitor of gas. It should be noted that the reduction in the price of gas in most of the cities listed was 50 per cent or more.

A second reaction to electric lighting was to provide more service and better-quality illumination. Some gas companies offered to install gas pipes and fixtures without charge. Others adopted better jets or increased the illuminating power of their gas. But the most important means of increasing the quality of gas light was the introduction of the gas mantle. Fortunately for the gas industry, Carl Auer von Welsbach, working in R. W. Bunsen's laboratory in Germany, invented a practical gas mantle in 1885. It was made of cotton fabric which was impregnated with rare earths. When placed near a gas flame, the mantle became incandescent and gave off a steady, white light. This light was not only vastly superior in quality to that from an open gas flame but also much more economical. The mantle increased the light that could be obtained from a given quantity of gas about sixfold.

The United Gas Improvement Company of Philadelphia, a firm which operated gas plants in over fifty cities and also constructed them on contract, purchased the American patent rights to the Welsbach mantle and began manufacturing it at Gloucester, New Jersey, in 1890. The mantles were used in both interior and outdoor lighting and were extremely successful. Mantle gas light was much cheaper than incandescent electric light and nearly as good in quality. The gas mantle was thus able to retard the countrywide trend to electric illumination. By 1900, after only ten years, there were ten million Welsbach mantles in use in the United States, an amount half as great as the number of incandescent electric lights in use. As late as 1935, some 150,000 gas-mantle street lamps were still in service in American cities, mostly in slums and fashionable suburbs.[1]

TABLE 20

Price of Gas in American Cities, 1878–1888

(per thousand cubic feet)

City	*1878*	*1883*	*1884*	*1888*
New York	$2.75	$2.25	$1.75	$1.25
Chicago	...	2.75	1.25	1.50
Boston	...	2.80	1.80	1.50
Philadelphia	2.30	...	...	1.50
Baltimore	2.75	...	...	1.00
Cleveland	2.50	...	...	1.00
Cincinnati	2.25	...	...	1.15
Richmond	3.00	...	...	1.50
Sunbury (Pa.)	...	3.00	0.75	...

Sources: 1878 and 1888 data from A. R. Foote, *Economic Value of Electric Light and Power* (1889), p. 147, and *EW*, X (December 31, 1888), 348. 1883 and 1884 data for Chicago from *EW*, III (March 8, 1884), 79; for Boston, from *EW*, III (March 22, 1884), 92; for New York, from *EW*, V (January 31, 1885), 42; and for Sunbury, *EW*, III (January 12, 1884), 11.

The preceding measures taken by the gas companies — price reductions and product improvements — were scarcely more than delaying actions. They could retard but not prevent the shift to electric lighting. The rapidly developing technology of the electrical industry was to bring cost reductions and quality improvements which meant that eventually the use of gas for illumination was to be negligible.

The gas industry undertook a more fundamental readjustment to electric lighting by seeking to popularize non-lighting uses of gas. The gas mantle was actually a step in this direction. For it was patterned after its chief competitor in employing the principle of incandescence, and it did not depend on the direct illuminating properties of gas at all. It utilized the heat-giving characteristic of a gas flame. The burner which Bunsen had invented in 1855 was used in the gas-mantle lamp. This burner mixed air with the gas to achieve more complete combustion and was very efficient in obtaining heat energy from gas. It did not matter that the flame was blue and not light-giving. What did matter was that the burner could produce a very intense heat with a small amount of gas.

The gas-mantle lamp clearly embodied the conception that gas was a fuel. It was this conception that led half a dozen New York City gas companies to coöperate, early in 1884, in promoting the use of gas stoves for domestic cooking. Each company was assessed approximately a thousand dollars a month. The funds so obtained subsidized three retail stores established as outlets for the manufacturers of gas stoves. The gas companies also paid part of the installation costs of the stoves.[2]

The replacement of the coal range by the gas stove was a slow process. As a fuel, gas was high in price. Another retarding factor was the fact that the gas stove was an incomplete substitute for the coal range, which served the threefold function of cooking, space heating, and water heating. The last function could be performed by a gas water heater, but space heating continued to be a substantial advantage of the coal range until widespread adoption of central heating in the first decades of the twentieth century. These decades also saw periodic interruptions in the supply of coal, principally because of strikes. The uncertainty about the availability of coal hastened the adoption of gas for domestic cooking.

The gas industry also sought employment of gas as a fuel in commercial establishments, such as hotels and restaurants, and in industry. The success of the gas industry in developing fuel markets is shown in Table 21. The data bear out the prediction of Edison in 1878, when he wrote that "gas will be manufactured less for lighting as a result of electrical competition and more for heating, etc. Thus enlarging its market and increasing its income." [3]

In searching for new uses for gas, the gas industry has operated in a rapidly changing environment where a new market may be developed only to be lost to a competitor. Gas engines, operated from the regular gas mains, became common in the 1880's and replaced small steam engines in many places. The gas companies expected an expanding power market, but development of the electric motor and the gasoline engine forced the gas engine into relative obscurity. Similarly, the gas clothes iron came into use in the first decade of the twentieth century, but it too was replaced by an electrical device.

The second fundamental readjustment of the gas industry was to offer electric-lighting service to its customers. This step involved acceptance of the view that a gas company was essentially selling illumination, which could be obtained from either gas or electricity. It was not easy for gas-company officials, who had derided, belittled, and fought electric lighting, to admit its merit. But those who could bring themselves to appreciate electric lighting found that they were in a favorable position to supply it at low cost. They already had land, buildings, coal-handling facilities, and a going organization. And coke from coal-gas manufacture that was not needed for water gas was available as a fuel for the steam-power plant.

By the mid-eighties, gas companies in a number of cities were offering electric-lighting service. Some did so reluctantly. The Brookline (Massachusetts) Gas Company, for example, announced in 1886 its intention to furnish electric lights when its customers requested them. Under no circumstances were orders to be solicited.[4] Other gas companies actively sought to expand their electric-lighting business. From the very first appearance of electric lighting, its greater illumination tended to increase the demand for light and hence the demand for gas. This additive, rather than substitutive, relationship between gas and electricity encouraged gas companies to install electric equipment. The additive relationship was to prove only temporary, but its influence on the acceptance of electricity by gas companies was considerable.

TABLE 21

Manufactured Gas in the United States, 1880–1931

	1880	*1899*	*1919*	*1931*
Uses				
Illumination (per cent)	100	75	21[a]	Negligible
Fuel: Domestic (per cent)	Negligible	25 (domestic, industrial and commercial combined)	54[a]	76
Industrial and commercial (per cent)	Negligible		25[a]	24
Annual Sales				
Value (millions of dollars)	[b]	69	282	435
Quantity (billions of cubic feet)	[b]	67	308	391

Sources: Uses data for 1899 from *Brown's Directory of American Gas Companies* (1900), *passim*; for 1919, from Louis Stotz and Alexander Jamison, *History of the Gas Industry* (1938), p. 187; for 1931, from G. B. Cortelyou, *The Gas Industry* (1933), p. 5. Annual Sales data for 1899, 1919, from census reports; for 1931, from Cortelyou, *The Gas Industry*, p. 5.

[a] These percentages are for 1920.

[b] The Tenth Census did not include the gas industry.

By early 1887, there were about 40 gas companies which supplied electric lighting. Two years later the number had increased to 266. This was about 25 per cent of all gas companies in the United States. By 1899, the number had climbed to 362 and the percentage to nearly 40. As previously indicated, Thomson-Houston was a leader in supplying the gas companies with electrical equipment, both arc and incandescent. Of the 20,000 arc lights and 55,000 incandescent lamps operated by the 266 gas companies in 1889, Thomson-Houston had furnished the equipment for more than half of the arc lights and about 15 per cent of the incandescent lights.

Westinghouse was responsible for one-half of the incandescent lights and Edison for one-fifth.[5]

The shift from gas lighting to gas heating and the production of gas and electricity by one firm were electric lighting's principal permanent effects on the gas industry. It is interesting to note that electric lighting also brought about minor technical changes. A plausible interpretation of these changes is that the gas industry sought to imitate the techniques of its successful rival, just as Edison had imitated the gas industry years before. It will be recalled that the gas mantle utilized the principle of incandescence, the same principle that underlay Edison's electric light. The Welsbach light can be correctly called the gas analogue of the incandescent electric light. Edison also exerted an influence on the gas-distribution system. Gas engineers adopted the feeder-main principle. The effect here was the same as in an electrical network. Gas pressure at the jets was equalized without the expense of larger pipes.[6]

The principal thesis of this chapter is that both the kerosene lamp and the electric lamp retarded the growth of the gas industry until it changed either its production methods or its markets. This thesis is consistent with variations in the rate of growth of the industry in the last half of the nineteenth century. Although available statistics are incomplete and far from satisfactory, it is possible to gauge the industry's growth in broad terms.

In an economy with an increasing population, an industry may grow absolutely and yet not grow relative to the population. Two kinds of growth may be distinguished; growth to meet the demands of a larger group of consumers, and growth to meet a wider acceptance of the industry's product among existing consumers. To make this distinction, the characteristics of the population which are relevant to the product under consideration must be taken account of. If the product is baby buggies, for example, the number of children under eighteen months of age is relevant. Per capita figures of product sales can reveal the degree of consumer acceptance of a product if that segment of population which is the potential market for the product can be identified. This procedure is valid unless the number of persons in the potential market changes as a result of the product itself. To use the baby buggy example again, if the existence of attractive and inexpensive baby buggies makes raising children so much easier and cheaper that more children are born, then it would not be valid to take the ratio of the number of baby buggies sold to the number of children under eighteen months of age as a measure of the growth of the industry.

In the gas industry, only the urban population, not the entire population, was the potential market. Before the days of bottled gas, the industry could serve only urban areas. The minimum-sized urban area which could sustain a gas company decreased as technological advance lowered production costs. At first only the largest cities had gas, but, by 1900, gas was found in communities as small as 5,000. For the analysis that follows, the urban population is defined as residing in cities of 5,000 or more. This figure is somewhat arbitrary, but the results would not have differed appreciably if the dividing line between urban and rural had been set at 10,000 or 2,500 inhabitants. It should be emphasized that the concept of the urban population as the potential market for gas is valid for this analysis only if the size of that population was not affected by the presence of gas illumination in urban areas. If people moved from farms and small villages to the cities, for example, because they could then enjoy gas lighting, the potential market would include the rural areas as well.

Lack of data on physical output (cubic feet of gas produced and/or sold) before 1889 makes impossible a single analysis of the 1849–1909 period. The earlier two decades, 1849–1869, are treated separately from the later two decades, 1889–1909. Omission of the gas industry from the 1880 census makes it difficult to treat the 1870's or to relate the earlier period to the later one, but an attempt can be made to secure an 1869 output figure comparable to the 1889 figure.

The indicator of physical output for 1849, 1859, and 1869 is the average number of wage earners employed. The use of these data for this purpose is open to the objection that productivity per worker may have changed appreciably during the twenty-year period. Increases in productivity probably did occur, but it is likely that they were small. The methods and raw materials of gas manufacture changed very little. The number of gas workers is the best index of gas output in the absence of physical-output or price data which could be applied to the census value of output figures.

The growth data of the gas industry are given in Table 22. Population data are employed as if they applied to the year of the census of manufactures (1849, 1859, etc.) instead of for the year of the population census (1850, 1860, etc.). The error in this procedure is probably small. The third column of figures shows that the gas industry grew approximately three times as fast as the urban population in the decade 1849–1859. In the following decade, the industry grew only in proportion to the growth in urban population. It is suggested that this slower rate of growth was primarily the result of competition from the kerosene lamp.

To continue to use wage earners as a measure of total output for 1889 and later is not defensible. The water-gas process, introduced in the 1870's, substantially increased worker productivity. The same effect resulted from other improvements such as new types of retorts and new techniques of handling coal and coke. It is therefore fortunate that physical-output data are available for 1889, 1899, and 1909. To link these years to 1869 (it will be recalled that the 1880 census omitted the gas industry), the output for 1869 was estimated by the following procedure: The average price of gas per thousand cubic feet in 1890 was $1.42.[7] The estimate is then made that the price twenty years earlier was at least two and one half times the 1889 price, or $3.50. That this figure is conservative is indicated by the fact that one estimate of the average price of gas in 290

TABLE 22

Growth of the Manufactured-Gas Industry in the United States, 1849–1909

Year	Urban population (millions)[a]	Wage earners in the gas industry	Gas wage earners per million urban population	Gas sold (billions of cubic feet)	Gas sold per capita of urban population (thousands of cubic feet)
1849	3.2	952	298	..	..
1859	5.6	5,730	1023	..	..
1869	8.9	8,723	980	9.2	1.0
1879[b]	12.5	..	..	..	..
1889	19.8	..	..	43.8[c]	2.2
1899	27.3	..	..	67.1	2.5
1909	38.3	..	..	150.8	3.9

Sources: Census reports. Derivation of the figure for gas sold in 1869 is explained in the text.

[a] Population in places of 5,000 inhabitants or more.

[b] The Tenth Census did not include the gas industry.

[c] This figure is revised upward, as explained in the text, to allow for gas establishments omitted in the Eleventh Census.

cities in 1878 is $3.15.[8] General price data indicate that the period after the Civil War was one of declining prices, and this fact is additional support for a high 1869 price. Dividing the 1869 value of gas produced by the 1869 price gives the physical-output figure which is shown in Table 22. The value figure is actually for all products of the gas industry, but the error involved in assuming that gas was the sole product is very small.

The 1889 output figure, as given by the census, was adjusted upward to compensate for the fact that over 250 gas companies failed to report in the 1890 census. The number of establishments which reported was 742. On the conservative assumption that each company which did not report operated only one establishment, the number of unreported establishments was one-third as large as the number that were reported. No information on the size of the omitted companies is available. If their establishments were, on the average, the same size as the 742 which reported, the industry output figure should be increased by one-third. In view of the lack of informaiton, a more conservative correction was made. The 1889 output figure was increased by only one-fifth.

Table 22 shows that the gas industry grew more than in proportion to the population in the twenty-year period, 1869–1889. The per-capita consumption of gas more than doubled. With no data available for 1879, it is possible only to speculate on the changes in the rate of growth within the period. It is probable that growth was most rapid in the decade 1875–1885. These years would reflect the stimulus from water gas and precede the serious inroads of electric lighting.

Growth only slightly exceeded the population increase in the last decade of the nineteenth century. The retardation in the rate of growth was probably caused by electric lighting. Without the gas mantle, this decade might have registered an actual decline in the per capita consumption of gas. The increasing rate of growth of the industry in the first decade of the twentieth century reflects the use of gas as a fuel, principally in domestic cooking.

To summarize, this chapter has attempted to outline briefly the effects of electric lighting on the gas industry. The industry was first forced to lower its prices and improve the quality of its product. To insure long-run survival, two additional steps were taken. The gas companies found new markets for gas and undertook to supply electric lighting. These measures were very successful. Today gas and electricity are commonly produced by the same enterprise, and gas is widely used as a convenient and economical source of heat.

XIII

The Dynamics of the Industry

TECHNICAL CHANGE IN INCANDESCENT-LIGHTING EQUIPMENT

THE incandescent-lighting system which Edison developed for the first central stations had four main components — the generator, the conductor network, the meter, and the lamp. During the twenty years that followed, the generator and the lamp were not altered in any fundamental way, but were constantly improved in reliability, durability, and efficiency. The impetus behind these changes was the desire to lower the cost of incandescent lighting to enable the central stations to compete more easily with the suppliers of other forms of illumination. As manufacturers learned more about the energy losses in a generator, machines of higher efficiency could be designed. Various small improvements were made from time to time, such as the use of carbon brushes instead of copper ones, the design of armatures with smaller heat losses, and the construction of longer-wearing commutators. In lamps, the filament was carbon until after 1900, but the exact nature of the carbon changed, and processes were developed to deposit a coating of graphite on the filament to increase its life and efficiency. Methods of fastening the filament to the lead-in wires were altered to lower manufacturing cost and to produce lamps nearer to the desired voltage. The platinum lead-in wires were reduced in length in order to economize this expensive metal. By 1900, the cost of an incandescent lamp was about one-fifth of what it had been in 1880, and its efficiency had nearly doubled.

The other two components, the conductor network and the meter, underwent major changes by 1900. The conductor network, employing direct current, was first the simple two-wire system, then the two-wire feeder-main system, and finally the three-wire feeder-main system. Westinghouse replaced direct with alternating current, which meant higher voltages and still lower transmission costs. After the introduction of alternating current, the major change in distribution was the development of rotary converters. These enabled an a.c. generating station to supply direct current at the place of utilization for d.c. networks, which could thereby be kept in economic use.

The change from direct to alternating current required a change in the meter. Edison's chemical meter gave way to the Westinghouse direct-reading mechanical meter. After the latter type came into general use, meter development followed two paths. The first was to replace current-reading meters with energy-reading meters. The latter were called watt-hour meters and appeared in the early 1890's. They permitted the electric light and power companies to charge their customers for what they actually consumed, electric energy.

The second path of meter development was the design of meters for special demand conditions. General Electric, for example, brought out a prepayment meter for low-income areas where a light company might experience difficulty collecting regular monthly bills. As the rate structures for electric energy became more complex, special meters were frequently required. Two-rate meters to record the energy used during peak periods separately from the energy used at other times were placed on the market. Because such meters made it possible to use a rate structure which more accurately reflected cost conditions, they were a step in the direction of a more rational use of resources.

The technical changes in the main components of the incandescent-lighting system were in the direction of lower costs, increased reliability, and better performance in the production of electric lighting for interior illumination — the use Edison had in mind from the beginning. Another series of technical changes resulted from the desire to widen the incandescent-lighting market to include large-space lighting and, in particular, street lighting. It was first necessary to produce lamps of large candle power. The Edison Lamp Works began making 32-c.p. lamps about 1881, and within a few years was making a 50-c.p. lamp. Still larger sizes were added until, by 1886, lamps of 250 c.p. were being produced. These large lamps enabled the Edison lighting companies to compete with arc lights in many uses. But, in street lighting, more than a large-size lamp was needed. The many miles of circuits and the relatively long distance between lights necessitated a higher voltage than usual in order to save copper. To enable incandescent-lighting companies to enter the street-lighting business, the Edison company brought out its municipal system in 1885. This was a series system which required special equipment. The dynamos were the constant-current type. The lamps took 4 amperes of current and were designed to last about 3,000 hours. They were fitted with automatic cutouts to keep the circuit continuous when a lamp burned out. Compared to arc lighting, incandescent street lighting had two important advantages. The individual lights were lower in candle power, and they required very little maintenance. The first Edison municipal system was installed in Lockport, New York, in 1885. A gas company used it to light the streets of a suburb beyond reach of its gas mains. By the middle of 1887, seven other installations had been made.[1] Thomson-Houston brought out an incandescent street-lighting system in 1888 employing alternating current. This was also a series system.

THE GROWTH OF INCANDESCENT LIGHTING, 1880–1900

Best available estimates indicate that incandescent lights in use had reached 250,000 by 1885, 3,000,000 by 1890, and 18,000,000 by 1902. Of the 250,000 in use in 1885, over 200,000 were Edison lights on Edison equipment. Most of the rest were United States company lamps on its equipment. Of the 3,000,000 in use in 1890, nearly 1,300,000 were Edison, about 600,000 were Thomson-Houston, and 500,000 were Westinghouse. By 1902, General Electric and Westinghouse accounted for nearly all incandescent-lighting equipment in use.[2]

The pattern of growth in incandescent lighting was similar to that in arc lighting. During the first years the pioneer innovator, Edison, produced most of the output. By 1885, many firms had begun the production of incandescent-lighting equipment, but only two, Thomson-Houston and Westinghouse, were to be successful enough to challenge Edison. In 1892, the pioneer innovator consolidated with the principal imitative entrepreneur, Thomson. Westinghouse then was the only other large firm in the industry. The part played by patents was similar to the role of patents in arc lighting. In the beginning, very little attention was paid to patents, and manufacturers could make the entire incandescent system. The dynamo could not be patented, and lamp patents were not respected. The Edison patents did not prevent the rise of Thomson-Houston and Westinghouse, just as the Brush patents did not prevent the rise of Thomson-Houston and other producers of arc-lighting equipment.

The rapid growth of incandescent lighting can be partly attributed to the fact that the demand for interior lighting from a central-station source had been well established by the gas companies. The incandescent electric light was about the same as gas in cost and much superior in quality. Home owners and business firms could easily recognize its superior quality and were willing to adopt it. As the electric light was improved, it could compete more effectively with other light sources. When lamps of larger candle power were made, the incandescent light could move into street and other large-space lighting. When the a.c. distribution system was developed, electric lighting could compete with oil lamps and candles in areas where consumer density was too low to permit gas distribution. When a more efficient incandescent lamp was made, it could be combined with batteries in portable and mobile uses where no system illumination was possible. Because the incandescent light was more adaptable to widely varying illumination requirements than the arc light, its growth potential was much greater. By 1902, the number of arc lights in use was over two-thirds of what it would be in 1912, but the number of incandescent lights in use, which had increased sixfold from 1890 to 1902, increased nearly fivefold in the decade after 1902.

As in arc lighting, the very rapid growth in incandescent lighting was partly due to the initiative taken by the manufacturers in promoting lighting companies. The manufacturers created a market for their products by creating the firms to buy them, and they demonstrated their belief that a demand for light existed by incurring much of the risk in establishing these new firms. Liberal guarantees of equipment performance were given, and stocks and bonds were accepted in payment for the equipment. The interests of the manufacturer and his customers were practically identical. Unless the lighting company had reliable, efficient equipment and provided good lighting service at a low cost, it would not prosper and electric lighting would not grow. There was, therefore, a strong incentive on the part of the manufacturer to produce lamps and equipment which could provide light at the lowest possible cost.

The incandescent-lighting system was not nearly so simple to install and operate as the arc-lighting system. The circuits were more complex, and accessories such as fuses, switches, and meters were needed. The establishment of central stations was extremely complicated, and this phase of the business developed much more slowly than the isolated plants. By 1885, Edison had nearly twice as many lamps burning in isolated plants as in central stations. The incandescent-lighting central stations, with complex distribution networks, difficult voltage-regulation problems, elaborate switchboards, many dynamos feeding one circuit, meters to be adjusted and read, and continuous 24-hour service, required expert management. The first rapid growth came in the simpler isolated plants, and the rapid growth of central-station lighting came later.

PART III

Electric Power

XIV

The Setting

THE electric motor is based upon the same fundamental principle as the dynamo. In the dynamo, an external force is used to move an electric conductor in a magnetic field, and the result is a current in the conductor. In the motor, a current is passed through an electric conductor in a magnetic field, and the result is a force acting on the conductor. This force can be viewed as arising from the conflict between the original magnetic field and a second magnetic field produced by the current in the conductor. The crucial fact that current in a conductor will create a magnetic field was discovered by Hans Oersted in Copenhagen in 1820. The following year Faraday exhibited in London a simple electrical device which rotated. In this crude electric motor, Faraday used a permanent magnet as the source of the stationary electric field. A little later, Ampere also constructed an elementary electric motor, and other scientists carried on similar work in electromagnetic rotation. In the early 1830's, Professor Joseph Henry of Princeton made an electric motor and expressed hope that the mechanical force it produced could be utilized.

These early scientists did not themselves apply their electric motors to any industrial purpose. The first to demonstrate their utility was Thomas Davenport, a blacksmith at Rutland, Vermont. In 1837, he constructed a motor which he employed to drill holes up to one-fourth inch in diameter in iron and steel. This motor weighed fifty pounds and was capable of rotating at over four hundred revolutions per minute.[1] Davenport's work was followed by the application of the electric motor to transportation. In 1839, Professor H. M. Jacobi, of St. Petersburg, Russia, fitted out a small craft with a motor which drove a paddlewheel. He conducted experiments on the River Neva. About this same time, Robert

Davidson mounted an electric motor on a railway car in Scotland and reached the speed of four miles per hour. In the United States, C. G. Page worked on electric motors during the 1840's, making a number of industrial applications and finally building an electric locomotive. The latter was tested in 1854 on the Baltimore and Ohio Railroad tracks near Washington, D. C., and attained the speed of nineteen miles per hour.

In every case, the applications of the electric motor to industry and transport were experimental and short lived. The explanation is simple. The only source of current was the primary battery, and electric power from that source was over twenty times as costly as the power supplied by a steam engine. Until a more economical source of current was available, there was no possibility of electric power's coming into general use. The original idea that electricity could be produced economically by chemical means from the consumption of zinc, as heat is produced by the consumption of coal, showed a misconception of the role of electric power. Electricity was not to be important as a form of primary energy. The sources of power — falling water, expanding gases, and steam generated by coal, oil, gas, or some other combustible — were to remain as before. Electricity was to serve as a means to transmit power from the prime mover to the place of use more economically and more conveniently than any other method ever known. Electricity would primarily replace the belts, the cables, and the shafts. And it would permit the transmission of power where, for economic or physical reasons, transmission by mechanical means had never been practical.

The work of Gramme, Pacinotti, Siemens, and others that made available the dynamo as a cheap source of current stimulated the development of electric power just as it had arc lighting. Gramme gave one of the first exhibitions of a motor operated by current from a generator in 1873 in Vienna. Since his motor was identical with his dynamo, he at the same time made clear the similarity between motor and dynamo action. Later he successfully applied his motors to a number of industrial uses in France; and as current became more generally available because of the growth of arc lighting, the use of electric motors increased.

By 1880, therefore, three fundamental facts about the electric motor had become widely known among electricians. The motor was essentially a dynamo running in reverse, and what was learned about dynamo construction could be utilized in motor construction. Like the dynamo, the motor had a group of conductors (the armature) which rotated in the magnetic field established by two or more electromagnets (the field poles). Furthermore, the motor required brushes and a commutator to convey the current from the stationary supply wires to the rotating armature.

The second fundamental fact was that the motor was to be the key component in the electric transmission of power. It could replace other methods of transmitting power, but would not be a substitute for prime movers. The third fact was that the electric motor could be operated by current from dynamos — the same current that was used for lighting.

These three facts and the technical knowledge that accompanied them were basic to the commercial success of the electric motor. What was needed were a reliable and efficient dynamo, a suitable network to connect the dynamo to the motor, and a reliable and efficient motor. The Gramme dynamo and motor were not efficient enough in transforming mechanical energy into electrical energy and back to mechanical energy to admit of serious competition to other forms of energy transmission. The constant-current network employed by arc-lighting circuits, though well adapted to the Gramme dynamo, was not suitable for motor operation. Widespread commercial use of electric power thus necessitated technical changes in the dynamo, the motor, and the connecting network.

The potential market for electric-power apparatus, as that market appeared in the early 1880's, comprised applications of electric power to industry and public transport. In those industries which were heavy consumers of power, the electric motor could eliminate costly and inefficient transmission equipment and at the same time permit individual or group control of machines with small power losses. Where firms were consumers of small amounts of power, the electric motor would make possible the purchase of power from a central station, which would be much more economical than the operation of a small steam engine. In cases where steam power had been too expensive to use by reason of the small amount or infrequency of power consumption, electric power would allow the substitution of mechanical power for human or animal power. Electric motors are adaptable to varied power requirements and could serve to drive machines such as lathes, drills, presses, and looms, and could also operate elevators and intraplant transport systems. Mines would be an especially fruitful application of the last kind.

In public transport, the electric motor could be substituted for the animals and cables pulling the streetcars and the steam locomotives drawing the elevated trains. On the regular steam railroads, electric motive power could also find special uses. In tunnels where the stack gases of ordinary coal-burning locomotives were dangerous and inconvenient, or in crowded terminals where the smoke and cinders were equally undesirable, the electric motor, clean and quiet, would be welcomed. Not for many years, however, would electric power be developed to the extent that there could be general substitution of electricity for steam on the main-line railroads.

The potential market for electric motors and other power apparatus in 1879 can be partially estimated. At that time there were 56,483 steam engines, with a total capacity of 2,185,458 horsepower, in use in manufacturing in the United States. In addition, there were 55,404 water wheels in use with a capacity of 1,225,379 horsepower.[2] These figures indicate the extent to which motive power, other than animal and human, was employed in industry, and electric power could conceivably serve as the means of transmission of most of it.

The potential demand in urban transportation is indicated by the fact that in 1880 there were about 19,000 streetcars in operation on nearly 3,000 miles of track in the United States. The motive power was supplied by 100,000 horses and mules.[3] These animals were costly, dirty, slow, and ill suited to long-distance runs. But they could be eliminated only if a mechanical means of car locomotion were developed. Because few cities would permit steam locomotives on the streets, it was necessary to resort to a more indirect use of steam power. The technique finally developed was the cable system, which was installed by a few street railways in the early 1880's. A stationary steam engine was employed to revolve an endless steel cable which ran in a slot between the two rails. On each streetcar was mounted an arm which reached down into the cable slot. The arm could be made to grip the moving cable, thereby placing the car in motion. The operation of this gripping mechanism involved considerable physical exertion and could be undertaken only by men of above-average strength.

The cable system gave reasonably satisfactory operation. Its chief merit was its speed — about twice that of horse railways. Its chief disadvantage was its cost. The initial investment, the power consumption, and the maintenance costs were so high that it was profitable only where the traffic load was very heavy. Furthermore, it was not well adapted to large transportation systems, utilizing hundreds of cars. If the cable broke, all traffic was suspended; the individual cars could not go faster than the cable and could not, therefore, make up time; and turnouts, sidings, single tracks, and other variations from straight double tracks could not be made part of the system. There was clearly a need for a motive power cheaper and more flexible than cables and cheaper and faster than animals.[4]

Almost all buyers in the potential market for electric-power apparatus were business firms. They operated factories, shops, mines, and street railways. The decision to replace other power-transmission methods with electricity or to replace animal and human power with electric power would thus be based almost entirely on cost considerations. "Cost" is used here to refer to all costs, and for the businessman this means not only the price of the motor but also its power consumption and maintenance expense. If electric power could show marked cost advantages over alternative methods, it would be adopted. In some uses, it could substantially expand revenues by increasing the quality or quantity of output. In these cases, cost would not be the only factor. In other applications, electric power would have advantages because only two small wires are needed to carry the power or because the motor is clean and quiet. Here, too, cost would be only one factor considered. But in the vast majority of instances, cost would be of prime importance. If electric-power equipment of such price, efficiency, reliability, and durability could be manufactured so that electric power would be low in cost, the other kinds of motive power employed in industry and transport would be discarded in favor of electric power. In short, here was a primarily economic problem.

XV

Electric Traction

THE PROBLEM OF ELECTRIC TRACTION

THE technical problems of designing an electric railway were numerous and difficult. Nearly a decade of effort by engineers and inventors, beginning with Edison in 1880, was required before solutions to the major problems of electric traction were found. And these solutions applied only to the electric street railway. Still another decade was to pass before the superiority of electric power in elevated urban railroads could be demonstrated.

The most fundamental problem of the electric railway was to supply the motor, mounted on a moving vehicle, with electric current. One possibility was to install a secondary battery on the vehicle. Another was to connect the stationary generator to the moving vehicle by a network of conductors. This network could consist of the rails. One rail could carry the current to the motor, and the second rail could return the current to the generator. If the two rails were used only as the return circuit, a special conductor would have to be installed, or, if the rails were not part of the electric circuit at all, two conductors would be needed. These conductors could be placed on poles above the track, on the ground beside the track (a third rail), or in an underground conduit.

Because the motor moved relative to the generator and the conductor network, a special pick-up device was required to transfer current from the conductors to the motor. If the regular rails were used as conductors, the wheels of the vehicle could pick up the current. If special conductors were installed, some kind of wheel, plow, or shoe was necessary to maintain continuous contact between the vehicle and the conductor network.

A second basic problem grew out of the fact that the motor was mounted on a vehicle which had to travel at varying speeds and start and stop frequently. These were conditions that required a specially designed motor, because the ordinary electric motor of the 1880's simply could not function satisfactorily under such conditions. The principal source of trouble was what electrical engineers call "commutation." A d.c. motor, like a d.c. generator, has brushes and a commutator. The brushes connect the current-supplying conductors to the rotating elements of the motor. These elements, the armature and the commutator, are mounted on the same shaft. The stationary brushes maintain contact with the rotating commutator through which the current passes en route to the armature. The commutator translates the supplied direct current into the alternating current which the motor must have to operate. It was the contact between the brushes and the commutator that caused serious difficulty. The copper brushes had to press firmly against the commutator in order to pass the heavy currents required by the motor. The result was much wear on both the brushes and the commutator.

This brush-commutator wear was increased by the constant starting and stopping. The heavy currents and changing voltages which accompany starting caused sparking and arcing at the points of contact. These electrical fireworks were extremely destructive. Stopping also brought troubles. The slight reverse movement of the vehicle in coming to a complete stop was usually sufficient to cause the brushes to cut into the commutator. Such cutting was especially damaging because the brushes were not set perpendicular to the circumference of the commutator at the point of contact but at an angle.

The unusual brush and commutator wear to which a streetcar motor was subjected meant high operating expense and unreliable performance. The brushes had to be replaced frequently and the commutator either machined down or replaced. The problem of commutation was therefore one that had to be solved before the electric railway could be a success.

A third basic problem was to devise a method of transmitting the power developed by the motor to the axles of the vehicle. Belts, chains, friction discs, or gears could be used. The ratio between the motor speed and the vehicle speed had to be chosen, and the position and manner of mounting the motor had to be determined. The motor (or motors) could be placed on or beneath the floor of the vehicle and could be rigidly or flexibly attached.

Solution of the three basic problems — current supply, the motor, and motor-axle power transmission — required scientific and engineering work of a high caliber. Judging correctly what were and were not acceptable solutions to these problems was only possible if the electric-railway system were viewed as a coördinated operating unit. The difference between failure and success in electric-railway design was to depend in no small measure on the ability to take such an over-all view. Many men attempted to design electric railways and failed. Several of these men and their unsuccessful efforts to innovate in electric traction will now be discussed.

UNSUCCESSFUL ENTREPRENEURS IN ELECTRIC TRACTION

1. *Thomas A. Edison*

To develop an electric-lighting system Edison had to design a suitable dynamo. Because it was generally known that dynamos could be reversed — that is, they could convert electric into mechanical energy — it is not surprising that Edison should have experimented with motors as well as generators. He was aware from the beginning of his work on the electric light that a central station which supplied electricity for lighting could also supply electricity for power. In one of his notebooks, an entry made sometime in 1878 mentioned electricity for use by small motors, which would be much more convenient than small steam engines, and concluded with the statement: "Generally poorest district for light, best for power, thus evening up whole city — note effect of this on investment." [1]

Edison used electricity from his Menlo Park central station for power purposes. The lamp factory, set up in the fall of 1880, employed only electricity for power transmission from the steam engine to the points of power consumption. A sewing machine and a water pump in Edison's Menlo Park home were operated by electric motors. A motor was also employed in Edison's electric pen, one of his early inventions and a forerunner of mimeograph stencil-cutting devices. A tiny electric motor, driven by a battery, imparted a reciprocating motion to a needle-like point which punctured the paper and produced a stencil.

In view of Edison's practical experience with motors and his success with dynamo design, it is strange that he did not develop an industrial motor which could be supplied by current from Edison central stations. He left that task to others, however, and concentrated on electricity for lighting.

Edison's almost complete neglect of electric power for industry was not repeated in his interest in electric power for transportation. In the summer of 1878 he made a western trip, which gave him a chance to observe the need for better transportation facilities in the Great Plains area. He noticed that many farmers had long and expensive hauls in transporting their grain and other produce to the railroads. It was clear that the small amount and seasonal character of this farm freight did not justify regular heavy steam railroads, but Edison believed electric power might here find an application. Light, narrow-gauge electric railroads could act as feeders to the main steam railroads and solve the transportation problem of many farmers. This was the vision that Edison had in mind when he began his railway experiments in January 1880. By that time he had developed an efficient dynamo, but the electric light and other components of his lighting system still occupied nearly all of his time. He engaged a mechanical engineer to design and build an electric locomotive and had a crew of men construct a track one-third of a mile long. In May 1880, the locomotive was first operated. Current was carried to the motor by the two rails of the regular track, and the locomotive wheels acted as current pick-ups. The motor was an ordinary Edison dynamo laid on its side. The technical details of the locomotive were the object of experiments for about a year, but no definitive results were obtained. Numerous railroad officials visited Edison's railway and witnessed it in action. The locomotive operated very well. It was reliable, well controlled, and achieved speeds as high as forty miles per hour. Many of the visiting railroaders, however, viewed it as a toy and refused to give it serious consideration.

The one railroad executive who thought that Edison's railway might have commercial value was Henry Villard, a director of the Edison company and president of the Northern Pacific. He made arrangements with Edison in the fall of 1881 for the construction of a three-mile experimental railway at Menlo Park in order that tests on a scale sufficient to determine the practicality of the railway might be carried out. If these tests were successful, Villard agreed to pay the expenses of the Menlo Park railway and to build at least fifty miles of electric railway in the wheat-growing regions. Success was defined as achieving a cost per ton-mile which was less than that of a steam railroad.[2] On the basis of Villard's promise, Edison worked out the plans for the projected road quite carefully. He secured all the data he could on the winds of the Great Plains area and proposed to drive the generators for the wheat trains with large windmills.

During the time of the building and operation of the second railway at Menlo Park, Edison was no longer there and could spare little time for railway work. The two locomotives which were constructed were nearly identical to the 1880 locomotive in their electrical features but resembled steam locomotives in appearance. The roadbed was well built, and the track was carefully laid. Three sidings and two turntables were included. The tests took place in 1882 and indicated that the railway was a success in contract terms. But Villard was unable to carry out his plans for an electric railroad in the west. The Northern Pacific had gone into receivership and was no longer in his contol. Edison later refunded to Villard the

$40,000 which he had advanced for the construction of the Menlo Park railway.

The Edison company was not willing to invest in the railway experiments, and Edison could find no financial backing after Villard was forced to withdraw. When another electric-railway experimenter, S. D. Field, wanted to consolidate with Edison in railway work, the Edison company thought that it was a good opportunity to realize a return on Edison's railway patents without any investment by the Edison company or any further work by Edison. Field and Edison had been in an interference proceeding on a railway patent in the Patent Office, and Field's financial backers feared that Edison would win. To avoid losing their investment in Field's railway system, they wanted to form a company to hold both the Field and the Edison electric-railway patents. That company, the Electric Railway Company of the United States, was organized in May 1883 with an authorized capital of $2,000,000. Field became the electrical engineer of the new company and tried to develop a practical electric-railway system. Edison did not play an active role in the enterprise. Experiments were first carried on at Menlo Park and later were transferred to New York City, where a short spur was constructed on the Twenty-Ninth Street elevated line for experimental purposes. The expected commercial use of the electric railway had by that time been shifted from a steam-railroad feeder in the western farming areas to the elevated railroads in New York. This shift was probably made upon Field's recommendation, although Edison expressed the opinion late in 1884 that the best place to introduce electric railways was the elevated railroads of New York.[8] Experiments were conducted on the New York elevated lines for a number of years, but Field never succeeded in convincing the elevated-railroad officials that electricity should be substituted for steam.

The Electric Railway company carried out only one successful installation. Field built a 3-ton, 9-miles-per-hour locomotive which operated in the main exhibition building of the Chicago Railway Exposition in June 1883. The locomotive used a wire brush to pick up current from a third rail and was very successful. Thousands of passengers were carried over a track one-third of a mile in length, and the company seemed to be off to a good start. But nothing except the experiments on the elevated lines was ever done. Field and Edison strongly disliked each other, and their animosity precluded a unified organization. The patent interference between Edison and Field had been settled by the granting of a patent to the latter. Edison claimed that this result followed the withdrawal of his patent application. Field, who insisted that his receipt of the patent proved that Edison's application had no merit, wanted to take his patents out of the company. The dissension between Field and Edison continued until 1890, when the Electric Railway company assigned Edison's patents to Edison General Electric. In 1896, the Field patents were sold to Westinghouse, and in 1897 the company was dissolved.

Edison did no railway experimenting after 1883 until 1890, when Henry Villard, then president of Edison General Electric, asked him to develop an electric railway suitable for large cities where overhead trolley wires were not permitted. Villard wanted a method of conducting the current to the streetcars which was cheaper and more reliable than the underground-conduit method. In trying to fulfill Villard's request, Edison returned to the current-transmission system he had used on the two Menlo Park railways. He employed the rails as the conductors. Because the rails were completely exposed to all vehicle and pedestrian traffic, the current was transmitted at a potential of only 20 volts. Such a low voltage requires very large current, and Edison displayed considerable ingenuity in devising wheels and rail joints which could pass the heavy currents. To reduce transmission losses, he planned to install motor-generator units in manholes beneath the tracks. These units would transform the 1200-volt feeder voltage to the 20 volts needed on the rails. Although Edison claimed that his low-voltage system was practical, it was never adopted on any railway. It proved to be as expensive as the underground-conduit system; and overhead trolley wires were permitted in more large cities than had originally been expected.[4] By 1900, the subway was receiving serious consideration as the answer to the transportation problem in the largest cities, and Edison's system was forgotten.

Edison's railway work was not successful. He failed to become the pioneer innovator in electric railways. The reason for this failure is not obvious. His work in developing the incandescent-lighting system proved that he possessed unusual technical talent. He had a well-equipped laboratory and his own experimental tracks. He was in electric-railway work very early and was the first person to operate from dynamo current an electric railway of steam-railroad dimensions. In spite of all of these advantages, his railway work in the early 1880's and the early 1890's did not terminate in any commercial installations.

One reason for Edison's failure in electric railways was lack of time. Edison himself gave that reason in an interview in the summer of 1884. Referring to the Menlo Park railway, he said: "I could not go on with it because I had not time. I had too many other things to attend to, especially in connection with electrical lighting."[5] The 1883 annual report of the Edison company expressed the same opinion. "No especial progress has been made with the Edison Electric Railway since the last meeting. The development of the Edison light, with its attendant demands upon Mr.

Edison's time and thought, has left him no leisure for perfecting the details of his System of Electric Railways." [6]

There can be no quarrel with the fact that Edison's work on lighting required his full attention and prevented him from carrying on simultaneously the development of an electric railway. But he was free to choose, at least in the beginning of his electrical work, whether to develop the electric light or the electric railway. He evidently chose the former because he was more certain of success. The question, therefore, still remains: why did electric railways look relatively unprofitable to Edison?

The principal reason for his initial failure to develop a practical electric railway is that he did not visualize correctly the place that the electric railway could occupy in the economy. He did not expect commercialization of electric railways to be attained in replacing the horsecars on street railways. He envisioned an electric railway serving as a feeder to the steam railroads on the western plains. The locomotives and trailer cars made and operated at Menlo Park resembled those of steam railroads and not horsecars. Use of the rails for current transmission at 220 volts also indicates that Edison was not thinking of electric cars traveling in city streets. Comparison with his work in the electric light is relevant. There Edison imitated technically and commercially a kind of lighting — gas — which he thought his electric light could displace. If he were to be successful in the electric railway, he should have seen that the horsecar could be displaced by an electric car. But he envisioned the electric railway as serving the function of the steam railroad. He believed that the smaller investment required for a light electric railway and its lower operating costs would enable it to operate profitably in areas with traffic insufficient to support a steam railroad.

It is to Edison's credit, however, that he did not expect the electric railway to replace steam railroads completely. In this respect, he revealed an insight keener than many electric-railway enthusiasts twenty years later, who confidently predicted electrification of all American railroads within a decade. Edison felt that complete electrification of steam railroads would have to await the production of electricity directly from coal.[7] Such a system would not be closely akin to electrification in the usual sense because no conductor — third rail or overhead wire — would be needed. Each locomotive would generate its own electricity from coal, and the electricity would drive an electric motor. This kind of electric locomotive would be similar in principle to the ordinary steam locomotive, which generates steam from coal and uses it to drive a steam engine.

Other factors help to explain Edison's lack of success in electric railways. His work on an electric streetcar in the early 1890's revealed his distrust of the overhead-trolley system. Five hundred volts on bare copper conductors a short distance above crowded city streets seemed to him dangerous and unnecessary. As his views on alternating current showed, he wanted to keep high voltages from any possible contact with the public. This was perhaps the main reason that he never got beyond using the two regular rails as the conductor network, a method which did not become standard practice. In motors, Edison also failed to establish the pattern for railway development. He made no effort to design a special railway motor. The emphasis in his early work on an electric railway designed for long hauls permitted him to be content with an ordinary lighting dynamo. As late as 1889, Edison was of the opinion that railway motors should not be stopped or reversed except at long intervals.[8] In effect, he wanted to avoid subjecting a motor to the abuses of street-railway service rather than to design one which could withstand those abuses.

Edison's failure to develop an electric railway of commercial significance should not obscure the fact that through his work in electric lighting he made fundamental contributions to the electric railway. His efficient dynamo was suitable for railway power generation and became the prototype of the early railway generators. The concepts of parallel conductors, a feeder-main arrangement, and the three-wire system — all of which were embodied in the current-distribution network of his lighting system — found a place in the current-distribution network of the electric railway.

2. *E. Julien*

E. Julien, an electrical engineer who lived in Brussels, Belgium, began experimenting with an electric-railway system in 1881. He used a secondary battery as the source of current in order to avoid the expense and complication of conductors and current-collecting devices. Julien's battery car attracted the attention of a New York lawyer, William Bracken, who had gone to Brussels in May 1886 on patent business. Bracken thought that the Julien battery streetcar could be marketed in the United States, and he made arrangements with Julien for the formation of an American company, the Julien Electric Company. Julien built a thirty-passenger car and sent it to New York, where it arrived late in 1886.[9] Julien followed his car to the United States and undertook to demonstrate its performance on various street railways. The batteries were placed under the seats, and the motor was installed beneath the car. A link chain transmitted the power to the car axle. These items of electric equipment were so designed that they could be mounted on ordinary streetcars. Special cars were not needed.

The Julien company restricted itself in manufacturing to the batteries. The motors were purchased. Julien cars were tried by a number of street-railway companies in Boston, New York, St. Louis, and other cities. The very low investment required by the Julien system unquestionably made it attractive. No conductor, overhead, surface, or underground, had to be installed; nor did the regular streetcar tracks have to be altered in any way. The batteries, the motors, and the accessories were practically the only equipment required. A special generator to charge the batteries was not usually needed, because almost any arc-lighting company was willing to charge the batteries at low rates during daylight hours.

The many trials of Julien equipment resulted in only a few permanent installations. At times very optimistic reports were made of tests held in New York and elsewhere, but the actual performance of the batteries did not justify such optimism. One New York street-railway company that had a Julien battery car on trial for over a year was unable to tell whether it was cheaper than horses.[10] The batteries were expensive and unreliable and an unpredictable expense item. Under ideal conditions, they performed fairly well, but the shaking and jolting to which they were subjected and the occasional heavy surges of current were very destructive. Battery cars were not usable at all where steep grades or extra-heavy loads were encountered. The energy loss in the batteries and the time and expense entailed in removing them for frequent charging were also major disadvantages.

Julien was not the only inventor who tried to apply batteries to electric traction. The idea was so attractive that good judgment was often put aside in the hopes that a successful battery could be found. But the battery car could not give economical and reliable service under the difficult and unpredictable conditions met in street railways. The fact that Julien did not realize the limitations of the battery kept him from becoming a pioneer innovator in electric traction. His battery car was unsuited for the job it was intended to perform.

The ultimate failure of the battery streetcar did not prevent it from playing a key role in the history of electric traction. When overhead conductors for electric streetcars were first being erected, considerable opposition to them developed. The unsightly spectacle of the overhead telegraph, telephone, fire-alarm, police-alarm, and electric-lighting wires, which literally blackened the skies in many cities, left urban residents unwilling to countenance the erection of additional wires. This opposition was overcome in a number of cities through initial use of a battery car which, of course, required no overhead wires or conductors of any kind. The battery car gave the public a chance to experience the benefits of electric traction and to realize that trolley wires were a small price to pay for these benefits. After a short period of battery-car operation, a street-railway company often found it relatively easy to secure permission from the municipality for the erection of trolley wires.[11]

3. *Bentley and Knight*

Edward M. Bentley, formerly an examiner in the electrical section of the United States Patent Office, and Walter H. Knight, an electrical inventor, began work on an electric street railway late in 1883 in the shops of the Brush Electric Company in Cleveland. A short track was built at the Brush works in November, and experimenting continued through the winter. In the spring, a contract was secured with the East Cleveland Street Railway Company to electrify a mile of track and equip several cars to operate on it. Bentley and Knight decided to use an underground wooden conduit, placed between the rails, to carry the two copper conductors. The conduit had a slot through which a plow from the streetcar could reach to obtain current for the motor. The rails were not part of the electrical circuit. Current was supplied by a 500-volt Brush arc-lighting dynamo, placed in the carbarns of the street-railway company. The motor, also a Brush dynamo, was mounted beneath the car.[12]

The electric railway commenced regular operation in July 1884 and had the distinction of being the first commercial electric street railway in the United States. After operation began, many technical difficulties were encountered. The wire belts which connected the motor to the car axle broke and were replaced by friction wheels. These also proved to be unsatisfactory, and finally a set of gears, built of paper to lessen the noise, was installed. The rails were irregular, and much trouble was encountered with cars jumping the track. The plow suffered considerable damage when such an event occurred. After two cars had been equipped and were in service, the difficulties of operating more than one car in a parallel system supplied by a constant-current dynamo became apparent. In spite of all these technical defects, the electric railway seemed to operate well enough to justify the organization of the Bentley-Knight Electric Railway Company in September 1884. The president of the new firm was Roland R. Hazard, a New York capitalist.[13]

The first reports on the Bentley-Knight installation at Cleveland were very optimistic. The president of the East Cleveland road was interviewed late in August 1884, after the electric cars had been in operation over a month. He expressed the opinion that complete electrification of his company's transport system would increase passenger revenues and save $50,000 in annual operating costs. He discussed the comparative advantages of horse, cable, and electric streetcars, and seemed convinced that electric power was the cheapest of the three. His plans had gone far enough to include calculation of the cost of a 500-horsepower electric generating plant, which he thought could be nearly paid for by sale of the real estate and the horses no longer needed.[14] In October, Knight sent a letter to the Committee on Electricity as Motive Power of the American Street Railway Association in which he stated that he expected extension of the Bentley-Knight system over the entire twenty miles of track of the East Cleveland company.[15] Bentley and Knight thus took it for granted that electricity would soon be the only motive power in use on the East Cleveland road. The same optimism appeared in a booklet published in the spring of 1885 by the Bentley-Knight company. It was stated that the Cleveland installation had given satisfactory service all during an exceptionally hard winter.[16]

The expectation that the Cleveland street railway would be further electrified was not realized. Late in the summer of 1885, the mile-long electric railway was discontinued. A year's operation had demonstrated that it was too costly and unreliable to warrent further use. A decision to continue or abandon the railway could not be avoided when the street on which it ran was torn up for a sewer installation. The East Cleveland Street Railway Company chose not to replace the conduit and the conductors which it contained.[17]

By the time of the abandonment of the electric railway in Cleveland, the Bentley-Knight company had established an office in New York City and had severed relations with Brush. Arrangements were made for experimenting at the Rhode Island Locomotive Works in Providence. All equipment necessary for the experiments was made in the locomotive shops. This arrangement continued through 1886, and a short section of track and conduit was laid. In addition to electric-streetcar development, some time was spent designing an electric locomotive for steam-railroad service. When the streetcar work showed promise of success, the locomotive firm made preparations for the manufacture of Bentley-Knight streetcar motors and other electric-railway apparatus. During 1886, a number of street-railway executives visited the Providence works and viewed the operation of the Bentley-Knight system.

A sales pamphlet issued by the Bentley-Knight company in 1885 indicated the nature of its sales arguments and the use it contemplated for its electric-railway system. The main argument for electric power as compared to cables, horses, or steam (used in urban transportation mainly on elevated lines) was the lower cost. Other advantages of electricity were also mentioned, such as the cleanliness and speed compared to horses, the flexibility and safety compared to steam. Complete cost estimates, for construction and operation, were given for horse, cable, and electric railways. For a five-mile, double-track, 40-car street railroad, the estimates of investment required were: electric, $462,000; horse, $204,000; and cable, $803,000. The annual operating expenses were estimated to be: electric, $52,000; horse, $107,000; and cable $101,000.[18]

The annual-expense figures supposedly included all costs, taking account of depreciation and a reasonable return on the investment. Figures were also given which showed the cost of changing existing horse and cable systems to electricity. Especial point was made of the fact that the regular horse and cable cars could be converted to electricity very easily by being mounted on the Bentley-Knight motor truck. It was not necessary to alter the tracks in any way. In the case of a cable road, the conduit which carried the cable could be used to carry the two copper conductors.

The Bentley-Knight company received its first contracts in 1887. It bid on a new three-mile, double-track, 37-car street railway which was to be constructed on Fulton Street in New York City. The Bentley-Knight bid of $214,000 was accepted. The second contract was for an electric railway in Woonsocket, Rhode Island, and the third for one in Allegheny City, Pennsylvania. To carry out these contracts, Bentley-Knight decided not to rely on the Rhode Island Locomotive Works. Arrangements were made with the Thomson-Houston Electric Company to supply the generators, the motors, and the other items of equipment.

Thomson-Houston designed a 15-horsepower, 400-volt railway motor which drove the car axle by means of metallic gearing. The latter consisted of two sets of gears which reduced the motor speed in two steps. This double-reduction gearing, as it was called, was necessary for two reasons. Motor design was not very well understood, and the only way to obtain a motor of sufficient capacity which would fit into the small space allotted it beneath the car was to make it high speed. Moreover, the cars ran relatively slowly, about ten miles per hour. The combination of a high-speed motor and a low-speed car required double-reduction gears. These gears were one major improvement added by the Thomson-Houston engineers. Another was the capacity of the motor. Fifteen horsepower was much more powerful than previous Bentley-Knight railway motors.

The regular Bentley-Knight underground conduit was installed in Fulton Street. One mile of the four-mile Allegheny City line was conduit, and the rest used overhead conductors. The entire Woonsocket road used overhead conductors. The Bentley-Knight overhead system was like the conduit system in that two conductors were used. In neither instance was the track part of the circuit. The current collector in the overhead system was a small wheeled carriage, called a trolley, which ran along on top of the conductors and was connected by a flexible cable to the streetcar.

The Woonsocket road went into operation in October 1887 and seemed to give satisfactory service. The Allegheny City road opened in January 1888 and also performed well for a short period. But before very long, serious troubles arose. The principal difficulty was the excessive wear of the copper brushes on the motor commutators. The brushes had to be replaced frequently, and the commutators required constant repair. The material and labor costs that had to be incurred to keep the cars running were very heavy. Bentley-Knight tried to solve the brush-commutator problem, but they were unable to devise a remedy. It seemed clear that a reliable and economical electric-railway motor was yet to be developed.

In 1888, Thomson-Houston began to market its own electric-railway system and no longer could supply Bentley-Knight. The latter firm therefore made arrangements with a Pittsburgh company for the manufacture of its railway motors and generators, and opened shops in New York City to make the minor components of its system and to carry on development work. The only contract that Bentley-Knight is known to have received during 1888 was awarded by the West End Street Railway Company of Boston. The West End company was building an electric railway from Boston to Brookline. The overhead-conductor system was used throughout, except in the section running from Park Square to Charlesgate, where the Boston city officials ruled against overhead wires. An underground conduit was needed, but it could not be supplied by the regular contractor because of the Bentley-Knight patents. The contract for the Park Square – Charlesgate section of the railway was therefore awarded to Bentley-Knight. Under this contract, Bentley-Knight provided two miles of conduit and a number of double-motor streetcars for operation on the conduit section of the line. The West End order is evidence that substantiates the following statement which appeared in Bentley-Knight advertising literature: "The Bentley-Knight Electric Railway Company absolutely controls all efficient and economic methods of operating electrically equipped cars by means of conductors contained in and protected by sub-surface conduits." [19]

Although many electric-railway installations were made in 1888 and 1889, Bentley-Knight was unable to do an appreciable amount of business. It had over fifty electric-railway patents, however, which covered not only the conduit but also other electrical and mechanical features of an electric-railway system. In August 1889, Bentley-Knight was purchased by Thomson-Houston.[20] Because Thomson-Houston had done its first electric-railway work with the Bentley-Knight company, the systems of the two companies strongly resembled and in some respects were identical with each other. For this reason, and to gain control of the conduit patents, Coffin thought it wise to buy out Bentley-Knight. Bentley joined Thomson-Houston as head of the patent department, and Knight became a design engineer in the railway department.

Bentley and Knight fell short of pioneer innovation in electric railways. They were closer to success than Edison, because they concentrated on street railways, not regular railroads, and did not try to use the two rails for current-transmission purposes. But they did not achieve success. Their railway system was technically unsatisfactory and too costly.

The high cost of the Bentley-Knight system is mainly attributable to the use of an underground conduit. Bentley and Knight started out in Cleveland with an underground conduit and continued to propose only conduits until the Woonsocket and Allegheny City installations of 1887. This was in accord with an influential body in street-railway work, the Committee on Electricity as Motive Power of the American Street Railway Association, as the following quotation from its 1885 report indicates: "In the crowded streets of American cities no system of overhead wires would be permitted by municipal authorities. The rails could not be used to carry the currents, for obvious reasons; therefore a conduit system offers the only practical solution." [21]

After the Woonsocket and Allegheny City installations, the Bentley-Knight sales literature suggested overhead conductors for small cities and the suburban areas of large cities. The cost of the conduit was $25,000 per mile, and the cost of the overhead system was only $3,000 per mile. Bentley and Knight did not realize early enough that the conduit system was too costly for the electric railway to displace horses and cables in any general fashion. They made the same kind of mistake in recommending the double trolley for both the conduit and the overhead systems. The double trolley requires two conductors and therefore more copper than the single-trolley system. Although the use of two conductors saves the expense of the rail bonding which is necessary to insure a good current path if the rails are part of the circuit, the overhead structure is complicated and costly to construct and maintain. Bentley and Knight chose the more expensive method rather than the cheaper and thereby lessened their chances of success.

From a technical standpoint, the Bentley-Knight railway system was deficient. It was undependable and not well suited to continuous daily use. Before coming in contact with the Thomson-Houston engineers, Bentley and Knight were content to connect the motor to the car axle by uncertain and makeshift methods such as wire belts, friction discs, and paper gears. They were also satisfied with weak motors which were unreliable and uneconomical. Not until the Thomson-Houston engineers began to design Bentley-Knight components were positive metallic gearing and more powerful motors adopted. These two features were absolutely essential to any practical and commercially feasible system.

Bentley and Knight thus made major mistakes in designing their electric railway. Their techniques had to be substantially altered by succeeding entrepreneurs before the electric railway could be a commercial success. Some of their mistakes resulted from a lack of boldness. Bentley and Knight were afraid to do what had to be done to give the electric railway a permanent and important place in the economy. They recommended the expensive underground conduit because they feared the reaction of the public and municipal authorities to overhead trolley wires. They employed the costly two-conductor system because they feared the reaction of the telephone companies. At that time, telephone circuits were grounded, and a grounded railway circuit produced "static" in the telephones. They used friction wheels and paper gearing because they feared public reaction to the noise created by metallic gears.

All these fears proved to be without foundation. When the speed and convenience of electric traction became known, the public readily accepted overhead trolley wires in all but a few cities. The telephone companies were unable to prevent grounded streetcar circuits and were forced to use metallic instead of grounded returns to avoid streetcar interference. The noise of metallic streetcar gears was accepted by the public, even though the gears could be heard as far away as two miles. The entrepreneur has to be able to judge what the public will permit. If he is overcautious, his innovation may be so costly and unreliable that it will not succeed; if he is too bold, public opinion or public authority may prevent him from acting at all.

4. *Charles J. Van Depoele*

Charles J. Van Depoele was born in Belgium and during his youth served as an apprentice to a cabinetmaker there. In 1869, at the age of twenty-three, he came to the United States and established a furniture-manufacturing business in Detroit. As this firm grew and prospered, he began to spend time and money on electrical experiments which interested him. These experiments led him to construct a laboratory in his furniture factory in 1877, and there he made a number of dynamos and arc lights. By 1879, he was lighting his own shops and had given several arc-lighting exhibitions in Detroit. In 1880, he began thinking seriously of manufacturing and selling arc-lighting equipment. At first he planned to set up a factory in Detroit, but, as a result of the financial support of Aaron K. Stiles, a Chicago capitalist, the new firm was located in Chicago. The Van Depoele Electric Light Company was incorporated on April 25, 1881, and very shortly afterward began marketing an arc-lighting system. With his arc light out of the development stage and in commercial production, Van Depoele soon lost interest in it. He turned to electric motors and, in 1882, started work on an electric railway. During the winter of 1882–83, his first railway experiments were conducted on a short temporary track laid near the Van Depoele plant in Chicago. Two copper conductors were stretched between the rails. Contact was made with these conductors by two small brass pulleys which were placed beneath the car. The current was supplied by a dynamo located in the plant.[22] The next Van Depoele electric railway was operated at the Chicago Industrial Exposition in the fall of 1883. The following summer, Van Depoele installed a half-mile electric railway at the Toronto Exhibition in Canada. A locomotive powered by a 30-horsepower Van Depoele dynamo (used as a motor) pulled three cars, each with a capacity of sixty persons. The two copper conductors were placed in a wooden conduit between the rails. The purpose of this railway was to carry passengers into the Exhibition grounds.

In the summer of 1885, Van Depoele extended the Exhibition track to a mile in order to connect with a horsecar line from the city of Toronto. As before, one motorcar pulled three trailers. The principal change was the employment of an overhead conductor with an underrunning trolley attached to the end of a pole which was mounted on the roof of the motorcar. A strong spring pressed the pole upward and thereby kept the trolley wheel continuously in contact with the overhead conductor. Van Depoele had conceived of this new method of current pick-up early in 1885.

The Exhibition railway again operated satisfactorily. It ran all during the Exhibition and carried from 6,000 to 10,000 passengers daily. The success of the Toronto railway led to the first contracts to install the Van Depoele system on regular street railways. In the fall of 1885, a street railway in South Bend, Indiana, was equipped by the Van Depoele company. Four cars were fitted with motors and an overhead conductor was installed. The first car was operated on November 14, 1885. The cars performed fairly well, but a change in the management of the railway company occurred about this time, and the electrification was not made permanent. The autumn of 1885 saw one additional Van Depoele railway, which was also only temporary. It supplied transportation service at the New Orleans Exposition during December.

Early in 1886, Van Depoele received an order for an electric locomotive from a Minneapolis steam-railroad company which was not permitted to use steam locomotives in the thickly settled part of the city. This installation and the ones preceding it were either temporary — as in South Bend — or employed the locomotive principle.[23] Although these early roads were of value in helping Van Depoele develop an electric-traction system that would be suitable for street railways, he had not yet equipped a regular and permanent electric street railway. He had invented the overhead trolley-pole method of current transmission and pick-up. He had experimented with various kinds of motor mountings and axle drives. But much additional work remained to be done before his system could give economical and reliable operation under the exacting and difficult conditions of street-railway service.

Van Depoele began making permanent electric street-railway installations in the spring of 1886. He was awarded a contract to equip two cars for operation over two miles of track at Montgomery, Alabama. This installation, and the ones that followed it, employed the single overhead conductor with the track as part of the return circuit. The trolley, a small wheeled traveler connected by a flexible cable to the car, was of the over-running type, and in this respect Van Depoele retrogressed. Following the Montgomery installation, Van Depoele constructed electric street railways at Appleton, Wisconsin; Detroit; Port Huron, Michigan; Windsor, Ontario; and Scranton, Pennsylvania. By the end of 1886, Van Depoele installations totaled twenty-eight cars and thirty miles of track. During 1887, additional cars were added to the Montgomery, Appleton, and Scranton lines, and new installations were made at Binghamton, New York; Dayton, Ohio; Jamaica, Long Island; Lima, Ohio; Harrisburg, Pennsylvania; Ansonia, Connecticut; and Omaha, Nebraska. By the end of 1887, the Van Depoele company had installed a dozen electric street railways which used nearly a hundred cars and over sixty miles of track.

This number of installations placed Van Depoele far ahead of his competitors in the electric-traction field. Other firms had only one or two to their credit, and none of these approached the Montgomery railway in size. At the end of 1887, Bentley-Knight was fulfilling the Allegheny City contract, and Sprague was making a very large installation in Richmond, but neither of these roads was yet in operation.[24] That the Van Depoele system was the best available was the conclusion reached by the Scranton street-railway company on the basis of a survey it conducted before awarding a contract to Van Depoele. A committee was appointed to make a thorough study of electric-railway systems, and the committee members visited all electric railways in operation or in the experimental stage in America. One member of the committee was sent to Europe to examine electric railways there.[25]

In marketing its electric-railway system, the Van Depoele company stressed the fact that the cost of electric traction was lower than other kinds of motive power. In some cases, guarantees on power costs were given. At Lima, Ohio, Van Depoele guaranteed that the cost of electric power per car would not exceed $2 per day. A six months' trial was to be allowed before the guarantee was to apply.[26] The operating-cost figures of the various installations were used to buttress the sales arguments of the Van Depoele salesmen. At Montgomery, Alabama, for example, the replacement of mules by electric power cut operating costs by a third. In addition to this stress on lower costs, the point was usually made that electric cars could travel faster than horsecars and therefore could carry more passengers in any given period. The result was increased revenues.

The increasing business of the Van Depoele company required larger manufacturing facilities and more working capital. A. K. Stiles, the manager and chief stockholder, was not convinced that the electric-railway equipment business would ever be very profitable. He was consequently unwilling to increase his investment in the company. He first hoped to sell the railway business to Sprague, but because of his work at Richmond the latter had neither the time nor the money to give the matter serious consideration. Then, in the spring of 1888, Thomson-Houston offered to buy the Van Depoele railway business, and the purchase was arranged. The services of Van Depoele and the railway patents of the Van Depoele company (now the Van Depoele Electric Manufacturing Company) were sold to Thomson-Houston for a royalty of $25 on each streetcar that would be equipped under the Van Depoele patents. Van Depoele, himself, received a royalty of $5 per car and joined the railway department of Thomson-Houston at a regular salary. Several months later, Stiles became dissatisfied with the sale terms. He was not optimistic enough about the future of the electric-railway business to believe that $25 per car could ever add up to a very large sum. He asked for a cash settlement of the royalty contract and received $300,000. He must have regretted this step later, for the royalties would have totaled several million dollars before the patents expired.

The sale of the Van Depoele railway business to Thomson-Houston in March 1888 prevents a definitive answer to the question: was Van Depoele the pioneer innovator in electric traction? The reason no answer can be given is that Van Depoele's work up to that time had not arrived at the stage of pioneer innovation, although it was clearly heading in that direction. The Van Depoele installations were successful in the sense that reliable operation at a cost below that of animal power was generally attained. But the act of pioneer innovation had not yet been performed. There was doubt that the Van Depoele system could be commercially successful on a large-scale railway system. And the technical features of Van Depoele's system were different enough from the features of those systems which later were commercially successful on a large scale—the Sprague system and the Thomson-Houston system—to give credence to that doubt. Had Van Depoele continued in his own company, he might have improved his system and become the pioneer innovator. As it was, he joined the Thomson-Houston engineering staff in March 1888 and worked with Professor Thomson and other Thomson-Houston engineers from that time on. The role of pioneer innovator cannot, therefore, be assigned to Van Depoele as an individual. The Thomson-Houston railway system was the result of the joint effort of a number of men in the Thomson-Houston organization, and it is the company, not Van Depoele alone, that shares with Sprague the title of pioneer innovator in electric traction.

The limitations of the Van Depoele system are revealed by an examination of some of the installations. In a few places, Van Depoele mounted the motors beneath the cars, but at later and larger installations (Scranton, Montgomery) he placed the motor on the platform near the motorman. The purpose of this location was to make the motor easily available for adjustment of the brushes if the sparking became serious. This was a makeshift solution to the sparking problem, and it necessitated use of the inefficient and unreliable chain drive. Another difficulty resulted from the fact that the motor was mounted directly and firmly on the car body. Such a fixed mounting complicates the motor-axle connection and increases wear and breakage, because the wheels and axles move with respect to the car body as a result of track irregularities encountered in normal operations. Placing the motor on the platform thus had definite mechanical disadvantages. Moreover, keeping the motor near the motorman prevented Van Depoele from adding to his system features which were needed for large-system operation. The two-motor car (one motor for each axle) and the double-ended car, which could be controlled from either end, were completely overlooked.

The other major technical fault of the Van Depoele system was the use of the overrunning instead of the underrunning trolley. The overrunning trolley is satisfactory only under the ideal conditions of low speeds and relatively straight tracks. It does not provide the positive contact which is needed for reliable performance under all kinds of operating conditions, and it makes switching and the overhead-conductor installation more complicated. Van Depoele abandoned the underrunning trolley, which he used at Toronto, because he could not make it operate in a satisfactory fashion. He tried to use it on regular street car installations, but could not keep it against the trolley wire. He sometimes resorted to the expedient of having a man ride on top of the car to hold the trolley pole against the overhead conductor. With the overrunning traveler, no such difficulty was experienced. The trolley and the motor mounting both indicate that Van Depoele was willing to use a method which would be successful only on a small scale rather than carry out the development work necessary to find a method suitable for a large-scale system. Van Depoele's innovational vision was thus deficient in an important respect. He did not see clearly the technical features an electric railway had to have to be workable where there were many miles of tracks and dozens of cars.

TABLE 23

Summary of Four Early Attempts to Develop an Electric Railway

			Techniques to meet the three basic problems of an electric railway		
	Intended Use	*Commercial Installations*	*The current-supply problem*	*The motor-axle power-transmission problem*	*The motor problem*
Edison (at Menlo Park; 1880–1882)	Long freight hauls	None	The two rails as the only conductors	Friction discs, then leather belt	No attempt to design a special motor. Used a lighting dynamo
Julien	Street railway	1887–1889, several (New York, Boston, St. Louis); all temporary	Storage battery carried in the streetcar	Link chain	No attempt to design a special motor. Purchased motors
Bentley-Knight	Street railway	1884–1885, Cleveland (temporary) 1887, three 1888, one 1889, company purchased by Thomson-Houston	Underground conduit containing two copper conductors	Wire belts, then friction discs, then paper gears	Worked with Thomson-Houston to design special railway motor. Did not give satisfactory service
Van Depoele	Street railway	1883–1885, special installations for exhibitions, etc. 1886, six 1887, seven 1888, company purchased by Thomson-Houston	One overhead conductor. Rails part of the electric circuit. Overrunning trolley (after underrunning trolley proved unworkable)	Link chain	Worked on motor problem but without success. Mounted motor on front platform of car to permit frequent adjustment and easy repair

The work of the early electric-railway entrepreneurs described in this chapter is summarized in Table 23. The progress from Edison's 1880 efforts to Van Depoele's 1887 installations is evident. Electric-railway design moved toward a reliable and commercially feasible system as various of the technical possibilities were shown to be unworkable by Edison, Julien, and Bentley-Knight. The successive stages are most apparent in the attempts by these men to solve the current-supply problem. The problem was almost solved by Van Depoele. Had he been able to develop a workable underrunning trolley, he would have solved it. The other two basic electric-railway problems were still far from solution in Van Depoele's railway. It was here that Sprague and Thomson-Houston, whose work is described in the following chapter, made the greatest advance over Van Depoele's work.

The engineer-entrepreneurs treated in this chapter all made contributions to electric traction, and one of them (Van Depoele) achieved moderate success in isolated commercial installations. But none performed an act of pioneer innovation in electric railways because all of them failed to apply electric power to a large-scale transportation system. On the basis of their work alone, it was quite certain that electric railways would never have been more than an oddity. Electric cars would never have replaced to any appreciable extent the horsecars, the cable cars, and the elevated steam railroads. The nearly complete substitution of electricity for these other kinds of motive power had to await the work of Sprague and Thomson-Houston.

XVI

The Pioneer Innovators in Electric Traction

FRANK JULIAN SPRAGUE

FRANK JULIAN SPRAGUE,[1] a native of Milford, Connecticut, was graduated from the United States Naval Academy in 1878 at the age of twenty. After two years at sea, he returned to the United States in the spring of 1880. He then received several shore assignments, including a tour of duty at the Newport Naval Station, where he was permitted to carry on electrical experimenting of his own choosing. He next sought assignment as the assistant to the officer representing the United States Navy at the 1881 Paris Electrical Exhibition. When this attempt failed, he secured orders for temporary duty on a naval vessel which was sailing from New York to join the Mediterranean squadron. Because the ship was delayed, he did not reach Europe until the spring of 1882, after the close of the Paris exhibition. Fortunately for Sprague, the Crystal Palace Electrical Exhibition had just opened in London, and he went there instead. Although only twenty-five years of age, he was given the opportunity to serve as secretary of an award jury which included a number of distinguished scientists. As a jury member, Sprague was in an excellent position to study and test the numerous electrical devices on display.

In London, Sprague rode occasionally on the Metropolitan District Railroad, an underground steam railroad. The smoke, gas, and dirt emitted by the locomotive in the small confines of the tunnel led him to consider the possibility of a cleaner kind of power, the electric motor. He first contemplated carrying the current to the car motor by means of a conductor at track level, but the probable complications of switching caused him to consider an overhead conductor instead. To pick up the current he envisioned an underrunning contact mounted on the roof of the car.[2]

At the Exhibition, Sprague met E. H. Johnson, who was representing the Edison company and in charge of the Edison exhibit. Johnson was impressed by Sprague's knowledge of and interest in electricity and suggested that he work for Edison when he returned to the United States. Sprague accepted this offer. On his arrival in the United States in May 1883, he was given a job by Edison in the construction department. He helped in the installation of the first overhead three-wire central station at Sunbury, Pennsylvania, which was completed on July 4, 1883, and the first underground three-wire central station at Brockton, Massachusetts, which was completed on October 1, 1883. Sprague remained at the Brockton station as operating engineer. In his free time, he carried on motor experiments and constructed a railway motor. He made such good progress in developing a practical and efficient motor that he resigned from Edison's employ in the spring of 1884 and devoted all his time to motor work. Edison was stressing illumination to the practical exclusion of motive power, and Sprague was pessimistic about opportunities in the Edison organization for anyone interested primarily in electric power.

Sprague continued work on his motors during the summer of 1884. By fall he was ready to market a motor explicitly designed for industrial use. The motor was well engineered and contained several new features. It sparked very little, and the speed was constant regardless of changes in load. Sprague displayed the motor at an electrical exhibition in Philadelphia in the fall of 1884, and its merits were quickly recognized. The reception given the motor encouraged Sprague to go ahead with plans to market it. In November 1884, he and Johnson formed the Sprague Electric Railway and Motor Company. The authorized capital was $100,000. Except for a few shares owned by Johnson, for which he paid cash, Sprague held all the stock. The company undertook to sell its motors through sales agents located in all sections of the United States. The manufacturing was done by the Edison Machine Works, and Sprague continued to spend most of his time on development work. He obtained the necessary funds from Johnson, who received stock in return.

For several years Sprague's enterprise was not much more than a paper one. Since the manufacturing was subcontracted to Edison, no manufacturing personnel or facilities were needed. The selling was handled by independent sales agents who invested their own funds in the inventory they carried. The operation of the Sprague firm consequently required very little capital investment and almost no employees. Johnson and

Sprague could easily take care of the administrative problems that arose. Sprague was truly operating on a shoestring, for the company was established with only $16,000 paid in.[3] Even this small amount was not required for ordinary business operations, and Sprague was able to apply the funds to research and development work. Profits which arose as sales expanded were used in the same way.

The market for Sprague motors was composed principally of business firms which could obtain electric current from their own incandescent-lighting generators or from an Edison-type central station. The Edison Electric Light Company recognized that a motor load would be very profitable for its central stations. The motors would usually be operated in the daytime, in contrast to electric lights, which were used mainly at night. The additional cost of supplying current during the daylight hours would consequently be very low. A circular encouraging the development of a motor load was issued to the licensee stations by the Edison company in 1885. This circular suggested the Sprague motor, as the following quotation shows: "A practical motor has been a want seriously felt in our system. . . The Sprague motor is believed to meet . . . all the exigencies of the case and the Edison Electric Light Company feels that it can safely recommend it to its licensees as the only practical and economic motor existing today."[4]

The use of Sprague motors for industrial purposes increased during 1885 and 1886, when they were first installed in clothing factories, printing presses, and various kinds of mills. In the fall of 1886, a Sprague motor was used to operate a freight elevator in a six-story building in Boston. A little later, a Boston furniture dealer installed a Sprague-driven passenger elevator and used this fact to attract patrons to his store.[5] Both of these elevator motors were operated on current supplied by the Edison central station and are evidence of the enterprise shown by the station management in securing motor business. The president of the Boston Edison Company was E. H. Johnson, Sprague's business associate, and Johnson is probably responsible for the large number of Sprague motors in use in Boston. By the end of 1887, seventy-three customers were receiving electric power from the Boston station. These customers had purchased Sprague motors totaling 240 horsepower in capacity.[6]

By the beginning of 1887, two hundred and fifty Sprague motors of sizes from one-half to fifteen horsepower were in operation throughout the United States. The increasing motor sales led Sprague to decide to establish his own manufacturing plant. He leased a New York factory for that purpose in October 1886. To finance this expansion and to provide additional working capital, the authorized capital stock of the Sprague company was increased to $1,000,000 a few months later. The factory was acquired to make motors for special purposes. The standard types of motors, which were made in quantity, were still manufactured by the Edison Machine Works.[7]

The Sprague company envisioned a widespread application of electric power in industry. An early Sprague booklet listed five uses of electric power: (1) the transmission of power over considerable distances; (2) the distribution of power within a single plant; (3) auxiliary power; (4) portable apparatus for pumping, hoisting, and so forth; and (5) tramways for the transportation of freight.[8] The first use was restricted to relatively short distances under the low d.c. voltages which were available. But the other four became common in the late 1880's. A Springfield, Massachusetts, steam-power station which had been distributing power to various firms by means of shafting and wire rope adopted Sprague motors for this purpose in 1887.[9] A Sprague motor was used for hoisting building materials in the construction of the Kansas State Capitol that same year.[10] In this use, the main advantage of the electric motor, which received current from an Edison central station, over a steam engine was that the hoist was needed only at long intervals. The first application of a Sprague motor to industrial tramways was in a Boston sugar refinery. Seven hundred feet of railway were constructed to carry the raw sugar from the waterfront to the refinery. Current was obtained from the sugar company's isolated plant, which supplied the lighting circuits at night.[11]

Sprague's main contribution to stationary electric power was to develop a reliable and efficient motor in large sizes. The motors made by other manufacturers in 1884 and 1885 were all very small — under one horsepower — and suitable only for a limited range of application. Sprague marketed motors of 15 horsepower in 1885, and by 1890 he was building them as large as 30 horsepower. A minor contribution was that he designed his motors for operation on the regular Edison circuits. Any firm within the range of an Edison central station or which owned an isolated Edison plant could use them.

The sales of the Sprague Electric Railway and Motor Company during 1885, 1886, and 1887 were almost entirely motors for industrial uses. But Sprague was not spending much time during these years on the development of industrial motors. He was concentrating on the problem of electric traction and, in particular, on the application of electric power to the New York elevated railroads. Although Van Depoele, Bentley-Knight, and a few other electric-railway entrepreneurs had begun to install electric-streetcar systems, it is quite logical that Sprague should consider the New York elevated railways as the ideal place to introduce electric traction. There the advantages of electric traction would be the greatest and the technical problems would be easiest to solve.

The principal advantages of electricity over steam on elevated railways were the clean and quiet operation of the electric motor and the promise of relief from traffic congestion. By the mid 1880's, the four elevated lines of New York were reaching the limit of their carrying capacity. The trains could not be appreciably increased in number because they were being run as close together as safety permitted. Faster or longer trains would be possible only if heavier locomotives were employed. But heavier locomotives would require a stronger elevated structure, and that would mean a substantial increase in capital expenditures. An alternative would be the construction of additional elevated lines. The city inhabitants objected strongly, however, to the erection of more elevated structures, and it became almost impossible for the elevated-railway companies to secure permission from municipal governments to build additional lines.

Electric power promised a way out of this dilemma because motors could be placed on each car and locomotives would be thereby eliminated. The trains could then be of almost any length (up to the limit set by the length of the station platforms) without changes in the elevated structure. They could run faster and closer together. Furthermore, the electric system, with power generated in a few, large, stationary steam plants instead of in hundreds of locomotives, would reduce fuel costs.

The technical problems of electric traction — the motor, current supply, and motor-axle power transmission — were easier to solve on an elevated railway than on a surface street railway, because the railroad right-of-way was out of reach of street traffic and because stops were less frequent. The private, inaccessible right-of-way meant that the very simple third-rail system of current supply, using an economical high voltage, could be employed. The less frequent starting and stopping meant that both the motor and the transmission mechanism would be subject to much less abuse. The fact that the roadbed was much smoother was also an important advantage. The equipment did not have to be nearly so durable and rugged.

Sprague made a very thorough study of the New York elevated lines and their transportation problems.[12] In 1885, he began experimenting on the short elevated test track at Twenty-Ninth Street, which had been built by the Edison-Field railway company. He soon felt that he needed a longer track to study operating problems and switched to the Thirty-Fourth Street branch of the Manhattan Elevated Railway to continue his experiments. By the end of 1886, Sprague was putting on successful demonstrations of his electric car, which showed reliability, good pulling power, and fast acceleration. These tests were so impressive that the Edison company considered buying the Sprague company.[13] Although this purchase was not consummated, several Edison directors invested a total sum of over $50,000 in the Sprague company. The elevated-railway officials could not be convinced, however, that electric traction was the answer to their transportation problems.

Just why the management of the New York elevated railroads was so uninterested in electric power is not easy to explain. They were quite aware that the existing elevated lines had nearly reached the limit of their carrying capacity. They were also conscious of the objections of the people of New York to the noise and dirt of the steam locomotives. In the early 1880's, they commissioned Edison to make a study of the effects of the noise and vibrations on the residents and structures along the elevated lines. But no changes were made. It is probable that the officials hoped that the public would overlook the discomforts resulting from steam locomotives and that permission would be granted for the erection of additional elevated structures, particularly on Broadway. With these hopes in mind, they refused to take any steps to increase either carrying capacity or the comfort of the New York populace.

The four New York elevated lines of the 1880's — Second, Third, Sixth, and Ninth Avenues — were under control of a single firm, the Manhattan Elevated Railway Company. It is therefore possible that the prejudice of Jay Gould against electric traction may have been a factor in the attitude of the company management. Gould was one of the financiers who controlled the Manhattan company. He was present at one of the demonstrations given by Sprague. It just happened that Gould was riding on the motorcar when, as a result of a heavy surge of current, a fuse blew with an explosive flash. Gould was so startled that he attempted to jump from the car and refused ever again to take the slightest interest in electric traction.[14]

Unable to interest the New York elevated railroads in electric traction after nearly two years of experiments and tests, and unwilling to finance more such development work himself, Sprague turned to urban surface traction in the hopes of achieving more success. He secured his first railway contracts in the spring of 1887. One of these contracts — calling for electrification of a new street railway to be built in Richmond, Virginia — was to decide whether the horse, the mule, and the cable were to give way before electric power. The significance of this contract derived mostly from its size. The Richmond railway marks the first attempt in the United States to electrify a large-scale streetcar system. Forty cars, twelve miles of track, a power plant of 375 horsepower — no electric railway then in operation even approached these figures.

Sprague received the Richmond contract from a group of New York capitalists, including Maurice B. Flynn, who had visited Richmond early in 1887 in search of a site for a manufacturing plant. They noticed that Richmond had only one street railway, and they thought a second one could be profitably operated. But the route they chose included steep grades, sharp curves, and unpaved clay streets. In these conditions, the use of animal power, except at prohibitive cost, was almost impossible. In order to be reasonably sure of a profit, they needed more power than horses or mules could provide, and they turned to electricity as a possible solution to their problem.

Flynn contacted Sprague, who had received considerable publicity as a result of his experiments on the elevated lines, and suggested that he electrify the street railway to be built in Richmond. The track was not yet laid, nor was the route completely determined, and therefore the exact conditions in which the cars would operate was not known. In spite of this uncertainty, Sprague signed a contract early in May 1887. He agreed to bear all the risk of failure and to guarantee an early completion date. The contract stipulated that Sprague was to supply forty cars with two motors and accessory equipment for each car, a complete overhead current-supply system for twelve miles of track, and an electric generating plant of 375 horsepower. Thirty of the forty cars were to be operated simultaneously, and grades of 8 per cent were to be ascended. The completion date was to be ninety days after the track construction had proceeded far enough to permit the electrical installation work to begin. When the railway had operated satisfactorily for sixty days, Sprague was to receive $110,000 in cash.[15]

The problems Sprague faced in trying to fulfill the Richmond contract were numerous and difficult. A decade later, he said: "When the Richmond contract was signed, we had only a blueprint of a machine and some rough experimental apparatus. The hundred and one details that were essential to success were as yet undetermined. Fortunately for the future of electric railways, the difficulties ahead could not be foreseen or the contract would not have been signed."[16] As a further handicap, Sprague was stricken with typhoid fever in July and was unable to work for over two months. Precious time slipped by, and it was early fall before he could give his personal attention to the Richmond project.

The condition of the track and roadbed was a major obstacle. The track was light, poorly joined, and insecurely fastened. It was unevenly laid on red clay. There were twenty-nine curves — including five of radius less than thirty feet — and grades as high as 10 per cent. A wet fall and winter converted the red clay into a sticky mass which often submerged the rails and made travel impossible. A more unfavorable situation in which to place the first large-scale electric street railway can hardly be imagined.

The technical problems that Sprague encountered were even more difficult. The source of most of these was the magnitude of the project. There were no more than sixty electric streetcars operating in the entire United States in the spring of 1887, and on no one railway were there more than eight or ten cars. For Sprague to undertake a forty-car railway, when he had yet to make a street-railway installation and when only a few much smaller installations had been made by other electric-railway entrepreneurs, was courageous indeed. He surely knew, moreover, that none of the installations had been very successful and that many were kept in operation only at considerable expense. His experience with railway motors and the problems of mounting and controlling them on the elevated lines was to be very useful. But there were numerous problems peculiar to streetcar operation that he never had before met. And the design of a forty-car system would require many features that no other electric-railway entrepreneur had put into practice.

In essence, Sprague had set out to show that electric power could be economical and reliable for a large street-railway system. This goal guided him in the design of what became the prototype of the modern street railway. But before that prototype was evolved, numerous and costly experiments were required. Sprague's predecessors, the most important of whom have been discussed in Chapter XV, had employed techniques which could never be successful on a large scale. These techniques were temporary, makeshift, awkward, expensive, and unreliable. They could not be employed on a large-scale street railway if that railway were to provide speedy, reliable, and efficient service over many miles of track. Sprague understood the fundamental errors of his predecessors and knew what a large-scale system needed. He had the technical ability to meet these needs and the determination to overcome any obstacle that might stand in his way.

The first serious technical trouble Sprague encountered was in the motors. An attempt to climb the 10 per cent grades burned out the armatures and field coils. To obtain more power, Sprague was forced to alter the gearing. He contacted Brown and Sharpe, machine makers of Providence, Rhode Island, who agreed to manufacture the new gears as rapidly as possible. The first test runs were made in November 1887, but by the following January it was apparent that Sprague could not meet the ninety-day deadline. The owners of the railway were disappointed and, even more important, considerably alarmed. They threatened to cancel the contract. To obtain an extension of time, Sprague was forced to make financial concessions. The total payment was reduced to $90,000, and only half of that was to be in cash. The remainder was to be in bonds of the street-railway company.

By almost superhuman effort, Sprague, aided by S. D. Greene, formerly a naval officer, and O. T. Crosby, formerly an army officer, succeeded in opening the railway for regular travel early in February 1888. During the succeeding months service was maintained, but only with great difficulty and at enormous expense. Overhead switches, insulation, lightning, and the motor brushes gave the most trouble. Of these four, the last was by far the most serious. The brushes had to be replaced frequently and the commutators machined. Each car was inspected after every trip and the necessary repairs made. The Edison factory in Schenectady and the Sprague factory in New York continuously shipped motors and motor parts by the fastest available means in order to keep the cars running.[17]

The electrical and mechanical problems were matched by difficulties with the track and roadbed. The rails often spread apart or sank into the mud. There were no guard rails on the curves. Derailments were so common that each car was equipped with a large timber and a scaling ladder. The timber was used for leverage, and the scaling ladder enabled a man to connect the trolley pole to the overhead wire. The ladder and the timber, which resembled a battering ram, gave an amusing medieval appearance to the parties of men who pushed the derailed cars back on the tracks.

Gradually the troubles were overcome. The mudholes were filled and the tracks straightened. A special electric connector and sections of rail were devised so that a derailed car could get back on the track under its own power. The substitution of carbon brushes for metallic ones solved the brush-commutator difficulties. Lightning arresters were installed, and it was learned that if the car lights were turned on during a thunderstorm, most of the lightning would discharge harmlessly through the lighting circuit. Over fifty different trolley poles were tried before a successful one was developed. The motor armatures and field coils were completely redesigned and rewound. Lubrication was found to loosen the motor gears which tended to lock. By the fall of 1888, reliable and economical operation had been achieved.

The real significance of the Richmond installation was that it contained the technical features which permitted successful operation on a large scale and set the pattern for electric street-railway development. An overhead conductor was used, and the current was picked up by a universal swiveling, underrunning trolley. The motors — two on each car — were mounted beneath the car and suspended by what was called the wheelbarrow suspension. Each motor was mounted by three points, two on the car axle and one on the car. This arrangement permitted the car to move relative to the axle and motor without misaligning the gearing. The double-reduction gear was used, although Sprague had at first tried to use the single-reduction gear which later became standard. The motor brushes were fixed in position, and motor control was achieved by a device, invented by Sprague, called the series-parallel controller. This controller placed the two motors in series when the streetcar was starting from standstill. After running speed was attained, the motors were placed in parallel across the supply voltage. The advantage of this technique was that the motors could operate more effectively and more efficiently.

One controller was mounted on each end of the car, permitting operation from either end. The tracks were part of the return circuit, and only one overhead conductor was used. The parallel system at 500 volts with a main conductor and a working conductor (the trolley wire) was adopted. Lightning arresters were installed. All these features — except the double-reduction gear which was replaced by the single-reduction gear in the early 1890's — became standard on American street railways and have remained so until the present. The motor mounting, the current pick-up device, the current-supply system, the method of motor control, the motor brushes — all these were so well chosen and so well adapted to reliable and economical operation that the improvements that could be made in later years were not fundamental in nature.

Sprague's Richmond installation, like Edison's Pearl Street station, cost far more than had been anticipated. To fulfill the contract, Sprague spent over $160,000, or nearly twice what he was paid. The high cost is easily accounted for. Sprague had not worked out the technical details when he took the contract, and the necessary experimentation was expensive. Furthermore, he was working against time, and the attempt to achieve results in a minimum of time was very costly. Changes in equipment were frequent and had to be decided upon instantly, without careful deliberation. Motors and other apparatus were manufactured quickly and sent by express to Richmond. When Sprague ordered the special gears from Brown and Sharpe, he told them to make them as soon as possible without regard for expense. The race against time led Sprague to open the road to the public in February, long before operation was reliable. Much effort and expense were necessary to keep the cars running.

Sprague was able to withstand the heavy Richmond loss because of the good earning capacity of the Sprague Electric Railway and Motor Company. And he made up the loss many times over when the success of the Richmond installation became known. Not only was continuous service by a large number of cars maintained at Richmond, but, even more important, operating costs were only 40 per cent of what they would have been with animal power. When thirty cars were first in operation at one time, on May 4, 1888, the Union Passenger Railway Company notified Sprague that the clause concerning satisfactory operation had been fulfilled and that the electrical equipment was formally accepted.[18] By July, the operation of the electric cars was so satisfactory that Flynn was willing to expand their use. He ordered forty more cars from Sprague for the Union Passenger Lines. In addition, he purchased control of the other Richmond street-railway company and announced plans to electrify it. This firm, the Richmond City Railway Company, had been established in 1865 and by 1888 was using 225 horses and mules to operate 50 cars over 13 miles of track. Flynn was particularly anxious to gain control of this company, because it had a much better route than his new Union Passenger company. The prospects for high profits as a result of electrification were very good.[19]

The excellent performance of the Sprague installation at Richmond exerted a powerful influence on the growth of electric street railways in the United States. One example is the West End Street Railway Company of Boston. This company had been formed originally by Henry M. Whitney to build a horse railway from Boston to Brookline to aid a real-estate-development project he had undertaken. He soon enlarged his plans and secured control of seven of the eight street railways in Boston and amalgamated them with his West End company. This step, completed in 1887, created the largest street-railway system in the United States, with 212 miles of tracks, 1,700 cars, and 8,000 horses. Whitney decided that a motive power better than horses was needed, and plans were made to install a cable system. Land for the power stations was purchased, and some of the contracts were awarded. Then Whitney heard of the Richmond electric railway and halted all the cable preparations while he made a study of electric traction. He visited Richmond three times. On one of these visits, Sprague staged a special demonstration for him in which twenty-two cars were lined up and started at once. Whitney decided that electricity, not cables, should provide the motive power for his streetcars, and he awarded Sprague the contract for the Boston-Brookline section. Twelve miles of track and twenty cars were involved.

The West End company's decision to electrify can be contrasted to the decision made by the Third Avenue Street Railway Company of New York City two years earlier. Late in 1886, the Third Avenue company decided to change from horses to either electricity or cables. To investigate electricity a committee of the company visited the Bentley-Knight experimental railway at the locomotive works in Providence. The committee learned that the electric railway would cost 25 per cent more to operate than a cable railway. The result of this visit was that the Third Avenue company "with some reluctance . . . abandoned all idea of electricity on account of its expense in the present stage of manufacture and control" and adopted the cable system.[20]

The impetus which the Richmond railway gave to the business of the Sprague company and to electric railways in general is indicated by the following data. In the spring of 1887, at the time that Sprague signed the Richmond contract, there were in operation in the United States eight electric street railways, using a total of 60 cars on 35 miles of track. Of these eight, five were Van Depoele.[21] By the fall of 1889, eighteen months after the Richmond road began regular operation, there were 180 electric street railways under construction and in operation, with 1,260 miles of track and nearly 2,000 cars. The number of roads equipped by various manufacturers were as follows: Sprague, 67; Thomson-Houston, 67; Van Depoele, 10; Bentley-Knight, 1; and all others, 35.[22]

The expansion of the sales of the Sprague company as its industrial and railway business grew necessitated an increase in its capitalization by 1889. An additional $200,000 of common stock and $600,000 of preferred stock were issued. The preferred stock was purchased by the Edison Electric Light Company. A few months later the Sprague company was merged into the newly formed Edison General Electric Company. By absorbing Sprague, Edison made sure its largest customer would not take his business elsewhere and, at the same time, entered the fields of electric power and electric traction. Sprague went along with his company and assumed the post of consulting engineer to Edison General Electric. He held this position only a short time. Henry Villard, Edison General Electric president, had decided that overhead trolley wires would not be permitted in large cities and had requested Edison to develop a low-potential rail system. Sprague tried to prevent Villard from taking this step, but failed; he resigned in protest and shortly thereafter organized his own company to make and install electric elevators. It was generally believed at the time that Sprague resigned because Edison General Electric began to call its railway system the Edison system instead of the Sprague system. Sprague unquestionably was very bitter about this change of name and considered it an act of injustice. He later wrote, however, that he had resigned over the low-potential issue before he learned that his name was going to be erased from the railway system he had worked so long and so hard to develop.[23]

Edison General Electric continued to produce and sell the Sprague motor until the formation of General Electric in 1892. This motor, called by Sprague the No. 6, was extremely successful and by far the best railway motor of the period. Over 4,000 were sold in the years 1888–1892. At Richmond, Sprague used his No. 5 motor, but learned that a more powerful motor was needed. Toward the end of 1888, he brought out the No. 6 motor, which at 15 horsepower was twice as powerful as the No. 5. The No. 6 was the first thoroughly successful railway motor in the United

States. It tends to support the view that a pioneer innovator must have more than a clear vision of the place his innovation can occupy in the economy and the judgment to decide what technical features are necessary to the innovation so it can occupy that place. He must also possess inventive and engineering ability of a high order. The technical features must be created and must be made reliable. Otherwise the vision cannot be translated into reality.

THE THOMSON-HOUSTON ELECTRIC COMPANY

Thomson-Houston entered the field of electric power in 1887. In the spring of that year, a contract was made to supply Bentley and Knight with railway motors and generators. In the summer, a full line of stationary electric motors of sizes from 1 to 15 horsepower was put on the market. The experience gained in motor manufacture, particularly from those made for the Bentley-Knight installations at Woonsocket and Allegheny City, led Coffin to believe that Thomson-Houston would find it profitable to enter the electric-railway business. According to W. J. Clarke, a Thomson-Houston official and later a high-ranking executive in General Electric, Coffiin stated early in 1888 that he considered the possibilities of electric lighting exhausted and that he consequently wanted to branch out into electric railways.[24]

One obstacle to this contemplated move was the Thomson-Houston charter. Coffin was not certain that it permitted the company to produce electric-railway equipment. The incorporation statute, passed by the Connecticut legislature in April 1883, gave Thomson-Houston the right to use, buy, sell, and lease electric apparatus for the production and use of electricity for "electric lighting, electric transmission of power, electro-telegraphic, electro-metallurgic, and other useful purposes."[25] Although no specific mention was made of electric railways, they could conceivably be included under electric transmission of power. To play safe, Coffin undertook to have the charter amended. Eighteen months later, on February 28, 1889, the Connecticut legislature approved a charter amendment which gave Thomson-Houston the explicit right to produce and sell electric-railway equipment and to hold securities in electric-railway companies. In addition to initiating the legislative process for amending the charter, Coffin applied for a franchise to build and operate an electric railway at Crescent Beach, Massachusetts, near Lynn. This railway would be operated as a commercial enterprise, but it could also be used for experiments and demonstrations.

Following these preliminary arrangements, a very important decision had to be made. Should Thomson-Houston enter electric traction by developing its own system, or should it purchase one of the companies currently marketing an electric-railway system? Thomson, confident of his ability to design an electric railway superior to any then being manufactured, favored the first alternative. Coffin favored the second. He believed that electric-railway development had proceeded too far for Thomson-Houston to take the time to develop its own system. The risks of being left behind were too great.

Coffin's desire to buy prevailed, and Thomson recommended Van Depoele. It was the only company with an appreciable number of reasonably successful commercial installations, and Thomson believed the Van Depoele patents might prove of great value. Coffin's subsequent offer to purchase the Van Depoele railway business came at a time when Stiles was seeking a buyer. Van Depoele also favored the sale, because he saw a chance to continue work on electric railways with a better engineering staff and stronger financial backing. The sale was completed in February 1888, and Van Depoele went to Lynn in March to begin work on the Thomson-Houston electric-railway system. The fact that Thomson recommended Van Depoele and not Bentley and Knight, whom Thomson-Houston had worked with, is an indication that Van Depoele was ahead of the other two inventors. Van Depoele and Bentley and Knight had been in the railway business about the same length of time, but Van Depoele had shown greater inventive ingenuity and had achieved greater commercial success.

Van Depoele, Thomson, and A. L. Roher, the Thomson-Houston engineer who had been assigned to the Bentley-Knight contracts, were mainly responsible for the Thomson-Houston railway system. What Thomson and Roher did, in essence, was to convert Van Depoele's small-scale system into a large-scale one. They tried to change those elements of his system which had restricted it to street railways of only a few cars. The goal was a system which could give efficient and reliable service on the largest street-railway systems in existence. Thomson decided to place the motors beneath the cars and to use direct mechanical gearing to drive the car axle. Like Sprague, Thomson realized that a motor suspension independent of the car bodies was needed in order that the gears could be properly engaged at all times. Experience with the Bentley-Knight installation at Allegheny City had shown the need for a 15-horsepower motor and two motors per car. The trolley pole and underrunning trolley which Van Depoele had abandoned were the subject of numerous experiments, and finally a reliable underrunning trolley was developed.

With these changes in the Van Depoele system, the Thomson-Houston company possessed a railway system which promised reliable and economical service on any scale. The system was first installed on the Lynn railway, which went into operation on July 4, 1888. Except for brush and commutator troubles, the cars ran very well. A number of orders were received in the summer and fall of 1888. Among these was an installation in Washington, D.C., where the Senate at first objected to overhead wires but later consented to their use.

Although these first Thomson-Houston installations were successful and brought about many additional contracts, both Coffin and Thomson realized that the problem of brush sparking had to be solved. Dependable and low-cost operation was not possible until some method of reducing brush and commutator wear had been devised. Van Depoele was in favor of mounting the motor on the platform near the motorman so he could adjust the brushes from time to time as necessary. Thomson rejected this solution as a step backward. Finally, Van Depoele solved the problem. He suggested the use of carbon instead of copper for brushes. In his early experiments with arc-lighting dynamos, he had used an arc carbon as a makeshift brush when a copper one was temporarily unavailable. The carbon brush worked well, and later he tried it on small motors. The immediate reaction of Thomson was that the resistance of carbon was so much greater than that of copper that a carbon brush could not be expected to carry heavy motor currents. He soon realized, however, that the brush could be made larger in cross section to counterbalance the high resistance of carbon. This was done, and carbon brushes were placed on several railway motors.[26] It was then obvious that the solution to the sparking problem had been found. Carbon brushes were installed on all the Thomson-Houston railway motors in operation and on all future ones. The success of the brushes was phenomenal. The streetcars could run for over a month with no attention to the motors. Reliable and economical operation had at last been achieved.

The exact date of the adoption of the carbon brush by Thomson-Houston is not known. An item in the *Electrical World* of March 9, 1889, stated that the Thomson-Houston company had substituted carbon brushes for copper brushes in its railway motors.[27] The date can thus be placed at no later than March and probably earlier. Either the latter part of 1888 or the early months of 1889 is most likely. It is also not definitely known whether Sprague arrived at the carbon-brush solution independently or whether he adopted it after hearing of Thomson-Houston's success with it. An article on the Richmond installation which included material supplied by Sprague himself stated that carbon finally solved the brush trouble at Richmond, but the exact date is not given.[28] The carbon brush is that kind of innovation which, when made known, can be immediately put into use by almost anybody. No elaborate instructions or technical details were needed. Although the Thomson-Houston company possessed a patent on the carbon brush, there is no evidence that any manufacturer was kept from using it. Sprague, for example, employed the carbon brush in his railway motors without interference by Thomson-Houston. The Westinghouse company secured the United States rights to a British patent which covered the carbon brush and was thereby protected when it brought out its railway system in 1890.[29]

By the spring of 1889, Sprague and Thomson-Houston, the two pioneer innovators of electric railways, had developed electric-railway systems which could be used successfully on the largest streetcar lines of the United States. The first large street railway to adopt electricity was the West End Street Railway Company of Boston. It will be recalled that Whitney, president of the West End company, had visited Sprague's Richmond installation a number of times and that he had given Sprague a contract for electrification of the Brookline division. This contract involved two sections of the overhead system, one from Charlesgate to Reservoir, a distance of three miles, and the other from Charlesgate to Oak Square, Brighton, a distance of five miles. Because the overhead conductor was not allowed in downtown Boston, Bentley-Knight was given the contract for the section from Charlesgate to Park Square, where the conduit system was used.[30] The contract for the electrification of the remainder of the West End's tracks was not awarded to Sprague immediately. Whitney wanted to test the operation of the Sprague system on the Brookline division. To make certain of reaching the right decision, he decided to give the Thomson-Houston system a trial also. The Thomson-Houston company received a contract to electrify the Cambridge division in the fall of 1888, about the same time that Sprague received the Brookline contract. The Sprague installation was completed in January 1889, and the Thomson-Houston installation in February. Both gave satisfactory service. The Bentley-Knight conduit did not work well, however, and eventually had to be replaced by the overhead system.

No records remain to indicate whether Whitney preferred the Thomson-Houston to the Sprague installation. But he expressed satisfaction with the Thomson-Houston line, which ran from Harvard Square to Bowdoin Square, Boston. In March 1889, he wrote to Thomson-Houston and disclosed that the electric power of one streetcar was equivalent, in terms of daily runs, to twenty-two horses. In conclusion, he remarked: "My confidence in the electric system of street transportation has been strengthened and confirmed by the success of the work in Cambridge." [31]

The Sprague and Thomson-Houston installations were both sufficiently satisfactory to place the decision of awarding the contract for electrification of the entire West End system on another basis. Whitney did not want to assume the risk that the electrical equipment might turn out to be unreliable and expensive to maintain. He therefore asked that guarantees of reliable operation be written into the purchase contract. He wanted the equipment manufacturer to take the responsibility for the upkeep and repair of the equipment at agreed-on rates. The Sprague company, however, was unwilling to make these guarantees and perform this repair service. In view of the fact that Sprague had lost over $75,000 on the Richmond contract, his refusal to make strong financial guarantees on a contract which probably would run over $1,000,000 is understandable. Moreover, his company was short of capital in the face of an increasing business and could hardly commit resources to a large contract without assurance of payment. But the Thomson-Houston company was in a different position. With a large and profitable business in arc and incandescent lighting, it could more easily assume the financial risks of the West End contract without danger of bankruptcy.

Thomson-Houston met Whitney's terms, and the first contract was signed on June 27, 1889. Thomson-Houston was to furnish between 240 and 600 railway motors and was to keep these motors, along with all other electrical equipment, in repair for five years. The repair charges were to be based on car-miles run. The contract included elaborate schedules stating the rate per car-mile which decreased with time in three-month steps.[32] Thomson-Houston also agreed to correct any interference with telephone and telegraph circuits, and gave specific performance guarantees. The first contract, which included the overhead line and the car equipments, came to nearly $1,000,000. Some months later, $500,000 worth of railway generators were ordered and, in September 1891, 500 more railway motors. By 1892, the West End contracts awarded to Thomson-Houston totaled over $3,000,000.

In 1891, when the repair contract had run for two years, the West End company took advantage of an escape clause and canceled it. The necessary repairs had been so infrequent and inconsequential that Thomson-Houston was making thousands of dollars annually on the repair arrangement. A two-year period was long enough to demonstrate that the Thomson-Houston equipment merited the faith that led Coffin to make the guarantees desired by the West End company.

The growth of the Thomson-Houston railway business necessitated the formation of a separate railway department. The man chosen to head the new department was Eugene Griffin, formerly an Army captain. When the Washington, D.C., electric railway was projected, Griffin, then in the Army engineers, was directed by the Board of Commissioners of the District of Columbia to make a complete report on the investment and operating costs of horse, electric, and cable street railways. Griffin traveled extensively in the United States and gained a thorough knowledge of urban transportation. In his report to the District of Columbia Commissioners, he included data which indicated that an electric railway using the overhead conductor had a decisive cost advantage over all other types, electric and nonelectric. Table 24 summarizes Griffin's findings.

Griffin's study convinced the District of Columbia authorities that an electric railway with an overhead conductor should be installed in Washington. Griffin himself concluded from the study that the electric railway

TABLE 24

Griffin's Street-Railway Data, 1888

	Type of Street Railway				
	Electric			*Cable*	*Horse*
	Overhead Conductor	*Conduit*	*Battery*		
Investment (construction and equipment) per mile of single track	$23,400	$40,400	$38,500	$56,650	$20,200
Annual running expenses per mile of single track	$3,325	$5,025	$8,862	$8,508	$10,682

Source: These data, from a Thomson-Houston publication, *Engineering News* (no date; GE Files), originally appeared in Griffin's report to the Board of Commissioners of the District of Columbia.

was destined to replace the other types. It therefore seemed likely that the manufacture of electric-railway equipment would be a growing and profitable business. He resigned from the Army early in 1889 and joined Thomson-Houston. He had first come into contact with Thomson-Houston in the summer of 1888 when it was awarded the contract for the

TABLE 25

Electric Streetcars in the United States, 1888–1892

Year (on Jan. 1)	*Number of electric streetcars in operation*	*Number of cars equipped by Thomson-Houston* [a]	*Number of cars equipped by Sprague* [b]
1888	130	70	none
1889	400	200	150
1890	2350	700	700
1891	5500	1530	1500
1892	8000	2770	2300

Sources: Data on cars equipped by Thomson-Houston and Sprague are from various company documents and publications in GE Files. Data on number of cars in operation for 1888 and 1889 from *EW*, XIV (August 17, 1889), 113; for 1890 from *EW*, XV (April 5, 1890), 245. Datum for 1892 is an estimate based on September 1891 statistic in *EW*, XVIII (October 31, 1891), 323. Datum for 1891 is an estimate based on miles of electric-railway track in use in November 1890, given in *EW*, XVI (November 22, 1890), 375.

[a] Includes Van Depoele.

[b] After 1889, Edison General Electric.

Washington street railway. At Lynn, Griffin proved to be an able salesman and administrator. When General Electric was formed, Griffin became first vice-president and was placed in charge of all sales. He held that position throughout the 1890's.

The growth of electric street railways in the United States and the participation of the two pioneer innovators, Sprague and Thomson-Houston, in that growth are shown in Table 25.

XVII

The Electric-Railway-Equipment Business

WESTINGHOUSE ENTERS THE FIELD

George Westinghouse first showed an interest in electric traction in 1886 when the electric-railway inventions of a Pittsburgh dentist, Joseph Finney, came to his attention. On the basis of these inventions, Westinghouse organized the Overhead Conductor Electric Railway Company in 1887. Although the activities of this company never progressed beyond the experimental stage, they taught Westinghouse that direct current faced a double handicap in electric traction. The motor had to have brushes and a commutator, and the voltage of all the transmission lines had to be as low as that in the conductor at the track. He then endeavored to use alternating current for electric traction. He expected that the Tesla a.c. motor, which had no brushes and no commutator, would give service more reliable and economical than any d.c. motor. In addition, alternating current would permit higher voltages on the transmission lines leading from the powerhouse to the conductor located at the track. The result would be lower transmission costs.

These optimistic hopes for alternating current were tested in 1888 and 1889 by the Westinghouse company in a series of experiments with an a.c. traction system. The experiments showed beyond doubt that, contrary to Westinghouse's expectations, the Tesla motor was totally unfitted for traction work. With a.c. motor design then in its infancy, the engineers were unable to design a better a.c. motor for that purpose. The Tesla motor was essentially a constant-speed motor. This means that it ran efficiently at only one speed. Since electric traction requires that a motor run at widely varying speeds, the Tesla motor promised inefficient operation. Another defect was its inability to exert a large force when starting from standstill. Again a fundamental requirement of electric traction was violated. The motor was not well suited to the task of bringing stationary vehicles into motion. A motor with small starting force, called by engineers a low starting torque, would need an elaborate power-transmission system to permit it to rotate at high speed when the vehicle was stationary. An example of such a system is the gear-shifting mechanism of the modern automobile, required because the gasoline engine also possesses low starting torque. By the fall of 1889, Westinghouse realized the unavoidable limitations of the Tesla motor and decided to bring out a d.c. electric-railway system of the conventional type.

A group of Westinghouse engineers were assigned to the task of developing an electric-railway system, and, to aid them, several Sprague engineers were induced to resign and join the Westinghouse organization. A study was made of the existing systems, and design of the railway equipment proceeded rapidly. In May 1890, the Westinghouse company issued a circular announcing and describing its forthcoming electric-railway system. It was a d.c. 500-volt overhead system with a single underrunning trolley. The motor was bipolar, with a surface-wound armature and double-reduction gearing.[1] Like the Thomson-Houston and latest Sprague motors, it was 15 horsepower.

Orders for seventeen installations were taken in May and June, and manufacturing operations began in July. By January 1891, the equipment for forty railways had been shipped. By May 1893, Westinghouse railway apparatus was in use on 233 railways.[2] Altogether, 300 of the original Westinghouse railway motors, known as the No. 1, were sold. A No. 2 motor was also produced. It was like the No. 1 except that it was designed for narrow-gauge railways. These motors were followed by the No. 3, which was marketed in the spring of 1891. The No. 3 was the first railway motor of modern design and gave Westinghouse an excellent reputation in the railway field. It contained most of the features which were to be standard in American railway motors. These included single-reduction gearing, four field poles, and the slotted-drum armature. The armature coils were machine wound, and the motor was partially enclosed as a protection against water and dirt.

Westinghouse was not satisfied with the overhead conductor system. Like Edison, he wanted to develop a surface conductor which could be safely used in a city street. He tried to devise a system in which there would be no current through the conductor unless the streetcar were passing over it. Such a surface-contact system was the goal of experiments he conducted in the vacant fields near his Pittsburgh home in 1894. No results were obtained, however, and the experiments were abandoned. The following year Westinghouse heard of a surface-contact system which was being tried in Washington, D.C. He purchased the company which owned this system, the Electro-Magnetic Traction Company, and moved it to East Pittsburgh, where two miles of the surface-contact system — popularly called the button system — were constructed around the Westinghouse works. Experiments were conducted for three years. The buttons were installed on the ground between the rails and, by means of a complex switching arrangement, were energized only when the car was overhead. The car thus obtained current from the various buttons in succession as it moved down the track.

There was agitation during the period 1895–1900 for legislation to outlaw overhead trolley wires in some cities. The button system, costing much less than the conduit system, might have found a fairly wide market if such legislation had become widespread. The 1895 Westinghouse annual report was very optimistic over the button system and hailed it as the complete solution to the problem of streetcar propulsion in large cities.[3] A Westinghouse railway booklet, issued in 1900, described the system in detail.[4] The Westinghouse company prepared a complete estimate of the cost of the surface-contact system for a New York City street railway, but no commercial installation was ever made. The system had too many technical defects. The general complexity of the switching mechanisms and the possibility that one of the switches might fail to work and render a button, of which there were over 400 to the mile, "alive," meant expense and danger. Furthermore, the buttons were found to wear very rapidly and to be inoperative in sleet.[5]

Westinghouse never completely abandoned his original idea of using alternating current in railway work. About 1904, the Westinghouse company came out with an a.c. system for street railways, and, several years later, an a.c. system was installed on the main line of the New Haven railroad. The New Haven electrification was the first large-scale single-trolley a.c. installation ever attempted. Its success, in the face of strong criticism and numerous predictions of failure, was a tribute to the courage and vision of Westinghouse.

COMPETITION IN RAILWAY MOTORS

The standard railway motor in 1890, the year that Westinghouse entered the railway business, was the bipolar, double-reduction-gear type with carbon brushes and a surface-wound armature. Sprague, Thomson-

Houston, and others had installed motors of this design on hundreds of streetcars. These motors had several defects. The two sets of gears were expensive to maintain and extremely noisy. Access to the motor parts was difficult, increasing repair expenses, and the motor was completely open to dirt and water thrown up from the streets. These faults were partially remedied by the first Westinghouse motor, which appeared on the market in July 1890. The gears were enclosed in grease to decrease noise and wear, the upper field pole was hinged to permit easy access to the armature, and the motor was enclosed on the underside and at one end to keep out some of the dirt and water. The next motor type to appear was the gearless motor which Westinghouse tried with no success. It placed too much weight directly on the axle, and severe pounding of the track resulted. Another disadvantage was the difficulty in removing the motor armature from the axle for repair. The purpose of the gearless motor was to eliminate completely the expensive and noisy reduction gears. When complete elimination was not possible, partial elimination was attempted. Motor gearing had been the subject of almost universal complaint by street-railway managers. It was so clear that motor development had to move in the direction of solving the gearing problem that the leading railway-motor manufacturers, independently and almost simultaneously, undertook the design of a single-reduction-gear motor.

The Westinghouse company began work on a single-reduction-gear motor — to be called No. 3 — in the fall of 1890. Since it was thought to be a very radical step, it was considered advisable to take ample time in getting the motor ready for market. But the appearance of a single-reduction-gear motor made by a small and relatively unknown firm, the Wenstrom company, in October 1890, forced Westinghouse and the others to market their single-reduction-gear motors much sooner than they had planned. The Thomson-Houston motor appeared in February 1891, the Westinghouse No. 3 in April, and the Sprague-Edison motor in May. Once the Wenstrom motor had been marketed, the other motor makers felt that they had to have their single-reduction-gear motors ready for the spring and summer trade. Railway construction, like most construction, was a seasonal activity.

Of the various single-reduction motors, only the Westinghouse No. 3 was a successful design. Edison General Electric followed its first single-reduction motor with a number of different models, but none was satisfactory. Thomson-Houston brought out a second single-reduction motor late in 1891. It was totally enclosed but inefficient and unreliable. In contrast, the Westinghouse No. 3 gave such good performance that after it had been on the market only a year, the railway business of Westinghouse made serious inroads on the sales of General Electric (which by this time had been formed to consolidate Thomson-Houston and Edison General Electric). It became clear that General Electric would have to turn out a motor better than those produced by its predecessor companies.

In the summer of 1892, the engineers in the railway department of General Electric undertook the task of redesigning the General Electric railway system with particular attention to the motor. An immense amount of experimental and design work was done, and finally the GE-800 motor was developed. It was first shipped in February 1893. The GE-800 was similar to the Westinghouse No. 3 in many respects. The slotted-drum armature, four field poles, single-reduction gearing, and a 25-horsepower rating were features of both motors. But the GE-800 was an improvement over the Westinghouse No. 3 in weighing much less (1,450 pounds as compared to 2,700 pounds) and in being totally enclosed and completely waterproof. The total enclosure, which made waterproofing possible, was itself possible only because the heat losses in the motor had been so reduced that closing in did not result in destruction of the insulation.

The report of the General Electric railway department covering the period during which the GE-800 motor was developed said:

> The GE-800 motor, our present standard railway motor, has been perfected and put into full production. An immense amount of time of engineers was given to the development of this motor as it was believed to represent the final effort in railway motors for some time to come. Every detail of the motor has been given the closest scrutiny and the most careful investigation has been made as to the best quality of material to be used. Probably not less than 10,000 of these motors will be made, and possibly double or treble this amount. Greater expense has therefore been gone to in the perfection of this piece of apparatus than would have been justified in any special work. Both a drum and a Gramme armature have been developed and put into manufacture so that we have a motor we can offer to either those who favor the drum or to those who favor the Gramme method and we have the further advantage that both of the armatures are interchangeable in the same machine. It is hard to see where the machine can be improved upon, and we may easy rest that our troubles with it during the coming winter will be the minimum of possible troubles. It is the only motor on the market that is entirely closed in.[6]

The GE-800 motor was extremely successful; over 3,000 were sold within a year. Because it was light, waterproof, and offered two alternative armatures, it found a wide market. The choice of the drum or Gramme armature was evidence of good marketing ability in the General Electric organization. Many street-railway managers and engineers believed, without good reason, that the ring-type armature was superior to the drum, and General Electric was willing to cater to their prejudices. In contrast, the Westinghouse engineers firmly believed that the drum was superior and refused to design a ring armature for the Westinghouse No. 3. The Westinghouse engineers were correct, as time has proved, but leaving the choice of the armature to the buyer probably increased sales of the GE-800. The Westinghouse No. 3 still could be sold in considerable quantities, however, because in some ways the GE-800 was inferior to it. The statement in the General Electric engineering report, quoted above, which implies that the GE-800 had no faults and could not be improved upon must be discounted. While the GE-800, like the Westinghouse No. 3, had four field poles, it had only two field coils, and as a result commutation was poor. The sparking, the brush wear, and the commutator wear were much greater than in the No. 3.

The GE-800 was, all things considered, an improvement over the Westinghouse No. 3, and the Westinghouse company was forced to redesign its motor in the direction taken by the GE-800 — that is, for lighter weight and total enclosure. The redesigned No. 3 was called the No. 12 and appeared on the market late in 1893. General Electric secured a No. 12 motor, had it examined by engineers in its railway department, and sent the results to its railway-equipment salesmen. "It is doubtless known to you that the Westinghouse company is now presenting a new machine following in many respects our design of the GE-800 motor. For your information, the following comparison of the merits of the two machines is sent you." [7]

The following points were included in the comparison.

GE-800	*Westinghouse No. 12*
1450 pounds	1750 pounds
Watertight	Open slot, one inch wide, two inches long over commutator and brushes; opening in gear side needs to be protected by canvas flaps
Easy to inspect commutator; armature and upper field can be taken up through the car; parts easily handled from below	Hard to inspect commutator; armature cannot be taken up through the car
	3/16-inch air gap — will tend toward hot fields
3000 sold (some 25,000 miles of service with no repair expense)	2 at West End Railway, Boston 2 at Pittsburgh

Because the No. 12 was not entirely waterproof, although it was enclosed and protected against dirt and water, the Westinghouse company in May 1895 brought out a new 25-horsepower railway motor, the No.

38. Like the GE-800, the Westinghouse No. 38 was made of steel castings, had the improved type of machine-wound armature coils, and was completely waterproof. The principal new feature of the No. 38 which was a decided improvement over the GE-800 was the use of laminated pole pieces. These pole pieces were cast with the motor frame.

The appearance of the No. 38 was predicted by General Electric, because a comparable motor in the 40-horsepower size had been marketed in January 1895 to replace the Westinghouse No. 10, the 40-horsepower counterpart of the No. 12. A circular letter was sent to salesmen in March 1895 showing them how to use the fact that the No. 38 was coming out as a point in competition against Westinghouse salesmen.

> Although the No. 12 has not been successful, the No. 10 was less so and has apparently been discarded as they are now offering for sale as a standard 40 hp motor, the No. 36, with an enclosed frame and in other respects similar to our GE type. It is probable that this same type will be produced on a smaller scale to supersede the No. 12.
>
> A good argument can be made of the fact that the No. 12 is liable to be soon superseded as this may induce purchasers to insist on having from Westinghouse agents bids on a new form 25 hp motor.[8]

This circular letter was followed in June 1895 by a 30-page booklet which provided additional information and arguments for the General Electric salesmen. Almost all of the booklet was directed at the Westinghouse company, because "at present, the Walker company is practically our only other competitor on car equipments."[9] The alleged technical defects of the No. 12 were listed in detail. The No. 12, as compared to the GE-800, supposedly sparked more, ran hotter, was inefficient, was not waterproof, and had a mechanical weakness in the upper-frame casting. It was further pointed out that the GE-800 motors had been made for over two years and that the repair parts were still interchangeable. The inference was that the GE-800 had proven in practice to be a well-designed motor.

The Westinghouse No. 38 possessed the characteristics of light weight and watertightness which had been the main selling points of the GE-800. In addition, the No. 38 had four field coils, which was a feature of all Westinghouse motors beginning with the No. 3, and laminated field poles. These two characteristics made the No. 38 superior to the GE-800 in an important respect. Commutation could not be nearly so good in the GE-800 with solid field pieces and two field coils. To correct these faults, General Electric brought out a new railway motor in the spring of 1897. This motor, called the GE-52, was rated at 27 horsepower and had four field coils and laminated pole pieces. The pole pieces were bolted in and not cast with the motor frame, however, and this method worked so well that the bolted construction was soon adopted by Westinghouse and other motor manufacturers.

The product competition in railway motors between General Electric and Westinghouse in the period 1890–1897 has been described in detail. It should be noted that although this is an instance of duopoly, there was no collaboration or effort of any kind to limit the product competition that took place. The competition in reality was between the engineering staffs of the two companies. If the engineers of one company were able to design a motor that met the customer's wants better than the second company's motor, the engineers of the second company had to improve their motor or run the risk of losing their market. The conditions in which the motor was to be used set the limits within which the competition took place. The goal was a motor which would give the best possible service when mounted in the small space beneath a streetcar and subjected to the abuse of frequent starting and stopping. Westinghouse and General Electric each tried to design a motor for that need, and each borrowed successful technical characteristics from the other's motor. The opinions of the engineers and arguments of the salesmen were continually corrected by the actual operation of the motors in service. The improvement in railway motors from 1890 to 1897 can be attributed to the vigorous and unabated product competition between General Electric and Westinghouse. Or perhaps it would be more accurate to say that the motor improvement *was* the product competition.

The contrast of these competitors with the duopolists as pictured in modern price theory is marked. There was no tacit agreement between General Electric and Westinghouse to "set" the product and share the market. Two firms were sufficient to provide vigorous competition. The reasons for such duopolistic competition are many. A railway motor is, in the first place, very complex. When a product possesses many features and when the possible variations in these features are numerous, it is hard to see how agreement on the product could be tacit. And the process of reaching explicit agreement on the product would have been lengthy and elaborate, if possible at all. Railway-motor design was new, data and experience were limited, and engineers differed widely in their opinions on desirable motor characteristics. Secondly, nobody knew what experimental and developmental work would lead to. The Westinghouse and General Electric engineers, jealous of their reputations and proud of their abilities, were ready to go ahead on the premise that their product would be such an improvement over their competitor's that their company would increase its profits. Thirdly, the engineers were ambitious and wanted a chance to show their merit. They were willing to compete. More than that, they *desired* to compete, for they knew their personal success depended upon the quality of their work compared to that of other engineers. The outstanding engineering work of Benjamin Garver Lamme, who was primarily responsible for the Westinghouse No. 3 railway motor and for other major Westinghouse engineering achievements, led to his appointment in 1901, at the age of forty-two, to the post of Chief Engineer of the company. He held that position until his death twenty-two years later. The individual incentive was supplemented by a group or team incentive such as is characteristic in athletics. The General Electric railway engineers saw the Westinghouse railway engineers as one football team sees another and worked together to try to defeat them. The judges in this contest were the street-railway managers who bought and used the motors and, through their buying, gave the decision to one engineering staff or the other.

The significance of the duopolistic product competition was not confined to improvement of the product. Vigorous product competition stimulated price competition. The engineers who labored hard to design a superior product did not want to see it fail to gain a market because the price was too high. And the non-engineering executives of the company, aware of the heavy costs incurred in development, realized that a large volume was necessary to recover these costs. The belief that the product was really good and much superior to the competitor's product was likely to encourage a pricing policy based on a large volume. The GE-800 motor, it will be recalled, was expected to achieve a sales figure of at least 10,000 and maybe higher. The price could, therefore, be set on the assumption of heavy sales. This expectation was realized, as the sales figures in Table 26 show.

Product competition had two price effects. It tended to bring about lower prices because of the price competition it fostered. And the reductions in product cost which resulted from the product competition lowered the level to which price competition could drive prices. In practice, it is hard to distinguish these influences, but on an analytical level the price-lowering force of product competition can be separated into price competition and technological change.

The price trend of street-railway motors illustrates the price effects of product competition. The price of a two-motor equipment declined from $4,500 in 1889 to $2,600 in 1891 and still further to $1,650 in 1893. The 1894 price was $1,250 and the 1895 price $750.[10] The price decrease from 1889 to 1895 was partly the result of a fall in prices of raw materials in the 1893 depression and partly the result of lower production costs as the manufacture of railway motors grew to larger proportions. But the numerous and significant technical changes in the motors and the vigorous price competition which drove down profit margins were also important factors.

The relative importance of technological change in railway motors in cutting costs and thus permitting the price decline can be estimated by making a comparison with railway generators. Three of the four factors mentioned in the preceding paragraph as explaining the price decrease in railway motors were also present to approximately the same extent in railway generators. The fall in raw-material costs, the expansion of the scale of production, and the squeezing of profits by price competition played the same role. But product improvement was different. By 1888,

TABLE 26

Sales of GE-800 Motors, 1893–1900

Period	*Length of period (months)*	*Number of GE-800 motors sold*	*Average monthly sales rate*
Feb. 1, 1893 – Jan. 31, 1894	12	3,000	250
Feb. 1, 1894 – Dec. 31, 1894	11	5,500	500
Jan. 1, 1895 – June 15, 1895	5½	4,500	818
June 16, 1895 – April 30, 1896	10½	5,000	476
May 1, 1896 – Oct. 31, 1900	54	3,500	64
TOTALS	93	21,500	231

Source: GE Files.

the generator had been the subject of intensive development work for nearly a decade. Much more was known about generators than motors when electricity was first applied to street railways. Consequently, there was less opportunity for major technical advances in generators than in motors. Technological changes did not have the large impact on costs because the changes were more in the nature of refinements. Important technical improvements were made, however, and there was a product competition vigorous enough to induce price competition. Among the important changes were slotted armatures, multiple field poles, and larger sizes. In addition, design engineers began to take account of the difficult conditions under which railway generators operate, primarily a result of the rapidly fluctuating loads, and made many small design improvements to insure efficient and reliable operation. The price of a 1500-kilowatt railway generator declined from $48,000 in 1891 to $26,000 in 1895, a decrease of about 46 per cent. Railway motors declined from $2,600 to $750 in the same period, or 71 per cent. The extra 25 per cent decrease in motor prices can be attributed to the additional product improvement which was possible because of the primitive state of the motor art in 1891.

The existence of active, free, and vigorous product competition in railway motors has been proved by reference to internal company records. The statement that vigorous price competition existed can also be documented. Griffin, the General Electric vice-president in charge of sales, sent a letter to the local sales managers in July 1895 which included the following paragraph: "For your own *personal confidential information* we wish to say that we desire to secure all the railway business possible and whenever you have reason to believe that we cannot secure the business at these prices and when you think the circumstances warrant the making of a lower price, do not fail to confer with either W. J. Clark or myself." [11]

The Westinghouse company was apparently cutting prices also, and in September another communication was sent to the sales managers from the Schenectady office:

> It would appear that our principal competitor, the Westinghouse Company, is at the present time making extraordinary efforts to secure business by cutting prices on both generators and car equipments. It is therefore considered wise to authorize our Local Managers to use some discretion in modifying our quotation sheets No. 5 and No. 7, if found absolutely necessary. In extraordinary cases, generator prices may be cut 10 per cent and car equipment prices, 5 per cent. This authorization should, of course, be used with great discretion and all our Agents should distinctly understand that we must secure all business that is in sight, if possible. Do not hesitate to communicate with the Schenectady office by wire in all emergency railway matters. *We must get the business.*[12]

Product competition in a complex product like a railway motor has ramifications beyond the stimulation of price competition. The continual product changes create problems, because the effectiveness of the changes cannot be predicted with certainty and because the fact that they are made is subject to different interpretations. One of these interpretations is that if a product design is changed frequently the reason must be that the product has been inferior. The inference can then be made that the new design will be no better than the old. The General Electric sales literature stressed this point in the period of the GE-800, from 1893 to 1897, during which time Westinghouse changed from the No. 3 to the No. 12 and finally to the No. 38. The General Electric sales booklet of June 1895 listed the GE-800 motor opposite the three Westinghouse motors that were contemporary with it. The exact dates of introduction of the Westinghouse motors were given. The sales argument which could be deduced from the changes in the Westinghouse design was stated as follows:

It now appears that the Westinghouse Company is about to introduce still another railway motor, called the No. 38. . . From this record, it is evident that the Westinghouse Company are still experimenting on light weight motors, and our agents should impress on buyers the fact that in taking these new types they are sure to get a motor that will require some modifications, as the history of every motor that has been produced amply proves.[13]

Evidence of poor quality was found not only in frequent changing of design but also in the fact that a competitor had sold its product at a low price. The low price was taken as *prima facie* evidence of low quality. A buyer can tell if one price is higher than another; he cannot easily tell if the quality of one product is better than another. He may, therefore, take the price as the indicator of quality on the assumption that a high-quality product can be sold at a high price and a low-quality product has to be sold at a low price. In this circumstance, the salesman may argue that his product is good because it commands a high price, and that his competitor's product is inferior because it sells at a low price.

Cases of this kind occurred in the competition between General Electric and Westinghouse. In March 1895, the General Electric railway salesmen were told that Westinghouse was selling its railway-motor controllers for $125 per set. That price was contrasted to the price of $165 per set which General Electric had recently received on sales of over 600 controllers.[14] Nearly a year later, General Electric sold four hundred GE-800 motors to the West End Street Railway Company of Boston. Several newspaper stories appeared which stated that the price had been $200 per motor, about half the usual price. W. J. Clark, manager of the General Electric railway department, sent a letter to the railway salesmen, denying the newspaper stories and attributing them to Westinghouse. He remarked, "We did receive figures considerably above the price which the Westinghouse Company quoted."[15] The inference in regard to the GE-800 motor was the same as the inference in regard to the Westinghouse controller a year earlier. In each case, the low price supposedly indicated an inferior product.

Product competition in a complex product raises problems of educating the salesmen to understand that product and competitive products. Some of the General Electric documents already referred to in the description of product competition in railway motors were prepared for the benefit of the salesmen. Technical comparison of the GE-800 and the Westinghouse No. 12, for example, enabled the General Electric salesman to argue intelligently for the product he was trying to sell. Such comparisons were frequently made by General Electric and undoubtedly also by Westinghouse. In 1902, for example, the General Electric railway department furnished a complete engineering report to C. T. Hughes, manager of the Eastern Sales District, comparing the GE-57, a heavy-duty 50-horsepower railway motor, with its Westinghouse counterpart, the No. 56. The report was detailed and long. It covered five typewritten pages and discussed such technical points as bearings, coils, ventilation, insulation, efficiency, heating, and sparking.[16] The report illustrates that a thorough engineering knowledge of one railway motor is necessary before it can be compared to another.

The motor salesman must know not only how to compare his and his competitor's products; he must understand the designations of the various motor sizes and types and be able to help the customer choose which motor best meets his needs. One confusion that existed in the minds of salesmen was the distinction between the pulling power and the horsepower rating of a railway motor. Griffin sent a circular letter to the rail-

TABLE 27

General Electric Railway Motors

Motor name	*Number of motors in equipment*	*Horsepower*	*Speed (miles per hour)*	*Price*
GE-800	2	50	9	$ 800
GE-1200	2	50	8	1400
GE-1200	2	100	16	1400
GE-2000	2	100	11	2700

Source: General Electric Company, Circular Letter No. 112, December 6, 1894 (GE Files).

way salesmen late in 1894 on the subject of railway motors. The three standard General Electric motors — the GE-800, the GE-1200, and the GE-2000 — were described in detail, and the motor designations were carefully explained: "The numbers 800, 1200, and 2000 represent the *horizontal effort* which will be developed by the motors at their *rated capacity* and are proportional to the weights (and, therefore, the costs of the motors), the numbers being just about one-half the weight . . . The horsepower of the motors depends upon the speed for which they are wound; thus, the GE-2000 with two turn armatures gives no more horsepower than the GE-1200 with two turn, because the latter will run nearly twice as fast as the former."[17] A table was then given which included the data in Table 27.

On receipt of Griffin's letter, a General Electric salesman in Chicago studied the table and made a number of calculations. The results puzzled him. He wrote to Griffin for an explanation. His first question was: Since two GE-800 motors cost $800 and give 50 horsepower at 9 miles per hour and two GE-1200 motors cost $1400 and give 50 horsepower at

8 miles per hour, why should the customer pay $600 more for the same horsepower at one mile per hour less? His second question was: Since two GE-1200 motors wound for 100 horsepower at 16 miles per hour cost $1400 and two GE-2000 motors wound for 100 horsepower at 11 miles per hour cost $2700, why should the customer pay $1300 more for the same horsepower at 5 miles per hour less? [18]

The answer to these questions, provided by W. H. Knight of the railway department, was that price varies with *pulling power only*. The horsepower figure depends on the speed as well as the pulling power and gives no indication regarding motor cost.[19] These relationships between motor performance and motor cost were explained again in the June 1895 booklet on railway motors. The salesmen were instructed to sell the motors on the basis of pulling power and to eliminate the use of the expression "horsepower." They were also told to impress upon the customer the fact that horsepower ratings are arbitrary, and not to overlook such characteristics as the maximum capacity of the motor within given sparking, overload, and temperature limits.[20]

The Westinghouse company also had salesmen whose technical knowledge was deficient. The head of the Western Sales Office, Guido Pantaleoni, could not understand why railway motors for St. Louis with its hills had to be larger than for similar streetcars in Chicago. It is reported that his query was, "But don't the cars have to go down hill as much as they go up?" [21] Another Westinghouse salesman did not understand the significance of the machine-wound coils on the Westinghouse No. 3, the first railway motor to have prewound armature coils. He solemnly assured a customer that spare armature coils could be carried along in the streetcar. In case of a burnout, the trap door in the car floor above the motor could be lifted and the new armature coils dropped in place.[22]

The customers were frequently as deficient in technical knowledge as the salesmen. The bias of some buyers for a ring instead of a drum armature has already been mentioned. When the customer was unable to choose a railway motor on the basis of its merits, because he lacked the technical training to judge those merits, he often resorted to a test or competition between the motors of different manufacturers. One common procedure was to couple two streetcars with different makes of motors end to end and then determine which could outpull the other. The result depended mainly on the skill of the motorman and the speed characteristics of the motors and indicated nothing about which was the more desirable motor. Another test was to see which streetcar motor could climb a hill in the shortest time. The bias of this test would be toward a motor with a constant-speed characteristic — a motor which tends to remain at the same speed as the load increases — although the pulling contest would be biased toward a motor with a drooping-speed characteristic — a motor which decreases in speed as the load increases. The motor which was supposedly more powerful in hill climbing would thus be less powerful in straight pulling, and vice versa. This was a contradiction which puzzled many buyers.[23]

Both the tug of war and the race test were used by the Brooklyn Rapid Transit Company when it chose between the General Electric and Westinghouse railway motors. Although the engineers of General Electric and Westinghouse knew that such contests were not a sound basis on which to choose a motor, the general manager of the Brooklyn Rapid Transit insisted upon it. First the tug of war was held, and then the two cars raced on parallel tracks, starting from standstill. Fortunately for the Westinghouse company, its motor had a better gear ratio, better commutation, and better temperature characteristics for these particular tests. It won them and was awarded the contract for the Brooklyn equipment.[24]

General Electric and Westinghouse together account for most, although not all, of the railway motors sold during the 1890's. Of the two, General Electric's sales were higher. From 1890 to 1898, Westinghouse sold about 20,000 motors. During the period 1893 to 1898, General Electric sold about 30,000 motors. If the sales figures of Edison General Electric and Thomson-Houston for the years 1890–1892 are added to the General Electric figure, the disparity becomes greater.

ELECTRIFICATION OF THE ELEVATED RAILWAYS

When the electric street railway had proved its commercial worth, and when the art of railway-motor design had made substantial progress, the motor manufacturers sought to electrify the elevated railways of New York and Chicago. General Electric included an electric elevated railway using the third-rail system in its exhibit at the Chicago World's Fair in 1893. Several elevated railways had been partially electrified before the Fair; afterward, General Electric secured the first contract for the complete electrification of an American line, the Metropolitan Elevated Railway of Chicago.[25] The contract included 110 GE-2000 motors.

The Metropolitan electrification and others of the period utilized the so-called locomotive car, which was an ordinary passenger car fitted with two or four motors and capable of pulling one or two trailer (nonpowered) passenger cars. The first locomotive car was built by Sprague in 1886 for experiments on elevated lines. The other experimenters of that time worked only with the electric locomotive. The latter came into use in isolated instances on main-line steam railroads for service in tunnels and terminals where there were strong objections to a steam locomotive; it was not used on elevated railways. The locomotive car was preferred because it was lighter than the ordinary locomotive, resulting in less wear on the elevated structure, and it carried passengers, thereby saving track space. Electricity thus had advantages beyond the lack of noise, fumes, and dirt. The locomotive car was still in principle a locomotive, however, even though it was also a passenger car. The realization of the essential limitations of any locomotive system and the idea that electricity was the only motive power which could escape them occurred to only one man who had the vision, ability, and courage to translate his idea into practice. That man was Frank Sprague. He saw that the full possibilities of electric power in handling heavy passenger traffic had not been achieved.

Sprague went into business for himself after he resigned from Edison General Electric. In 1891, he formed the Sprague Electric Elevator Company. During the succeeding years, he developed and installed electric elevators for fast passenger service in the tall buildings in New York. He also continued to show an interest in electric traction and especially in urban rapid transit. In June 1891, he publicly offered to install on the Second Avenue Elevated, at his own financial risk, two six-car trains, one to be powered by an electric locomotive and the other by electric motors under each car. He repeated these offers of test trains to the elevated-railway companies in 1895 and 1896, but each time was refused. His work on electric elevators during these years led him to devise various methods for controlling the elevator motors from within the elevators and from outside. Sprague soon realized that he could apply the same control methods to electric-motor cars, and he went on to develop what he called the multiple-unit system of control. If this system were applied to an elevated railway, every car would be equipped with electric motors, and any car could be operated alone or with any others in any numbers, in any end relation, and in any sequence. The entire train could be controlled from either end of any car. The maximum conceivable flexibility in train make-up and car handling would thus be achieved. Each car would be powered, lighted, heated, and braked independently, reducing train make-up time, permitting trains of any length, and making storage, repair, and inspection easy.

A major advantage of the multiple-unit system of control would be that each car would possess the correct amount of motive power for it alone. No heavy locomotives, which waste power on short trains and deteriorate the elevated structure, would be needed. Tractive power on a railroad is a function of the weight on the driving wheels. If the locomotive principle is employed, the locomotive itself must be heavy enough to provide the desired traction. If each car is self-powered, the entire weight of the train (including the passengers) can be used as traction weight. Furthermore, individually powered cars allow much faster acceleration. This increases the average running speed with no decrease in safety and gives greater economy in energy consumption. All of these advantages are permitted by no form of motive power except electricity. Electricity employed in the multiple-unit system is, therefore, ideal for urban rapid transit. But until the advent of Sprague, no person or firm had developed a multiple-unit system of control. Sprague had the vision of what multiple-unit control could do in cutting costs and increasing the revenues of the elevated lines, and he had the technical ability to translate this vision into reality.

Sprague's opportunity to carry out the multiple-unit scheme came in 1897. The South Side Elevated Railway of Chicago was reorganized in the spring of that year, and the new officials decided to adopt electricity. This decision was undoubtedly a result of witnessing the operation of the electrified Metropolitan Elevated Line. Equipment bids were called for, and General Electric, Westinghouse, and Siemens and Halske responded. All the bids proposed locomotive cars. The South Side company was not satisfied, however, that locomotive cars could provide the faster schedules that were desired. A. D. Lundy, an electrical engineer who was acting as a consultant to South Side in connection with the proposed electrification, suggested that Sprague, whom Lundy had worked for in Richmond, be called in.[26] At first Sprague refused. He had made plans to go to London to try to secure a $500,000 elevator contract for a new underground railway being constructed from the Bank of England to Shepherd's Bush. Furthermore, he had recently fallen while installing elevators at the Waldorf Hotel in New York and had suffered serious injury. He was still on crutches when Lundy asked him to draw up plans for the South Side electrification.

His friendship with Lundy plus the chance to propose his multiple-unit system of control finally induced Sprague to accept the offer. He suggested to the South Side management that his control system was the answer to their need for greater carrying capacity. The novelty of his proposal and the opposition of the equipment companies, who ridiculed it as impractical, led to some hesitation before it was accepted. Sprague at last secured the contract, early in April 1897, by agreeing to take upon himself all risk that his plan might fail. He signed the contract as an individual, and the railway company, for its protection, required him to furnish a $100,000 bond for penalties in case he did not fulfill the terms. He agreed to have six cars completely equipped and ready for test on or before July 15 on a standard track, at least one mile long, to be supplied by him at his own expense. Further tests were to be conducted when the remaining 114 cars had been equipped. South Side was to have no obligation to accept any of the equipment until it performed as Sprague promised it would. And Sprague was to do all the installation and testing without interrupting the elevated service. For supplying and installing motors, lights, heaters, control mechanisms, cabs, and braking systems on the 120 cars, and for fulfilling all performance and testing conditions, Sprague was to receive $300,000.

When Sprague signed the South Side contract, his equipment plans were no more fully developed than they had been on acceptance of the Richmond contract ten years before. The multiple-unit control system existed only on paper. No controlling mechanism had been constructed and subjected to experiments and tests. But the large amount of development work still to be done was only part of Sprague's difficulty. He was physically handicapped, and he decided to go ahead with his London trip. His chances of meeting the July 15 deadline thus did not seem very good. In London, the negotiations for the elevator order went very slowly, and Sprague did not arrive back in New York until June. On his return, he found that the small amount of development work that he had been able to direct by cable and letter from abroad was nearly at a standstill because of a strike in the Sprague shops. It is not surprising that he later referred to 1897 as "one of my most difficult years." [27]

W. J. Clark, manager of the General Electric railway department and a good friend of Sprague's, followed him to England in the hopes of securing the order for the 240 motors that were needed for the South Side electrification.[28] Clark promised Sprague the use of the General Electric test track at Schenectady and got the order, although the generators for the power station were purchased from Westinghouse. By very intensive labor, Sprague was able to put two cars in operation on that track on July 16. Ten days later, he demonstrated a six-car train there before South Side officials and engineers. To indicate the ease with which the six cars could be operated, he permitted his ten-year-old son to handle the controls. In November, a five-car train was put into service for test purposes on the track of the Metropolitan Elevated Railway in Chicago. The operation of this train for several weeks proved the reliability of the Sprague system. The following April twenty cars were placed in service on the South Side tracks. Seventeen of these—one in flames—had to be taken off the first day because of defective rheostats, but after that no serious trouble was encountered. By August 1898, 120 cars were in operation and steam locomotives had been removed from service.[29]

The South Side installation worked remarkably well. From the beginning, it gave efficient and reliable service. The increase in average speed to fifteen miles per hour, the better adjustment of train lengths to variations in traffic, and the greater facility in car handling resulted in increased revenues and lower costs. The earnings of the South Side Elevated Railway before and after the conversion to electricity are shown in Table 28.

The effect of the multiple-unit control system on the earnings of South Side was quickly reflected in the value of its stock. Before reorganization, the stock was selling at $32 per share. After electrification, the market price rose to $105.[30] Capitalists and elevated-railway officials could not afford to ignore the Chicago installation. It was evident that the basis for the increase in the South Side's earnings was the multiple-unit system of control. The adoption of the Sprague system by other elevated railroads in the following years was almost a certainty because of its demonstrated effect on costs and revenues.

Sprague's success in Chicago aroused the interest of General Electric and Westinghouse. Both firms had supplied equipment for the South Side

TABLE 28

Effect of the Sprague Electrification on the Earnings of the South Side Elevated Railway

Month	*Year*	*Motive power*	*Net earnings*
November	1897	steam	$10,603.80
November	1898	electricity	39,448.56
December	1897	steam	14,691.69
December	1898	electricity	45,355.68

Source: *Cassier's Magazine*, XVI (August 1899), 460.

electrification, and both were quick to see the advantages of multiple-unit control. Within a short time, the two companies were marketing their own elevated electrical systems. The General Electric system was an all-electric one, very similar to Sprague's, while the Westinghouse system was electropneumatic. Compressed air was used in combination with electricity in the controlling mechanism. In spite of this competition from the two large companies, Sprague secured a number of contracts, including the Boston Elevated Railway and the Brooklyn Elevated Railway.

General Electric came to the conclusion that Sprague was infringing its motor-control patent in his multiple-unit control system and refused to supply him with any more motors or other equipment. To counteract this measure, Sprague purchased his motors from Westinghouse. General Electric's next step was to bring suit against Sprague for infringement of the General Electric series-parallel controller patent. Oddly enough, this patent was originally Sprague's, granted for one of the inventions he had made while working on the Richmond contract in 1887. The patent had been assigned by him to the Sprague Electric Railway and Motor

Company, which had been absorbed by Edison General Electric, which, in turn, had been consolidated into General Electric. Sprague countered this second move by bringing suit against General Electric for infringement of his multiple-unit system of control. This suit proceeded very well for Sprague. It began to appear that he would win. General Electric became alarmed, because it had made important installations of its multiple-unit control system — on the Manhattan Elevated Railway, on the Brooklyn Heights Railroad, and others — and these installations as well as future business would be jeopardized by a Sprague victory. In 1902, General Electric purchased the Sprague Electric Company, "as in no other way could we get possession of a patent which was absolutely necessary to our business." [31] Sprague received over $1,000,000 for the patent on his multiple-unit control system.

Sprague was twice a pioneer innovator in electric traction. In each case, he stepped in after electric power had been applied for several years in commercial installations. By reorienting the development of electric-power devices, he altered completely the commercial significance of electric motive power. In street railways, he envisioned large systems with many cars, in contrast to the small systems which had been electrified, and he designed the motor and the auxiliary equipment for large-scale operations. Before Sprague, the electric streetcar had shown no superiority over the cable and only a slight superiority over the horse. After Sprague, it was clear that horses and probably cables would be replaced by electricity. In elevated railways, he perceived the limiting element in traction — the weight upon the driving wheels — and he saw how the entire weight of a train could be used as driving-wheel weight through electricity. He discarded the locomotive principle, which had been carried over by others from steam railroading into the electrification of elevated lines, and designed the multiple-unit system of control. This gave electricity such an advantage over all other forms of motive power that it soon was recognized as the only motive power suitable for urban rapid transit. Before Sprague, the electric elevated had not shown very much superiority over steam. After Sprague, it was clear that no elevated railway could continue to use steam power. In both street and elevated railways, Sprague showed outstanding vision, stamina, technical ability, and courage. He signed large contracts with hardly more than ideas and blueprints. Yet within relatively short periods, he developed reliable, practical, and economic systems of electrical transport.

XVIII

Alternating Current

THE pioneer work in the application of direct-current electric power to industrial uses by Sprague has already been described. In 1887, there were fifteen manufacturers of small motors (one horsepower and under) in the United States, and they had produced about 10,000 motors. Some of these manufacturers had originally designed motors for battery operation in such devices as fans and sewing machines, but as the direct-current low-voltage central stations became more common, more and more motors were designed for operation on central-station circuits. Thomson-Houston joined Sprague in the production of large motors in 1887, and other manufacturers soon entered that field. The use of motors, large and small, continued to increase. By 1890, electric motors were employed for many industrial purposes and had become quite common, though far from universal. Industrial electric power was handicapped in its competition with steam engines and the various nonelectric forms of power transmission by the relatively high cost of central-station electric power. The high cost resulted from the use of low transmission voltages. These voltages severely limited the area which one central station could economically serve and forced the central station to locate with reference to the power customers instead of low power-generation costs. There was clearly a need for higher transmission voltages in order that the full advantages of central-station power generation could be achieved. Higher transmission voltages for power as for lighting required alternating current. But no a.c. motor or any practical method of converting alternating to direct current existed. For reasons discussed below, the a.c. system which Westinghouse had developed for incandescent lighting could not be applied to electric power without fundamental changes.

THE EARLY WORK OF WESTINGHOUSE

The activities of the Westinghouse company in bringing a.c. power to the commercial stage extended over a period of about six years. The first two years, 1888 and 1889, were spent in obtaining patent rights and doing development work of an exploratory nature. The next two years saw the temporary suspension of these efforts. Work was resumed in 1892, and by July 1893 Westinghouse was ready to supply a.c. power equipment on a regular commercial basis.

It will be recalled that Westinghouse was anxious to have a meter for his a.c. lighting system and that Shallenberger accidentally discovered a principle upon which to construct one in the spring of 1888, when he was working on an a.c. arc light. This principle could also be utilized to build an a.c. motor. Shallenberger and others in the Westinghouse organization were aware of this fact, but, before any development work could be undertaken, two announcements of a.c. motors were made. The first appeared in an article by an Italian scientist, Galileo Ferraris, published in an Italian scientific journal in April 1888. The second was part of a paper which Nikola Tesla, a Hungarian-born electrical engineer, presented before a meeting of the American Institute of Electrical Engineers in May 1888.

Westinghouse realized what a workable motor could mean to the alternating-current system of transmission, and he took immediate steps to acquire the patent rights of both these inventors. He sent Guido Pantaleoni to Italy to buy the a.c. motor and meter patents of Ferraris; and H. M. Byllesby, a Westinghouse vice-president, to New York to inquire about Tesla's patents. Byllesby learned that these patents were owned by the Tesla Electric Company. After visiting Tesla's laboratory in New York City and witnessing several demonstrations, he reported to Westinghouse that the motors seemed to operate satisfactorily. Although Tesla explained the operation of his motor, Byllesby remarked that "his description was not of a nature which I was enabled, entirely, to comprehend. However, I saw several points which I think are of interest. In the first place, as near as I can get at it, the underlying principle of this motor is the principle which Mr. Shallenberger is at work on at the present moment. The motors, as far as I can judge from the examination which I was enabled to make, are a success. They start from rest and the reversion of the direction of rotation can be suddenly accomplished without any short-circuiting."[1]

Byllesby observed that the motors required a third wire in addition to the two wires of the usual lighting circuit. The third wire was connected to a special coil on the armature of the generator. When he told Tesla's associates that he might be interested in purchasing the Tesla patents, they informed him that a San Francisco capitalist had offered $200,000 plus a royalty of $2.50 per horsepower on all apparatus. Byllesby's reaction to these figures was to remark: "The terms, of course, are monstrous; and I so told them. . . I told them there was no possibility of our considering the matter seriously but that I would let them know before Friday. . . In order to avoid giving the impression that the matter was one which excited my curiosity I made my visit short."

While Byllesby kept in contact with the Tesla Electric Company and tried to secure more favorable terms, Pantaleoni reached an agreement with Ferraris in Italy. Pantaleoni paid him 5,000 francs for the American rights to his a.c. patents. Fuller investigation of Tesla's patents revealed, however, that the Ferraris patents would have little, if any, value. Byllesby was therefore in an unfavorable bargaining position for the Tesla patents. He finally secured a ninety-day option for $5,000. If Westinghouse took the option, it would pay $20,000 in cash and $50,000 in notes (payable in three installments at six-month intervals) and, in addition, a royalty of $2.50 per horsepower for each motor. Minimum royalties were to be $5,000 for the first year, $10,000 for the second year, and $15,000 for each succeeding year.[2]

The reaction of Westinghouse to these terms was contained in a letter he wrote to one of his associates in the company: "If the Tesla patents are broad enough to control the alternating motor business, then the figures that have been named by Mr. Byllesby . . . are not unreasonable; in fact the Westinghouse Electric Company cannot afford to have others own the patents that are necessary to enable it to make motors to work on the alternating current system. . . A successful alternating current motor . . . together with our meter will materially advance our interests."[3] A week later, he expressed a similar view: "With reference to the Tesla motor patents, the price to be paid seems rather high when coupled with all of the other terms and conditions, but if it is the only practicable method for operating a motor by the alternating current, and if it is applicable to street car work, we can unquestionably easily get from the users of the apparatus whatever tax is put upon it by the inventors."[4]

The Westinghouse company purchased the Tesla a.c. motor patents late in July. Tesla accompanied his patents to Pittsburgh and worked there for a year with members of the Westinghouse engineering staff in an effort to bring his motor to the commercial stage. The results of this early work were mostly negative. As previously indicated, it was soon learned that the Tesla motor was completely unsuited for traction purposes, and the attempt to use it as a railway motor was given up. It was also discovered that the motor did not perform well on the high-frequency (over 100 cycles per second) lighting systems that Westinghouse, Thomson-

Houston, and others were manufacturing and installing. Another difficulty arose out of the third wire that Byllesby had observed the motor needed. This third wire supplied to the motor an additional voltage which, in alternating from a positive peak to a negative peak and back to a positive peak again, reached these peaks a little earlier (or later) than the alternating voltage supplied by the other two wires. In technical terms, the additional third-wire voltage was out of phase with the other voltage. For best operation, the Tesla motor required at least two voltages differing in phase or, again to use engineering terminology, polyphase voltages. Because the ordinary a.c. lighting circuits supplied only one voltage, they were not a satisfactory voltage source for the Tesla motor. In short, what the Westinghouse engineers found was that the Tesla motor could not be operated from the a.c. circuits then in commercial use. Development of a complete power system, including generators and transformers as well as the motor, was necessary. And this power system would have to be polyphase and low in frequency.

The polyphase development work continued during 1889, but had to be suspended in December 1890 because the Westinghouse company encountered financial difficulties.[5] In 1888 and 1889, it will be recalled, Westinghouse purchased control of a number of companies and in this process incurred relatively large liabilities. During the same period, sales rose from $800,000 in 1887 to over $4,000,000 in 1889, and there was a corresponding increase in working-capital requirements.[6] Part of this increase was reflected in a large increase in accounts payable. By the middle of 1890, when total assets were about $11,000,000 and current assets about $2,500,000, short-term liabilities totaled about $3,000,000, exclusive of $1,200,000 owed to George Westinghouse for a cash advance.[7] The charges on these liabilities plus the fixed rentals on the leased companies and the heavy legal expenses arising out of the increased tempo of patent litigation meant a severe drain on the cash resources of the company. At the same time, the fact that so many liabilities were short term made it necessary to accumulate cash to meet these obligations when they came due. In these circumstances, the company officials felt that only experimental work that promised immediate results was justified.

The efforts to develop a single-phase motor seemed to promise early results, and this work was continued. The previous work had revealed that the single-phase motor was likely to give good operation under special conditions. In 1891, Westinghouse installed a single-phase power system, the first a.c. power-transmission system in the United States, at Telluride, Colorado. An a.c. generator, wound for 3000 volts and driven by a water turbine, generated electricity which was transmitted four miles to a 100-

horsepower synchronous motor located in a mine.[8] Since the motor was not self-starting, a small Tesla motor was used for that purpose.

During the years that development work on a polyphase power system was suspended, attention was given to the problem of what frequency and phase would be most suitable for power circuits. If the frequency and number of phases could be chosen, work could go ahead rapidly as soon as funds were again available. It was recognized that the high frequency of the lighting system was undesirable not only for Tesla motors but also for the large direct-connected alternators which were coming into use. There is a fixed relation between the rotation speed of a generator, the

TABLE 29

Speed, Frequency, and Field-Pole Relations in Alternating-Current Generators and Motors [a]

Frequency of alternating current (cycles per second)	*Number of field poles required in a slow-speed generator (100 rev/min)*	*Maximum speed attainable in an induction motor* [b] *(revolutions per minute)*
10	12	600
20	24	1200
30	36	1800
60	72	3600
120	144	7200

[a] This table is based on the following equation which applies to alternating-current machinery: $f = PN/120$, where f is the frequency of the current in cycles per second, P is the number of field poles, and N is the speed of rotation of the rotating element of the a.c. machine in revolutions per minute.

[b] Induction motor is the engineering term for the Tesla motor. Maximum speed is obtainable with the minimum number of field poles, two.

number of field poles in that generator, and the frequency of the current generated. A low-speed steam engine (say 100 rev/min) connected directly to a generator meant a low-speed generator. As Table 29 shows, the number of poles required is much larger for higher frequencies. More poles add to the construction cost of the generator and make operation more difficult.

A low frequency has the additional advantage of being more suitable for long-distance transmission. This results from the fact that a transmission line impedes the flow of the alternating-current power less when lower frequencies are used. At the same time, a low frequency requires larger transformers and makes it difficult to operate high-speed induction motors. Table 29 indicates the maximum speed of induction motors operating on various frequencies. A group of Westinghouse engineers studied the frequency problem early in 1891 and recommended 30 cycles per second for power circuits. This recommendation was accepted by the company management.

The decision on frequency was followed by another on the number of phases. The choice was between two-phase and three-phase. That is, two voltages or three voltages could be supplied to the Tesla motor, which could operate satisfactorily on either arrangement. The three-phase system furnished a steadier flow of power to the motor, just as a 4-cylinder gasoline engine provides a steadier flow of power than a 2-cylinder engine. Moreover, three-phase required about 15 per cent less copper for transmission lines than two-phase. Two-phase, on the other hand, had the advantage of fitting readily into single-phase lighting circuits. While it was recognized that eventually the demand for electric power would justify separate 30-c/sec power circuits, the big demand in the early 1890's was for lighting. If a frequency were chosen for lighting circuits which was suitable (although not ideal) for induction motors, power and lighting could be supplied from the same circuits until the demand for power warranted special power circuits.[9] Lighting circuits, of course, required only a single-phase voltage. Because a two-phase system can be viewed as two single-phase systems, lights could be supplied from each circuit independently, while the two circuits could be connected to each Tesla motor. Three-phase, on the other hand, required a complicated network which could not be easily operated as three separate single-phase circuits. The advantages of two-phase during the period of transition from combined lighting-power circuits to separate circuits was thought to outweigh the long-run advantages of three-phase, and the Westinghouse company chose two-phase.

The development work on the power system was resumed in 1892. The work progressed well, and the complete system was finished in time for demonstration the following year at the Chicago World's Fair. It will be recalled that Westinghouse secured the Fair lighting contract. The generating plant consisted of twenty-four 500-horsepower, 60-c/sec, single-phase alternators. An ingenious method, suggested by Westinghouse himself, was employed to secure two-phase voltage from each pair of these generators. This two-phase voltage was used to operate a 300-horsepower induction motor which drove an a.c.-d.c. generator which, in turn, delivered 550 volts d.c. and 390 volts, two-phase, 30 c/sec, a.c.[10] This alternating current was then taken, via step-up and step-down transformers, to a rotary converter which delivered 500 volts d.c. A railway motor was operated by the voltage from the rotary converter, which thus showed how electric power could be transmitted as alternating current but changed into direct current for railway systems. A second rotary converter, which operated on 60-c/sec alternating current, was shown delivering current for electroplating. Several additional a.c. motors — both induction and synchronous — were also in operation. As can be inferred from this description, the Westinghouse company had a complete polyphase system on display. The induction motor, the transformer, the rotary converter, and the a.c.-d.c. generator were all part of the system and showed its great flexibility in providing direct current of any voltage and alternating current of any voltage, any frequency, and for lighting or power. General Electric also had polyphase apparatus on display, but there were only a few equipments and none was in operation.

ELECTRIC POWER AT NIAGARA FALLS

Efforts to utilize the water power of Niagara Falls began about the middle of the nineteenth century. The Falls were ideal for power development because of their proximity to populated areas and trade routes. In 1890, about one-fifth of the population of the United States lived within four hundred miles of Niagara Falls, and Buffalo, a city of 250,000, was only twenty miles away. A second important attribute of the Falls was the evenness of flow. The Niagara River rarely varies more than a few feet in depth, primarily because it is the outlet for a huge drainage area in which four of the Great Lakes act as reservoirs. The twin characteristics of good location and steady flow — very seldom found in natural water falls — gave great potential value to the millions of horsepower at Niagara.

The very abundance of power was primarily responsible for the failure of the early attempts to harness Niagara Falls. There was too much power relative to the amount of land available to permit local use by rope or belt transmission from water wheels. Any project which attempted to capture more than a tiny fraction of the power would have incurred heavy capital costs for canals, wheel pits, and tunnels. This investment would not be justified by the amount of power that could be sold to factories located near enough to receive that power by mechanical transmission. One estimate showed, for example, that on the basis of water-power projects in New England, the space required for industrial consumption of 120,000 horsepower would be about thirty square miles.[11] Utilization of Niagara power on a large scale had to await either a method of transmitting power over considerable distances or a method of power consumption which required much less space than ordinary industrial uses. Without one of these changes, the conditions of 1885 could not be altered appreciably.

By 1885, a canal had been built for power purposes at Niagara. This canal was a hypotenuse of a right triangle formed by the canal and the Niagara River, which makes a ninety-degree turn at the Falls. The canal, about one mile in length, carried water from above the Falls to eight or ten mills located on the bank of the river below the Falls. Each of the mills had its own water wheel and utilized only a fraction of the available 200-foot head. All together, these mills, most of which made flour or paper, used no more than 10,000 horsepower.[12]

An occurrence in 1885 made the problem of space at Niagara even more acute and the prospects of power utilization correspondingly dimmer. In that year, the New York State Niagara Reservation was established with the object of preserving the scenic beauty of the Falls. The Reservation consisted mainly of a thin strip of land which extended from one mile above the Falls to the suspension bridge below. Goat Island, located in the Niagara River at the brink of the Falls, was also included. The effect of the Reservation was to remove permanently from use as factory or powerhouse sites exactly that land which would have been the best location for a major power development. The canals and tunnels which such a development would require would now have to be much longer and therefore more expensive. At the same time, the number of possible power customers was reduced.

Interest in a substantial development of Niagara power was aroused in 1886 by the plan of Thomas Evershed, a civil engineer employed on the Erie Canal. Evershed had done surveying work in the Niagara vicinity as early as 1843 and had played a leading role in the establishment of the Niagara Reservation. He realized that the Reservation made the space problem even more difficult than it had been, and he tried to demonstrate in his plan that a large power development was possible without destroying the beauty of the Falls. He proposed the construction of a tunnel, two and a half miles long, which would serve as a discharge path for the water after it had given up its energy to water wheels. The tunnel was to be approximately parallel to the river above the Falls and would empty into the river below the Falls, near the suspension bridge. Twelve canals would carry water from the river to vertical shafts leading to the tunnel. These shafts were to be the wheel pits for 238 water wheels, each of 500-horsepower capacity. The water would flow from the Niagara River above the Falls, through the canals to the shafts, fall and strike the water wheels, and be carried to the Niagara River below the Falls by the discharge tunnel.[13]

It can be seen that the long tunnel was to serve two purposes. It would place the power project far enough upstream to avoid the Reservation, and it would permit the erection of mills and factories along a dozen canals spread over a considerable distance. The latter was to insure that enough power users could be accommodated to make the project feasible. The 238 water wheels, serving that number of users, would develop a total of 119,000 horsepower. This was a very large amount of power compared to any previous Niagara project.

Evershed's plan led to the formation of the Niagara River Hydraulic Tunnel, Power and Sewer Company in March 1886. Initial attempts to raise the necessary capital failed. The efforts to interest capitalists in the United States and England continued, and finally, in 1889, a New York group agreed to support a large-scale development of Niagara power. This commitment involved at least several million dollars, but the exact amount needed was not of much import because the group included the leading investment bankers of the United States. The best-known Niagara supporters were J. Pierpont Morgan, William K. Vanderbilt, and various partners in the following investment-banking houses: Drexel, Morgan, and Company; Winslow, Lanier, and Company; and Brown Brothers and Company. Three representatives of the group — F. L. Stetson, J. P. Morgan's attorney; W. B. Rankine, also an attorney; and E. A. Wickes, a business associate of W. K. Vanderbilt — went to Niagara Falls in July 1889 to meet with the directors of the Niagara River company. The New Yorkers agreed to organize the Cataract Construction Company. This firm would prepare the plans for utilizing the power of Niagara Falls and would act as financial agent for the Niagara River company. In April 1890, the Cataract company purchased all of the capital stock of the Niagara Falls Power Company (the name had been changed from Niagara River Hydraulic Tunnel, Power and Sewer Company in September 1889) and took over its options for land and the right of way for the discharge tunnel. The price of the capital stock was $174,000, and a total of $308,500 was paid for the land and the tunnel right of way. Of the grand total of $482,500, slightly over $100,000 was paid in cash, the remainder in bonds of the Niagara Falls Power Company.[14]

It will be recalled that the original Evershed plan specified a long tunnel, a dozen short canals, and numerous vertical shafts. These would require a total of ten miles of excavation, much of it in hard limestone. The construction cost was so high (some estimates placed it at $10,000,000) that the Cataract officials were reluctant to go ahead with the Evershed plan. To secure a firm basis for any action that might be undertaken, they decided to seek advice from prominent engineers and inventors.

Edison was among the first consulted. In November 1889, he submitted a report calling for a main tunnel, water turbines with rope or cable transmission to dynamos on the surface, and transmission of d.c. electric power to Buffalo. Sprague and Westinghouse were also called in. Sprague said that he doubted the commercial feasibility of a transmission of electric power from Niagara to Buffalo. Westinghouse was also dubious that Niagara electric power could compete in Buffalo with steam power. He recommended compressed air, which could be used directly in existing steam engines. Among the other experts consulted were Henry Morton, president of the Stevens Institute of Technology; Henry Rowland, professor of physics at Johns Hopkins; and Coleman Sellers, a prominent consulting engineer in Philadelphia.

It is significant that the Cataract officials were chiefly concerned with the transmission of power to Buffalo. They did not believe that the city of Niagara Falls, which had a population of about 10,000 and little industry, could consume much power. They looked instead to a large city where some 50,000 horsepower was in daily use, nearly all of it supplied by steam engines.

Faced by a wide range of opinions on power generation and transmission, the Cataract officials did not know how to proceed. By this time it was apparent that nothing in current engineering practice even approached the magnitude of the problems encountered in the Niagara planning. What was needed was a thorough and systematic study of the generation and transmission of hydraulic power. To carry out such a study, Edward Dean Adams, a partner in Winslow, Lanier and Company and president of the Cataract Construction Company, went to Europe in the spring of 1890. His intention was to consult with leading European scientists and engineers and to examine the most advanced hydraulic-power techniques, a branch of engineering in which Switzerland excelled. Before Adams left, the Cataract company floated a $2,500,000 bond issue in order to have sufficient funds to cover planning and initial construction.

In June 1890, Adams established the International Niagara Commission, with headquarters in London. The members of the Commission were Sir William Thomson (Lord Kelvin), chairman; Professor W. C. Unwin of London, secretary; Lieutenant-Colonel Theodore Turrettini of Switzerland; Professor Elie Mascart of the Collège de France; and Coleman Sellers. All of these men were famous scientists and engineers.[15]

The Commission sponsored a contest to determine the best method of generating and transmitting the Niagara power and requested twenty-eight firms in Europe and the United States to submit proposals. Twenty thousand dollars in prize money was offered. When the contest was announced, L. B. Stillwell, a Westinghouse engineer, was in London. He asked Westinghouse for permission to submit a plan based on the polyphase alternating-current system. Westinghouse refused on the grounds that the prize offered was too small a sum to pay for $100,000 worth of advice. He remarked: "When the Niagara people are ready to do business, we shall make them a proposal." [16]

While awaiting the contest entries, the Commission and several other engineers collaborated on a careful study of the Evershed plan. It was soon decided that a basic feature of any plan for power development at

Niagara was the discharge tunnel. The tunnel was reduced in length to about a mile and was designed to handle water enough to generate 110,000 horsepower. Tunnel construction was begun in October 1890.

Concomitant with the decision to begin construction of the tunnel was a decision of far greater importance. The central-station method of power generation was adopted in place of the many small water wheels, each serving a single customer, specified in the Evershed plan. The central-station idea resulted from two influences at Niagara. The belief on the part of the Cataract officials that most of the power would have to be sold in Buffalo tended to lead to the idea of a single central station. And the desire to avoid the enormous excavation costs of the Evershed plan with all its wheel pits and canals made the central-station idea attractive. One short inlet canal, a single large wheel pit, and a shortened discharge tunnel meant that excavation costs would be less than half those of the Evershed plan.

The Commission awarded the prizes in its Niagara-project contest in the spring of 1891. Of the fourteen entries, none was thought by the Commission to be suitable for Niagara Falls. Although the Commission learned much from studying the various proposals, it could make only two major recommendations in its report to the Cataract Construction Company, dated April 13, 1891. First, the power generators — either electric or compressed air — should not be placed down in the wheel pit beside the water turbines. Because the generators would require constant supervision and repair, they should be installed on the surface, above the turbines, and be driven by vertical shafts. Second, "The general opinion of the Commission was in favor of the adoption of electrical methods as the chief means of distributing power, though perhaps not as the only means. In the selection of electrical methods they were not convinced of the advisability of departing from the older and better understood methods of continuous currents in favor of the adoption of methods of alternating currents." [17]

By the summer of 1891, the Cataract officials had made considerable progress in the Niagara project. Construction of the tunnel was well under way, and construction of the inlet canal and the wheel pit for the powerhouse was begun. The big question marks remaining were the size and design of the water turbines and the method of power transmission. The central-station idea called for large water turbines, if possible, but the 150-foot head combined with a turbine capacity of at least several thousand horsepower went far beyond any water turbines yet constructed. Preliminary negotiations with several Swiss firms were being conducted, however, and by the spring of 1892 tentative designs for 5000-horsepower water turbines had been worked out.

The other question mark — power transmission — was temporarily eliminated in the summer of 1891 by the conclusion that the local distribution of power (within a few miles of Niagara Falls) should utilize d.c. electricity. Transmission to Buffalo was to employ compressed air. Nothing was done, however, to translate these decisions into reality, because it was apparent that power transmission was in a stage of very rapid development. This view was substantiated a few months later when a.c. electric power was transmitted more than a hundred miles at 77 per cent efficiency in Germany. This transmission involved only 100 horsepower, but it was polyphase and at a potential of 30,000 volts.

By 1892, the Cataract company had given up all thought of compressed air. Electric power was the choice. But there still was the question of alternating or direct current. During 1892 and early 1893, the success of several a.c. installations tended to swing the balance in favor of the newer current. The Westinghouse Telluride installation of 1891 had proved to give satisfactory service. By early 1893, Westinghouse had completed a hydroelectric installation at Pomona, California, involving a 10,000-volt, 35-mile transmission line.[18] The award of the Chicago World's Fair lighting contract to Westinghouse in 1892 was further evidence of the trend to alternating current. Added to these a.c. installations was the fact that, in 1892, a 5000-horsepower water turbine was chosen. The construction of a d.c. generator of that size would have been very difficult because of commutation problems. Against the advice of Lord Kelvin, who cabled from England on May 1, 1893, "Trust you avoid gigantic mistake of alternating current," the Cataract company formally decided on alternating current in May 1893.[19]

The negotiations to obtain electrical equipment were not left until the choice between alternating and direct current was made. As soon as compressed air was definitely abandoned in favor of electricity, the Cataract company contacted several electrical manufacturers. In December 1891, the company sent a letter to Westinghouse, Edison General Electric, Thomson-Houston, and three Swiss firms, asking for estimates on the electrical equipment that would be needed at Niagara.[20] By September 1892, only the three foreign companies had submitted designs and estimates. A little later, General Electric presented a plan calling for direct current for local distribution and alternating current for transmission to Buffalo. In December, Westinghouse announced that it had completed a plan for Niagara and was ready to submit definite proposals. At this response of the American companies, the Cataract company decided to cease serious consideration of the Swiss firms because they would not give satisfactory guarantees against patent suits and because transportation charges and the tariff would add about 50 per cent to the cost of foreign-made equipment.

The Cataract officials and their engineering advisers visited the Westinghouse plant at Pittsburgh in January 1893 and the General Electric plants at Schenectady and Lynn in February to make sure that each firm possessed adequate manufacturing facilities. In March, General Electric and Westinghouse submitted their complete plans for an electric-power generation and transmission system at Niagara Falls. Westinghouse proposed a two-phase, thirty-cycle system; General Electric, a three-phase, forty-cycle system. The three principal advisers to the Cataract Construction Company — Professor Forbes of England, Dr. Sellers, and Professor Rowland — favored the Westinghouse plan. Sellers and Rowland preferred its mechanical features. Forbes liked its electrical characteristics. He believed the prospect of a large lighting load in Buffalo made two-phase more desirable than three-phase. The Cataract officials rejected both plans, however, and directed Forbes to prepare designs for the generators and other apparatus. The principal objection to the General Electric and Westinghouse generator designs was that they did not give sufficient recognition to the water turbines which had already been contracted for. Rather unusual flywheel effects were necessary in the generators if the turbines and their governors were to function properly.

The turbines were of 5000-horsepower capacity and rotated at 250 revolutions per minute. The generator Forbes set out to design had to have the same characteristics. To obtain the necessary flywheel effect, he made the field the revolving element of the generator and placed it outside the stationary armature. For the electrical characteristics, he chose two-phase, 16⅔ cycles per second, and 20,000 volts. His reason for the low frequency was that he expected the a.c. motor of commercial importance to be, not the induction motor, but the commutating type. The latter is very similar to a d.c. motor and has both brushes and a commutator. The more similar the supply voltage is to direct current — that is, the lower the frequency — the better this motor works. Forbes selected the high voltage because it would permit direct connection to the transmission line without the interposition of transformers.

When Forbes had completed the generator design, the following letter, dated August 10, 1893, was sent to General Electric and Westinghouse.

> The preliminary design of the generator adapted to the electrical system most advantageous in our case is now sufficiently elaborated to enable us to present the entire scheme for your careful consideration, and in such form as will enable you to make tenders for what you require.
>
> That you may fully understand what we want, we desire that you send to Niagara Falls at your earliest convenience on or after the 14th inst. a competent

representative or representatives to receive explanations, and be furnished then with the necessary drawings and documents to enable you to make an intelligent study of this subject. . . *Any alterations that you may propose in the design will be carefully considered, and if acceptable, will be appreciated in awarding the contract.* We desire your offer to be accompanied by guarantee as to quality of workmanship and efficiency of operation. Time of completion and installation will be considered an important factor in award of contract.[21]

Westinghouse reacted to this letter in somewhat the same way he had reacted to Stillwell's suggestion that his company enter the Niagara Commission contest three years before. He feared that the Cataract company might be seeking advice which the Westinghouse company had learned at great expense. He wrote to Dr. Sellers a week later:

We have given several years time to the development of power transmission, and have spent an immense sum of money working out various plans, and we believe that we are fully entitled to all of the commercial advantages that can accrue to us from the utilization of the knowledge that we have, and we do not feel that your company can ask us to put that knowledge at your disposal so that you may in any manner use it to our disadvantage. If you were stating a general proposition, and asking us to prepare plans and specifications and submit designs, that would be one thing. We would then have the benefit of the advantages that we claim to possess over our competitors. If, on the contrary, you perfect plans as the result of suggestions and observations made by us, and these plans are submitted to other manufacturers, they will have all of the advantages that should accrue to us solely. . . We must, of course, treat this matter entirely from a business standpoint.[22]

The Forbes generator design was thought by the Westinghouse engineers to be defective in important respects. The frequency of 16⅔ c/sec produced very noticeable flickering in incandescent lights and provided a limited choice in the maximum speed and speed range of induction motors.[23] Furthermore, 16⅔ c/sec was too low for satisfactory operation of most polyphase power equipment.

The Westinghouse engineers also sharply criticized the high generating voltage. The insulation problems would be difficult to solve and perhaps impossible. In choosing such a high voltage, as in choosing a low frequency, Forbes seemed to be neglecting the two principal advantages of the a.c. system. When alternating current is used, a low voltage can be generated because it is easy to increase that voltage for transmission. The second advantage is that alternating current allows use of a simple and rugged noncommutating motor. The recognition by the Westinghouse engineers that Forbes was not capitalizing on the inherent advantages of alternating current is good evidence of the advanced position held by the Westinghouse company in the field of a.c. lighting and power.

Both General Electric and Westinghouse submitted bids for three 5000-horsepower generators early in October 1893. Negotiations then took place between the Cataract engineers and the engineers of the manufacturing companies. The Westinghouse engineers refused to guarantee operation of the Forbes design and insisted upon many changes, including a higher frequency and a lower voltage. As a compromise, agreement was reached on 25 cycles per second and 2200 volts. On October 6, the Cataract engineers recommended to the board of directors that the contract for the three generators be awarded to Westinghouse. Details of the contract were not completed until October 27, when it was signed and a public announcement was made.

The generator contract was a victory for electricity over compressed air, cables, and ropes, a victory for central-station power over that of individual plants, a victory for alternating over direct current, and a victory for Westinghouse over General Electric. Exactly why Westinghouse won is not easy to determine. Both Westinghouse and General Electric had assigned their best engineering talent to the Niagara project. In Westinghouse, this meant Albert Schmid, an excellent mechanical engineer; Lewis B. Stillwell, chief engineer; and Benjamin G. Lamme, an engineer destined to make important contributions to the design of electrical machinery. In General Electric, the men working on the Niagara generators included E. W. Rice, head engineer and later president of the company; Charles P. Steinmetz, one of the outstanding electrical engineers of the time; and Horace F. Parshall, a famous designer of electrical machinery. Both Westinghouse and General Electric had good manufacturing facilities.

It seems probable that the Westinghouse engineers were more experienced in a.c. machinery design as a result of the extensive efforts by the Westinghouse company to develop a polyphase power system. The reputation of Westinghouse was also a factor. The company had long been the chief exponent of alternating current and it had made a number of successful a.c. long-distance-transmission installations. The very successful demonstration of a complete polyphase system at the Chicago World's Fair in the summer of 1893 further added to the prestige of the company.

The receipt of the contract by Westinghouse can, in essence, be attributed to the company's reputation and experience in alternating currents. The Edison General Electric part of General Electric was, of course, completely disqualified on these grounds, and even Thomson-Houston was a follower, not a leader, in alternating currents. It is interesting to note that the General Electric sales committee attributed their failure to secure the contract to the pro-Westinghouse bias of Professor Forbes.[24] There was undoubtedly some truth in this view. Forbes had been favorably impressed from the first by the mechanical and electrical excellence of Westinghouse equipment. He also saw the extent to which the Westinghouse engineers had improved upon his generator design. And Forbes was unquestionably highly regarded by the Cataract officials. It is likely that in the generator contract he was especially influential. Of the four engineers who signed the statement recommending Westinghouse, only Forbes was primarily an electrical engineer.[25]

The question arises why pressure from the financial interests who held investments in both General Electric and the Cataract Construction Company was not exerted to throw the contract to General Electric, or, if such pressure was exerted, why it was not effective. J. P. Morgan was a heavy investor in both companies. His representatives on the Cataract board were his partner, George S. Bowdoin, and his lawyer, F. L. Stetson. Morgan's close friend, Charles Lanier, and Lanier's business associate, E. D. Adams, were also on the Cataract board. Morgan himself sat on the General Electric board along with two members of his banking firm, C. H. Coster and Harrison Twombley. One man, Darius O. Mills, actually sat on both boards.

The financial ties between Cataract and General Electric seem strong enough to have been effective. The most probable reason these ties did not result in the contract's going to General Electric is that the financiers were afraid to go against the judgment of their engineering advisers in view of the large investment at stake in the Niagara project. One recorded event supports this hypothesis. Edward Dean Adams, the president of the Cataract Construction Company, sold his shares in the Edison Illuminating Company of New York late in 1889 and resigned from its board of directors. Previously (1881–1885), he had been a director of the Edison Electric Light Company. He sold his Edison shares "in order to remove all question of personal interest, which might restrict the freedom with which information might otherwise be supplied . . . [because he anticipated that] questions would arise regarding electrical transmission, particularly as to the use of direct or alternating current."[26]

Adams wanted to be in an objective position for the important decisions in the Niagara project. The other financiers, not actually responsible for Cataract decisions, did not have to take Adams' drastic step to insure objectivity. But they apparently tried to act in the Cataract affairs without regard to their General Electric investment.

It is very unlikely that any financial tie of significance between Cataract and Westinghouse existed. The Cataract company issued only 500 shares of stock. The obvious reason for such a small number was that ownership by only a handful of men was contemplated and a large number of shares was not needed. Stetson, Wickes, and Rankine owned 100 shares.

The eleven Cataract directors accounted for almost the entire 500 shares. The few shares not held by directors were spread quite thinly, usually one share to a person. Two Westinghouse directors—August Belmont and Brayton Ives—were among those who held a share or so each, but it is hardly conceivable that they were able to influence the operation of the Cataract company.

The rivalry between General Electric and Westinghouse over the Niagara contract was very keen. On one occasion, charges of industrial espionage were made. In the spring of 1893, Westinghouse suspected a leak of the Niagara-project designs, prices, and contract proposals to General Electric. After learning that some of the missing blueprints were located in General Electric's Lynn factory, Westinghouse secured a court order directing a sheriff to search the Lynn works. He found several Westinghouse blueprints. A janitor in the Westinghouse engineering department was thought to have stolen the plans from the company files. Charges of conspiracy to cheat and defraud the Westinghouse company of certain letters and documents were brought against General Electric officials in September 1893. The accused officials admitted some of the espionage, but claimed that their only purpose was to learn of possible violations by Westinghouse of the Sawyer-Man injunction (relating to the manufacture of incandescent lamps). The jury split, six to six.[27]

Westinghouse received the contract for the first three generators, the switchgear, and auxiliary equipment in the powerhouse. General Electric was awarded contracts for the transformers, the transmission line to Buffalo, and the equipment for the substation there. General Electric also supplied transformers and rotary converters for aluminum and carborundum plants erected near Niagara Falls. By 1905, two powerhouses of the Niagara Power Company were in operation at Niagara Falls. Of the twenty-one generators in these powerhouses, ten were Westinghouse and eleven were General Electric. Although General Electric received the first contract for transformers, Westinghouse received the second contract some years later. In water turbines, the Cataract company adopted the policy of using the design of more than one firm as an "encouragement of competition among Swiss turbine builders."[28] The ten turbines in Power House No. 1 were designed by Faesch and Piccard, of Geneva, Switzerland; the eleven turbines in Power House No. 2 were designed by Escher, Wyss and Company, of Zurich. The first award in turbines and electrical equipment was on the basis of merit, but the nearly even split in generators and the division of the other business between General Electric and Westinghouse lend credence to the hypothesis that the policy of encouraging competition was extended to manufacturers of electrical equipment.

The first two Niagara generators went into service in August 1895. The first customer was the Pittsburgh Reduction Company (later the Aluminum Company of America), which erected a plant a half mile from the power station in order to be near a low-cost source of electric power. Pittsburgh Reduction contracted for 5,000 horsepower on a 24-hour basis. The Carborundum Company, which also erected a plant near the power station, was another early customer. Within two years, an additional half-dozen electrochemical firms making calcium carbide, sodium peroxide, soda ash, sodium, chlorine, and other products had located at Niagara Falls. This local demand for power far exceeded the Buffalo demand, which was only 1,000 horsepower when the transmission line to Buffalo was first opened in the fall of 1896. In 1897, when four generators were in service, 13,500 was sold at Niagara Falls and 5,000 was transmitted to Buffalo. Of the 13,500 horsepower for local consumption, 12,500 was for electrochemical plants.[29] These figures show that local consumption was nearly three times Buffalo consumption and that the electrochemical industry accounted for over 90 per cent of the local consumption.

The electrochemical industry was very new (especially in the production of aluminum and carborundum), and its appearance at Niagara Falls as a heavy, 24-hour-per-day customer had not been anticipated by the Cataract company. The crucial aspect of the electrochemical industry as a user of electric power was that it required electricity *qua* electricity for chemical processes and for heating. These applications of electricity could use much more electric energy per square unit of floor space than the usual mill or factory. The concentrated use of electric energy was one answer to the limited space available for industrial purposes at Niagara. The successful transmission of electric power to Buffalo was the other answer, but, as it turned out, not as important as had been expected. Even in more recent times, about half of the electric energy generated at Niagara Falls is consumed there by electrochemical plants.

The successful operation of the Niagara Falls Power Company's power station and the appearance of the electrochemical industry at Niagara Falls led to further development of the surface canal. This canal, it will be recalled, led water from above the Falls to a number of mills located on the bank of the river below the Falls. In 1895 and 1896, the owner of the canal, the Niagara Falls Hydraulic Power and Manufacturing Company, constructed a central station at the water's edge below the end of the canal. The water from the canal fell down huge metal tubes and drove fifteen water turbines with a total capacity of 34,000 horsepower. About three-fourths of the power was sold to three electrochemical firms. The remainder was used for general lighting and power in the Niagara area.

The Niagara Falls Power Company continued to add generating capacity. By 1900, when the Cataract Construction Company was liquidated, ten 5000-horsepower generators, all made by Westinghouse, were in use. Further expansion took the form of a second powerhouse and wheel pit, located on the same inlet canal but on the opposite side. Power House No. 2 contained eleven rather than ten turbine-generator units, but in other respects was practically identical to Power House No. 1. The completion of the second, in 1904, meant that the limit of the discharge tunnel had been reached. The 110,000-horsepower project thus was finally finished, nearly twenty years after Evershed's first proposal and fifteen years after the New York financiers gave it their support.

By 1900, the investment of the Niagara Falls Power Company in the tunnel, wheel pit, powerhouse, turbines, and electric equipment (including the transmission line to Buffalo) was more than $7,000,000. Another $3,000,000 was required for Power House No. 2. This money was all supplied by Morgan and the other financiers backing the Niagara project. No securities were offered publicly. The financial success of the project was proof that the millions of dollars had been committed on an economically feasible venture. Even more important, the Niagara Falls electrification established beyond a doubt the supremacy of alternating current in power generation and distribution. The 25-c/sec frequency became the standard power frequency in the United States. Two-phase did not, however, become standard. By the time of the construction of the transmission line to Buffalo, it was recognized that three-phase would have been a better choice. Fortunately, the invention of the two-phase–three-phase transformer permitted conversion of the two-phase generated power into three-phase for transmission without difficulty.

The Niagara electrification is an interesting exception to most innovational applications of electricity. The leading role was *not* performed by a manufacturer of electrical equipment. The planning for the innovation was initiated by financiers who went to great lengths to obtain advice from the most eminent scientists and engineers in Europe and the United States. Only after the basic features of the project had been decided were the electrical manufacturers invited to submit designs for electrical equipment. That these designs were subsequently rejected in favor of the Cataract company's own design is convincing evidence that the financiers were playing a leadership role. It is true that this design was later modified and considerably improved by an electrical manufacturer, but his role was confined to minor technical matters and the actual manufacturing operations. If it is accepted that the Niagara project was the pioneer innovation in large-scale electric-power generation and transmission, the vision of the place the innovation could occupy in the economy and the choice of its general characteristics should be attributed to the officials of the Cataract Construction Company and their advisers. Westinghouse supplied only the engineering skills necessary to design and manufacture equipment of the desired technical characteristics.

XIX

The Alternating-Current-Equipment Business

THE year 1893 can be taken as the beginning of the commercial application of polyphase alternating-current power in the United States. No installations of importance took place before 1893. During that year, the Westinghouse polyphase system was exhibited in Chicago; the Niagara Falls contracts for polyphase generators were awarded to Westinghouse; General Electric made its first polyphase installations in New Hampshire, South Carolina, and California; and the Stanley Electric Manufacturing Company, formed in 1891 by William Stanley after he left Westinghouse, began the manufacture of a polyphase motor. These three companies — Westinghouse, General Electric, and Stanley — were to carry out the principal acts of pioneer innovation in polyphase a.c. power in the 1890's. Full realization of the economic possibilities of polyphase power required innovations in three areas. The first was in the application of this power to industry and transport by means of induction motors and rotary converters. The second was in long-distance transmission, which would permit larger central stations and the use of water powers located in inaccessible places, far from population centers. The third was in prime movers. Reciprocating steam engines were too uneconomical in the larger sizes to permit central stations of the large capacity that seemed justified by the widespread application of electric power and economical transmission methods.

APPLICATIONS OF POLYPHASE POWER

The growth of polyphase power depended primarily on two devices, the induction motor and the rotary converter. Both General Electric and Westinghouse engaged in a.c. motor development in the early 1890's, and each had a motor ready for market by 1894. Because these first motors were based on an analysis of the elementary principles of the induction motor, they were much alike. Within a short time, General Electric brought out a second induction motor. The new motor was needed for operation in the monocyclic system which General Electric placed on the market late in 1894. The monocyclic system was thought to be, as the name suggests, a single-phase system and therefore not covered by the Tesla polyphase patents. In reality, it was an unbalanced three-phase system. One phase had much more capacity than the other two. The large-capacity phase supplied all the lighting and nearly all the power to motors. The other two phases, conducted to the motors by a third wire, supplied only a small current.

The General Electric monocyclic induction motor was a better motor than its predecessor. It had to be well designed and constructed in order to operate satisfactorily on the monocyclic circuits. Westinghouse also brought out a new and improved induction motor late in 1894. This motor, called Type B, was so successful that some of the Westinghouse engineers believed that it was useless to try to improve it.[1] Like the General Electric motor, the Type B motor was reliable and gave good service.

In spite of their similarity in providing reliable service, the improved Westinghouse and General Electric induction motors of early 1895 were different in important respects. The chief difference lay in the choice of the moving and stationary elements. In the General Electric motor, the secondary was the rotating element; in the Westinghouse motor, the primary rotated. The primary of an induction motor is that part which is connected to the current supply. The secondary is not so connected. It can be seen that in the Westinghouse motor, some device was necessary to connect the current-supply wires to the rotating primary. This device consisted of slip rings mounted on the shaft of the rotor (the rotating element) together with stationary brushes which were in contact with the slip rings. The current-supply wires were connected to the brushes, and the slip rings were connected to the coils in the primary. In the General Electric motor, the primary was the stator (the stationary element) and the secondary the rotor. Here slip rings and brushes were not needed. The current-supply wires could be directly connected to the primary.

Both motors used a resistance for starting. It will be recalled that Westinghouse learned in experimenting with the first Tesla motor that its starting torque was very low. Engineers subsequently found that if resistance were added to the secondary of the motor, it would have more starting torque. The motor could then start from standstill while connected to its load. A disadvantage of this method of starting was that the resistance had to be removed when the motor came up to speed if it were to operate efficiently and satisfactorily. Westinghouse could meet this requirement fairly easily. The secondary was the stator and the resistance was short-circuited (that is, taken out of the secondary) by the throwing of a hand switch when the motor came up to speed. In the General Electric motor, the resistance had to be placed in the rotor. Taking out the resistance after the motor had come up to speed was therefore more complicated. General Electric resorted to a switch actuated by centrifugal force. The switch short-circuited the secondary resistance when the rotor had reached a predetermined speed.

The need for a secondary resistance explains why the Westinghouse engineers chose a rotating primary instead of a rotating secondary.[2] But in both motors the built-in resistance was expensive to construct. Another defect in both motors was that they could not be operated with supply voltages greater than 400 volts. The wires were so placed that insulation for high voltages was virtually impossible.

The fact that the General Electric motor did not possess slip rings and brushes gave it an important competitive advantage over the Westinghouse Type B. A General Electric salesman made much of this difference, for example, at a meeting of the Cotton Manufacturers Association in Atlanta in the fall of 1895. The two motors were on exhibit there, and the General Electric salesman pointed out to the mill operators the great fire danger because of possible sparks from the Westinghouse motor.[3] The fire threat was only one disadvantage of the collector rings and brushes. They were exposed to injury, dirt, and grit, and were a potential source of wear and expense. Their use made it harder to enclose the motor and protect it from dust and oil.

The need for a Westinghouse motor with no rings or brushes became apparent to at least one Westinghouse engineer, B. G. Lamme. He set out to design such a motor and to make it superior to the General Electric motor. By a very careful analysis of motor-test data and by excellent analytical reasoning, he developed a motor which measured up to the goal he had set. To eliminate the rings and brushes, he adopted the rotating secondary. To eliminate the starting resistance, he made an ingenious change in the secondary circuit. And to permit high voltages, he devised the bar winding (the so-called squirrel-cage winding) for the rotor. Lamme thus removed the major weaknesses of the induction motor. His new motor, named Type C, was extremely rugged and reliable. It was inexpensive to manufacture; it had a high starting torque; and it could be loaded down to standstill without burning out. It was very successful, and, within a year, General Electric was forced to bring out a new motor similar to Type C. The induction motor which was to be standard thus owed its rotating secondary to General Electric and the squirrel-cage rotor without starting resistance to Westinghouse. By 1914, over 95 per cent of the induction motors manufactured in the United States possessed these characteristics.[4]

The competition in induction motors between General Electric and Westinghouse was not confined to the obvious physical features. It also extended to the performance characteristics. General Electric made complete and careful analyses of the various Westinghouse motors as they appeared on the market. The Type B motor was tested and compared with its General Electric counterpart in the 10-horsepower size by General Electric engineers in February 1896. This comparison involved the listing of over twenty technical features and performance characteristics of the two motors. The comparison showed that the Type B could develop more torque and more horsepower, but its efficiency was less, its starting current higher, and its speed regulation poorer.[5] A similar comparison was made later of the General Electric 10-horsepower motor and the Westinghouse Type C. In performance characteristics, the same differences appeared as before. It was clear that the General Electric and Westinghouse motors were designed for different purposes. The Westinghouse motor had a greater power output, but the efficiency of the General Electric motor was higher. The Westinghouse motor was best suited for operation where the power requirements would vary considerably and where efficiency and speed regulation could be profitably sacrificed to secure flexibility. The General Electric motor gave its optimum performance under conditions of steady load. A predictable load of constant amount permitted the selection of a motor of the correct size to deliver power at high efficiency.

The competition between General Electric and Westinghouse thus concerned both the physical features and the performance characteristics of induction motors. General Electric's stress on the absence of slip rings and brushes in its motor in 1895 has already been mentioned. When its Type C had been placed on the market, Westinghouse emphasized the lack of resistance-switching devices and any delicate mechanism which could cause trouble or delay. In performance, the main arguments for the Type C motor were its reliability under diverse operating conditions, its ability to carry a standstill overload without burning out, and the ease with which it handled a variable load. The main arguments for the General Electric motor were its operating economy and good speed regulation.

The differences in physical features and performance characteristics were paralleled by differences in manufacturing costs. The Westinghouse Type C motor, with a bar-rotor winding and no starting resistance, was cheaper to produce than the General Electric motor. A detailed part-by-part cost analysis of the two motors in the 10-horsepower size was carried out by General Electric engineers. This study showed that the cost of the General Electric motor was over 25 per cent greater.[6]

The interest of General Electric in Westinghouse cost data probably resulted from a desire to explain the fact that Westinghouse could regularly sell induction motors at lower prices. Table 30 shows the prices of General Electric and Westinghouse induction motors on August 24, 1897. Most of the General Electric sales took place at the 50 per cent plus 10 per cent discount from list. Most of the Westinghouse sales probably occurred at the 33⅓ per cent plus 10 per cent discount. The price differentials shown in the table could persist because a purchaser who had a steady load would find it more economical to buy the General Electric motor in spite of its higher price. Its efficiency was from 2 to 10 per cent

TABLE 30

Induction Motor Prices, August 24, 1897

	General Electric			*Westinghouse*			
Horsepower	*List price*	*Per cent discount from list price*		*List price*	*Per cent discount from list price*		
		50 + 10	60		33⅓	33⅓ + 10	33⅓ + 10 + 10
1	$ 375	$146.25	$130.00	$180	$119.80	$107.82	$ 97.04
3	437	196.65	174.80	330	219.50	197.55	177.80
5	600	270.00	240.00	380	253.00	227.70	204.93
7.5	675	303.75	270.00	500	333.00	299.30	269.37
10	875	393.75	350.00	600	399.50	359.55	323.60
15	1,150	517.50	460.00	760	506.00	455.50	409.95
20	1,375	618.75	550.00	960	639.00	575.10	517.59

Source: GE Files.

higher than the Westinghouse motor, and lower consumption of current could more than make up for the higher price.

The rotary converter was equal in importance to the induction motor in stimulating the growth of polyphase power systems. It provided a simple and economical way to convert alternating to direct current and permitted a.c. power lines to supply d.c. for uses where only direct current was suitable, such as urban electric traction and electroplating, and for the d.c. light and power networks which had been installed in the 1880's. C. S. Bradley, who had worked for Edison at Menlo Park, invented the rotary converter in the early 1890's and established a factory at Yonkers, New York. General Electric soon bought out Bradley and thereby secured a strong position at an early date in the rotary-converter field. But the major development work in the perfection of the rotary converter and its adaptation to various phases, frequencies, and other operating conditions was carried out by Westinghouse. Particular concern with the extension of the a.c. power system was responsible for the intensive work done on the rotary converter by Lamme and other Westinghouse engineers. The emphasis on rotary converters gave Westinghouse a lead in that field which was a substantial source of profits during the late 1890's.

The sale of induction motors and rotary converters in the first years was difficult because a.c. power circuits were almost nonexistent. The problem of marketing the motors and converters was discussed at a Westinghouse executives' conference in 1893, and the conclusion was reached that if every effort were made to sell polyphase generators for general lighting service, the market for motors and converters would naturally follow.[7] This conclusion proved to be a correct one, and, within a few years, the sales of polyphase apparatus increased rapidly because of the polyphase circuits which had been installed.

The Westinghouse approach to the marketing problem was based on the fact that the main reason for the success which alternating current had achieved in competition with direct current was the saving in transmission costs made possible by the higher transmission voltage. The transmission savings did not encourage the ordinary manufacturer who owned his own electric plant to adopt alternating current, however, because the transmission distances were small and d.c. motors, which were well understood and highly developed, gave excellent service. On the other hand, the manufacturer who purchased power from a central station and who could benefit from the transmission economies of alternating current could not install a.c. motors until he was supplied with a.c. power. Efforts were made, therefore, to induce the central stations to install polyphase generators in the expectation of selling electric power in the future to firms within a large radius of the power plant. Westinghouse thus began with the central station because in that kind of installation the transmission advantage of alternating current was in its favor.

The approach of General Electric to the problem of marketing polyphase equipment differed from that of Westinghouse. General Electric recognized that alternating current had advantages over direct current in addition to the saving in power-transmission costs. One such advantage was the constant-speed characteristic of the induction motor. It will be recalled that General Electric manufactured a motor with much better speed regulation than Westinghouse. The General Electric engineers succeeded in designing a motor with as good a speed characteristic as the d.c. constant-speed motor, the shunt motor.[8] But the induction motor did not have a *better* speed characteristic.

The speed of a motor can be considered with respect to another variable. How does the speed vary as the voltage applied to it changes? This was an important question in the 1890's because the voltage regulation of many electric circuits, and particularly those which were supplied by isolated plants, was quite poor. The voltage fluctuated considerably as lights and motors were turned on and off. If the motor speed were affected by a change in line voltage, the motor could not give constant-speed operation on a circuit with poor voltage regulation. Here was where the induction motor was superior to the d.c. shunt motor. The speed of the induction motor is less affected by small changes in line voltage than is the shunt motor. A 10 per cent drop in line voltage, for example, will cause the speed of a shunt motor to decrease about 5 per cent. The corresponding decrease in the speed of an induction motor is only about 1 per cent.[9] The induction motor thus runs at a more nearly constant speed where the line voltage is not steady. The superiority of the induction motor as a constant-speed device was further enhanced by the fact that no warm-up period is necessary. The field coils of a d.c. shunt motor increase in temperature after the motor is in operation. About three hours are necessary for the coils to reach a stable temperature, and during this period the speed of the motor increases about 8 per cent.[10]

Other advantages of the induction motor over the d.c. shunt motor derived mainly from the fact that the induction motor of the rotating-secondary type made by General Electric had no commutator, no collector rings, no brushes, and no moving electrical contacts of any kind. As has been discussed, this meant no sparking and cheaper, more reliable operation.

The superiority of alternating over direct current because of lack of sparking and a more constant speed served as the basis for General Electric's recommendation of alternating current for textile mills. The General Electric salesman mainly responsible for the first a.c. electrification of a textile mill was Sidney B. Paine. He was graduated from Brooklyn Polytechnic Institute in 1875 and spent the next six years as a textile-mill engineer. He then became a salesman for Edison and sold incandescent-lighting plants to New England textile firms.[11] His textile-mill experience proved to be valuable preparation for sales work. No other manufacturer of lighting plants had a salesman as familiar with the textile industry, and Paine achieved an outstanding sales record. In 1893, shortly after the formation of General Electric, a sales department for textile-mill power was established with headquarters in Boston and Paine in charge. The selection of Boston as the location of the new sales department suggests that the first power-equipment sales were expected to be made in New England. This expectation turned out to be wrong, primarily because the New England firms were conservative and well situated near water power. The first sales took place in a region where new enterprises faced difficult power-transmission problems. This region was the South.

In 1893, a textile mill was under construction at Columbia, South Carolina. The location had been chosen to utilize water power available there. Ordinary mechanical-power transmission from the water wheels to the mill machinery was not possible because of a canal which had been built to carry river traffic around the falls. The thin strip of land between the canal and river was wide enough for the powerhouse and the water wheels, but the power would have to be transmitted about one thousand feet to the mill. One alternative was to build a flume from the canal to the mill site to permit installation of the water wheels there. The construction costs made this method too expensive, and it was rejected. A second alternative was to use ropes or cables, but this method of power transmission for a distance as great as a thousand feet was expensive and inefficient.

A third alternative, electric power, was seriously considered only after it became clear that the more conventional methods of power transmission were unsatisfactory. When the mill management called for bids on electrical equipment, Siemens and Halske, Westinghouse, and General Electric responded. Westinghouse and Siemens and Halske proposed electric-transmission systems which were in accord with the practice of the time. These systems employed direct current, the only form of electric power used to any appreciable extent, and they did not alter the shaft-belt-pulley system of power transmission within the mill. Large d.c. motors were to be installed to drive the mill shafting. Electric power was merely to be a substitute for the thousand feet of rope or cable from the powerhouse to the mill.

Paine proposed an electric-power system which differed considerably from the other two. He believed that electric power was more than a substitute for the thousand feet of cable and that alternating current was better than direct current for textile-mill power. For high-quality output, the textile machinery needed a constant-speed drive. The same dynamo was to supply both motors and lights, however, and as the lights were turned off and on, the line voltage would change. The result would be a noticeable change in the speed of a d.c. shunt motor. In addition, the heating of a d.c. motor as it warmed up would affect its speed. In these conditions, induction motors could give better constant-speed performance.

Paine also realized the true significance of the fact that his induction motors did not spark and were well protected against dirt. This meant that they could be placed almost anywhere with no danger to the motor or its environment. Paine proposed that a large number of small motors be placed in the mill proper to drive groups of textile machines. He saw that electric power was so flexible that overhead shafting was not needed. Its elimination was, of course, very desirable. Friction losses in the shafts, belts, and pulleys could be avoided; particular groups of machines could operate without requiring the shafting throughout the entire mill to rotate; and much of the pollution of the atmosphere (and consequently the fabrics) from rotating belts and shafts would be dispensed with. In spite of the advantages of individual motor drive, an engineer might hesitate to place a sparking d.c. motor in the lint-filled atmosphere of a textile mill. With the induction motor, the question of safety did not have to be raised.

Paine's selling task was extremely difficult. He was advocating the unknown alternating current and a new kind of drive system. Because he was supplanting the mechanical-power transmission system within the mill, his bid for electric equipment was higher than the other two. He was offering to supply many small motors rather than a few large ones, and this plan meant increased manufacturing costs per horsepower. Siemens and Halske bid $55,000, Westinghouse bid $65,000, and General Electric bid $75,800.[12] The General Electric bid included two three-phase, 500-kilowatt, 36-c/sec generators (to be driven at 108 revolutions per minute by direct connection to horizontal water turbines), two 15-kilowatt exciting generators,[13] seventeen 65-horsepower motors, seven hundred 16-candle-power lamps, and auxiliary switchboard and powerhouse equipment. General Electric guaranteed 80 per cent efficiency between the water turbines and the motor shafts.[14]

Paine finally convinced the textile-mill management that his proposal was superior to the other two and secured the contract. But then he was faced with the problem of getting it accepted by his superiors. The sales committee, in an August 1893 meeting, approved, but the executive committee did not. It feared too great a departure from established practice. Coffin wrote to Paine, remonstrating him, and said: "We have never yet manufactured an ac motor larger than ten horsepower and have never sold any larger than five horsepower. You have sold motors for this installation rated at sixty-five horsepower. You must use dc motors for such a job as that." [15] In reply, Paine explained the circumstances and the need for alternating current. Coffin finally accepted the contract.

When the motors had been designed and manufactured, Paine made two important innovations in the technique of motor installation. He mounted the motors on the ceiling in order that they would take up no floor space and attached belt pulleys to both ends of the motor shafts. The motors went into operation in April 1894. It turned out that they had to develop 85 instead of 65 horsepower, but their performance was entirely satisfactory. Over thirty years later they were still in service.[16] The Columbia installation established two precedents in textile-mill electrification. The kind of power was polyphase alternating current and the method of applying that power was the individual- or group-machine drive. The success of the Columbia electrification led to an even larger contract at a textile mill in Pelzer, South Carolina, the following year. Here electric power was transmitted nearly three miles, and twenty-one motors, including fourteen of 110 horsepower were installed. The Pelzer installation permitted the use of additional water power without constructing a mill or a mill village at the power site.[17]

General Electric, sparked by Paine, maintained for many years the leading position in textile-mill electrification that it first attained as a pioneer innovator in that field. As late as 1925, Paine did not want data published on General Electric's textile-mill electrification business. He believed that other electrical manufacturers did not realize how great a proportion of the textile industry had been electrified by General Electric.[18]

Textile-mill electrification was an example of General Electric's emphasis on polyphase-power installations which included both generators and motors. The contrast with the Westinghouse policy of concentrating on central-station polyphase generators was evident, and General Electric salesmen were told how to profit by the difference in policies. In November 1894, they were told of seven General Electric polyphase-power installations, and in December the manager of the power and mining department, J. R. McKee, informed them as follows:

> The remarkable fact cannot escape your notice that while this company has installed or received orders for this large amount of apparatus (25,000 horsepower), none of our competitors, as far as we are aware, has any multiphase plant at the present time in successful operation. This is a fact which certainly ought to have weight with practical men who appreciate the difference that exists between a system that is an assumed success, tested by actual use, and one that simply exists on paper.[19]

The work in applying polyphase power that Westinghouse and General Electric carried out in the middle of the 1890's was largely complementary. The General Electric induction motor was designed for one kind of operation; the Westinghouse motor was designed for another. Westinghouse approached polyphase power through the central stations; General Electric concentrated on the isolated industrial plants. As the use of polyphase power grew, each company expanded its line of equipment and sales policy until, by 1900, the two were in a competitive relation with regard to nearly all polylphase equipment.

THE TRANSMISSION OF POLYPHASE POWER

When financial difficulties forced curtailment of development work in alternating current at Westinghouse in 1890, William Stanley resigned his position. The following year, he formed the Stanley Electric Manufacturing Company with a capital stock of $25,000. The factory was located in Pittsfield, Massachusetts, a city in the Berkshires near Stanley's home in Great Barrington. Stanley planned to manufacture only a.c. equipment and first brought out a line of transformers. In 1893, he added a.c. motors. In 1894, he began to make a.c. generators because Westinghouse would not sell its generators to buyers of Stanley transformers.[20] Both the generators and motors were different from any others on the market. The purpose of the new designs was to avoid infringement of the Tesla patents.

The Stanley motor differed from the regular Tesla induction motor in its magnetic field. In the Tesla motor, the two (or three) alternating currents of different phases produced a magnetic field which *rotated*. The magnetic field in the Stanley two-phase motor allegedly *alternated*. Because the Tesla motor patent specifically claimed a rotating magnetic field, Stanley hoped that his motor would avoid infringement. It was not as good a motor as the more conventional induction motor, but it had a high starting torque and gave satisfactory service. Its chief fault was that it had what engineers call a low power factor. The alternating current through the motor lagged behind the voltage. The current reached positive and negative peaks later than the voltage and thus was out of step. This lack of synchronism decreased the effectiveness of the electric energy supplied to the motor. Stanley corrected the lagging current by installing on each motor a device, called a condenser, which tended to place the current ahead of the voltage and thus to bring the two into synchronism.

The Stanley generator also differed from its counterparts manufactured by Westinghouse and General Electric. Called an inductor alternator, it was fundamentally an induction motor driven by a prime mover and made to act as a generator. Like the induction motor with rotating secondary, the inductor alternator did not need brushes and slip rings. This gave it an advantage over the usual (synchronous) alternator. Other advantages were its simplicity and ruggedness. It was relatively inexpensive to manufacture and could not be easily damaged. Its principal defects were that it was difficult to operate and the current it generated was not suitable for all a.c. devices. As a general-purpose generator, it was distinctly inferior to the synchronous type.

The principal selling point of the Stanley alternator was its lack of brushes and collector rings. If the buyer were not a trained engineer, it seemed obvious that a generator with no moving electrical contacts, admittedly a possible source of trouble and expense, was a superior piece of equipment. The superficial appeal of the Stanley generator was sufficient to make both General Electric and Westinghouse feel its competition. After the Stanley machine had been on the market for nearly two years, a General Electric technical report made the following comments on the competition experienced by General Electric: "The most serious difficulty that we have encountered in such competition lies in the fact that the Stanley dynamo has certain features which look well although they are of very little significance from a practical engineering standpoint. We allude to the absence of collector rings and moving wire. It is, of course, folly to sacrifice good engineering for such considerations." [21]

Table 31 indicates the large amount of business in polyphase generators which Stanley was able to secure. General Electric and Westinghouse were forced to meet this competition by making a product change. In Westinghouse, the sales department demanded an inductor alternator. The engineering department advised against this on the grounds that the inductor alternator was not a good machine and only a temporary stage in a.c. generator development. The salesmen insisted that they had to

TABLE 31

Polyphase-Generator Sales, 1893–1897

Manufacturer	*1896 (kilowatts)*	*1893–1897 (kilowatts)*
Stanley	11,000	40,000
Westinghouse	[a]	120,000
General Electric	19,000	90,000

Sources: Figures for Stanley and General Electric are estimates based on data in GE Files. Figures for Westinghouse estimated from data in WE Files.

[a] No data available.

have one, however, and in 1896 Westinghouse brought out a line of inductor alternators.[22] In General Electric, the engineering department also advised against the inductor alternator. This advice prevailed. In 1896, General Electric brought out a new line of polyphase generators, the revolving-field type.[23] It will be recalled that the synchronous generator required collector rings and brushes to carry away the electric current generated in the rotating armature. The armature currents and voltages were large, especially in the large generators, and that made the moving electrical contact a weak point in the machine. What the General Electric engineers did was to design a generator in which the armature was stationary and the field rotating. No moving electrical contacts were required to obtain the current generated in the armature. Moving contacts (collector rings and brushes) were necessary to supply current to the rotating field, but here the current and voltage were so small that the moving contacts posed no problems of reliability or expense. By changing to the rotating-field generator, General Electric combined in one machine the general-purpose characteristic of the synchronous type and the reliability of the inductor type.

After only two years of producing an inductor alternator, Westinghouse switched to the revolving-field, synchronous type. Stanley's inductor alternator thus served the important function of forcing a fundamental improvement in the a.c. generators made by General Electric and Westinghouse. These firms could have adopted the revolving-field construction much earlier. It was common in Europe by 1894. But the stimulus of competition was required to bring about the change. The new design quickly became standard for a.c. generators and has remained so until the present. As in railway motors and induction motors, the type of a.c. generator that was standard by 1900 resulted from product competition among the electrical manufacturers.

During the period 1891–1900, the work force of the Stanley company increased from fifteen men to three hundred, and the annual sales grew to over $1,000,000. Compared to the 1900 sales of General Electric, which totaled over $28,000,000, the figure $1,000,000 may seem inconsequential. It must be remembered, however, that Stanley produced only a.c. equipment. If lamps and d.c. apparatus are not included, the General Electric sales figure was approximately $5,000,000. The Westinghouse figure for a.c. apparatus was of the same magnitude. In a.c. motors, generators, meters, and transformers, Stanley's sales cut noticeably into the business of his two large competitors.

Evidence that Stanley provided competition for General Electric and Westinghouse is available. Numerous references to the company appear in General Electric internal communications in the years 1894–1900. Stanley's catalogue describing his polyphase system was carefully examined in the summer of 1894 by a General Electric engineer, who prepared a report on it for the manager of the power and mining department.[24] In 1895, General Electric salesmen received many reports on faulty Stanley installations. Westinghouse took more direct steps. In the words of William Stanley: "One of the high officials of the Westinghouse Company [made] a visit to our principal bank at Pittsfield, at which he stated that they were going to 'drive me out of business no matter how much it would cost' and advised them 'not to loan the company or myself any money as they would certainly wreck us.' "[25]

Stanley's significance for the development of the electrical industry went beyond furnishing product competition in a.c. apparatus. In 1892, Stanley and his principal assistants, Cummings C. Chesney and John F. Kelley, set out to discover the voltage limits for the transmission of electric power. It was clear that the higher the voltage, the lower the cost in terms of energy lost in transmission and copper required. The limits arose from the insulation problem. If inexpensive and reliable insulators for fastening the transmission wires to the poles could be developed, higher transmission voltages would be possible. To develop such insulators, Stanley constructed an experimental line near Pittsfield and operated it during the winter of 1892–93.[26] Additional high-voltage work followed, and eventually the Stanley company was advocating higher transmission-line potentials than either General Electric or Westinghouse. In 1897, Stanley made a 40,000-volt installation in California. Several years later the voltage was increased to 60,000 volts. This high voltage made possible the use of water power over two hundred miles distant from the place of the consumption of the electric energy. General Electric and Westinghouse were not willing to install transmission lines operating above about 40,000 volts at this time. Stanley's contract for a 60,000-volt line was reported by the General Electric San Francisco sales manager, Dr. T. H. Addison, to J. R. McKee, manager of the power and mining department, who, in turn, reported to Coffin as follows:

> We invite particular attention to the statement in Dr. Addison's letter that Mr. Eckart told him that the Stanley Company "take responsibility for line transmission at a pressure of 60,000 volts."
>
> This is far ahead of anything, in fact very far ahead, which the General Electric Company's engineers have so far been willing to assume responsibility for; and we have not learned that the Westinghouse Company will ensure the successful operation of anything like so high a voltage.
>
> We take it from this that the Stanley Company are willing to be quite courageous in their exploiting power transmission work and that they also propose to be hereafter considerably more of a factor in this line of work than they have been in times past.[27]

Steinmetz recommended against guaranteeing the satisfactory operation of a 60,000-volt transmission line. He wrote: "This voltage has never been used or approached on any transmission line. . . I do not believe it can be operated successfully at the present."[28]

The 60,000-volt line was a success, however, and within ten years transmission voltages of over twice that figure had come into use in the West Coast mountain regions. These high voltages permitted utilization of hitherto inaccessible water powers and allowed the construction of larger and more economical steam-generating stations which could supply electric energy to large areas at low cost.

THE GENERATION OF POLYPHASE POWER

By the mid-1890's, it was beginning to appear that the limit in the size of the direct-connected a.c. generator would be reached within a few years. Because the large steam engines which drove these generators were slow moving, the size of a generator needed to obtain a large output was enormous. The cost per horsepower of the copper and other materials and the expenses for installation made the construction of generators of over 10,000 kilowatts in size uneconomical. It was cheaper to buy, install, and operate two 8,000-kilowatt generators than one 16,000-kilowatt generator. This limitation prevented the full economies which the large central stations, made possible by the growing demand for electric energy and the high transmission voltages, could lead to. While a multiplication of steam engine–generator units in one central station resulted in a lower average cost per kilowatt, this lowering of cost was much less than that which could be achieved by the installation of larger units if a high-speed prime mover were available.

An important step in the development of a high-speed prime mover occurred in 1882, when C. G. P. de Laval, a Swedish scientist, built his first steam turbine. This turbine was the impulse type and operated at very high speeds. Two years later, C. A. Parsons, an English scientist, built a reaction-type turbine which was also high speed.[29] Both Laval and Parsons coupled their turbines to generators, but the high speed of the turbines required reducing gears, and the turbogenerator units were necessarily of small capacity. Parsons carried on intensive development work to increase the size and efficiency of the turbogenerator units. By 1895, over four hundred of these Parsons units, in sizes up to 400 kilowatts, were operating in central stations and isolated plants. When news of Parsons' success in turbine work reached the United States, General Electric and Westinghouse showed an interest in what he had done. General Electric had the first opportunity to buy the United States rights of Parsons' turbine patent, but refused. Steinmetz advised against it. "Referring to the question of steam turbines," he said, "I consider this field very promising, and believe we should push experimental work in this regard with the greatest possible speed to see what we can do in this matter. I do not think very much of Parsons' steam turbine but think that a simpler design, even if not quite as efficient in steam consumption, would be desirable. . . I prefer to delay closing any agreement with Mr. Parsons."[30]

Westinghouse sent a high-ranking executive to England in 1895 to investigate the Parsons turbine. On the basis of his recommendation, Westinghouse purchased the American patent rights for the Parsons turbine in the fall of that year.[31] Plans were then made for the Westinghouse Electric and Manufacturing Company to build the generators and the Westinghouse Machine Company to build the turbines for the turbogenerator units.[32] The first unit was completed in 1896. The generator was a d.c. machine which rotated at 5000 revolutions per minute and had a capacity of 120 kilowatts. The high speed was necessary to secure good turbine efficiency. Direct coupling between the turbine and the generator eliminated the cost, repair expense, and energy loss of reduction gears. It soon became clear, however, that commutation at such a high speed was unsatisfactory. The next experimental unit embodied an a.c. generator. The armature was the rotating element. The difficulty of collecting heavy currents at high voltages from a rapidly revolving shaft led to the rotating-field design. A rotating field, it will be recalled, means that only the small, low-voltage current for the field excitation needs to be passed through the revolving collector rings. Westinghouse made its first commercial installation of turbogenerator units in 1898 at the Westinghouse Air Brake Company works near Pittsburgh. This installation consisted of four 400-kilowatt, 3600-rev/min, 60-c/sec units. Two years later, the first central-station installation was made at Hartford, Connecticut. This unit rotated at 1200 rev/min and delivered 2000 kilowatts.[33]

During the years just before the turn of the century, General Electric was also engaged in developing a turbogenerator. After the Parsons turbine had been refused, little was done until late in 1896, when an American inventor, C. G. Curtis, attempted to interest General Electric in his steam turbine. He was successful and was provided with a staff and facilities for experimentation. By 1899, the engineers had not succeeded in building a workable turbine, and there was some thought among the General Electric top management of abandoning the turbine project altogether.[34] It was finally placed in charge of another engineer, however, and by 1901 a successful turbine had been developed. First a 500-kilowatt turbogenerator unit and then a 1500-kilowatt unit were constructed. The first commercial installation was a 5000-kilowatt unit which was erected in Chicago in a central station of the Commonwealth Edison Company. The unit began operation in 1903 and, after some preliminary difficulties, gave satisfactory service. This unit differed from the Westinghouse units in two respects. It was vertical instead of horizontal, and it rotated at a slower speed. Later General Electric turbogenerator units were built in the horizontal form because, as higher speeds were attained, the vertical type became increasingly difficult to construct.

The principal advantages of the steam turbine as a central-station prime mover lay in its high speed and low operating cost. A speed of 1000–2000 rev/min as compared to the 100 rev/min of the large reciprocating steam engines permitted a much smaller prime mover and generator and meant large savings in materials, construction costs, and installation costs. The contrast between an engine-type alternator and a turbogenerator, both designed to deliver 400 kilowatts at 50 cycles per second, is shown in Table 32.

In larger sizes and faster speeds, the turbogenerator had a still greater advantage over the engine-type. In the 5000-kilowatt size, for example, a 3600-rev/min turbogenerator weighed only one-fifth as much as the 100-

TABLE 32

Comparison of Engine-Type and Turbine-Type Alternating-Current Generators
(three-phase, 3,000 volts, 50 cycles, 400 kilowatts)

	Engine-type	*Turbine-type*
Speed (rev/min)	93.75	1500
Rotor diameter (inches)	146.0	29.5
Rotor length (inches)	9.9	23.6
Weight of copper (pounds)	2,760	1,040
Weight of iron (pounds)	8,050	5,890
Weight of generator (pounds)	30,870	14,332
Manufacturing cost	$3,100	$1,400

Source: *Standard Handbook for Electrical Engineers* (1908), pp. 315–320.

rev/min engine-type. The zenith in physical size of the engine-type was reached in 1901, when Westinghouse installed seventeen 6000-kilowatt engine-type alternators in New York City for the Manhattan Railway. These machines were 42 feet high and weighed nearly a million pounds each.[35] In later years, engine-type alternators up to 10,000 kilowatts were constructed, but none of these was as large as the 1901 machines.

The saving in first cost in turbogenerator sets was accompanied by a substantial saving in operating costs. A steam turbine is more economical in steam consumption than a reciprocating steam engine, and maintenance costs are only about a fifth as much. A turbine can run for weeks and months with almost no attention. A steam engine must be oiled, adjusted, and inspected very often.

Increasing transmission voltages and the growing demand for electric energy led to larger central stations. But these stations would have had relatively high generation costs if alternating current and the steam turbine had not combined forces. Because of commutation difficulties, a d.c. generator could not be designed for more than 3000 kilowatts. Alternating current removed this limit. Because of the low speed and efficiency of the reciprocating steam engine, the optimum size for an engine-driven alternator was under 10,000 kilowatts. The steam turbine removed this limit. Turboalternators were built in 10,000-kilowatt sizes by 1907, 30,000 kilowatts by 1917, and 200,000 by 1935. These large production units reduced the cost of electric energy sufficiently so that it no longer was economical for a manufacturer to produce electricity for lighting and power in his own generating plant. The phenomenal growth of the central stations in the first decade of the twentieth century is largely accounted for by the shift of electric-power production from the isolated plants in factories, office buildings, hotels, apartment houses, and elsewhere to the central stations.

STANDARDIZATION OF THE A.C.-SYSTEM CONSTANTS

The a.c. polyphase system involved two major technical characteristics, phase and frequency. It will be recalled that Westinghouse, the first firm to develop a complete polyphase system, chose two-phase in order to simplify the transition from single-phase to polyphase. In the matter of frequencies, Westinghouse decided on 30 cycles per second for power circuits, but was forced to accept 25 cycles at Niagara Falls. The latter frequency became the standard Westinghouse power frequency.

Twenty-five and 30 cycles were too low for lighting purposes. The Westinghouse engineers who studied the frequency problem in 1891 came to the conclusion that two frequencies were required, one for lighting and small power and one for heavy power. The original Westinghouse frequency of 133⅓ cycles was too high for the slow-speed engine-type alternators then coming into use.[36] Any frequency below 60 cycles did not give good arc-light operation.[37] At 25 cycles, incandescent lights tended to flicker.[38] At least 60 cycles seemed necessary, and that frequency was low enough for small induction motors to operate satisfactorily. Sixty cycles was therefore chosen by Westinghouse as its standard lighting and small-power frequency.

General Electric did not follow the lead of Westinghouse in either phase or frequency. Originally, General Electric chose three-phase and several different frequencies. The Thomson-Houston frequency was 125 cycles. Like Westinghouse, General Electric saw that a high frequency was undesirable, and 66⅔ cycles was chosen for general light and power installations. For circuits which supplied mainly power, General Electric made a number of installations at 36 cycles. The General Electric Niagara bid specified 40 cycles. For a short period, the company recommended 40 cycles for all a.c. work and hoped that this compromise figure would eliminate the need for two frequencies.

The change in frequency during the early years of the 1890's was accompanied by a change in phase. It will be recalled that General Electric brought out its monocyclic system late in 1894. The main purpose of this system was to avoid the Tesla polyphase patents. It also had another advantage over the regular three-phase system. Because the monocyclic system was an unbalanced three-phase system, it was, like the two-phase, a good way to bridge the gap between single-phase systems and full-fledged polyphase systems. The large-capacity phase of the monocyclic system supplied all the lighting and resembled an ordinary single-phase circuit. The third wire, supplying the other two phases, was connected only to the motors.

The monocyclic system performed satisfactorily. Its main disadvantage was that induction motors do not operate well on an unbalanced system unless carefully designed and constructed. Another disadvantage was its theoretical complexity. The two-phase or three-phase system was less difficult to understand and to explain to purchasers. Polyphase alternating current was then so new that trained engineers sometimes had difficulty understanding it. The monocyclic system only added to the confusion. General Electric's competitors were aware of how little it was understood and used the inadequate knowledge as a competitive weapon. In 1895, shortly after the new system had been introduced, the Stanley and Westinghouse salesmen told prospective customers that in the monocyclic system a slightly loaded motor could deliver current to a heavily loaded one. The inference was that the first motor owner would pay for power used by the second. When questioned about this point by General Electric salesmen, Steinmetz replied that the allegation was not true, because the only current delivered by one motor to another would be the third-wire current, which did not affect the meter of either customer. But Steinmetz was not certain whether the meter in the monocyclic system needed to be only in the main phase. He said that he was carrying on tests to find out.[39] If a prospective buyer were reluctant to purchase monocyclic equipment, he could hardly be censured, when Steinmetz, the inventor and a brilliant engineer, was uncertain about the operation of the monocyclic system.

The Stanley company, like Westinghouse, favored two phases. The reason for choosing two phases was that such a system was "well suited for increasing existing single phase plants."[40] In frequency, Stanley used 132 cycles, 125 cycles, and 66⅔ cycles. These relatively high frequencies were used for both lighting and power installations. The emphasis of Stanley on high frequencies grew out of the need for a condenser, as was discussed above, to make the motors operate properly. In order for the condenser to be small and cheap, the frequency had to be high.

As polyphase power became more common, the advantages of three-phase — steadier power and smaller copper cost — assumed greater importance. C. F. Scott, a Westinghouse engineer, invented a phase-changing transformer and thereby helped the Westinghouse company retrieve itself from its earlier advocacy of two-phase. Three-phase could be used for transmission even though two-phase was generated. The economic value of the Westinghouse two-phase generation plants was maintained by Scott's invention just as the rotary converter maintained the value of the Edison d.c. networks. Westinghouse began to make three-phase installations in 1895. When the 1896 patent agreement between General Electric and Westinghouse gave General Electric the right to use the Tesla patents and therefore the balanced three-phase system, three-phase soon came into general use.[41] The Stanley company, however, continued to make two-phase equipment until it was absorbed by General Electric in 1903.

Frequencies differed from phases in that frequencies were not so closely identified with particular companies. The standard power frequency became 25 cycles and was established by the Niagara Falls installation. The 60 cycles chosen by Westinghouse in 1891 eventually won out over the various General Electric and Stanley frequencies. General Electric and Westinghouse, along with other electrical manufacturing firms, deserve much credit for standardizing at 25 and 60 cycles when it became clear that these frequencies were satisfactory. It is very convenient and very tempting for the electrical manufacturer to consider the frequency as a variable in designing electrical equipment. A single design can often be used for equipments of various capacities if only a few changes, which result in a different frequency, are made. In general, the American electrical manufacturers refused to follow the easy path of treating frequency as a variable. They incurred the extra design and production expenses involved in redesigning machines for particular requirements in order to produce equipment for one of the standard frequencies. George Westinghouse compared the frequency problem to the gauge problem of the railroads and was mainly responsible for the Westinghouse adherence to two standard frequencies. The long-term result of the frequency policy of the electrical firms was the use of 25 and 60 cycles over almost the entire United States. Power systems could easily be interconnected in times of emergency; electrical equipment could be moved from one place to another; and the entire United States became the market for the standard items of equipment which could be produced in large quantities at substantial savings in design and production costs. The foresight and wisdom of the American firms avoided the chaotic conditions concerning frequencies which have prevailed in much of Europe.

After 1900, the 60-cycle frequency took over more and more of the power work in addition to lighting. By 1920, 25 cycles remained only in a few heavy power applications such as a.c. main-line railways. The almost universal use of 60 cycles resulted in part from the ability of manufacturers to design rotary converters and induction motors (except in large sizes for slow-speed work) which operate satisfactorily on 60 cycles. Similarly, engineers invented a device, called the synchronous condenser, which neutralized the greater extent, compared to a low frequency, to which a high frequency is impeded by a transmission line.[42] It can be seen in retrospect that 25 cycles was a transitional frequency which gave the engineers time to learn how to make 60 cycles useful for general power purposes.

In addition to the foregoing technical advances which removed the drawbacks of 60 cycles for power purposes, certain advantages of this frequency over 25 cycles began to be important and helped accelerate the trend to 60 cycles. The high-speed steam turbine brought one such advantage to the fore. An examination of the speed formula for a.c. machines will reveal that because two field poles is the minimum number possible, the maximum speed for a 25-cycle generator is 1500 rev/min.[43] When steam turbines of speeds up to 3000 rev/min and higher became possible, the 25-cycle generators had to be abandoned in favor of a 60-cycle generator (maximum speed: 3600 rev/min) if the higher-speed turbine were to be directly connected to the generator. Speed of rotation also gave 60 cycles an advantage in motors. Again, because of the relationship between speed, frequency, and number of field poles, it turned out that 60-cycle induction motors could be constructed at any one of a wide choice of speeds in the most commonly used range, while 25-cycle motors were restricted to only a few speeds. Table 33 lists some of the possible speeds at the two frequencies.

In summary, the history of alternating-current frequencies in the United States began with a single frequency, the 133 cycles per second of the Westinghouse system when it was used only for lighting. The late 1880's and early 1890's saw a large number of frequencies in use, but by 1900 two had become accepted as standard: 60 cycles for lighting and small power, and 25 cycles for heavy power. By 1920, most alternating-current circuits in the United States were operated at the same frequency, 60 cycles per second. In thirty-five years' time, the pendulum had swung back to a single frequency, half as high as the original one and suitable for all types of lighting and power devices.

PRODUCT COMPETITION AND THE PERFECTION OF KNOWLEDGE

The most common kind of competition in the electrical manufacturing industry in the 1890's was product competition. Just as economists have envisioned a price competition in which the product of each producer is identical, so it is possible to envision a product competition in which the price of each producer is identical. But in the traditional price-competition case, the prices of all producers are also identical, and the question may arise how these theoretical extremes of price and product competition can be distinguished. The answer lies in the variance of the price through time. An analogy will bring out the point. Assume a homogeneous product and many producers. The price for all will be the same. Assume a homogeneous product and three producers who have

TABLE 33

Induction-Motor Speeds

Number of field poles	*Twenty-five cycles*		*Sixty cycles*
2	1500		3600
4	750	Comparable speed ranges: 1500–750 (25 cycles) and 1800–720 (60 cycles)	1800
6	500		1200
8	375		900
10	300		720
12	250		600

Source: This table is based on the formula given in Table 29, p. 280.

a tacit understanding on price. The price for the three producers will be the same. Yet the first market is competitive and the second is monopolistic. How are they to be distinguished? By the fact that the first price, which is competitive, will fluctuate, while the second price, which is monopolistic, will be very stable and will change only at relatively long intervals. Dynamic considerations — taking account of movement through time — permit a clear and unambiguous distinction between the two cases of price competition.

Similarly, movement through time permits an unqualified distinction between price and product competition. In both cases, the price and product of all producers are identical in a state of equilibrium. But in price competition, the product is fixed and competition takes place through changes in price. In product competition, the price is fixed and competition takes place through changes in the product. Time-series data in price competition exhibit a stable product and a fluctuating price. Time-series data in product competition exhibit a stable price and a fluctuating product.

The problem of knowledge in price competition relates to whether buyers and sellers know the prices at which all sales take place. In product competition, the problem of knowledge relates to whether buyers and sellers know the qualities of the products that have been sold. In the first case, since the product is homogeneous, it is outside the knowledge problem, just as in the second case, the price is homogeneous and outside the knowledge problem.

The electrical manufacturing industry is more complicated than the ideal cases of price and product competition in two respects. *Both* price and product competition existed, and the number of producers was not many but few. In some lines of equipment, duopoly existed; Westinghouse and General Electric were practically the only producers. In others, there were more than two; and in some (incandescent lamps, for example), there may have been enough producers to go beyond the number which can be treated as oligopoly. The knowledge problem in this market of price-product competition and small numbers can be viewed through the eyes of the individual producer. He wanted to know the kind of product his competitors were producing, how many sales they were making of these products, the prices they were charging, the success of their designs, the capacity of their factories, and what product changes were being contemplated. The manufacturer cannot tell how effective his competitor is unless he knows his competitor's sales. When the competitor is making large sales, the firm will take steps to change its product or price or both to keep from losing its market. Knowledge of the competitor's capacity is useful in judging whether he is in a position to supply the entire market if a particular price or product should be especially successful.[44]

The alleged General Electric espionage in 1893, when an attempt was made to learn the Westinghouse designs for the Niagara Falls contract, is an example of a manufacturer's effort to secure knowledge about his competitor which is useful in product competition. Another General Electric attempt to secure information concerning Westinghouse occurred in the spring of 1895. Westinghouse charged that General Electric had paid $25 to a Westinghouse employee for furnishing information about the company. By some unexplained means, the Westinghouse officials secured a copy of a letter which had been sent from the Philadelphia sales office of General Electric to the Pittsburgh General Electric manager, E. G. Waters. The letter stated that the Schenectady office desired to find out "in any manner possible, even approximately" the Westinghouse output, weekly or monthly, of street-railway motors, alternators, and so forth.[45] Other correspondence indicated that such information had been obtained and paid for. The reply of Mr. Waters to these charges was: "There is no manufacturing concern in this country that is not more or less interested in the capacity and output of its competitors. The Westinghouse Company has recently completed a factory for which extravagant claims have been made as to capacity and output. . . Nothing other was done than to verify reports as to capacity and output of the Westinghouse plant as published."[46]

Waters went on to remark that for some time prices and other information had been escaping from his office to competitors, but that he had been unable to discover who was responsible. Then an employee of his office resigned and accepted a job in New York with a rival firm. Waters implied that the rival was the Westinghouse company. The correspondence from Waters' files which was in the hands of Westinghouse lends weight to the correctness of this implication.

The desire of one firm to learn the sales and capacity of an important rival is partly a phenomenon of oligopoly and could exist in the absence of product competition. It is conceivable that if two firms were producing identical and unvarying products, one firm would like to know the sales and capacity of the other in order to judge that firm's probable reactions to his price moves and, in particular, whether it has the ability to supply the entire market. Where product competition is present, a company has additional reason to want information concerning sales and plant capacity of his rivals. Such information makes it possible to judge the effectiveness of a competitor's product. If the competitor's product is successful, the firm has to alter its product or lose most of its sales.

The need for data on a competitor and his product in the course of product competition in the electrical manufacturing industry is illustrated by the following paragraph from a General Electric letter sent to meter salesmen: "I wish to impress upon you that this meter question is a serious one and that it is quite necessary that you keep us advised fully concerning any competition which you may meet, so that we can combat it, and give you necessary data to fight the Stanley meter."[47]

The kind of data on the Stanley meter which General Electric could supply its salesmen was contained in a letter sent out to sales managers some weeks earlier. General Electric had made exhaustive tests of four Stanley meters. The principal object was to determine their accuracy. When new, they were found to be from 1 to 2 per cent slow at light loads. After seven and a half months of regular use, they would not run steadily at light loads. The General Electric salesmen were told to get the users of Stanley meters to test them after three months' service, because at that time the unsatisfactory operation would be noticeable.[48]

General Electric also wanted data on the number of central stations using the Stanley meter and the total number of these meters in service. This information was needed, as were the reports direct from the salesmen on the competition they met, to determine the effectiveness of the

Stanley meter in securing a market. If the meter were effective, it was important to know why it had sold so well in order that General Electric could put out a better or lower-priced meter and thus maintain its own meter sales.

The plan adopted by General Electric to secure data on the Stanley meter was explained to the sales managers in a circular letter sent out by the general manager of the supply department, J. R. Lovejoy. Each local sales manager was to obtain the coöperation of a *friendly* central-station manager, who would be requested to send the following letter in his name to the Stanley salesman of that area: "We understand that your induction meter is extensively used in this region, and we should like to enquire if you can give us a list of such users, together with the number of meters in service in each station, together with such information relative to your meter as would be of value to us in determining the kind of meter which is best suited to our work." [49]

The circular letter also suggested a form letter which the friendly central station could send out to other stations in the area if the letter to the Stanley salesmen did not secure the desired information. This second letter also requested extensive data on use of the Stanley meter. The central stations were asked for performance data, meter life and accuracy, the general satisfaction it gave, and so forth.

Whether General Electric's plan to obtain data on the Stanley meter succeeded is not known. The fact that General Electric had to resort to this roundabout procedure is good evidence that no direct methods of getting data from Stanley employees in the head office were available.

XX

Interfirm Relations

INTERFIRM relations in the electrical manufacturing industry during the 1890's were basically determined by two events: the formation of General Electric in 1892 and the patent agreement between General Electric and Westinghouse in 1896. General Electric was a combination of two of the three largest firms in the industry and established practically a duopoly in many lines of equipment. This consolidation of Edison General Electric and Thomson-Houston resulted primarily from the patent holdings of each. The patent situation again became an important influence on interfirm relationships in 1896, but this time consolidation did not occur. Instead, General Electric and Westinghouse agreed to a patent cross-licensing arrangement which made the duopolistic character of the industry even more pronounced.

The first section of this chapter describes and analyzes the formation of General Electric. The second section discusses the conditions which led to the 1896 agreement and the effects of that agreement on the industry. Postponement of these two topics until this time is justified by the fact that patents on power equipment played a leading role in both events.

THE FORMATION OF GENERAL ELECTRIC

Available evidence indicates that the consolidation between Thomson-Houston and Edison General Electric which was to create General Electric in 1892 was under consideration as early as 1889. After completing the arrangements for the formation of Edison General Electric in the early months of 1889, Villard began making plans for a consolidation. Edison was opposed to this. "If you make the coalition, my usefulness as an inventor is gone. My services wouldn't be worth a penny. I can invent only under powerful incentive. No competition means no invention."[1] Planning for a consolidation continued, however, and, in May 1890, reference to an impending merger was made in a letter issued to Thomson-Houston stockholders. The letter mentioned a stock-pooling agreement and said: "Negotiations have for some time been in progress for a sale of the whole or a majority of the common capital stock of the company. Though material advance has been made, we are not yet warranted in stating the terms of the proposed sale or disclosing who the purchasers are. We can only say at present that the price and terms are satisfactory to us."[2]

In February 1891, Villard visited the Lynn factory of Thomson-Houston, and for some time thereafter negotiations took place at the Boston home of a Morgan associate, H. M. Twombley. Coffin and F. P. Fish, counsel for Thomson-Houston, represented the Lynn firm, and Twombley represented the Morgan-financed Edison firm. By the end of 1891, terms had been agreed on, and in the spring of 1892, steps were taken to organize the new company which was to be called General Electric. A committee to carry out the financial details of the consolidation was formed. On the committee were J. P. Morgan and two associates, D. O. Mills and Twombley, and three Boston financiers, F. L. Ames, T. Jefferson Coolidge, and Henry L. Higginson. Arrangements were completed to exchange Edison General Electric and Thomson-Houston stock for General Electric stock, and, on April 15, 1892, General Electric was incorporated in New York.

The directors, officers, and executives of the new company are shown in Table 34. Of the six Edison General Electric men on the eleven-man board, Morgan and his associates account for four. Only Hastings and Edison cannot be classed as Morgan men. Of the five Thomson-Houston men, two — Coffin and Griffin — were Thomson-Houston executives, and the other three were Boston capitalists who had invested in Thomson-Houston for a considerable period of time. It should be noticed that the management of the company was principally in the hands of men who had previously been with Thomson-Houston. If cognizance is taken of the early replacement of Crosby by Clark, three out of the four general managers also came from the Lynn firm. The president of General Electric succeeding Coffin was Rice, Thomson's assistant in the early Thomson-Houston days.

Of the five officers and executives who came from Edison General Electric, only Ord, Kruesi, and Upton were associated with the early Edison activities. Greene and Crosby were both in the Sprague company when it was purchased by Edison General Electric in 1889. And Kruesi and Upton, it should be noted, were not high-ranking executives con-

TABLE 34

Previous Affiliation and Status of the Directors, Officers, and Executives of General Electric

Name	*General Electric status*	*Previous company*[a]	*Previous status*
Directors			
F. L. Ames	Director	TH	Influential stockholder
C. A. Coffin	"	TH	Chief executive
T. J. Coolidge, Jr.	"	TH	Influential stockholder
C. H. Coster	"	EGE	Director
T. A. Edison	"	EGE	Director
Eugene Griffin	"	TH	Head of Railway Dept.
F. S. Hastings	"	EGE	Treasurer and Asst. Sec'y.
H. L. Higginson	"	TH	Influential stockholder
D. O. Mills	"	EGE	" "
J. P. Morgan	"	EGE	" "
H. M. Twombley	Chairman of the Board of Directors	EGE	" "
Officers			
C. A. Coffin	President	TH	Chief executive
Eugene Griffin	First Vice-President	TH	Head of Railway Dept.
J. P. Ord	Second Vice-President	EGE	Comptroller
F. P. Fish	General Counsel	TH	General Counsel
E. I. Garfield	Secretary	TH	[b]
B. F. Peach	Treasurer	TH	[b]
Executives			
S. D. Greene	General Manager, Lighting Dept.	EGE	[b]
O. T. Crosby[c]	General Manager, Railway Dept.	EGE	[b]
J. R. McKee	General Manager, Power Dept.	TH	Head of Commercial Dept.
J. R. Lovejoy	General Manager, Supply Dept.	TH	[b]
E. W. Rice[d]	Technical Director	TH	Asst. to Elihu Thomson
John Kruesi	Manager, Schenectady Works	EGE	Manager, Schenectady Works
G. E. Emmons	Manager, Lynn Works	TH	Manager, Lynn Works
F. R. Upton	Manager, Harrison Works	EGE	Manager, Harrison Works

Sources: Based on *Annual Reports* of Thomson-Houston, Edison General Electric, and General Electric, and on documents in GE Files.

[a] TH stands for Thomson-Houston; EGE for Edison General Electric.

[b] Previous status unknown.

[c] W. J. Clark, formerly of Thomson-Houston, replaced Crosby in 1894.

[d] Rice became Third Vice-President (in charge of manufacturing) in 1895 (or early 1896).

cerned with the activities of the corporation as a whole. The business leadership of General Electric clearly did not come from personnel associated with Edison in the early 1880's. The significance of this fact is discussed below.

The consolidation of Edison General Electric and Thomson-Houston brought a number of organizational problems. Administrative practices of the two companies differed in many ways. The choice of which procedures to use in General Electric had to be made. The department type of organization and the cost-accounting system developed by Thomson-Houston at Lynn were taken over by the new company. The geographic sales districts of Edison General Electric served as administrative units for the combined sales force. In manufacturing, the main problem was that of duplicate facilities. It was decided to concentrate the heavy and nonstandard work at Schenectady and to confine Lynn to the manufacture of the lighter, standard items which were produced in quantity. The lamp works to be used was selected on the basis of a competition. The Lynn factory and the Harrison factory each produced a lot of fifty lamps. These lamps were tested, and the Edison lamps proved to be superior. All incandescent-lamp manufacture was henceforth carried on at Harrison.

The consolidation problem even extended to the central stations. In many cities there was an Edison station, supplying d.c. incandescent lighting and power, competing with a Thomson-Houston station which was supplying arc lighting or a.c. lighting and power or both. General Electric did not desire to antagonize either company, because both were valuable customers. Coffin finally evolved the plan of inducing the two companies to merge under the Edison name. This can be looked upon as a concession by Coffin to the Edison local companies and the former Edison personnel in General Electric. These groups were conscious of the fact that General Electric, at the top-management level at least, was in reality a Thomson-Houston organization. Coffin wanted to receive the business of the Edison central stations and the complete coöperation of the Edison personnel in General Electric.

The formation of General Electric can be attributed to a number of influences. One of the most important was patents. F. P. Fish, who was present at the preliminary negotiations, stated that the reason for forming General Electric was the patent situation.[3] He had reference to the fact that certain patents of each company were needed by the other company if its equipment was to be of high quality. Edison General Electric, through Sprague, owned a number of very important railway patents, including those on the series-parallel controller and the wheelbarrow type of motor suspension. Other basic patents, such as those on the incandescent lamp and the three-wire and feeder-main networks, were derived from the original Edison company. Similarly, Thomson-Houston held basic patents needed by Edison General Electric. The Van Depoele trolley and overhead-turnout patents, a patent on the flashing process which lengthened the life of lamp filaments, and various arc-lighting patents were the most important of those belonging to Thomson-Houston. Because of the patents held by each company, neither could manufacture railway, lighting, or power equipment of the best quality without fear of infringement suits or injunctions. In some cases, a product less good than the best was manufactured. Edison General Electric, for example, did not use a flashing process for its lamps. In other cases, an infringing product was produced. Thomson-Houston made a series-parallel railway-motor controller. But in all products there was a strong desire on the part of each company to manufacture the best product possible without fear of patent difficulties.

The influence of patents in bringing about the consolidation can be stated in more general terms. Attention can be focused on the lines of equipment produced by each company instead of on particular patents. Edison General Electric had evolved from the pioneer innovator in d.c. incandescent lighting and had developed a good business in lighting equipment for central stations and isolated plants. Through acquiring Sprague, it had gained a strong position in d.c. electric power and street railways. In arc lighting, however, it was weak, and in alternating current it had done nothing in either light or power. The contrast with Thomson-Houston is particularly marked in the last two lines. Thomson-Houston had developed a very strong position in arc lighting, both in isolated plants and central stations, and it had secured control of Brush, the pioneer innovator. In alternating current, Thomson-Houston had entered the field shortly after Westinghouse and had had a long period of experience in a.c. equipment. Only in electric railways were the product lines of Thomson-Houston and Edison General Electric competitive instead of complementary. Here both firms had the experience, the reputation, and the patents of a pioneer innovator.

Each company desired to expand the lines in which it was weak and to begin the manufacture of those products which showed promise. Lack of patents and manufacturing experience made such expansion difficult. The increasing use of alternating current in lighting and the start of its use in power was an incentive to Edison General Electric to take up a.c. equipment. But a five-year handicap was hard to overcome. In d.c. power equipment, Thomson-Houston had not developed its line to the same extent as Sprague. For Thomson-Houston had few contacts with central stations supplying direct current for incandescent lighting, and a market for d.c. power equipment was more difficult to find. In electric railways, the strength of each company was so great that merger seemed to make possible a position in electric-railway equipment equal to the dominance in incandescent-lighting equipment long enjoyed by Edison and the dominance in arc lighting long held by Thomson-Houston. The consolidation of Thomson-Houston and Edison General Electric thus presented the prospect of an extremely strong company covering the entire field of electrical equipment.

Another influence, besides patents and equipment lines, leading to the consolidation can be inferred from the fact, indicated in Table 34, that the top management of General Electric consisted principally of Thomson-Houston men. The Edison firms had never had, apart from Edison himself, a forceful, imaginative, dynamic, and aggressive leader. Edison had provided the leadership up to about 1885, but was kept from having a free rein by the conservatism and caution of the financial backers. Furthermore, he had had to take charge of the technical and inventive work, as well as production, and the time he could devote to integrating and coördinating the general policies was severely limited. E. H. Johnson showed considerable promise as a leader, but never came up to expectations; and Henry Villard gave only part of his time to the electrical industry. J. P. Morgan no doubt perceived that the Edison firms had been held back by the lack of leadership. When he became acquainted with Coffin and his excellent record in bringing Thomson-Houston to an important position in the industry, Morgan probably realized that Coffin could supply what Edison General Electric needed. Coffin undoubtedly was well enough acquainted with one of his most important competitors to know that consolidation with Edison General Electric would give him a chance to increase the area in which his leadership abilities could function. To secure the top position in the new company, he would not have to compete with an able leader from Edison General Electric, nor would he have to share the powers and responsibilities of the top position with any Edison executive.

In the opinion of Edison, there was still another reason for the consolidation. When interviewed by a newspaper reporter in February 1892, Edison stated: "Recently there has been sharp rivalry between the companies, and prices have been cut so that there has been little profit in the manufacture of electrical machinery for anybody. The consolidation of the companies . . . will do away with a competition which has become so sharp that the product of the factories has been worth little more than ordinary hardware." [4]

The desire to eliminate competition was probably present, but it is difficult to evaluate its importance. There was apparently no attempt to form a combination of the three leading firms in the industry, and it would consequently be misleading to classify the union of Thomson-

Houston and Edison General Electric as a "trust" similar to the "Whisky Trust," the "Oil Trust," or the "Tobacco Trust." Since any serious effort to achieve a monopoly could hardly neglect Westinghouse, it is extremely doubtful that elimination of competition was a major motive in the formation of General Electric.

It is perhaps legitimate to ask why Thomson-Houston joined with Edison General Electric and not with Westinghouse. A consolidation between Edison General Electric and Westinghouse would have been impossible because of the antagonisms engendered in the a.c.-d.c. controversy, but the patent-license relationship between Westinghouse and Thomson-Houston could have led to a union. Westinghouse was strong only in alternating current and needed the arc lighting and electric railways of Thomson-Houston. Thomson-Houston could have used some of the a.c. patents of Westinghouse. And since Westinghouse and Thomson-Houston were the two largest producers of a.c. equipment, their consolidation would have created a firm very strong in that line. But it is clear that the influences of patents and lines of equipment were not nearly so favorable to their consolidation as to that of Thomson-Houston and Edison General Electric. Alternating-current power was not yet important in 1891, and the significance of the Westinghouse a.c. power patents was not generally understood. In a.c. lighting, Thomson-Houston had been able to develop its own system without patent difficulties. Westinghouse did not possess patents such as the Edison lamp and circuit patents or the Sprague railway patents, which were of great value to Thomson-Houston. Furthermore, the leadership factor did not encourage consolidation. George Westinghouse was the unquestioned leader of his firm, and it is doubtful that he would have joined forces with Thomson-Houston except on the condition that he be president of the new company. On his part, Coffin would not have assented to a consolidation which relegated him to a minor position. A combination may be extremely difficult to effect if the leader of each company is aggressive and ambitious.

The newly formed General Electric was condemned by some contemporary writers as a typical monopolistic trust which was heavily overcapitalized.[5] Although it is true that the assets of General Electric shrank considerably in the following years of depression, the consolidation itself does not seem to have involved overcapitalization. Prior to consolidating, Edison General Electric and Thomson-Houston each listed assets of about $20,000,000. The first General Electric balance sheet (January 31, 1893) listed assets of over $50,000,000, but a $10,000,000 bond issue had been sold for cash at par soon after the formation of the company. The funds received from the bond issue account for the extra $10,000,000 of assets on the General Electric balance sheet as compared to $40,000,000, the sum of the assets reported by the two companies prior to consolidation.

For the first two years after the consolidation, sales and profits continued at about the levels that would have been expected if the corresponding figures for Thomson-Houston and Edison General Electric had been added together. In 1891, Edison General Electric had sales of $11,000,000 and profits of $2,000,000. Thomson-Houston had sales of $10,000,000 and profits of nearly $3,000,000. In the eight-month period, June 1, 1892, to January 31, 1893, General Electric had sales of $12,000,000 and profits of $3,000,000. Converted to an annual basis, these figures become $18,000,000 and $4,500,000. During 1893, in spite of the beginning of a general business depression, sales did not drop below $16,000,000. Profits, however, fell to $2,000,000, and the value of certain assets declined considerably. Hit hardest were the securities of local companies that had been accepted for patent licenses or in part payment for equipment. The nationwide cash stringency made collections difficult, and accounts receivable were also affected. The severe price declines reduced inventory values. Losses sustained in these three classes of assets — securities, current receivables, and inventories — were estimated to be $12,500,000 by January 31, 1894, and $15,000,000 by January 31, 1895.

The scarcity of cash in 1893, which made it impossible for General Electric to collect anything on most accounts and difficult to collect even in part on the best accounts, created problems for the company, because it had some obligations which required settlement in cash. For the annual interest on the $10,000,000 bond issue, $500,000 was needed; a $600,000 cash dividend had been declared but not paid; and notes and accounts payable totaled $7,000,000. All sales were put on a cash basis so that receipts from sales would provide the cash for wages and materials. But the cash obligations which were not part of current operations could not be met by cash received from current sales. Cash on hand, which was nearly $4,000,000 on January 31, 1893, fell to $500,000 by January 31, 1894. Additional cash of $4,000,000 was raised by selling local-company securities of face value several times that figure to a syndicate of bankers led by J. P. Morgan. With this aid, General Electric was able to meet enough of its legal obligations to avoid receivership, which for a time during 1893 seemed imminent.[6]

Sales fell to $12,500,000 in 1894 and remained at that level until 1898, when they rose to $16,000,000. They increased rapidly after that, reaching $22,000,000 in 1899 and nearly $29,000,000 in 1900. Profits were about $500,000 in 1894 and varied little until 1898. They then increased to $4,000,000. As these figures suggest, the period 1893–1898 was one of generally depressed conditions in the electrical manufacturing industry. Because over 60 per cent of the output represented new capital investment in lighting, power, and street-railway companies, the orders for this part of the output decreased markedly during a time when general business prospects were unfavorable.

The large asset losses sustained by General Electric in 1893 and 1894 exceeded the surplus item on the balance sheet, but the write-down of the capital-stock account did not occur until 1899. A 40 per cent reduction was then voted, and the patents were reduced in value from $8,000,000 to $4,000,000. By 1900, the General Electric balance sheet listed assets of only $27,000,000, as compared to $50,000,000 in 1893. It is clear, however, that the write-down of assets was necessary because the asset valuations as originally set by Thomson-Houston and Edison General Electric were too high in view of the price decline of raw materials, finished products, and securities which occurred during the 1890's. The write-down was not a process of eventually setting true values on assets overvalued as a result of overcapitalization at the time of the consolidation.

PATENTS

By 1894, both General Electric and Westinghouse possessed hundreds of patents. Some of these had been obtained directly from inventors and engineers in the employ of the company, some by purchase from outside inventors, and some by merger with other firms. These patents were wanted for one of two reasons. Either the patent could serve to prevent any other firm from producing an identical or very similar product; or it could protect the firm's customers against patent-infringement suits by other manufacturers. Examples of patents of the first kind are the Edison lamp patent, the Tesla induction-motor patent, the Van Depoele trolley patent, and the Bentley-Knight conduit patent. Each of these was considered to be basic and controlling. If a firm wanted to manufacture incandescent lamps, induction motors, underrunning trolleys, or conduit equipment of an economical and reliable type, access to the corresponding patent was necessary. Examples of patents of the second kind are the Westinghouse patent on the electropneumatic multiple-unit system of control, the various flashing-process, arc-lamp, and railway-motor-control patents. In these cases, the intent was not to gain control of all methods of accomplishing a certain technical result but merely to protect one method against other patents. The Westinghouse multiple-unit-control system accomplished the same result as the Sprague multiple-unit control, but by use of electricity and compressed air instead of electricity alone. Similarly, in the flashing process, arc lamps, and railway-motor-control devices, there were enough alternative methods to permit each firm to own a patent covering its product. In these çases, the possession of a patent did no more than permit a company to make a product or use a process without interference. The patent could not serve as a means to monopolize the entire field.

When General Electric and Westinghouse had expanded their business to include nearly all lines of electrical apparatus, the two objectives of patent ownership came into frequent conflict. If each firm owned patents on a certain line of apparatus with the objective of controlling the field, a conflict was inevitable. If one firm entertained the control objective while the other was satisfied with the protection objective, a conflict was also the result. The control objective and the protection objective are logically incompatible. Only if each firm had been content with the protection objective alone in all lines would patent trouble have been avoided.

Westinghouse and General Electric had long been accustomed to giving patent guarantees on all equipment. They were willing to accept complete responsibility for patent-infringement suits against the equipment purchaser. But the existence of the control objective was a continual threat to strong patent guarantees. By the mid-1890's, in fact, they could no longer be made by both companies on all kinds of equipment. Westinghouse could not sell the underrunning trolley and continue to give patent guarantees when General Electric held the controlling patent. General Electric could not market the induction motor and continue to give patent guarantees when Westinghouse held the controlling patent. This impasse resulting from basic patents in various equipment lines could have been resolved in a number of different ways. General Electric could have retired from polyphase power and Westinghouse from electric railways. Or General Electric could have marketed an inferior non-infringing polyphase system and Westinghouse an inferior non-infringing railway system. A third alternative was a merger of the two companies; and a fourth was a patent cross-licensing agreement under which each company could continue to produce all types of equipment and give strong patent guarantees to its customers.

The recognition of an impasse and the choosing of one of the four alternatives could not occur until General Electric was convinced that Westinghouse held the controlling patents in polyphase power and Westinghouse was convinced that General Electric held the controlling patents in electric railways. During 1894 and 1895, Westinghouse and General Electric took patent action against each other which made it clear that an impasse existed. Westinghouse instituted a number of suits against General Electric and its customers charging infringements of the Tesla patents. In other instances, threats were made. When General Electric undertook a three-phase installation in a municipal power plant at Canandaigua, New York, early in 1895, a Westinghouse official wrote the mayor of Canandaigua as follows: "You will of course understand that should you persist in using the multiphase motors we will be compelled to bring suit for injunctions and damages. We have already instituted suit against the General Electric Company."[7]

The General Electric salesmen were told to reassure the buyers of polyphase apparatus that there was nothing to worry about in the patent situation. Such reassurance was to be made verbally, however, and not in writing, because, "if put formally, the matter takes a degree of importance it does not correctly possess."[8]

In the spring of 1895, rumors spread of an impending patent agreement between General Electric and Westinghouse. Negotiations were conducted for a time and then called off. The patent situation was not yet serious enough to force action. During 1895, however, the Van Depoele trolley patent was upheld and adjudged to cover all underrunning trolleys. Although no court ruling on the Tesla patents was made, the strength of the Westinghouse company in polyphase power equipment became more clear as the use of alternating current for power increased. Experience and analysis showed that the Tesla inventions were necessary to a successful polyphase system. By 1896, over 300 patent suits were pending between General Electric and Westinghouse. It was obvious that something had to be done if both companies were to continue to produce full lines of equipment and give strong patent guarantees to their customers.

The solution to the difficulty must be viewed against the leaders of the two companies, Coffin and Westinghouse. Their ambition and aggressiveness were such that it is doubtful that serious consideration was given by either man to producing inferior equipment or less than a full line of electrical apparatus. What both wanted was a chance to carry on a normal business without interference from patents. The solution to the patent impasse was thus a cross-licensing agreement. This permitted the two companies to produce full lines of good-quality equipment and carry on the price-product competition that had been characteristic of their relationship.

Negotiations, which extended over a number of months, finally resulted in a patent agreement which was signed March 12, 1896, and which became effective March 31, 1896. The General Electric patents were considered to represent 62½ per cent of the value of the patents in the pool, and the Westinghouse patents, 37½ per cent. The business in the equipment lines covered by the patents was to be divided in that proportion without royalty payments. If either company exceeded its share of particular equipment types, royalty payments were to be made. The agreement was to run for fifteen years and was to be administered by a board of patent control which had two members each from General Electric and Westinghouse. A fifth member, from outside the industry, was available to arbitrate in case of a deadlock.

The patent agreement thus called for the pooling of patents and the manufacture of the patented equipments by both companies. There was an exception, however, to each of these features of the agreement. In railway apparatus, General Electric produced the motor controllers for the two firms, and Westinghouse, through its wholly-owned subsidiary, R. D. Nuttall Company of Pittsburgh, produced the trolleys. The only patents not pooled were those on incandescent lamps. The reason for this exception was that the Edison licensees demanded it. Because of the patent-license agreements between these companies and General Electric, the licensees had strong legal grounds on which to base their claim that a pooling of the incandescent-lighting patents would be an unwarranted interference with their long-standing position as the exclusive sellers of Edison lamps in their territories.

It was this issue of licensee interference that led to a dispute over the interpretation of the agreement that finally had to be settled by the courts. The dispute arose over the use of three-phase power apparatus in New York City. Westinghouse was of the opinion that its licensee station there, the United Electric Light and Power Company, had the sole right to use three-phase equipment. General Electric, however, sold polyphase generators and rotary converters to the Edison Electric Illuminating Company of New York. In March 1899, Westinghouse went to court to obtain an injunction to prevent delivery of the General Electric equipment, but the court refused to grant the injunction.[9] The equipment involved was worth about $250,000.

The competitive effect of the patent agreement is not easy to determine. A distinction should be made between the effect on the competition between General Electric and Westinghouse and the competition among all the firms in the industry. With reference to the first effect, the contract contained no clauses concerning price or product agreements. The price and product competition could be more vigorous than previously because patent conflict had been removed. The patents now could serve as the framework within which competition could take place. The General Electric sales managers were told how to view the patent agreement shortly after it became effective: "A contract has been made with the Westinghouse Company for exchanging licenses under our patents upon an agreed basis. This contract does not affect the conduct of our commercial business, except from the patent standpoint, does not increase prices or interfere with competition. This fact must be impressed upon our agents and customers."[10]

The agreement does not seem to have lessened competition between General Electric and Westinghouse. The 62½–37½ arrangement was for royalty purposes and should not be looked upon as indicating output quotas. The agreement had other important effects, however. The strongest possible guarantees against patent-infringement suits could be placed in all sales contracts. General Electric guaranteed the purchaser against any possible loss or expense by reason of adverse claims under patents, and Westinghouse could make a similar guarantee. Another effect was the elimination of the costly patent litigation between the two firms.

The effect of the agreement on the rest of the industry was probably to strengthen the relative position of General Electric and Westinghouse. The legal talent freed by the agreement was directed to carry on patent suits against the other firms in the industry. It is doubtful whether litigation among electrical manufacturing firms actually declined much. In August 1896, Griffin sent out a circular letter on the patent situation in which he listed the important General Electric patents and remarked that "suits on practically all of these patented inventions are being vigorously prosecuted." [11] The effort to prevent infringement was thus intensified. With basic patents in all the main lines of equipment, General Electric and Westinghouse were in a very powerful patent position relative to the small companies. The latter were unable to make strong patent guarantees, which was a sizable competitive handicap, and, beyond that, were in danger of being forced out of business by injunctions which could prevent them from manufacturing at all. Certain contracts which General Electric and Westinghouse were using in the sale of railway apparatus by the end of 1896 indicate that the intent was to prevent their customers from using General Electric or Westinghouse patented apparatus, such as the overhead trolley, with car equipments made by other manufacturers.[12] These contracts, like the patent suits, tended to weaken the competitive position of the smaller firms.

That the 1896 agreement strengthened the general competitive position of Westinghouse and General Electric with respect to the rest of the industry is shown by the companies which found it desirable to sell out to one firm or the other. The Stanley company was under suit by Westinghouse for infringement of the Tesla patents from 1895 on. Finally, in 1903, Stanley sold out to General Electric. He then formed the Stanley Meter Company, but that firm was also sued by Westinghouse for patent infringement and was soon dissolved. Stanley was thus unable to stay in the a.c. equipment business without the Tesla patents. A firm which was similarly situated, but with reference to the General Electric railway patents, was the Walker Manufacturing Company. This company, located in Cleveland, had been formed in 1883 to manufacture heavy machinery, including power-transmission plants and cable railways. When it became clear that electricity was going to replace mechanical methods of power transmission in many instances, Walker entered the electrical manufacturing field. In May 1894, it marketed its first railway motor and soon afterward was producing a fairly complete line of railway, lighting, and power apparatus. Walker, like Stanley, was a company which did a volume of business large enough to be noticed by General Electric and Westinghouse. In 1896, these two firms initiated a number of patent suits against Walker and its customers. Infringement was claimed of the Sprague motor-suspension patent, the Van Depoele trolley and overhead-switch patent, and several generator patents. The trolley patent was eventually declared invalid, but the others were sustained.[18] Walker continued to try to do business during these suits and secured a substantial number of contracts. Among these were a few large orders which were obtained because several of the owners of Walker had extensive investments in urban traction companies. It became more and more difficult to do business, however, and in the fall of 1898 Walker sold out to Westinghouse. The price was about $1,000,000.

During the 1890's, the Lorain Steel Company, also of Cleveland, started making electric-railway motors and other electrical equipment. A number of patent suits were instituted against Lorain by General Electric, and in the early 1900's Lorain sold its electrical business to Westinghouse. Another firm which sold out about the same time was the Siemens and Halske Company, of Chicago. It had been established in 1892 as a branch of the parent German company. In 1895, the Chicago firm enlarged its manufacturing facilities and carried on production of lighting and power apparatus. Financial difficulties together with a prolonged strike led the company to sell out to General Electric in 1900. While patents are not known to have played a direct part in the sale of Siemens and Halske, the worsening of its competitive position after 1896 is probably to some extent attributable to the increased strength of General Electric and Westinghouse.

The division between General Electric and Westinghouse of Stanley, Walker, Lorain, and Siemens and Halske is interesting from the patent standpoint. Westinghouse, weak in railway patents, purchased Walker and Lorain, the two which were strong competitors in railway equipment. General Electric, weak in power patents, purchased Stanley and Siemens and Halske, the two which were primarily in the power-equipment business.

XXI

The Dynamics of the Industry

TECHNICAL CHANGE IN ELECTRIC-POWER EQUIPMENT

The technical changes in railway motors have already been described at some length. It will be recalled that the first railway motors, used by Sprague at Richmond, were low in horsepower, unprotected against dirt and water, and so high in speed that double-reduction gears were necessary. During the succeeding years, the horsepower of the motors was increased from 7.5 to 15 to 25 and finally to 50 for ordinary streetcar work. Partial enclosure and eventually total enclosure were adopted. The increase in knowledge of motor design permitted motors of relatively light weight which could develop adequate horsepower at speeds sufficiently low so that single-reduction gearing could be used. Designers learned how to provide for easy access to the motor to enable faster and less expensive adjustments and repairs. Materials and manufacturing methods were changed to decrease cost and give better performance.

As electric traction spread from street railways to elevated lines, interurban lines, and finally to subways, motors of larger horsepower and the proper operating characteristics had to be developed. By 1900, there were a least a dozen types of railway motors, each designed for a specific use. The spread of electric traction beyond the street railway also called for new methods of current pick-up, such as the third-rail–shoe system used on elevated railways. Similarly, the motor controllers underwent change. As motor capacities increased, the controllers had to be designed to handle larger quantities of current without excessive sparking. For elevated railways, the multiple-unit system of control was developed. This system permitted great flexibility in car handling and was made almost completely automatic. The rate of acceleration was pre-set and out of control of the motorman. The dead-man's switch was evolved to prevent serious accident in case the motorman were suddenly incapacitated.

The first industrial applications of electric power used ordinary generators as electric motors. The performance of such motors was not completely satisfactory. Speed changes usually required shifting the brushes, and the speed variations caused by changes in the load were undesirable. When attention was paid to motor performance and when motor design became an art separate from generator design, motors were manufactured which were more suitable for most purposes. The brushes were fixed in position, and motors with constant-speed characteristics were developed. Motors of many sizes up to 50 horsepower were being made by the end of the 1880's for isolated-plant and central-station operation. All of these, like the railway motors, were d.c. motors. For purposes where a variable-speed, high-torque motor which had to start frequently from standstill was required, the series d.c. motor was one which would never be surpassed. In elevators, cranes, and streetcars, it gave excellent service. For constant-speed work, the shunt motor was very satisfactory.

The low voltages possible with direct current were a severe limit on the size of the area to which any one central station could supply power and forced central stations to locate with reference to power consumers instead of with reference to minimum costs of power generation. The use of a higher voltage which could reduce transmission cost was permitted by the adoption of alternating current. When a successful motor had been developed, it was found that it would not operate satisfactorily on the single-phase a.c. lighting circuits, and polyphase circuits had to be established before the induction motor could be widely used. The first induction motors required slip rings, collector brushes, and starting resistances. The elimination of these features in the rotating-secondary, squirrel-cage-rotor induction motor resulted in a motor with a minimum of moving parts and a low construction cost. This motor had a good speed characteristic and became universally used where a constant-speed motor was desired. The lack of brushes meant almost no repair expense and no sparking. The motor could safely be used in the presence of inflammable and explosive materials.

The induction motor permitted the direct use of a.c. power by the consumer; but for those uses where the d.c. series motor was superior to the induction motor, the employment of alternating current for power transmission depended upon the availability of an efficient and inexpensive method of converting alternating to direct current. The rotary converter met that need. At first, it could be made to operate well only for low frequencies, but, by 1900, 60-cycle converters were being made in large sizes.

Achievement of the economies in transmission possible with alternating current required high voltages. The limit on these voltages was the insulation on the transmission line. Considerable effort was directed toward developing a suitable high-voltage insulator, and finally the suspension type was invented. The first high-voltage transmission lines were confined to the western regions, where the climate was not very severe. Much more work on insulation had to be carried out before high voltages, above 50,000 volts, could be used in the areas of the United States where sleet, snow, and heavy storms were common.

The high-voltage transmission lines were first used to make available hitherto inaccessible water power. They later came into use in conjunction with steam-powered central stations. With a large market for electric power and with economical transmission possible, there was need for more economical methods of power generation. The steam turbine was developed to meet this need. Its steam economy was high, its maintenance cost low, and its size small. Alternating-current generators were designed which could operate efficiently at the high turbine speeds which permitted generators low in cost per kilowatt of output.

The growth of electric power raised problems of standardizing the various circuit constants in order that manufacturing costs could be reduced. The standardization problem was first encountered on a large scale in electric railways. Five hundred volts very quickly came to be the standard voltage, and this permitted a single railway to use equipment made by a number of manufacturers. Each equipment maker could design all his railway motors and generators for 500-volt operation with assurance that any street railway in the United States was a possible customer. In alternating-current power, voltage was only one of the circuit constants that had to be standardized. The frequency and the number of phases were also involved. Voltage standardization was not quite so important as in d.c. circuits, because voltages were easily adjusted by transformers. Frequency converters and phase-changing transformers were invented to permit systems of different frequency and phase to be interconnected. The need for these last two devices was reduced by the extent to which 60 cycles, 25 cycles, and three-phase became standard throughout the United States.

ENTREPRENEURSHIP IN THE MANUFACTURE OF ELECTRIC-POWER EQUIPMENT

Entrepreneurship in the manufacture of electric-power equipment was carried on by single individuals, groups of individuals in a single firm, and groups of individuals from a number of firms. In electric railways, the two pioneer innovators were Sprague and the Thomson-Houston company. Sprague as a single individual was a pioneer innovator; in the Thomson-Houston company a number of persons, including Thomson, Van Depoele, Roher, and Coffin, took part in the decisions that led to pioneer innovation. In d.c. electric power and in elevated-railway electrification, Sprague again was the pioneer innovator and made the responsible decisions. In the application of a.c. power, the Niagara Falls electrification was the pioneer innovation. Here many people and several firms were involved. The Cataract Construction Company played a primary role, but the Niagara Commission, the many advising experts, and the Westinghouse company also took part. In the a.c. electrification of textile plants, Paine, a General Electric salesman, acted on his own initiative in the pioneer innovation. He had to convince not only the mill owner but also his superiors in General Electric. In high-voltage transmission, Stanley and his two engineers, Chesney and Kelley, led the way in successful installations. In turbogenerator units, groups of individuals in General Electric and Westinghouse carried on work simultaneously that was to lead to successful installations. The Westinghouse company made the first central-station turbogenerator installation and adopted the horizontal, high-speed type which became standard. But General Electric made the first large turbogenerator installation and for that reason must also be viewed as a pioneer innovator.

Entrepreneurship in some lines of electric power differed considerably from the entrepreneurship in arc lighting and incandescent lighting. It will be recalled that where a central station was to furnish light for streets, offices, homes, or factories, a local lighting company was formed. The task of the electrical manufacturer, say Brush or Edison, was to secure backing from one or more local capitalists. The companies were usually started on a small scale, and little initial investment was needed. In isolated plants, the marketing problem was different. Here the owner of a hotel, office building, apartment house, or factory had to be convinced that arc or incandescent lighting was worth its cost to his business. Unlike the usual central station, where the entire investment was in the electric plant and a building to house it, the investment in an isolated plant was commonly no more than a small fraction of the firm's total investment.

The problem of introducing electric railways and a.c. central-station power equipment was different from either of the two cases in lighting.

New firms were not established at the initiative of manufacturers of electric-railway or power-generation equipment. And the firms that bought this equipment were making an investment that was a large proportion of their total investment. In these circumstances, the act of pioneer innovation had a publicity and advertising significance that was much greater than in either arc or incandescent lighting. It was Sprague's Richmond installation that led Whitney to decide to adopt electric railways. When the largest street-railway system in the United States decided to invest several millions in electric traction, the smaller street railways were no longer hesitant about electrifying. When Sprague secured a $300,000 contract for installation of the multiple-unit system on a Chicago elevated railroad, and when that installation proved to be successful, the other elevated railways were ready to invest millions of dollars in the same system. When the Niagara Falls Power Company chose alternating current as its method of power transmission, and when alternating current performed satisfactorily, the future of polyphase alternating current for central-station power was assured. Because a firm that had a multimillion dollar investment at stake chose polyphase alternating current, the hundreds of central-station owners and the entrepreneurs interested in water-power development were no longer reluctant to invest in polyphase power.

It is important to see that use of an innovation on a small scale in a few scattered installations is not of much significance. Almost no one is encouraged to follow and adopt the innovation. The Van Depoele railway installations did not convince Whitney that electric traction was the most profitable kind of motive power. In contrast, Sprague's Richmond installation, because it possessed the technical features which were necessary for economical and reliable operation on a large scale, led Whitney to abandon completely his plans for a cable road. Similarly, the Westinghouse hydro-electric-power installation at Telluride or the several General Electric polyphase installations in New England did not establish alternating current as the universal technique of long-distance power transmission. But the Niagara Falls electrification did. In these instances of pioneer innovation, the size of the investment and the publicity the installation received were the prime factors which distinguish it from the earlier cases which cannot be labeled acts of pioneer innovation. Underlying these factors of investment size and favorable publicity were the technical characteristics which permitted reliable and economical operation. These technical characteristics resulted from the vision of the pioneer innovator, who saw the place the innovation could occupy in the economy and had the technical ability to develop those characteristics.

The industrial use of electric power was in most cases an innovational problem akin to isolated lighting. If the firm already had an incandescent-lighting plant or if it had access to a central-station circuit, it could install one or two motors on a trial basis before making a heavy investment. In some cases, however, the amount invested was so large that the installation had the character of a pioneer innovation. The electrification of the textile industry is an example. Because of the peculiar power-transmission problem at the Columbia mill, the choice of all-electric or none had to be made. An investment of $75,000 in electric equipment alone was involved. The success of this installation was a stimulus to textile-mill electrifications of the same kind (that is, alternating current, group drive, motors on ceiling, and so forth) throughout the South.

One peculiar aspect of innovational entrepreneurship in the electrical manufacturing industry is the extent to which General Electric and Westinghouse, because of their size and the wide range of their manufacturing operations, could install innovational equipment in their own plants. They could thereby observe closely the performance of such equipment under actual operating conditions. Another advantage was that potential customers were sometimes easier to sell to when they saw the item of equipment in operation in the firm's own plant. Examples of this kind of installation were the new Westinghouse plant at East Pittsburgh, completed in 1894, which used induction motors extensively, and the turbogenerator unit which was installed in the powerplant of the Westinghouse Air Brake Company in 1899. It was on the basis of the Air Brake installation that Westinghouse adopted the revolving-field type of generator. An example from General Electric is a very large crane which was installed in the Schenectady shops. It demonstrated the possibilities of the electric crane for industrial purposes.

THE GROWTH OF ELECTRIC POWER, 1880–1900

The growth of electric traction in the United States is shown in Table 35. Of the 2,900 electric streetcars in use in 1890, about two-thirds were equipped by Sprague and Thomson-Houston. The share of these companies was about equal, each accounting for over 1,000 cars. Of the 51,000 electric cars in use in 1902, about 30,000 had been equipped by General Electric, about 15,000 by Westinghouse, and the rest by Walker, Lorain, and other smaller companies. The consolidation of the two pioneer innovators who in 1890 had divided between them nearly the whole market did not result in a firm which secured the entire market after 1890. Westinghouse began to manufacture railway equipment and, on the basis of several exceptionally well-designed motors, built up a large railway business. Total lack of basic railway patents was no handicap to this company. By the time infringement suits were started and decided, a patent agreement was reached which permitted Westinghouse to remain in the railway-equipment business.

The market for electric-railway equipment was made up of two segments; one can be called the substitution segment and the other the growth segment. The substitution segment consisted of existing street railways which used animal, cable, or steam as the motive power. The growth segment consisted of the new street railways which were constructed from year to year. Table 36 shows the miles of track for two years, classified by type of motive power. It can be seen that, during the period 1890–1902, street-railway trackage increased by 14,460 miles. Electric railways increased by 20,650 miles. Of the latter increase, 6,190 miles was the

TABLE 35

Street Railways in the United States, 1880–1902

	All Street Railways		*Electric Street Railways*	
Year	*Miles of Track*	*No. of Cars*	*Miles of Track*	*No. of Cars*
1880	3,000	18,000	0	0
1887	6,000	25,000	30	80
1890[a]	8,100	33,000	1,300	2,900
1902	22,600	60,000	22,000	51,000

Sources: 1880 data from J. A. Miller, *Fares Please!* p. 32. Data for 1887 based on speech by T. C. Martin, reported in *EW*, VIII (December 18, 1886), 296; also speech by G. W. Mansfield, reported in *EW*, XIV (August 17, 1889), 113; also *Transportation Business in the United States: Eleventh Census*, vol. XIV, pt. i, p. 692. Page 682 of the last-cited volume is the source of the 1890 data. Data for 1902 from *Abstract of the Twelfth Census*, p. 387.

[a] On July 1.

substitution segment and 14,460 miles the growth segment. The 6,190 miles of track in which electricity was substituted for another form of motive power included 5,400 miles of animal railway, 250 miles of cable railway, and 540 miles of steam railway. It seems clear that nearly the entire substitution segment of the market was composed of animal railways. The obvious reason is that most of the street railways were animal-powered before the coming of electric traction. The data are aggregates, however, and cannot give more than a rough breakdown of the electric-railway-equipment market. The buyers of this equipment were the street-railway companies, and, for an accurate analysis, it would be necessary to know how many horse-railway firms bought electric equipment and how many entirely new railway companies were formed to operate electric railways. Furthermore, the trackage figures do not reveal changes which took place during the twelve-year period. To the extent that nonelectric railways were abandoned, the growth segment is understated. To the extent that nonelectric railways increased after 1890 only to change to electricity before 1902, the substitution segment is understated.

The growth in street railways as a whole during the last decade of the nineteenth century can be attributed to two distinct factors. The population increase in the United States, particularly in the cities, called for more street railways and for enlargement of existing ones. Although some of the urban growth resulted from the fact that electric traction was available, there would have been a substantial urban growth with a corresponding increase in street-railway trackage even if horse railways had remained the dominant type. The second factor was the increase in the speed of streetcars when they were electrified. The maximum average speed which could be economically attained with horsecars was six miles per hour. Electric streetcars could average from eight to ten miles per hour in the crowded sections of the city and almost twenty miles per hour in the residential areas. The average speed of the trolley car was therefore at least twice the speed of the horsecar. An area four times as large as that served by horse railways was brought within the same travel time for the central business district of a city. The extension of electric railways to the outlying areas was profitable because the city would grow where fast transportation was available. The electric railway could be used in this fashion to build up its patronage; while the cable road, with an investment per mile at least five times as much, could be installed only in districts already heavily populated.

TABLE 36

Motive Power of Street Railways in the United States, 1890–1902

Type of motive-power	Miles of Track		
	1890	*1902*	*Change*
Electric	1,260	21,910	+20,650
Animal	5,660	260	−5,400
Cable	490	240	−250
Steam	710	170	−540
TOTALS	8,120	22,580	+14,460

Source: *Abstract of the Twelfth Census*, p. 387.

Sales in the substitution segment of the market were made almost entirely on a cost basis. The cost per car-mile of operating an electric street railway was about half the cost per car-mile of operating a horse railway. Although the cost differential was not this great in 1888, by 1890 very few new horse railways were being constructed. The cost differential permitted a rapid and complete substitution for horse motive power by 1900. The cost advantage over cable motive power was so small that it was nearly nonexistent until the mid-1890's. New cable roads continued to be built after 1888, and, by 1891, there were over fifty of them. By 1895, however, electric-railway equipment had been further developed and a measurable cost differential in favor of electric power had been established. Thereafter, substitution of electricity for cables proceeded rapidly. Eventually, cables were used only where steep grades prohibited the use of any motive power which depended on friction between the car wheels and the track.

Many sales in the growth segment of the market also depended on cost, but not on the cost of electric power compared to other forms of motive power. For a street railway that was to run in outlying districts, the horse was too slow and the cable too expensive. The decision involved estimating passenger revenues and comparing them to operating costs. If the road were built at all, it would use electric power.

Because the sales of electric-railway equipment depended so much on operating costs, the equipment manufacturers were willing to make cost guarantees. The West End Street Railway Company, it will be recalled, demanded guarantees of repair costs from Thomson-Houston. Another example is the electrification of a five-mile stretch of track in New York City in 1894–95. The railway company had intended to install the cable system, which it was using on some of its other trackage, but General Electric was ready to assume all the risk of an electric-conduit road, and the company consented to electrification. General Electric agreed to equip the road electrically and to allow the railway company to operate it for twelve months. If the operation proved to be unsatisfactory, General Electric was to remove its apparatus and receive no compensation.[1] Guarantees of this kind served to shift the risks of innovation to the manufacturer and were an important reason for the rapid increase in electric traction.

The growth of electric power in manufacturing in the United States is shown by the following data. In 1880, mechanical power used in manufacturing totaled 3,411,000 horsepower. Of this, a negligible amount was transmitted by electricity. By 1890, 16,000 out of a total of 5,955,000 horsepower was transmitted by electricity, and ten years later the corresponding figures were 495,000 out of 11,300,000.[2] The use of electric power in industry thus increased about thirtyfold during the 1890's, a rate of increase about fifteen times as large as the increase in total power in industry. Even with such a rapid growth, however, less than 5 per cent of industrial power was transmitted by electricity in 1900. Of this 5 per cent, about one-third was supplied by central stations and two-thirds by isolated plants. The central station was beginning to be important as a source of electric power, although electric power itself was still a minor element in manufacturing.

It is interesting to note the extensive use of electric motive power in the electrical manufacturing industry. The census classification "electrical apparatus and supplies" roughly corresponds to the electrical manufacturing industry as defined in this study. In 1900, the electrical apparatus and supplies industry employed 63,856 mechanical horsepower, of which 24,256 (nearly 40 per cent) was transmitted by electricity.

Electric power's greatest advantage over other forms of power transmission existed where long distances were involved. By 1900, this fact was universally recognized. In factories, where the transmission distances were relatively short, the advantages of electric power were not so striking but nevertheless of importance. The first advantage to be generally recognized was the elimination of countershafting and belting. The gains from this elimination were numerous. The expense of the shafting was saved, the power lost in transmission was reduced, working conditions were better, and maintenance expenses were less. Furthermore, there was much greater flexibility in production planning and control. The machines no longer had to be arranged in straight lines or in the same building, the buildings did not have to conform to a cubical shape, and speed control of individual machines was much easier. The clearance of overhead areas permitted the use of large cranes for the handling of materials inside the shops. This substitution of mechanical power for human power resulted in substantial cost reductions.

When electric current from central stations became generally available for power purposes, the small power consumers found the electric motor much more economical than the small steam engine. The motor required no attendant and could develop its full power any time it was needed. Electric power thus permitted the substitution of the large steam plant of the central station for the small isolated steam plants. In places where power use was so small that it did not justify an isolated steam plant, the electric motor encouraged the substitution of mechanical power for human power. The sewing machine in the home, the drill in the dentist's office, and the buffer, polisher, and grinder in the jeweler's shop are examples.

The problem of selling electric motors for use in shops, offices, homes, and factories was quite different from the problem of selling railway equipment. The motors were a relatively small expenditure for any one firm, and the publicity of big installations and the operating guarantees were not so important. The essence of the problem of selling was to have experienced salesmen contacting a large number of potential customers. The number of motors in industrial use consequently increased much more slowly than the number in street railways. The various industries had different power requirements, and the designing of motors to suit these requirements and the sale of them to the industrial firms was a process which had hardly more than started by 1900. Nevertheless, the basic technical advances in the generation, transmission, and utilization of electric power had been made, and the succeeding decades saw a widespread use of electric power throughout the economy.

Conclusion

Conclusion

It is now appropriate to summarize this study of the electrical manufacturing industry, stressing the general concepts, tendencies, and trends which run through it all. In addition, a few pages are devoted to suggestions which may be of use in the formulation of the public policies concerning industrial markets. It may seem presumptuous to advance the viewpoint that public policy in 1953 can in any way profit from an analysis of industrial experience in the several decades prior to 1900. Nevertheless, on the assumption that there are repetitive patterns in industrial development and that good public policy must take account of long-run as well as short-run objectives, it is hoped that a study in economic history of this kind will have relevance to modern economic problems.

COMPETITION

Competition in the electrical manufacturing industry during the period 1875–1900 can be summarized by listing in table form the principal factors which determined the nature of that competition. For analytical purposes, the industry can be thought of as composed of two segments: the equipment producers and the lighting-element producers. It has been shown that the competition which existed in arc carbons and incandescent lamps differed appreciably from competition in the heavy-equipment items such as dynamos and motors. Competition in the two markets was interrelated, of course, and the distinction between the two segments of the industry should not be overemphasized. Some of the firms which produced lighting elements also produced equipment. Another tie between the two markets was provided by the customers, who were present in both markets. Thus on the supply side and on the demand side, the markets were interconnected. Nevertheless, it is convenient to treat the segments of the industry and the corresponding markets separately and then to discuss the consequences of the interrelationships.

Table 37 lists the principal determinants of competition in the electrical manufacturing industry. It will be recalled that the competitive patterns in arc carbons and incandescent lamps were similar. In each case, the product was not durable, and therefore regular purchases by the lighting companies were necessary. The fact that the product was a capital good meant that there was an emphasis on cost. In addition, the product was homogeneous, or nearly so, relatively simple to make, and not subject to rapid technical change. The carbons and lamps could be produced, in the early years at least, without expensive or complicated equipment. The necessary raw materials were readily available. Patents were not significant

TABLE 37

Determinants of Competition in the Electrical Manufacturing Industry

	Heavy equipment (generators, motors, etc.)	*Lighting elements (carbons, incandescent lamps)*
Nature of the product	Durable, heterogeneous capital good; complex; many technical changes	Nondurable, nearly homogeneous capital good;[a] simple; few technical changes
Number of producers	Few	Many
Entry of new firms	Difficult	Easy
Patents	Very important in a.c. power and electric railways	Not important in arc carbons; important in incandescent lamps after 1892

This table follows Professor E. S. Mason's classification of the objective elements which help to explain business practices in an industrial market.

[a] Labeling incandescent lamps as a capital good is justified by the fact that prior to 1900 it was standard practice for central stations to furnish the lamps as well as the current and to make one all-inclusive charge for light. The lamps, like the generators, were a capital good used to produce the consumer good, light.

in either the product or the manufacturing process. In these conditions — a standardized product sold mainly to business firms, relatively free entry, many buyers, and more than fifteen sellers — the market closely approached the economist's concept of pure competition. The competition was almost entirely in prices, and these were driven down to cost by the additional supply from new firms. But these freely competitive conditions did not prevail for long. The year 1888 marked the end of pure competition in arc carbons, and 1896 saw the termination of pure competition in incandescent lamps.

Similar influences were present in both cases. The concentration in production of the equipment which provided the current for lighting elements was one factor. The large electrical manufacturing firms, which produced arc carbons and incandescent lamps as well as equipment, commonly required that the purchasers of their equipment also buy carbons and lamps from them. After most of the equipment was made by a few firms, the independent manufacturers of carbons and lamps had difficulty finding a market. Another influence was the increased mechanization in the production of lighting elements. The machines and processes, which were often patented, required a greater capital investment than the previous production techniques. Patents on arc carbons were never of importance, but in incandescent lamps, patents served as the framework for the price-output stabilization agreement of 1896 and 1897. In both arc carbons and incandescent lamps, the transition from competition to oligopoly was spurred by the experience of the producers under severe price competition. The low prices and chaotic conditions of 1886 and 1887 in arc carbons and of 1894 and 1895 in incandescent lamps "taught" the firms that some way must be found to stabilize the industry.

It is difficult to say, in retrospect, whether the public interest was better served by competition or stabilized oligopoly. In favor of competition, it may be said that the rapid increase in supply and the lowering of prices stimulated the demand for the lighting elements by reducing the price of electric lighting and encouraging its substitution for other forms of artificial illumination. In favor of the stabilized oligopoly is the fact that the quality of the product was somewhat higher than before. The severe price competition tended to deteriorate the product. In regard to prices, the effect of the stablization was less than one might expect. Prices were increased moderately at first, but later continued to fall in accordance with the previous long-term trend. Several reasons can be suggested for this price behavior. One is the identity of interest between the equipment manufacturers, who controlled a large proportion of the arc-carbon and incandescent-lamp production, and the lighting companies. The market for equipment depended upon the profitable operation of the central stations. The existing stations would not expand nor would new lighting companies be formed unless profit prospects were good. The equipment makers were therefore quite willing to supply lighting elements at low prices. A second factor was the influence of potential competition. If prices remained low and profit margins small, the production economies of large-scale operations and the use of efficient production processes, which were usually patented, kept new firms out of the industry. If high prices had been set, the entry of new firms would have been encouraged because the use of small-scale, obsolete manufacturing methods would have been profitable.

Competition in electrical equipment was considerably different from competition in the lighting elements. The product was durable, complex, and heterogeneous. As a durable capital good, it was sold to businessmen who were interested in the cost of light production, not the first cost of the equipment. Price was thus relegated to a position of secondary importance. What counted was the quality of the equipment. This included its life, operating costs, maintenance costs, and general reliability. Rapid technical changes improved equipment quality and decreased further the significance of price.

Patents also influenced competitive conditions. They were a prime cause of the numerous consolidations and mergers which finally resulted in only two full-line producers. Furthermore, patents permitted competition to take place on a system basis instead of with reference to single items of equipment. Manufacturers could refuse to allow the use of particular patented apparatus except as a part of a complete lighting or power system. While this kind of competition was intended to take advantage of certain key patents, it should be noted that the economical and reliable operation of a number of interconnected items of equipment was also involved. The seller could contend, with considerable justification, that he was merely protecting the reputation of his products in requiring that only items of his manufacture be combined into one system.

Considerable emphasis has been given in this study to product competition. Three cases — railway motors, induction motors, and polyphase generators — were examined in detail. The product competition was seen to exist even in the presence of duopoly. Moreover, a strenuous price competition was fostered. It is possible that these results also hold in other industries where the product is a durable good which is highly complicated and heterogeneous. Two important qualifications to this conclusion are necessary, however, because of the evidence upon which it is based. The data on competition in all three types of equipment cover the 1893–1896 period, which was one of depressed conditions in the electrical manufacturing industry. Even with a homogeneous product, a strenuous and perhaps cutthroat price competition might have occurred because of the desperate efforts to maintain sales. The second qualification is that the products of the industry were technologically immature. The product competition which took place may have been as vigorous and unrestrained as it was because the art of manufacturing electrical equipment was so young. It is legitimate to ask whether such competition continued after designs had become standardized. If technological change proceeded at a slower pace in later years, the traditional duopoly case, with a fairly homogeneous product and a recognition of mutual dependence, may have resulted. Product competition based on a static technology, in which product choices are made from a perfectly well-known and unchanging set of alternatives, may have an effect on duopolistic behavior different from that based on a rapidly advancing technology.

It is probable that continuous and unpredictable change in the technology of a product and its manufacture introduces the element of uncertainty which accounts for the competitive rather than the monopolistic behavior of the oligopolists. In his treatment of oligopoly with product differentiation, Professor E. H. Chamberlin recognizes that where the product is not homogenous, additional uncertainty concerning the effects of a rival's actions is introduced because of "a new unknown — the extent of buyers' preferences for his own product over others, expressed by the shape of the demand curves for the individual products." [1]

To this uncertainty which exists where the products are differentiated but fixed may be added the uncertainty due to the fact that one firm does not know which of various possible "products" will be chosen by its rival. If the products are selected from rapidly changing alternatives rather than from a fixed set of well-known ones, still more uncertainty is introduced. And when the product is a durable, highly complex capital good, there are also all the uncertainties relating to the economical and reliable performance of the equipment.

What is the significance of uncertainty for a theory of oligopolistic behavior? The classical theory of oligopoly, which considered only a homogeneous product, could present no definite results because the only uncertainties considered pertained to the expectations of one firm concerning the price and output policy of its rivals. It was certain, not uncertain, that the buyers would choose the product of one firm over another solely on the basis of price. In these conditions, variations in behavior could not be explained by objective elements but only by differences in entrepreneurial psychology. If it can be shown, however, that uncertainties exist because of market or production factors, then oligopolistic behavior patterns become determinate in terms of forces that economists are accustomed to handle.

Professor Chamberlin made the first step in the direction of such a theory of oligopoly when he considered a differentiated product. If to this is added product variation, a rapidly changing technology, and a durable, complex product, then the uncertainty of the effects of the actions of any firm on its rivals may be so great that all indirect effects may be neglected. If this is true, competition can exist in oligopoly and even in duopoly. And no theory of entrepreneurial psychology, blackmail, or warfare is necessary to explain why the relations among a small group of firms are completely competitive.

In his book on the aluminum industry, Professor D. H. Wallace suggested that a distinction should be made between oligopolistic situations on the basis of whether demand is changing slowly and predictably or rapidly and unpredictably. Another factor he considered relevant was the possibility of developing new variations in the basic product. In aluminum this meant finding new alloys and new uses of the ingot metal. Professor Wallace summarized his views as follows: "In a market characterized by great uncertainty surrounding a rapidly moving demand curve, where there is a large field for profitable development of new variations of the basic product, it seems unlikely that oligopolists would follow policies appropriate to more or less permanent division of the market in fixed proportions."[2]

In Professor Wallace's case, the uncertainty results from the moving demand curve and the changing technology of the product. Another economist who has dealt with the effect of uncertainties on oligopolistic behavior is Professor William Fellner. His view is that the quasi-agreements which are typical of oligopoly do not usually cover technological change, product variation, and advertising. The reason is that

> these variables are apt to be more nearly associated with inventiveness than are the variables regulated by quasi-agreement. The lowering of costs of production, product variation, and gains from advertising are more nearly related to inventiveness than pricing. Inventiveness is the faculty of improving the conditions under which one is operating, by adopting methods which are unpredictable. . . In all these cases, the essence of the matter is that it is impossible to discount the future changes in relative strength which will be brought about by these manifestations of inventiveness. . . Therefore, in many cases competition remains less restricted, or possibly even unhampered with respect to these variables, especially if the oligopolistic group is not quite small.[3]

Professor Fellner thus imagines agreements which cover price but not product variation, technological change, and advertising. The theory of oligopolistic behavior which has been put forth in this study differs from Professor Fellner's view in two respects. The evidence in the motor competition does not suggest an agreement on price with the other variables handled competitively. As far as can be determined, the vigorous product competition led to equally unrestrained price competition. It is hard to see how it could be otherwise, particularly where the product is a durable producer's good. To agree on price without agreement on all features of the product would surely be unlikely when product changes have measurable results in terms of the production cost. The complex nature of a durable producer's good, the possibilities of improving that good, and genuine disagreement among engineers regarding the features that the good should possess made any product agreement impossible. The result was a product-price competition with all variables handled competitively. A second modification of the Fellner theory is that the qualifying phrase, "especially if the oligopolistic group is not quite small," may be unnecessary. The electrical manufacturing industry shows that three firms or even two may compete vigorously.

One additional aspect of competition in the electrical industry should be mentioned. It will be recalled that in the Niagara Falls power development, purchases of electrical equipment were nearly equally divided between General Electric and Westinghouse and that it is highly probable that the Niagara Power Company consciously avoided buying from only one manufacturer because of an interest in maintaining alternative sources of supply. This purchasing policy, supposedly designed to maintain competitive conditions in the industry, was also used by other equipment buyers. After the formation of General Electric in 1892, the Westinghouse annual report stated: "It seems to be the views of your principal customers that all users of electric light and power apparatus must soon recognize that an independent concern, like your company, is essential to their prosperity; and that such a concern, conducted on good business principles should be supported, as failure to do so might lead to such a monopoly in the electric light and power business that consumers would be forced to purchase apparatus upon any terms that might be dictated."[4] A few months later, a Westinghouse advertisement called General Electric the "Electric Trust" and concluded with the remark: "We invite the cooperation and support of all users of Electrical Apparatus who desire to have the benefits of competition."[5]

Westinghouse thus tried to secure business not only on the grounds that its products were good and its prices low, but also because it was the only full-line producer other than General Electric. Potential customers were supposed to recognize that if Westinghouse were to go out of business, they would be able to buy electrical equipment from only one company, which would presumably act as a monopolist.

Whether many buyers based their purchase decisions on a principle as general as maintaining competition is not known. The existence of a competitive ideology among these buyers is probable because they were businessmen and aware of the importance of alternative sources of supply. It should also be noted that the contention of Westinghouse that it would provide effective competition for General Electric would be seriously discounted by an economist who applied the usual oligopolistic reasoning. He would doubt that anything but tacit or explicit agreements between the two manufacturers would result. In contrast to this view, the facts prove that Westinghouse did provide an effective competition. If some of the equipment buyers acted on the assumption that duopoly could mean genuine competition, they cannot, with justice, be accused of unrealism.

ENTREPRENEURSHIP

The entrepreneurial activities in three branches of electrical manufacturing have been examined. These activities seem to fit the following schema. First, the engineer-entrepreneur must visualize a place in the economy that the product he expects to develop — electric-lighting equipment or electric-power equipment — can occupy. With this vision before him, he must decide what technical features the product should have to insure its commercial success. He then must invent a product which possesses these technical features.

The three-stage schema applies most generally to the very beginning of an industry. Once the product is manufactured and sold at a price greater than cost, and if it gives reliable and economical performance, then the task of pioneer innovation is largely completed. The engineer-entrepreneur no longer is the key person in the firm, and as the industry grows and the producers are successful, the important problems shift to the areas of marketing, finance, and business administration.

The pioneer innovation by an engineer-entrepreneur which creates a new industry can be thought of as requiring an extension of entrepreneurship forward to product markets and backward to factor markets.[6] More is involved than the organization of *existing* factors to produce for an *existing* market. On the input side, labor has to be trained, machinery has to be designed, and raw materials have to be located. Brush had to find a new source of carbonaceous material before he was able to make satisfactory arc carbons. Thomson had difficulty in securing copper wire of sufficient purity, and he had to make his own meters for testing because no meters which met his requirements were on the market. Edison sent exploring parties all over the world looking for the bamboo best suited for lamp filaments. The search ended in Japan, which served as Edison's source of filament material for a number of years. All the engineer-entrepreneurs were handicapped by the lack of a labor force which could make, install, and operate electrical equipment. Edison at one time organized a school in New York to train electricians, and Brush traveled hundreds of miles to correct troubles in arc-lighting installations because no one else could determine what was wrong.

On the output side, markets for electrical equipment had to be created. The common procedure was to promote lighting firms and to help them get started in business. The manufacturer provided advice and general supervision and took much of the risk by accepting securities in payment for equipment and by giving cost and durability guarantees. When the electrical manufacturing industry was well established, entrepreneurship could shrink back to the confines of a single firm. The factors and supplies were available; the lighting companies were in existence.

It is legitimate to ask, although not in every case possible to answer, how the various engineer-entrepreneurs happened to become interested in electricity and its commercial applications. It will be recalled that Edison and Westinghouse had done inventing and manufacturing in other fields before taking up work in electric lighting and power. Edison was an engineer-entrepreneur on a full-time basis when he turned to the electric light. He made the move consciously and chose electric lighting as the best of a number of alternatives. Westinghouse was also fully occupied in innovational activities and was led from work in railroad switching and signaling devices to electrical manufacturing. Once in the latter field, he saw the commercial possibilities of alternating current. The entrepreneurial activities of both Edison and Westinghouse in the electrical industry should thus be viewed as the result of deliberate choices by experienced engineer-entrepreneurs who were looking for new areas in which to use their talents profitably.

Unlike Edison and Westinghouse, the other important engineer-entrepreneurs — Brush, Thomson, Sprague, and Stanley — confined themselves to the electrical industry, in which they had their first experience in innovational activities. Their decisions to enter the industry grew out of noncommercial backgrounds, and consequently a brief discussion of these backgrounds is necessary to an understanding of their choice of electrical manufacturing as a career.

Brush was interested in scientific literature while still a boy and constructed crude apparatus such as telescopes and microscopes to study natural phenomena. His interests included electricity and especially the arc light. He constructed his first arc light while still in his teens and thereafter set for himself the goal of making the arc light of commercial value.[7]

The story of Thomson is similar to that of Brush. From the age of ten, Thomson was intensely interested in scientific and mechanical subjects. Among other things, he made a camera, a static machine, and a telegraph. He cast type metal, carried on chemical experiments, and read voluminously in scientific books and periodicals. All this activity preceded his graduation from high school. After graduation, he joined the staff of the school and taught chemistry while he carried on electrical experiments. He then lectured at the Franklin Institute and was given the opportunity to test arc-lighting dynamos. This contact with arc lighting combined with what he saw in Paris led him to begin the manufacture of arc-lighting equipment on a commercial basis.

Sprague was introduced to electricity at the Naval Academy and at the 1876 Centennial Exhibition in Philadelphia. During his two years at sea, he found time to invent nearly sixty devices including a telephone, a telegraph, a motor, and a method for transmitting pictures by wire. On returning to the United States, he sought opportunities for electrical work here and abroad and finally resigned from the Navy to enter Edison's employ. His study and experiences led him to believe that the field of the future was electric motive power, and he organized a firm in 1884 to carry out the application of electric power to industry and transport.[8]

Unlike Brush, Thomson, and Sprague, Stanley's early life is quite obscure. After a short time at Yale, he left to enter electrical work. Although he was interested in several problems, he thought the crucial need was for a cheaper system of distribution, and he believed that alternating current could meet that need. As early as 1883, he made an entry in a laboratory notebook which showed that he was working on an a.c. distribution system.[9] By the spring of 1885, he was beginning to understand that parallel connection of transformers was the key to an a.c. system which would operate satisfactorily. He described his thought processes during this period in an article he wrote many years later.

> I realized that if we could make a transformer that would regulate the energy transformed by slight variations of its induced counter electromotive force in the same manner that a shunt-wound motor regulated for energy transferred by variation of its rotational counter electromotive force, the problem would be beautifully solved. I saw this analogy faintly at first, but soon with strong and clear conviction. I was very much excited by it. It seemed too simple and too easy to be true. I was almost afraid to believe or speak of it, for I had experienced a good many disappointments and was in a nervous and overworked condition; but as my convictions grew and strengthened I gained courage. Then I clearly saw that the solution was found. I told Mrs. Stanley, and, although she did not understand a word about it, she saw it too.[10]

After working for Westinghouse on a.c. problems for about five years, Stanley formed his own company to make a.c. equipment.

It can be seen that Brush, Thomson, Sprague, and Stanley followed similar paths in entering the electrical industry. They had unusual scientific and inventive interests early in life. After literally years of experimenting with various kinds of electrical apparatus, each engineer-entrepreneur selected one type of electrical equipment which he thought could achieve commercial use. He then carried on development work and organized a firm to make and sell that equipment.

One further aspect of entrepreneurship in the electrical industry should be briefly noted. As a general rule, the radically new developments came not from old, established firms, but from new firms and independent engineer-entrepreneurs. Arc lighting was brought to the commercial stage by Charles Brush. Edison made practical the incandescent light. Westinghouse introduced alternating current for light and power. Sprague pioneered in electric traction, and Stanley in high-voltage alternating current. In some of these cases, existing firms that could have carried out the innovational work were unable to see any commercial value in the innovations. Edison could see no economic worth in alternating current. Edison, Brush, and Westinghouse were not innovators in electric traction. General Electric and Westinghouse were hesitant in pushing toward higher transmission voltages. The idea of abandoning the locomotive principle did not occur to any of the electrical manufacturing firms of 1897.

There were, however, important exceptions to the rule that pioneer innovations require independent engineer-entrepreneurs and new firms. Thomson-Houston innovated in electric traction, although an outsider, Van Depoele, gave considerable assistance. Paine, a member of the General Electric sales force, accomplished a major innovation in the use of a.c. power. And a group of financiers were mainly responsible for the Niagara power development. They envisioned a power project which was far beyond anything then in existence, and they translated that vision into reality by directing and coördinating the activities of engineering experts and manufacturing firms.

In spite of these exceptions, the tendency of pioneer innovations to be the work of newcomers to the industry is general enough to receive special attention. Two studies similar to this one reveal the same tendency. In his work on the radio industry, Professor W. R. Maclaurin found that new firms were of critical importance. None of the established companies manufacturing electrical or communications equipment or operating telegraph or telephone systems thought radio was of any commercial value.[11] Similarly, A. A. Bright, Jr., includes material in his book on the electric-lamp industry which indicates that several of the new non-incandescent sources of light were not developed by General Electric or any of the other incandescent-lamp producers. Neon lighting was introduced into the United States by a newly organized subsidiary of a French firm, because General Electric refused to develop neon lighting on the grounds that incandescent lamps were superior.[12] In 1936, a Dutch firm offered General Electric and Westinghouse a license to make and sell a new type of photoflash lamp. Both companies rejected this offer. A small American firm, the Wabash Appliance Corporation, took the opportunity instead and by 1940 was supplying three-fourths of the domestic market in flash bulbs.[13]

It seems reasonable to conclude that for the commercialization of technical advances, society must depend on independent engineer-entrepreneurs and new firms. The reasons for this are several. New technical developments require new understanding. Engineer-entrepreneurs who have spent years in a particular field may find it difficult, if not impossible, to shift to another field. The time which would be needed is one limitation; the fresh point of view required is another. The personal qualities of engineer-entrepreneurs also are relevant. Such men tend to have faith in their own ideas to the exclusion of all others. This faith is necessary for success, but it precludes success in all but a few lines of endeavor for any one man.

New firms are needed because existing companies, especially if they are successful, tend to become bureaucratic. Mistakes are penalized; initiative is unrewarded. Success in a particular product creates a vested interest in that product, and there is considerable hesitancy about entering new fields. Another factor is the reputation of the company. It fears to try radically new developments when it has a record of excellent product quality at stake. Influenced by all these things, the company management may honestly feel that particular inventions have no chance of commercial success and that any resources devoted to them would be wasted.

Entrepreneurship in a new industry involves decisions which are extremely speculative and require strong faith in the future of the industry. A new firm which is small and unhampered by traditions and records of the past and an engineer-entrepreneur who has devoted himself to making commercial some new product, no matter what resistance he meets, are the functionaries through which scientific advances become of value to society. Many times the proposals of these engineer-entrepreneurs may be completely unsound and of no economic merit. It is not possible to tell beforehand, however, which of the proposals will achieve commercial success and which will not. All should be given an opportunity to appear on the market. The decision on the merits of the proposals then can be made by consumers acting through the market mechanism.

TECHNICAL CHANGE

Technical change in the electrical manufacturing industry can be described in terms of several broad trends. One was the increasing complexity of the product. The first electric system — arc lighting — was from a technical standpoint quite simple. A series circuit has a minimum of complications. Constant current meant that no fuses were required. Use in street lighting made meters, other accessories, and individual control of the lamps unnecessary. The next electric system — incandescent lighting — was much less simple. The parallel network was very complicated, especially after the three-wire and feeder-main techniques came into use. Fuses were required. In the central stations, ammeters and voltmeters were needed to check operations; in the homes and offices, a meter measured electric energy consumed. Switches, junction boxes, and numerous other devices were part of the system. The third electric system to come into use was alternating current, which was applied to both lighting and power. Complex relations, unknown to d.c. systems, had to be considered. Phase and frequency problems arose. Switching and intersystem connections became a special study. Devices were invented to change alternating to direct current, to convert from one frequency to another, and to alter the number of phases.

The transition from simple to complex systems and equipment can be interpreted as proceeding hand in hand with the training of people to design, manufacture, sell, install, and operate the apparatus. In the beginning, only a simple system could have achieved commercial success. As knowledge of electricity and electrical equipment increased, and as this knowledge became widespread, the more complicated systems could give economical and reliable performance. These more complicated systems fitted electricity into an ever-growing number of uses. The replacement of gas street lighting was relatively simple. Substituting electric lighting for interior gas illumination was less so. Most complicated of all was the general displacement of mechanical methods of power transmission.

Increasing complexity as a facet of technical change can thus be thought of as resulting from the necessity to conform to the degree of electrical knowledge. Other facets of technical change can be viewed as due to market forces. One of these forces was the pressure to reduce cost so that electrical equipment could come into more widespread use. The increase in size of individual items of equipment (generators, motors, transformers), the double-carbon arc lamp, the copper-plated carbons, the high-resistance lamp, the three-wire system, the feeder-main system, the efficient generators, the introduction of alternating current, the use of higher transmission voltages, the turbogenerator units — all these resulted from the efforts to decrease costs. The electrical manufacturers realized that only if costs were lowered could their products triumph over gas, oil, candles, horses, cables, belts, ropes, countershafts, and isolated steam-power plants.

Another market force affecting technical change was the desire to expand the market for electrical apparatus by making it suitable for more uses. Arc lights were reduced in intensity and enclosed to permit use in interior illumination. Incandescent lights were manufactured in large sizes for large-space lighting and in small sizes for surgical instruments and flashlights. The development of alternating current permitted the extension of lighting networks so that incandescent lights could be substituted for oil and candles as well as for gas. In transportation, larger motors and the multiple-unit system of control made electric power more economical than steam in elevated and interurban railways and led to the development of subways. In industry, motors of varied characteristics spurred the application of electric motors to more and more uses.

One further aspect of technical change in electric equipment should be mentioned. Concomitant with the trend toward diversity was a trend toward standardization. Because electrical equipment typically operates as part of a system, certain features of all apparatus on one system must be the same. The apparatus is supplied with energy from a central source and must be constructed with certain characteristics before it can make use of this energy. Arc lamps had to be designed for a certain amount of current, incandescent lamps and d.c. motors for a certain voltage. All the components of an electric-railway system had to be suitable for operation on one voltage. With the advent of alternating current, factors in addition to current and voltage had to be taken into account. The frequency and phase characteristics of the meters, transformers, a.c.-d.c. converters, and so forth, had to match the characteristics of the circuits to which they were connected. In all these system constants — current, voltage, frequency, and phase — the change was from many values to few. Early arc-lighting systems operated on a number of different current values. By 1900, nearly all used 9.6 amperes. The d.c. voltages also differed widely at first. For light and power, 110–220 volts became standard; and in electric-railway systems, 500 volts was nearly universal by 1890. In frequency, 60 cycles for lighting and 25 cycles for power were eventually accepted as standard. In phase, the three-phase system had largely displaced the two-phase and monophase systems by 1900. The fact that the design engineers were willing to treat these system characteristics as constants eventually led to production economies in equipment manufacture and encouraged the expansion of central-station circuits.

ECONOMIC GROWTH

The growth of the electric manufacturing industry was very rapid. Annual sales increased from a negligible amount in 1875 to over $100,000,000 twenty-five years later. The principal reason for this rapid growth was that the products of the industry were readily substitutable for other, less effective ways of doing things. Every new product is a substitute for something, but the substitution will take place much faster if a minimum amount of shift or alteration in the economic structure is necessary. In lighting, artificial illumination supplied from a central source was common in streets and homes. The electric light, arc and incandescent, provided a better light at a cost comparable to gas for these same uses. Street railways were widespread. The electric motor was a better kind of motive power than horses and mules because its cost was lower and it enabled cars to travel faster. Mechanical power was widely used in industry. Electricity was a more economical means of transmitting this power than cables, belts, chains, shafts, and compressed air.

The growth could thus be much faster than if streets and homes had not been lighted from a central source, if public-transportation systems had not been in existence, or if the only power used in industry had been human or animal. The rapid expansion in the use of electricity was possible because of the economic and technical changes that had preceded it and paved the way for it.

This part of the growth of the electrical industry resulted from a substitution of electricity where very little change in economic and technical procedures was required. Later, electricity replaced devices and methods where substantial alterations were required before it could be used. Alternating current permitted the formation of lighting companies and the employment of a system type of illumination where only non-system illuminants, such as kerosene lamps and candles, had previously been economic. Alternating current thus brought about the spread of incandescent lighting to small communities and the outlying areas of large cities which were so thinly settled that gas was not feasible. Similarly, the electric streetcar, because of its speed, permitted the extension of street railways to areas which could not be served by a public-transportation system when only animal power was available. Here the electric railway was substituted for non-system forms of transportation, such as private vehicles or taxicabs. In elevated railroads, electric power allowed, for the first time, the abandonment of the locomotive principle. The multiple-unit idea, combined with a clean form of power, eventually made possible an entirely new kind of urban transportation, the subway. Other applications of electric power were equally revolutionary. Electricity made mechanical power feasible in the home, a place where the only power had been human. The development of the electric sewing machine, the electric washing machine, and later all the other electric home appliances brought about significant changes in the daily life of the average housewife. Electric power also made available water powers which had been previously inaccessible and completely altered techniques of production. In all these uses, the substitution of electricity for other techniques involved major economic changes. These were the creative effects of the introduction of electricity into the American economy.

Another aspect of economic growth in the electrical industry was the trend within firms to expand from single products or closely related groups of products to the entire line of electrical apparatus. Brush started in arc lighting and spread into incandescent lighting, batteries, electric power, and electric-railway equipment. Thomson-Houston also began in arc lighting and later expanded into d.c. incandescent lighting, d.c. power, electric railways, a.c. incandescent lighting, and a.c. power. Edison was initially only in d.c. incandescent lighting but eventually went into d.c. power apparatus, electric-railway equipment, and arc-lighting systems. Westinghouse first manufactured d.c. incandescent-lighting equipment and then expanded to include a.c. incandescent lighting, d.c. power, electric railways, arc lighting, and a.c. electric power. Thus the economic growth of electrical manufacturing firms has meant not only an increase in sales, assets, employees, physical capacity, and profits, but also in the number of products manufactured. By 1900, there were two full-line producers. These companies manufactured nearly every kind of electrical apparatus other than communications equipment.

The existence of only two full-line producers after more than two decades of growth was largely the result of patents. The mergers and consolidations were prompted by the desire to avoid patent conflicts and the hope of obtaining a strong position in the industry through control of important patents. Patents also made possible the independence of Westinghouse. The 1896 patent agreement between Westinghouse and General Electric strengthened these two firms at the expense of the rest of the industry and hastened the trend toward duopoly.

SUGGESTIONS FOR PUBLIC POLICY

Two suggestions concerning industrial markets grow out of this study. The first is that free access to resources and free markets should be maintained. Innovations should be allowed to compete for consumer support, and the success of an innovation should be determined in the market place. Individuals who have faith in their ideas and who are willing to spend their time and invest their own and other people's money in developing new products should be allowed to do so, no matter how unsound their ideas may appear to be. The history of the electrical industry proves that many attempts to develop new products will seem preposterous, absurd, and a waste of resources. But the only way to find out whether this is true is to let the development of the new product proceed to the commercial stage and then submit the product to a market test. In the end, it was the consumers who proved Edison right and his critics wrong when he said he could develop a practical incandescent lamp. Similarly, the consumers proved that Westinghouse was right in advocating alternating current and that his critics (who included Edison) were wrong.

The fact that radical innovations usually seem valueless to established companies means that, in most cases, engineer-entrepreneurs have to found new firms to market the new product which they have developed. New firms thus play a critical role in economic progress and should be encouraged. They can present their products to the consumers, who then will judge whether further production is justified.

The second suggestion concerns policy on monopolies. One problem that has puzzled economists is this. If there is a monopoly in a certain industry, would the public interest be served by breaking up this company into two or three firms? Answers based on traditional oligopoly theory are in the negative, because tacit agreements resulting from recognition of mutual dependence lead to a pattern of action very similar to the original monopolist's price and output policies. It is here suggested that forming a small number of firms out of a single firm may result in genuine and effective competition under certain conditions. These conditions relate to the nature of the product and the amount of technical change taking place. If the product is durable, complex, and a capital good, and if technical change in the product and the techniques of making it are reasonably rapid, then the prospect of securing effective competition by establishing only a few firms is good. It would be important that the engineering talent of the original firm be divided about equally among the companies which are created and that each of these organizations be headed by an ambitious and aggressive leader. Free access to basic patents would have to be given to the various firms in order that they could start on an equal footing. On the basis of this study alone, it is not possible to say that any such scheme could succeed or exactly how it should be carried out. But this study does indicate that further analysis of oligopolistic behavior in areas where that behavior has been competitive would be fruitful. If the factors which produce genuine competition under oligopoly could be segregated and identified in a number of industries, general principles could be derived. In particular instances of monopoly, these principles would be of considerable assistance in determining whether competition could be obtained by establishing several firms in place of one.

Notes
Bibliography
Index

Notes

The following abbreviations have been used in the notes:

EW	*Electrical World*
GE Files	Historical files of the General Electric Company, Schenectady, New York
WE Files	Historical files of the Westinghouse Electric Corporation, East Pittsburgh, Pennsylvania

INTRODUCTION

1. E. C. Kirkland, *A History of American Economic Life* (1951), p. 702.

2. For a statement of the opposite view, see W. C. Kessler, "Business Organization and Management," chap. xxxi in *The Growth of the American Economy*, ed. H. F. Williamson (1946), pp. 732–734.

3. J. A. Schumpeter, *Business Cycles* (1939), pp. 130, 135, 145.

PART I. ARC LIGHTING

CHAPTER II. THE RISE OF LEADING FIRMS

1. C. F. Brush, "Some Reminiscences of Early Electric Lighting," *Journal of the Franklin Institute*, CCVI (July 1928), 5.

2. Made in Ansonia, Connecticut. Wallace and Sons began to construct dynamos in 1874. The first ones were for electroplating, not arc lighting.

3. *Journal of the Franklin Institute*, CIII (March 1877), 151.

4. *Ibid.*, CIV (September 1877), 11–12.

5. *Ibid.*, CV (May 1878), 290.

6. E. J. Houston and Elihu Thomson, "The Investigations of the Sub-Committee on Electrical Measurements," *Journal of the Franklin Institute*, CV (June 1878), 377.

7. A. A. Adams, "The First Electric Light Plant in Boston," *EW*, XXXIV (December 22, 1900), 954.

8. Copper cost means the cost of the copper conductors which carried the current from the dynamo to the arc light.

9. B. F. Miles, "Arc Light Carbons," *EW*, XXV (January 5, 1895), 8.

10. *Ibid.*

11. Brush, "Some Reminiscences of Early Electric Lighting," p. 11.

12. *EW*, VII (April 10, 1886), 167.

13. Copy of agreement between the Brush Electric Company and its local lighting companies (GE Files).

14. Report of the Superintendent of Lamps and Gas of New York City for 1881 (GE Files).

15. Brush Electric Company, sales pamphlet, 1881 (GE Files).

16. T. C. Martin, "The Electric Industry in America in 1887," *EW*, IX (January 29, 1887), 50.

17. American Electrical Directory (1885), p. 245.

18. Although the 1880 census reports do not identify either the Brush or the Weston firm by name, the available evidence lends strong support to the assumption that the data contained in these reports refers to these two companies.

In the 1880 census of manufactures, data on industries making electrical products were classified under three headings: electric lights, electrical apparatus and supplies, and telegraph and telephone apparatus. There was no industry classification labeled central electric stations or electric light and power stations. In the 1890 census, the two classifications, electrical apparatus and supplies and telegraph and telephone apparatus, were merged under the single heading, electrical apparatus and supplies. The classification, electric lights, was not used after the 1880 census. Beginning in 1902, special censuses have been taken of the electric light and power industry (the central stations) at five-year intervals.

It has been commonly assumed that the electric-lights industry in the 1880 census was the central-electric-station industry. Widespread acceptance of this assumption is primarily due to the fact that later census reports, in repeating the 1880 data for comparison with current data, have combined the 1880 classifications, electrical apparatus and supplies and telegraph and telephone apparatus, to secure data comparable to the electrical apparatus and supplies industry (see *Manufacturing Industry in the United States: Eleventh Census*, vol. VI, pt. i [1895], p. 76; *Manufactures: Twelfth Census*, VII [1902], 7). The electric-lights data of 1880 have been labeled electric light and power data in later censuses. The census bureau itself is therefore the authority for the view that the electric-lights industry of 1880 was not engaged in the manufacture of electrical products.

This interpretation of the electric-lights industry of 1880 was accepted by early writers on the electrical industry. In 1898, the *Electrical World* quoted statistics from the 1880 census and assumed that electric lights meant central electric stations (see *EW*, XXXI [March 26, 1898], 381, and XXXI [April 9, 1898], 445). T. C. Martin excluded the 1880 electric-lights data from the electrical apparatus and supplies industry, which he treated in a special report at the 1900 census; he interpreted the 1880 data in the same way two decades later (see *Manufactures: Twelfth Census*, X [1902], 157, and Martin, *Forty Years of Edison Service*, pp. 73–74). In accordance with the interpretation of the census bureau and early writers on the electrical manufacturing industry, A. A. Bright, Jr., has included the 1880 electric-lights data under the heading, "operation of electric and power systems" (*The Electric-Lamp Industry*, pp. 13 and 33).

The 1928 report of the Federal Trade Commission on the electric-power industry is the only study known to me which refers to the 1880 electric-lights industry as an industry *manufacturing* electric lights (Federal Trade Commission, *Supply of Electrical Equipment and Competitive Conditions* [1928], p. 37). Two defects blur this interpretation, however. On the same page, census data on the electrical manufacturing industry which do not include the 1880 electric-lights data are quoted with no indication of a contradiction between these figures and the previous statement. Furthermore, as will be shown presently, it is probable that not all of the establishments in the electric-lights industry were engaged in manufacturing electric lights.

The apparent confusion in 1880 and subsequently over the meaning of electric lights was grounded in the early failure to distinguish sharply between the manufacture of electric-lighting equipment and the use of that equipment in a central station to supply light to municipalities and business firms. Numerous instances of this confusion could be cited. The *American Electrical Directory* of 1886, for example, purported to list the electrical manufacturing companies in the United States. Of forty-two firms mentioned, at least three were central stations. There was also a tendency to classify sales agents and central-station construction firms as electrical manufacturers. Similarly, a list of the electrical companies in New York in 1885, as given by the property-tax records, made no distinction between three central stations and eight manufacturers of electrical equipment (*EW*, V [January 3, 1885], 1. See also, for example, *EW*, IV [December 20, 1884], 260, and VII [February 20, 1886], 77). This distinction was also usually lacking in statistics on newly formed electrical corporations.

Data on the electric-lights industry, as reported in the 1880 census, are given in Table A. My conclusion is that the first two establishments are electrical manufacturing plants and the third is an arc-lighting central station. It is hardly conceivable that a central station in 1879 would have employed as many as 150 or even 75 workers. As indicated in Table B, one decade later the average number of workers per central station was less than 15. The same table shows that 75 or 150 workers for an electrical manufacturing plant was apparently possible in 1879.

TABLE A

The Electric-Lights Industry (as reported in the 1880 census)

Number of establishments	*Location*	*Capital*	*Workers*	*Value of materials purchased*	*Value of product*
1	Ohio: Cuyahoga County	$200,000	150	$100,000	$300,000
1	New Jersey: Essex County	200,000	75	50,000	150,000
1	California (county not given)	25,000	4	650	8,400
TOTALS 3		$425,000	229	$150,650	$458,400

Source: *Manufactures of the United States: Tenth Census*, vol. II (1883).

How does the hypothesis that the first two establishments in Table A are electrical manufacturing plants and the third a central station accord with other known facts? In 1880, there were at least two firms making arc-lighting equipment, Brush in Cleveland and Weston in Newark. In June 1879, what is thought to be the first electric central station in the world was established in San Francisco. These facts do not contradict the hypothesis. Table A shows that the first two establishments were in Cuyahoga County, Ohio (where Cleveland is located) and Essex County, New Jersey (where Newark is located). Unfortunately, the county location of the third is not given, but the state (California) means San Francisco is a possibility. The listing of industries by cities in the 1880 census report recognizes that there was an electric-lights establishment in Cleveland, Newark, and San Francisco in 1879 (*Manufactures of the United States: Tenth Census*, II [1883], 396, 414, 436).

The data on workers per establishment of Table B give stronger support to the view that the Ohio and New Jersey electric-lights establishments were electrical manufacturing plants than to the view that the California establishment was an electric central station. Establishments in electrical aparatus and supplies and in telegraph and telephone apparatus were often as small as four workers and sometimes smaller. The California establishment could have been an electrical manufacturing plant.

TABLE B

Comparison of 1880 Data on the Electric-Lights Industry with Other Census Data

Year	*Industry*	*Number of establishments*	*Number of workers*	*Average number of workers per establishment*
	ELECTRICAL MANUFACTURING			
1880	Electric Lights			
	Cuyahoga County, Ohio (Brush?)	1	150	150
	Essex County, New Jersey (Weston?)	1	75	75
	Electrical apparatus and supplies			
	Three large establishments [a]	3	152	51
	Entire industry	36	378	10
	Telegraph and telephone apparatus			
	Three large establishments [a]	3	313	104
	Entire industry	40	893	22
1890	Electrical apparatus and supplies	189	9,485	50
1900	Electrical apparatus and supplies	580	45,877	79
	ELECTRIC CENTRAL STATIONS			
1880	Electric lights			
	California (San Francisco arc lighting?)	1	4	4
1890	Electric light and power [b]	144	2,004	14
1902	Electric light and power	3,620	30,326	8

Source: Census reports.
[a] These data are chosen from the state-by-state breakdown of all establishments in the industry.
[b] These data are for only New York State, Washington, D.C., and St. Louis, Missouri.

If the hypothesis that the electric-lights establishments in Ohio and New Jersey were Brush and Weston, respectively, is correct, then neither of these plants should be included under electrical apparatus and supplies or telegraph and telephone apparatus. An examination of the 1880 data on the electrical apparatus and supplies industry reveals that no New Jersey establishment is listed and that none of the six Ohio establishments is in Cuyahoga County. Similarly, the telegraph and telephone data show no New Jersey establishment, and none of the three Ohio establishments is in Cuyahoga County. As a further check, the cities data indicate that there was no establishment of either industry in Newark or Cleveland.

In summary, it is known from other than census data that Brush in Cleveland and Weston in Newark were making arc-lighting apparatus in 1879. These two establishments were not included in either the electrical apparatus and supplies industry or the telegraph and telephone industry. Nothing in the data on the electric-lights industry contradicts the hypothesis that two of the three establishments were Brush and Weston.

19. S. M. Hamill, "Beginning and Future of the Arc Lamp," *Engineering Magazine*, VII (August 1894), 700.

20. *EW*, VI (August 1, 1885), 43.
21. *EW*, I (May 26, 1883), 336.
22. See pp. 15–16, above.
23. D. O. Woodbury, *Beloved Scientist* (1944), p. 92.
24. *Ibid.*, p. 101.
25. William Parker *et al.*, "First Report of the Committee of Investigation," April 13, 1880 (GE Files).
26. William Parker *et al.*, "Second Report of the Committee of Investigation," April 27, 1880 (GE Files).
27. Letter from J. A. McManus, secretary to Elihu Thomson, to J. W. Hammond, February 21, 1929 (GE Files).
28. Quoted in a letter from Elihu Thomson to J. W. Hammond, July 25, 1923 (GE Files).
29. The air blast was not to *blow out* arcs which occurred in commutation. "It was, in fact, one way of insulating such a commutator for high voltage and nothing else" — letter from Elihu Thomson to J. W. Hammond, February 9, 1927 (GE Files).
30. Woodbury, *Beloved Scientist*, p. 124.
31. For a discussion of Weston and the United States Electric Lighting Company, see pp. 31–34, above.
32. Incorporation statute of the Thomson-Houston Electric Company (GE Files).
33. Memorandum from J. R. McKee to J. W. Hammond, April 20, 1927 (GE Files).
34. The Brush Electric Company had the Brush system on exhibition at the exposition but refused to enter the competition. See Woodbury, *Beloved Scientist*, pp. 149–150.
35. *EW*, VI (September 26, 1885), 135.
36. W. H. Preece, "Electric Lighting in America," *EW*, IV (December 27, 1884), 265.
37. Thomson-Houston Electric Company, Circular Letter to Agents No. 40, June 3, 1891 (GE Files).
38. Thomson-Houston Electric Company, *Annual Report* (February 2, 1891), p. 4.
39. Contract between the Thomson-Houston Electric Company and the Jamestown Electric Light and Power Company, August 9, 1887 (GE Files).
40. Thomson-Houston Electric Company, Circular Letter to Agents No. 37, April 20, 1891 (GE Files).
41. The shares in the last trust (October 1889) were not sold but were issued to the Thomson-Houston stockholders as a dividend. This trust paid $14.73 per share when dissolved in 1905.
42. *EW*, IV (August 9, 1884), 41.
43. D. O. Woodbury, *A Measure for Greatness* (1949), pp. 98–101.
44. The grounds for assuming that these data refer to Weston are discussed in note 18, above.
45. *Engineering* (London), XXXII (July 8, 1881), 42.
46. C. R. Flint, *Memories of an Active Life* (1923), pp. 289–292.
47. Woodbury, *A Measure for Greatness*, pp. 91–92.
48. Flint, *Memories of an Active Life*, p. 291.
49. Preece, "Electric Lighting in America," p. 265.
50. Woodbury, *Beloved Scientist*, pp. 134–135.
51. *EW*, III (June 21, 1884), 201.

52. *EW*, VII (January 2, 1886), 10.
53. *EW*, VII (January 9, 1886), 19.
54. *EW*, IV (August 30, 1884), 66.
55. *EW*, IV (July 5, 1884), v.
56. *EW*, V (May 16, 1885), 198.
57. *Boston Globe*, February 19, 1885.
58. The Fuller-Wood Company was formed in 1879. It was an outgrowth of the Fuller Electrical Company, organized in 1877 to exploit the arc-lighting patents of J. B. Fuller, a New York inventor. In 1879, the arc-lighting patents of James Wood were purchased, and the name of the company was changed. The Wood equipment was excellent, but Fuller-Wood had only mediocre success.
59. *EW*, VII (January 23, 1886), 39.
60. *EW*, IX (January 29, 1887), 59.
61. *EW*, IX (April 16, 1887), 196.
62. *EW*, X (October 29, 1887), 238.
63. *Fortune*, VII (April 1933), 38.
64. *EW*, VIII (November 27, 1886), 260.
65. Thomson-Houston Electric Company, sales booklet (October 1, 1888), p. 81 (GE Files).
66. *EW*, V (February 14, 1885), 64.
67. *EW*, VI (September 5, 1885), 102.
68. Edison General Electric brought out an arc-lighting system in 1890.
69. GE Files.
70. American Electric Manufacturing Company, *The American System of Electric Arc Lighting* (1887), p. 19 (GE Files).
71. *EW*, IX (May 14, 1887), 233.
72. *EW*, XI (April 28, 1888), 288.
73. The Gramme Electrical Company is discussed on p. 41, above; the Bentley-Knight Railway Company on pp. 225–230, above.
74. *EW*, XII (September 1, 1888), 110.
75. *EW*, XII (August 18, 1888), 89.
76. *EW*, XII (September 15, 1888), 152–153.

CHAPTER III. INTERFIRM RELATIONS

1. *EW*, II (September 1, 1883), 4.
2. *EW*, IV (August 9, 1884), 44.
3. *EW*, VII (February 13, 1886), 73–74.
4. Thomson-Houston datum from *EW*, III (March 29, 1884), 107; Brush datum from Preece, "Electric Lighting in America," p. 265.
5. Thomson-Houston Electric Company, sales pamphlet (1889), p. 4 (GE Files).
6. *EW*, V (May 9, 1885), 187.
7. Thomson-Houston Electric Company, Circular Letter to Agents No. 14, December 6, 1890; No. 21, January 26, 1891; and No. 63, January 1, 1892 (GE Files).
8. *EW*, IV (October 25, 1884), 155.
9. Thomson-Houston Electric Company, Circular Letter to Agents No. 11, October 3, 1890 (GE Files).
10. Light intensity at a point which is at a distance d from a light source is proportional to the intensity of that light and inversely proportional to d^2.

$$(1500/15)/100^2 = 1/100 = 1 \text{ per cent}$$

11. See p. 20, above.

12. The telephone is another example of this phenomenon. In the beginning, most people could not believe this instrument could be of any use. Once its utility had been demonstrated, however, the public refused to do without it.

13. Preece, "Electric Lighting in America," p. 265.

14. *EW*, X (October 15, 1887), 203.

15. *EW*, IV (July 5, 1884), 6; IV (August 6, 1884), 38.

16. A representative of the Edison Electric Light Company was also present. Flint hoped to include manufacturers of both incandescent- and arc-lighting equipment in his electrical combine.

17. Flint, *Memories of an Active Life*, p. 295.

18. *EW*, XIII (March 2, 1889), 139.

19. *EW*, XIII (January 19, 1889), 38.

20. *EW*, XIII (April 6, 1889), 211.

21. *EW*, XIV (July 20, 1889), 46.

22. See Chapter XV, above.

23. *EW*, XIV (October 26, 1889), 287.

24. Thomson-Houston Electric Company, "Report of the Meeting of the Standardizing Bureau," February 24–27, 1891 (GE Files).

25. *EW*, XII (December 1, 1888), 294.

26. Letter from the Trustees of the Fort Wayne Electric Company to the Common Stockholders of the Thomson-Houston Electric Company, August 13, 1889 (Baker Library, Harvard Business School).

27. Thomson-Houston Electric Company, *Annual Report* (February 2, 1891), pp. 4–5.

28. *EW*, XIV (October 26, 1889), 287.

29. For details of these transactions, see Chapters IV and XV, above.

30. For sources of data in this paragraph on arc lights in use, see Table 7, p. 65, and Table 9, p. 70. Data on market shares of the various companies are from GE Files.

CHAPTER IV. THE ARC-CARBON INDUSTRY

1. Wallace and Sons of Ansonia Connecticut produced carbons very early, but their arc-lighting system was not on the market after 1879.

2. *EW*, VI (December 12, 1885), 237.

3. *EW*, VIII (December 4, 1886), 277.

4. *EW*, VIII (December 18, 1886), 299.

5. *EW*, IX (April 23, 1887), 195.

6. *EW*, X (July 16, 1887), 25.

7. *EW*, (July 30, 1887), 51.

8. Miles, "Arc Light Carbons," p. 8.

CHAPTER V. THE DYNAMICS OF THE INDUSTRY

1. *Abstract of the Twelfth Census* (1904), p. 417.

2. *Manufactures: Twelfth Census*, X (1902), 170.

3. General Electric Company, Minutes of the Manufacturing Committee, November 24, 1893 (GE Files).

PART II. INCANDESCENT LIGHTING

CHAPTER VII. THE EDISON SYSTEM

1. For an early but surprisingly complete description of Edison's proposed incandescent-electric-lighting system, see the *New York Sun*, October 20, 1878. See also the *New York Herald*, December 21, 1879, and the *New York Times*, December 28, 1879.

2. Woodbury, *Beloved Scientist*, pp. 108–109.

3. A. A. Bright, Jr., *The Electric-Lamp Industry* (1949), pp. 110–111.

4. T. C. Martin, *Forty Years of Edison Service* (1922), p. 9.

5. *Ibid.*

6. Paget Higgs, *The Electric Light* (1879), p. 214.

7. R. H. Parsons, *The Early Days of the Power Station Industry* (1940), p. 8.

8. *The Telegraphic Journal and Electrical Review* (London), VII (February 15, 1879), 60. For a more complete discussion of the views of those scientists and engineers who believed that the subdivision of the electric light was impossible, see my article, "Electrical Science and the Early Development of the Electrical Manufacturing Industry in the United States," *Annals of Science* (London), VII (December 1951), 382ff.

9. Payson Jones, *A Power History of the Consolidated Edison System* (1940), pp. 28–29.

10. H. L. Satterlee, *J. Pierpont Morgan* (1939), p. 156.

11. Fabbri retired from Drexel, Morgan, and Company at the end of 1885.

12. Francis Jehl, *Menlo Park Reminiscences*, 3 vols. (1937, 1938, and 1941), I, 246.

13. Henry Villard, *Memoirs* (1904), II, 297–300.

14. Contract between T. A. Edison and the Edison Electric Light Company, November 15, 1878. The original contract is in the office of the Secretary, General Electric Company, Schenectady, New York.

15. Edison continued to receive royalties until General Electric paid him the capitalized value of future royalties in 1896.

16. Henry Villard Papers (Houghton Library, Harvard University).

17. Jehl, *Menlo Park Reminiscences*, I, 242.

18. The term "Edison company" is used throughout this book to designate the original and parent company, the Edison Electric Light Company.

19. Jehl, *Menlo Park Reminiscences*, II, 545–546.

20. *American Gas Light Journal*, XXXVII (July 3, 1882), 5.

21. For the calculation which shows that this price was equivalent to the price of gas, see p. 184, above.

22. Edison Electric Light Company, *Twelfth Bulletin* (July 27, 1882), p. 122.

23. *Review of Telephone and Telegraph*, I (August 1, 1882), 178.

24. *Edisonia* (1904), pp. 149–151.

25. The Edison Lamp Company was incorporated in 1884 with a capital stock of $250,000.

26. Contract between T. A. Edison and the Edison Electric Light Company, March 8, 1881. The original contract is in the office of the Secretary, General Electric Company, Schenectady, New York.

27. Edison Electric Light Company, *Eleventh Bulletin* (June 27, 1882), p. 107.

28. Jehl, *Menlo Park Reminiscences*, II, 768.

29. *Edisonia*, p. 161.

30. *New York Tribune*, August 14, 1882.
31. Samuel Insull, *Central Station Electric Service* (1915), p. xxxix.
32. *EW*, I (August 4, 1883), 489.
33. Edison Electric Light Company, *Annual Report* (October 24, 1882); reproduced in *Fifteenth Bulletin* (December 20, 1882), p. 235.
34. For an explanation of the three-wire system, see p. 178 and Diagram 3, p. 179, above.
35. *New York Herald*, December 21, 1879.
36. Edison Electric Light Company, *Annual Report* (October 23, 1883); reproduced in *Twentieth Bulletin* (October 31, 1883), p. 446.
37. Opinion of John W. Howell, stated in interview with John W. Hammond, July 13, 1925 (GE Files).
38. *EW*, IV (November 1, 1884), 167.
39. *EW*, VIII (December 18, 1886), 300.
40. The Sprague company is discussed in Chapter XVI. The Canadian Edison Manufacturing Company was formed to manufacture incandescent lamps in Canada, a necessary step if the Edison lamp patents were to be valid there.
41. The Edison Electric Light Company, the patent-holding company, continued to exist as a separate corporate entity although its stock was held by Edison General Electric.
42. Jehl, *Menlo Park Reminiscences*, II, 880.
43. Letter from T. A. Edison to Henry Villard, February 8, 1890 (Henry Villard Papers, Houghton Library, Harvard University).

CHAPTER VIII. MARKETING THE EDISON SYSTEM

1. Jehl, *Menlo Park Reminiscences*, II, 811–812.
2. General Electric Company, *Edison Incandescent Lamps* (September 20, 1897), p. 12 (GE Files).
3. Letter from S. D. Greene, General Manager, Lighting Department, to C. T. Hughes, Manager, Eastern Sales District, January 25, 1894 (GE Files).
4. General Electric Company, Minutes of the Meeting of Lighting Representatives, June 13, 1895, p. 22 (GE Files).
5. General Electric Lighting Department, Circular Letter No. 260, May 28, 1897 (GE Files).
6. *Electrical Engineer*, XXII (November 25, 1896), xiii.
7. General Electric Company, Minutes of the Meeting of the Sales Committee, December 12, 1893 (GE Files).
8. Letter from C. T. Hughes, Manager, Eastern Sales District, to Mr. Beran, January 21, 1893 (GE Files).
9. General Electric Company, Minutes of the Meeting of Lighting Representatives, June 13, 1895, p. 22 (GE Files).
10. Edison Electric Light Company, *Annual Report* (October 24, 1882).
11. *EW*, II (December 8, 1883), 251.
12. General Electric Company, Minutes of the Meeting of the Sales Committee, October 20, 1893 (GE Files).
13. *Electrician* (London), IX (June 1882), 107.
14. "Report on the Efficiency and Duration of Incandescent Lamps," published as a supplement to the *Journal of the Franklin Institute*, CXX (September 1885), 29–30.

15. Resolution of the General Electric Executive Committee, December 8, 1893 (GE Files).

16. Edison Electric Light Company, *Fourth Bulletin* (February 24, 1882), p. 3.

17. Edison Company for Isolated Lighting, *Bulletin for Agents No. 7* (August 19, 1885), p. 6.

18. Edison Company for Isolated Lighting, *Bulletin for Agents No. 2* (May 28, 1885), p. 3.

19. Edison Electric Light Company, *Twentieth Bulletin* (October 31, 1883), p. 431.

20. Edison Electric Light Company, *Eighteenth Bulletin* (May 31, 1883), p. 345.

21. These figures are from the following sources: *Electrical Review*, II (March 22, 1883), 6; Edison Company for Isolated Lighting, price list, March 1, 1885 (GE Files); Edison Company for Isolated Lighting, *Bulletin for Agents No. 9* (October 16, 1885), p. 4.

22. This list was published in the Isolated company's *Bulletin for Agents No. 5* (June 26, 1885), pp. 4–6. Paine continued in sales work after General Electric was formed and was mainly responsible for the important part played by General Electric in the application of electric power to textile mills. See Chapter XIX for a discussion of Paine's work in electric power.

23. The agreement between the Edison company and the Illuminating company of March 23, 1881, is reproduced in Jones, *A Power History*, pp. 273–278.

24. Edison Electric Illuminating Company of New York, *Annual Report* (December 13, 1881); reproduced in Jones, *A Power History*, pp. 328–329.

25. Edison Electric Illuminating Company of New York, *Annual Report* (December 11, 1883); reproduced in Jones, *A Power History*, pp. 321–324.

26. Jones, *A Power History*, pp. 37–40.

27. General Electric Company, "Information on Practices of Edison Licensees," January 26, 1893 (GE Files).

28. *Edisonia*, p. 185.

29. *Ibid.*, p. 186.

30. *Ibid.*, p. 187.

31. Report of the Eighth Semi-Annual Convention of the Association of Edison Illuminating Companies, Nantasket Beach, Massachusetts, August 8 and 9, 1888 (GE Files).

32. Report of the Tenth Semi-Annual Convention of the Association of Edison Illuminating Companies, Niagara Falls, New York, August 13–15, 1889 (GE Files).

33. A copy of this form is in GE Files.

34. The formation of General Electric is described in Chapter XX.

35. A copy of this agreement is in GE Files.

36. Letter from C. T. Hughes, Manager, Eastern Sales District, to Eugene Griffin, First Vice-President, November 3, 1893 (GE Files).

37. The ten questions as listed are condensed from the originals, which are given in the Minutes of the Meeting of Lighting Representatives, June 13, 1895 (GE Files).

38. General Electric Company, Circular Letter No. 80, May 20, 1900 (GE Files).

39. Letter from C. A. Coffin to District Sales Managers, April 28, 1893 (GE Files).

40. General Electric Company, Minutes of the Meeting of the Sales Committee, August 28, 1893 (GE Files).

41. Letter from Eugene Griffin to Department, District, and Local Managers, December 4, 1893 (GE Files).

42. Letter from S. D. Greene to Department and Local Office Managers, November 26, 1895 (GE Files).

43. Letter from C. T. Hughes to S. D. Greene, August 7, 1895 (GE Files).

44. Westinghouse absorbed the chief Edison competitor of the eighties, the United States Electric Lighting Company, in 1888. Stanley, a small firm specializing in certain types of alternating-current apparatus, is discussed in Chapter XIX.

45. Letter from C. T. Hughes to the General Manager of the Lighting Department, May 21, 1894 (GE Files).

CHAPTER IX. THE WESTINGHOUSE ELECTRIC COMPANY

1. Contract between William Stanley and George Westinghouse, March 5, 1884 (WE Files).

2. *EW*, IV (September 27, 1884), 115.

3. *EW*, VI (October 31, 1885), 185.

4. *Engineering* (London), XXXIX (May 1, 1885), 158–159.

5. Letter from G. Pantaleoni to C. E. Allen, March 11, 1941 (WE Files).

6. Alternator is a short term for alternating-current generator.

7. Reminiscences of G. Pantaleoni, April 1939 (WE Files).

8. Letter from G. Pantaleoni to H. W. Cope, November 5, 1935 (WE Files).

9. William Stanley, "Alternating Current Development in America," *Journal of the Franklin Institute*, CLXXIII (June 1912), 568.

10. Woodbury, *A Measure for Greatness*, p. 141.

11. *Telegraphic Journal and Electrical Review* (London), XII (June 9, 1883), 486.

12. *Ibid.*, p. 467.

13. *EW*, VI (October 24, 1885), 167.

14. *EW*, VI (November 14, 1885), 204.

15. Westinghouse Electric and Manufacturing Company, *Westinghouse: Past, Present, and Future* (1936), pp. 6–7.

16. Agreement between William Stanley and George Westinghouse, December 24, 1885 (WE Files).

17. *Electric Journal*, VIII (June 1911), 493. Converter, like secondary generator, was an early name for the transformer.

18. Stanley, "Alternating Current Development in America," p. 573.

19. Reminiscences of B. P. Rowe, January 10, 1936 (WE Files).

20. The Edison three-wire and feeder-main networks are explained on pp. 178–179.

21. Letter from P. A. Lang to H. W. Cope, November 18, 1935 (WE Files).

22. Westinghouse Electric and Manufacturing Company, *Shall We Use Meters?* (1892), p. 3.

23. Copy of license agreement, December 5, 1888 (WE Files).

24. Minutes of the Meeting of Lighting Representatives, June 13, 1895 (GE Files).

25. *EW*, XXVI (July 13, 1895), 60.

26. Contract between Westinghouse Electric and Manufacturing Company and the Missouri Electric Light and Power Company, February 20, 1892 (WE Files).

27. *EW*, IX (January 15, 1896), 33.

28. Sawyer-Man Electric Company, *Incandescent Lamps* (*c.* 1900). Sawyer-Man was a Westinghouse subsidiary.

29. Westinghouse Electric Company, *The Alternating Current System* (1888), p. 64 (WE Files).

30. Westinghouse, *Shall We Use Meters?* p. 9.

31. Reminiscences of W. R. Pinckard (WE Files).

32. *EW*, XX (December 10, 1892), 374.

33. Westinghouse Electric and Manufacturing Company, *Annual Report* (May 16, 1894), p. 4.

34. *EW*, IV (July 12, 1884), 14.

35. Bright, *The Electric-Lamp Industry*, p. 72.

36. *EW*, I (May 19, 1883), 309.

37. *EW*, X (October 8, 1887), 200.

38. Agreement between the Westinghouse Electric Company and the Thomson-Houston Electric Company, December 1887 (WE Files).

39. *EW*, X (November 19, 1887), 270.

40. *EW*, XII (October 20, 1888), 215.

41. Letter from F. P. Fish of General Electric to G. B. Gilbert of the Edison Electric Illuminating Company of Detroit, May 29, 1893 (GE Files).

42. *EW*, XII (December 15, 1888), 314–315.

43. *EW*, XII (August 25, 1888), 95.

44. H. G. Prout, *A Life of George Westinghouse* (1922), p. 96.

45. *EW*, XIII (February 2, 1889), 53.

46. *Scientific American*, XLIII (October 23, 1880), 255.

47. Jehl, *Menlo Park Reminiscences*, II, 611–613.

48. United States Electric Lighting Company, *Catalogue* (1882), p. 20.

49. *EW*, XIII (February 2, 1889), 53.

50. T. A. Edison, Reply to Thomson-Houston Memoranda of March 23, 1889, April 1, 1889 (Henry Villard Papers, Houghton Library, Harvard University).

51. Flint, *Memories of an Active Life*, p. 292.

52. Letter from George W. Hebard, President of the United States Electric Lighting Company, to the Westinghouse Electric Company, July 27, 1887 (WE Files).

CHAPTER X. INTERFIRM RELATIONS

1. Swan was an English inventor.

2. *EW*, III (January 26, 1884), 29.

3. *EW*, V (May 9, 1885), 186.

4. *EW*, V (May 16, 1885), 196.

5. *EW*, V (May 30, 1885), 216.

6. Edison Electric Light Company, *The Edison Electric Light* (1886), pp. 3–4.

7. *EW*, V (May 25, 1885), 207.

8. *EW*, VIII (July 3, 1886), 5–6.

9. *EW*, XI (May 25, 1888), 269.

10. Letter from W. J. Jenks to the members of the Association of Edison Illuminating Companies, February 1, 1890 (GE Files).

11. Opinion of J. W. Howell, stated in an interview with J. W. Hammond, July 13, 1925 (GE Files).

12. *EW*, XIV (October 12, 1889), 243.

13. Hammond, *Men and Volts*, p. 182.

14. *EW*, XXI (January 14, 1893), 34.

15. Letter from S. D. Greene to S. A. Duncan of the McKeesport (Pennsylvania) Light Company, February 13, 1893 (GE Files).

16. *EW*, VIII (August 21, 1886), 91.

17. Circular letter from S. D. Greene to Edison licensees, December 16, 1892 (GE Files).

18. Letter from A. E. Dow, Treasurer of the Edison Electric Illuminating Company of Fall River, Massachusetts, to S. D. Greene, April 8, 1893 (GE Files).

19. Letter from K. Clark, President of the Edison Electric Light and Power Company of St. Paul, Minnesota, to S. D. Greene, March 20, 1893 (GE Files).

20. Letter from the Chief of Construction of the Edison Electric Light Company of York, Pennsylvania, to W. S. Howell, General Electric lamp engineer, April 8, 1893 (GE Files).

21. Letter from S. D. Greene to K. Clark, April 8, 1893 (GE Files).

22. Letter from G. H. Fenn, Secretary of the Edison Electric Light and Power Company of St. Paul, to S. D. Greene, April 15, 1893 (GE Files).

23. Letter from E. Z. Wallourer, President of the Harrisburg Electric Company, Harrisburg, Pennsylvania, to S. D. Greene, March 17, 1893 (GE Files).

24. Letter from S. D. Greene to W. F. B. Stewart, lawyer at York, Pennsylvania, February 13, 1893 (GE Files).

25. W. S. Howell, "Report on the Westinghouse Stopper Lamp at York, Pennsylvania," March 15, 1893 (GE Files).

26. Letter from D. McCoy, President of the Edison Electric Light Company of Grand Rapids, Michigan, to S. D. Greene, February 10, 1893 (GE Files).

27. Letter from G. P. Yost, President of the Edison Electric Light Company of York, Pennsylvania, to S. D. Greene, March 8, 1893 (GE Files).

28. *EW*, XXIV (August 4, 1894), 114.

29. Reminiscences of L. M. Cargo (WE Files).

30. Letter from George Westinghouse, President of the Westinghouse Electric and Manufacturing Company, to C. A. Coffin, President of the General Electric Company, January 14, 1897 (WE Files).

31. United States Tariff Commission, *Incandescent Electric Lamps* (1939), pp. 32–33.

32. *EW*, XXIX (February 13, 1896), 226.

33. Lamp-patent license of 1897 (WE Files).

34. Letter from George Westinghouse to E. E. and E. S. Jackson, lawyers, January 15, 1897 (WE Files).

35. Letter from F. H. Taylor, Vice-President of the Sawyer-Man Electric Company, to Mr. Baker, of the same company, August 13, 1904 (WE Files). Mr. Jackson was counsel for the licensees.

36. Bright, *The Electric-Lamp Industry*, p. 104.

37. Letter, Westinghouse to Coffin, January 14, 1897 (WE Files).

38. Edison Electric Light Company, *A Warning* (February 1888; GE Files).

39. W. T. M. Motham, "The Westinghouse System," February 8, 1888 (GE Files).

40. *EW*, XII (December 22, 1888), xiii.

41. H. P. Brown, *A Test of the Efficiency of a Westinghouse Alternating Current Electric Lighting Plant* (1890).

42. Report of the Eighth Semi-Annual Convention of the Association of Edison Illuminating Companies, Nantasket Beach, Massachusetts, August 8 and 9, 1888 (GE Files).

43. Report of the Tenth Semi-Annual Convention of the Association of Edison Illuminating Companies, Niagara Falls, New York, August 13–15, 1889 (GE Files).

44. Quoted in Malcolm MacLaren, *The Rise of the Electrical Industry during the Nineteenth Century* (1943), p. 178. The source for this statement by Brown is not given.

45. *EW*, XII (August 4, 1888), 51.

46. H. P. Brown, "The New Instrument of Execution," *North American Review*, CXLIX (November 1889), 586.

47. *Albany Law Journal*, XL (October 19, 1889), 303.

48. *EW*, XIII (January 5, 1889), 4.

49. *New York Tribune*, July 9, 1889.

50. Data in WE Files.

51. Brown, "The New Instrument of Execution."

52. T. A. Edison, "Dangers of Electric Lighting," *North American Review*, CXLIX (November 1889), 632.

53. L. B. Stillwell, "Alternating Current vs. Direct Current," *Journal of the American Institute of Electrical Engineers*, LIII (May 1934), 708.

54. Letter from George Westinghouse to T. B. Kerr, July 11, 1888 (WE Files).

55. Westinghouse Electric Company, *Safety of the Alternating System of Electrical Distribution* (October 1, 1889).

56. George Westinghouse, "A Reply to Mr. Edison," *North American Review*, CXLIX (December 1889), 653.

57. George Westinghouse, "Sir Wm. Thomson and Electric Lighting," *North American Review*, CL (March 1890), 321.

58. A copy of this report is included in the Sprague Papers (Engineering Societies Library, New York City).

59. Comment of W. S. Andrews, stated in an interview with J. W. Hammond (GE Files).

60. Letter from T. A. Edison to Henry Villard, February 8, 1890 (Henry Villard Papers, Houghton Library, Harvard University).

61. Edison, "Dangers of Electric Lighting," p. 632.

62. *Ibid.*

63. Telegram from T. A. Edison to E. D. Adams, February 2, 1889 (Henry Villard Papers). The "his" in the telegram refers to George Westinghouse.

64. Report of the Eighth Semi-Annual Convention of the Association of Edison Illuminating Companies (GE Files).

65. *A Warning*, p. 72.

CHAPTER XI. ENTREPRENEURSHIP

1. The feeder had to be large enough, however, to preclude flicker in the lights as additional ones were turned on or off.

2. F. L. Dyer, T. C. Martin, and W. H. Meadowcroft, *Edison: His Life and Inventions* (1929), II, 914.

3. Jehl, *Menlo Park Reminiscences*, II, 862. This statement was made to C. L. Clarke, chief engineer of the Edison Electric Light Company.

4. *EW*, VII (May 1, 1886), 202.

5. *EW*, VI (July 25, 1885), 35.

6. W. H. Preece, "Progress of the Electric Light in England," a report submitted to the House of Commons, Ottawa, Canada, March 10, 1882. Quoted in the Edison Electric Light Company, *Ninth Bulletin* (May 15, 1882), p. 16.

7. Martin, *Forty Years of Edison Service*, p. 38.

8. This meter can be seen in the restored Menlo Park Laboratory, Edison Institute, Dearborn, Michigan.

9. The Edison Electric Light Company, *Sixteenth Bulletin* (February 2, 1883), p. 31.

10. *Ibid.*, pp. 33–34.

11. The Cincinnati Water Works installed an electric-light plant in 1884 and for a period of several months used almost no gas. But its gas bill each month was the same as before (*Cincinnati Enquirer*, February 16, 1885). Quoted in the Edison Company for Isolated Lighting, *Bulletin for Agents No. 6* (September 15, 1885), p. 3.

12. *American Gas Light Journal*, XXXVII (July 3, 1882), 5.

13. Edison Electric Light company, sales booklet, 1884 (GE Files).

14. Jehl, *Menlo Park Reminiscences*, II, 494.

15. Francis Jehl, "Electric Lighting at Brünn," *Electrician* (London), X (November 25, 1882), 38.

16. Jehl, *Menlo Park Reminiscences*, III, 985.

17. *Edisonia*, pp. 166–178.

18. For a good, short summary of the work of inventors immediately preceding Edison, see Bright, *The Electric-Lamp Industry*, pp. 42–56.

19. Dyer, Martin, and Meadowcroft, *Edison*, I, 16.

20. *EW*, IV (October 18, 1884), 151.

21. GE Files.

22. *Time*, LV (January 2, 1950), 54.

23. Prout, *George Westinghouse*, pp. 314–318.

CHAPTER XII. THE IMPACT ON THE GAS INDUSTRY

1. *Fortune*, XI (May 1935), 46.

2. F. L. Collins, *Consolidated Gas Company of New York* (1934), p. 220.

3. Martin, *Forty Years of Edison Service*, p. 11.

4. *EW*, VIII (December 11, 1886), 287.

5. The figures in this paragraph are from the following sources: *EW*, IX (February 12, 1887), 74; *EW*, XIII (March 30, 1889), 183; and *Brown's Directory of American Gas Companies* (1900), *passim*.

6. *EW*, XIV (July 20, 1889), 42.

7. *Manufactures: Twelfth Census*, X (1902), 712.

8. A. R. Foote, *Economic Value of Electric Light and Power* (1889), p. 146.

CHAPTER XIII. THE DYNAMICS OF THE INDUSTRY

1. Edison Electric Light Company, *Street Lighting by the Edison Municipal System* (1887).

2. The data in this paragraph on market shares of the various producers are from various documents and publications in GE Files and WE Files. The data on incandescent lights in use for 1885 are from *EW*, VII (February 20, 1886), 80; for 1890, from *EW*, XV (April 5, 1890), 236; and for 1902, from census data.

PART III. ELECTRIC POWER

CHAPTER XIV. THE SETTING

1. MacLaren, *Rise of the Electrical Industry*, p. 83.

2. *Manufactures of the United States: Tenth Census*, II (1883), 493.

3. J. A. Miller, *Fares Please!* (1941), p. 32.

4. For a more extended discussion of the merits and drawbacks of cable railways, see my essay, "Frank Julian Sprague: Father of Electric Traction," chap. viii in *Men in Business*, ed. William Miller (1952).

CHAPTER XV. ELECTRIC TRACTION

1. Martin, *Forty Years of Edison Service*, p. 11.

2. Dyer, Martin, and Meadowcroft, *Edison*, I, 460.

3. *EW*, IV (November 29, 1884), 221.

4. Edison estimated that for a six-mile, double-track, 60-car street railway, the cost of his low-voltage system (exclusive of the central station, the cars, and the original cost of the track) would be $31,000 per mile. If more cars were to be operated, the cost would increase in proportion. See letter from T. A. Edison to Henry Villard, October 5, 1891 (Henry Villard Papers, Houghton Library, Harvard University).

5. *EW*, IV (August 9, 1884), 42.

6. Edison Electric Light Company, *Annual Report* (October 23, 1883); reproduced in *Twentieth Bulletin* (October 31, 1883), p. 445.

7. *EW*, IV (November 29, 1884), 221.

8. W. D. Marks, "Report on Sprague Motor Number Six," April 15, 1889 (Henry Villard Papers, Houghton Library, Harvard University).

9. *EW*, VIII (December 4, 1886), 268.

10. *EW*, XI (March 17, 1888), 142.

11. See MacLaren, *Rise of the Electrical Industry*, pp. 102–103, and C. S. Sergeant, "Early Experiments in Boston," *Street Railway Journal*, XXIV (October 8, 1904), 534.

12. E. M. Bentley, "First Electric Streetcar in America," *EW*, XLII (March 5, 1904), 439.

13. Hazard was also active in other electrical enterprises. See p. 39, above.

14. *Electrical Review*, IV (August 30, 1884), 3.

15. "Report of the Committee on Electricity as Motive Power," October 15, 1884 (GE Files).

16. Bentley-Knight Electric Railway Company, booklet on electric railways (1885), p. 3 (GE Files).

17. *EW*, IX (January 15, 1887), 29.

18. Bentley-Knight Electric Railway Company, booklet on electric railways (1885), p. 12 (GE Files).

19. Bentley-Knight Electric Railway Company, *Electric Street Railways* (1888).

20. Letter from W. H. Lanman to C. M. Ripley, March 30, 1920 (GE Files).

21. *EW*, VI (November 21, 1885), 215.

22. *EW*, I (February 3, 1883), 67.

23. The locomotive principle means using a powered vehicle to pull (or push) other vehicles which are not self-powered.

24. Sprague's work in electric street railways is discussed in Chapter XVI.

25. *EW*, VIII (December 11, 1886), 281.

26. *EW*, X (August 27, 1887), 121.

CHAPTER XVI. THE PIONEER INNOVATORS IN ELECTRIC TRACTION

1. Much of the material in this section and in the last section of the following chapter appeared in my essay "Frank Julian Sprague" in *Men in Business*, ed. William Miller (Cambridge: Harvard University Press, 1952).

2. F. J. Sprague, "Digging in the Mines of the Motors," *Journal of the American Institute of Electrical Engineers*, LIII (May 1934), 697.

3. *New York Times*, October 26, 1934, p. 21.

4. *New York Times*, September 23, 1928, p. III–5.

5. *EW*, VIII (October 2, 1886), 168; and VIII (November 20, 1886), 254.

6. *EW*, X (September 3, 1887), 130–131.

7. *EW*, IX (February 12, 1887), 82.

8. Sprague Electric Railway and Motor Company, *Electric Transmission of Power* (1890).

9. *EW*, IX (February 12, 1887), 82.

10. *EW*, XI (January 7, 1888), 5.

11. *EW*, IX (May 7, 1887), 221.

12. Three articles by Sprague under the title, "Application of Electricity to the Propulsion of Elevated Railroads," appeared in the *Electrical World* early in 1886. See *EW*, VII, 27, 36, and 118.

13. Edison Electric Light Company, *Annual Report* (October 26, 1886), p. 13.

14. Hammond, *Men and Volts*, p. 84.

15. F. J. Sprague, "Lessons of the Richmond Electric Railway," *Engineering Magazine*, VII (September 1894), 789.

16. *EW*, XXXI (Febuary 12, 1898), 221.

17. F. J. Sprague, "Some Personal Notes on Electric Railways," *Electrical Review*, XL (February 15, 1902), 227.

18. *EW*, XI (May 26, 1888), 273.

19. For interesting details of Flynn's activities in Richmond street railways, see the Henry Villard Papers (Houghton Library, Harvard University).

20. *EW*, IX (January 22, 1887), 37.

21. *EW*, IX (June 4, 1887), 267.

22. *EW*, XIV (October 19, 1889), 264–265.

23. Sprague, "Digging in the Mines of the Motors," p. 702.

24. Federal Electric Railways Commission, *Proceedings* (1920), I, 140.

25. Thomson-Houston Electric Company, incorporation statute (GE Files).

26. Hammond, *Men and Volts*, pp. 135–136.

27. *EW*, XIII (March 9, 1889), 151.

28. *EW*, XXXI (February 12, 1898), 221.

29. C. A. Terry, *Early History of the Westinghouse Electric and Manufacturing Company* (1925), pp. 58, 59.

30. C. S. Sergeant, "Early Experiments in Boston," p. 534.

31. Letter from H. M. Whitney to the Thomson-Houston Electric Company, March 18, 1889 (GE Files).

32. Recollections of A. L. Roher (1926; GE Files).

CHAPTER XVII. THE ELECTRIC-RAILWAY-EQUIPMENT BUSINESS

1. The term "surface-wound" means that the coils of copper wire were placed on the surface of the iron drum around which they were wound. In the later slotted-drum armature, slots were cut in the drum for the copper coils. The tops of the coils were then flush with the surface of the iron drum.

2. *EW*, XXI (May 27, 1893), 397.

3. Westinghouse Electric and Manufacturing Company, *Annual Report* (July 2, 1895), p. 11

4. Westinghouse Electric and Manufacturing Company, *The Westinghouse Exhibit at the International Tramways and Light Railways Exhibition* (June 1900), pp. 14–15.

5. It is interesting to note that General Electric also experimented with a surface-contact system in the 1895–1900 period, but had no more success than Westinghouse.

6. General Electric Railway Department, "Report of Engineering Work: June 1, 1892 — June 1, 1893" (GE Files).

7. Letter from O. T. Crosby, General Manager of the Railway Department, to Sales Agents, February 18, 1894 (GE Files).

8. General Electric Company, Circular Letter No. 127, March 28, 1895, issued by W. J. Clark, General Manager of the Railway Department (GE Files).

9. General Electric Company, *Arguments and Information for Representatives of the Railway Department* (June 15, 1895), p. 6 (GE Files). The Walker Manufacturing Company of Cleveland was formed in 1883 to make heavy machinery, including cable equipments. In 1894, Walker began to manufacture electric-railway motors and generators.

10. These price data are from GE Files.

11. Personal and confidential letter from Eugene Griffin, First Vice-President, to Local Office Managers, July 25, 1895 (GE Files). W. J. Clark was General Manager of the Railway Department.

12. Letter from W. J. Clark to all Local Office and Department Managers, September 15, 1895 (GE Files).

13. *Arguments and Information for Members of the Railway Department*, p. 5.

14. General Electric Company, Circular Letter No. 128, March 21, 1895, from W. J. Clark, General Manager of the Railway Department (GE Files).

15. Letter from W. J. Clark to Local Office Managers, February 6, 1896 (GE Files).

16. Personal and confidential letter from the Railway Department Assistant Manager to C. T. Hughes, January 14, 1902 (GE Files).

17. General Electric Company, Circular Letter No. 112, December 6, 1894, from Eugene Griffin, First Vice-President (GE Files).

18. Letter from T. P. Bailey, Assistant Western Sales Manager, to Eugene Griffin, First Vice-President, January 14, 1895 (GE Files).

19. Letter from W. H. Knight to Eugene Griffin, January 16, 1895 (GE Files).

20. *Arguments and Information for Members of the Railway Department*, p. 14.

21. Letter from O. S. Lyford to H. W. Cope, November 4, 1933 (WE Files).

22. B. G. Lamme, "Development of the Street Railway Motor in America," *Electric Journal*, XV (November 1918), 457.

23. B. G. Lamme, "Development of the Street Railway Motor in America," *Electric Journal*, XV (October 1918), 412.

24. Letter from Lyford to Cope, November 4, 1933.

25. General Electric Company, Circular Letter No. 68, June 25, 1894 (GE Files).
26. F. J. Sprague, "The Electric Railway," *Century Magazine*, LXX (August 1905), 522.
27. Sprague, "Digging in the Mines of the Motors," p. 703.
28. F. J. Sprague, second affidavit, sworn December 5, 1900, in London (GE Files).
29. Sprague, "The Electric Railway," p. 524.
30. Federal Electric Railways Commission, *Proceedings*, I, 753.
31. Letter from A. G. Davis of the General Electric Patent Department to F. P. Fish, General Counsel of General Electric, February 1, 1910 (GE Files).

CHAPTER XVIII. ALTERNATING CURRENT

1. Letter from H. M. Byllesby to George Westinghouse, May 21, 1888 (WE Files). The quotation in the following paragraph is also from this letter.
2. Agreement between the Tesla Electric Company and the Westinghouse Electric Company, July 7, 1888 (WE Files).
3. Letter from George Westinghouse to T. B. Kerr, July 5, 1888 (WE Files).
4. Letter from Westinghouse to Kerr, July 11, 1888 (WE Files).
5. Letter from L. B. Stillwell to Lemuel Bannister, August 22, 1892 (WE Files).
6. *EW*, XV (March 15, 1890), 200.
7. *EW*, XVI (July 19, 1890), 46.
8. A synchronous motor is essentially an ordinary a.c. generator operated in reverse.
9. The factors involved in the choice of a lighting frequency are discussed on p. 313, above.
10. The term "induction motor" will hereafter be used to designate the a.c. motor invented by Tesla.
11. E. D. Adams, *Niagara Power* (1927), I, 325.
12. F. L. Stetson, "The Use of Niagara Water Power," *Cassier's Magazine*, VIII (July 1895), 178.
13. Adams, *Niagara Power*, I, 114–116, 143.
14. *Ibid.*, p. 134.
15. *Ibid.*, p. 172.
16. F. E. Leupp, *George Westinghouse* (1918), p. 74.
17. Adams, *Niagara Power*, I, 444.
18. *EW*, XXI (April 1, 1893), 254.
19. Adams, *Niagara Power*, II, 256.
20. This letter is reproduced in *Niagara Power*, II, 223–224.
21. Adams, *Niagara Power*, II, 233.
22. Letter from George Westinghouse to Dr. Coleman Sellers, August 19, 1893 (WE Files).
23. See Table 29, p. 280, above.
24. General Electric Company, Minutes of the Sales Committee, November 20, 1893 (GE Files).
25. The statement is reproduced in *Niagara Power*, II, 239. Of the other three signers, two were mechanical engineers and one a hydraulic engineer.
26. Adams, *Niagara Power*, I, 164.
27. *EW*, XXII (September 16, 1893), 208.
28. Adams, *Niagara Power*, II, 117.

29. S. D. Greene, "Distribution of the Electrical Energy from Niagara Falls," *Cassier's Magazine*, VIII (July 1895), 361. These data were not part of Greene's original article but were added by the editor in a reissue early in 1897.

CHAPTER XIX. THE ALTERNATING-CURRENT-EQUIPMENT BUSINESS

1. B. G. Lamme, "The Story of the Induction Motor," *Journal of the American Institute of Electrical Engineers*, XL (March 1921), 203.
2. B. G. Lamme, *Autobiography* (1926), p. 82.
3. General Electric Company, Bulletin Letter No. 14, November 1, 1895 (GE Files).
4. F. F. Fowle, *Standard Handbook for Electrical Engineers* (1915), p. 520.
5. "Speed regulation" refers to the ability of a motor to maintain a constant speed under different loads. The usual definition of the speed regulation of an electric motor is:

$$\frac{\text{no-load speed minus full-load speed}}{\text{full-load speed}} \times 100 = \text{speed regulation (per cent).}$$

6. General Electric Company, "Cost Report on General Electric and Westinghouse Motors," *c.* 1896 (GE Files).
7. Lamme, *Autobiography*, p. 80.
8. The d.c. constant-speed motor is known technically as a shunt motor. The field coils are in parallel with the armature. In the series d.c. motor, the field coils and armature are in series. The series motor is used in electric traction, elevators, cranes, and hoists. The shunt motor is used in industrial work where the load and speed are relatively constant.
9. These figures are only approximate and depend, in each case, on the specific characteristics of the motor. See C. V. Christie, *Electrical Engineering* (1925), pp. 213–214.
10. *Ibid.*, p. 214.
11. Recollections of S. B. Paine (GE Files).
12. Letter from S. B. Paine to B. S. Havens, April 15, 1925 (GE Files).
13. "Exciting generators" are d.c. generators used to supply the field current for generators.
14. General Electric Company, Minutes of the Sales Committee, August 11, 1893 (GE Files).
15. Recollections of S. B. Paine (GE Files).
16. S. B. Paine, *General Electric in the Development of the Textile Industry* (*c.* 1926).
17. *EW*, XXVII (March 14, 1896), 285.
18. S. B. Paine, Memorandum on the Textile Industry, June 9, 1925 (GE Files).
19. General Electric Company, Circular Letter No. 111, December 17, 1894, issued by J. R. McKee, General Manager of the Power and Mining Department (GE Files).
20. Letter from William Stanley to B. G. Lamme, December 29, 1913 (WE Files).
21. General Electric Company, Technical Letter No. 137, February 10, 1896 (GE Files).
22. Lamme, *Autobiography*, pp. 105–107.
23. Technical Letter No. 137.
24. Letter to J. R. McKee, August 7, 1894 (GE Files).
25. Letter from Stanley to Lamme, December 29, 1913.

26. Stanley, "Alternating Current Development in America," pp. 578–579.

27. Letter from J. R. McKee to C. A. Coffin, October 16, 1899 (GE Files).

28. Letter from C. P. Steinmetz, Head of the General Electric Engineering Department, to E. W. Rice, Third Vice-President, October 31, 1899 (GE Files).

29. In the reaction turbine, the steam expansion takes place both in the stationary nozzles and in the rotating blades. In the impulse turbine, the expansion takes place only in the nozzles. For a lucid explanation of the difference between the two types, see A. P. Usher, *History of Mechanical Inventions* (1929), pp. 357–358.

30. Letter from C. P. Steinmetz to E. W. Rice, Technical Director of General Electric, January 3, 1895 (GE Files).

31. *EW*, XXVI (October 12, 1895), 408.

32. The Westinghouse Machine Company was formed in 1880 to manufacture a high-speed steam engine invented by H. H. Westinghouse, brother of George.

33. Reminiscences of Francis Hodgkinson (WE Files).

34. Hammond, *Men and Volts*, p. 277.

35. B. G. Lamme, *Electrical Engineering Papers* (1919), pp. 607 and 664; *Autobiography*, p. 114.

36. See Table 29, p. 280, above.

37. Letter from L. B. Stillwell to C. A. Terry, March 11, 1933 (WE Files).

38. They still do. The 25-cycle Niagara Falls power has been used until very recently for general lighting in southern Ontario. Low candle-power incandescent lamps flicker noticeably in this region.

39. General Electric Company, Minutes of the Meeting of the Lighting Representatives of General Electric, June 13, 1895 (GE Files).

40. Letter from the Stanley Electric Company to its customers, April 8, 1895, quoted in General Electric Company, Power and Mining Department Bulletin Letter No. 1, April 15, 1895 (GE Files).

41. The 1896 patent agreement between General Electric and Westinghouse is discussed in Chapter XX.

42. For a more complete discussion of the technical developments which made it possible to use 60 cycles for heavy power work, see the excellent paper by B. G. Lamme, "The Technical Story of the Frequencies." This article was first published in the *Transactions of the American Institute of Electrical Engineers*, XXXVII (1918), 65, and was reprinted the following year in Lamme's *Electrical Engineering Papers*, p. 569.

43. See Table 29, p. 280, above.

44. For a theoretical treatment of the effect that the capacity of a firm may have on the reactions of a rival, see A. G. Papandreou, "Market Structure and Monopoly Power," *American Economic Review*, XXXIX (September 1949), 888ff.

45. *EW*, XXV (May 25, 1895), 603.

46. *Ibid.*

47. General Electric Company, Circular Letter No. 588, July 28, 1902, from C. E. Estabrook of the Supply Department (GE Files).

48. General Electric Company, Letter of Advice to Offices No. 149, July 11, 1902 (GE Files).

49. Letter from J. R. Lovejoy, General Manager of the Supply Department, to Local Office Managers, July 22, 1902 (GE Files).

CHAPTER XX. INTERFIRM RELATIONS

1. T. A. Edison, Reply to Thomson-Houston Memoranda of March 23, 1889, April 1, 1889 (Henry Villard Papers, Houghton Library, Harvard University).

2. Letter from H. A. Pevear, *et al.*, Trustees, to Thomson-Houston Stockholders, May 26, 1890 (Baker Library, Harvard Business School).

3. Recollections of F. P. Fish (GE Files).

4. *New York Times*, February 21, 1892, p. 2.

5. See, for example, the *Boston Commercial Bulletin*, April 15, 1893, and various issues of *Electricity* in May and June 1896.

6. Mrs. Charles Van Depoele was among those who expected the collapse of General Electric. Charles Van Depoele died in March 1892, leaving to his wife and five children the royalty income from his street-railway patents which were being used by General Electric. Mrs. Van Depoele sold out for a lump sum in 1893 because she expected General Electric to fail. See the *New York Times*, October 21, 1928, p. III–5.

7. General Electric Company, Bulletin Letter No. 3, May 15, 1895, from J. R. McKee, General Manager, Power and Mining Department (GE Files).

8. *Ibid.*

9. *EW*, XXXIII (April 1, 1899), 398.

10. Letter from Eugene Griffin, First Vice-President, to Department and Local Office Managers, April 4, 1896 (GE Files).

11. General Electric Company, Circular Letter No. 194, August 4, 1896 (GE Files).

12. *EW*, XXVIII (December 19, 1896), 747.

13. In 1898, an appeals court reversed the 1895 decision which had upheld the trolley patent.

CHAPTER XXI. THE DYNAMICS OF THE INDUSTRY

1. F. S. Pearson, "The Latest Developments in Electric Conduit Railways," *Cassier's Magazine*, XVI (August 1899), 268.

2. These data are from *Manufactures: Twelfth Census*, VII (1902), cccxvi.

CONCLUSION

1. E. H. Chamberlin, *The Theory of Monopolistic Competition* (5th ed.; 1946), p. 101.

2. D. H. Wallace, *Market Control in the Aluminum Industry* (1937), p. 338.

3. William Fellner, *Competition among the Few* (1949), pp. 183–185.

4. Westinghouse Electric and Manufacturing Company, *Annual Report* (May 18, 1892), p. 6.

5. *EW*, III (July 27, 1892), xiii.

6. For a more extended discussion of this phenomenon, see G. J. Stigler, "The Division of Labor is Limited by the Extent of the Market," *Journal of Political Economy*, LIX (June 1951), 185ff., especially p. 190.

7. Brush, "Some Reminiscences of Early Electric Lighting," pp. 3–5.

8. Sprague, "Digging in the Mines of the Motors," pp. 695–697.

9. Stanley, "Alternating Current Development in America," p. 566.

10. *Ibid.*, p. 568.

11. W. R. Maclaurin, *Invention and Innovation in the Radio Industry* (1949), pp. 21–29, 243–245.

12. Bright, *The Electric-Lamp Industry*, pp. 370–371.

13. *Ibid.*, pp. 340–341.

Bibliography

The major part of the material on which this study is based comes from the files of General Electric and Westinghouse and from the *Electrical World*, of which I read every issue from 1883 to 1901. The most important items in the company files are listed individually. The books, articles, and other sources, which follow the company material, are only those that I found especially useful. They are not intended to be an exhaustive listing of items which concern the electrical manufacturing industry or the economic problems discussed in this study.

I. COMPANY MATERIALS

A. PUBLICATIONS

1. GENERAL ELECTRIC (AND PREDECESSOR COMPANIES)

Arguments and Information for Representatives of the Railway Department (General Electric Company, June 15, 1895).

The Brush Electric Light (Brush Electric Company, *c.* 1883).

Bulletin, Nos. 1–22 (Edison Electric Light Company, 1882–1884).

Bulletin for Agents, Nos. 1–14 (Edison Company for Isolated Lighting, 1885–1886).

Economy of the Electric Railway (Edison General Electric Company, 1891).

The Edison Central Station System (Edison Electric Light Company, January 1, 1884).

The Edison Electric Light: The Legal and Commercial Status (Edison Electric Light Company, October 7, 1886).

The Edison Incandescent Electric Light (Edison Electric Light Company, *c.* 1887).

Edison Incandescent Lamps (General Electric Company, September 20, 1897).

The Edison System of Electric Railways (Edison General Electric Company, 1891).

The Edison System of Incandescent Lighting and Electric Motive Power from Central Stations (Edison Electric Light Company, 1888).

The Electric Motor (Thomson-Houston Electric Company, January 1889).

Electric Street Railways (Bentley-Knight Electric Railway Company, 1889).

Electric Transmission of Power (Sprague Electric Railway and Motor Company, 1890).

Haskins, C. D., *General Electric Meters* (General Electric Company, 1897).

Incandescent Electric Lighting (Edison United Manufacturing Company, *c.* 1889).

Paine, S. B., *General Electric in the Development of the Textile Industry* (General Electric Company, *c.* 1926).

Seventeen Years of Brush Arc Apparatus (Brush Electric Company, 1895).
Street Lighting by Incandescent Lamps (Thomson-Houston Electric Company, October 1, 1888).
Street Lighting by the Edison Municipal System (Edison Electric Light Company, 1887).
The Thomson-Houston Electric Railway System (Thomson-Houston Electric Company, 1890).
Thomson Recording Watt Meters (General Electric Company, 1895).
A Warning (Edison Electric Light Company, February 1888).

2. WESTINGHOUSE (AND PREDECESSOR COMPANIES)

Adventures in Power (Westinghouse Electric and Manufacturing Company, 1936).
The Alternating Current System (Westinghouse Electric Company, 1888).
Catalogue (United States Electric Lighting Company, 1882).
Electric Street Railway History (Westinghouse Electric and Manufacturing Company, 1898).
Forty Years Ago (Westinghouse Electric and Manufacturing Company, 1924).
George Westinghouse (Westinghouse Electric Corporation, 1946).
Incandescent Lamps (Sawyer-Man Electric Company, *c.* 1900).
Interesting Facts Concerning Alternating Current Generators and Converters (Westinghouse Electric and Manufacturing Company, 1893).
One-Fourth of a Million Horsepower of Polyphase Electric Transmission Apparatus (Westinghouse Electric and Manufacturing Company, 1898).
Railway Apparatus (Westinghouse Electric and Manufacturing Company, 1893).
Safety of the Alternating System of Electric Distribution (Westinghouse Electric Company, October 1, 1889).
Shall We Use Meters? (Westinghouse Electric and Manufacturing Company, 1892).
Transmission of Power (Westinghouse Electric and Manufacturing Company, 1893).
The Westinghouse Exhibit at the International Tramways and Light Railways Exhibition (Westinghouse Electric and Manufacturing Company, June 1900).
Westinghouse: Past, Present, and Future (Westinghouse Electric and Manufacturing Company, 1936).

3. OTHER ELECTRICAL MANUFACTURING FIRMS

The American System of Electric Arc Lighting (American Electric Manufacturing Company, 1887).
Arc Lamp (Adams-Bagnall Electric Company, *c.* 1895).

B. RECORDS

1. HISTORICAL FILES OF THE GENERAL ELECTRIC COMPANY, SCHENECTADY, NEW YORK

a. Contracts and agreements

Brush Electric Company and its local arc-lighting companies.
Edison and the Edison Electric Light Company, November 15, 1878; January 12, 1881; March 8, 1881. (These three contracts are in the office of the Secretary of General Electric, Schenectady, New York.)

Thomson-Houston Electric Company and the Jamestown Electric Light and Power Company, August 9, 1887.
Edison General Electric and the Edison central-station companies.
Edison General Electric equipment-sales contracts.
General Electric and local central-station companies, Type C and Type D.

b. Reports

Broderick, J. T. "Standardization: Its Influence on Costs, Deliveries, Quality, and Collections" (March 15, 1901).
General Electric Company, "Cost Report on General Electric and Westinghouse Motors" (*c.* 1896).
—— "Preliminary Report on the Electrical Equipment of the Brooklyn Elevated Railway" (April 6, 1897).
General Electric Railway Department, "Report of Engineering Work: June 1, 1892 — June 1, 1893."
Howell, W. S., "Report on the Westinghouse Stopper Lamp at York, Pennsylvania" (March 15, 1893).
"Information on the Practices of Edison Licensees" (January 26, 1893).
Miescher, P., "Report on the Power of Willamette Falls at Oregon City" (May 2, 1884).
Motham, W. T. M., "The Westinghouse System" (February 8, 1888).
Parker, William, *et al.*, "First Report of the Committee of Investigation" (New Britain, Connecticut, April 13, 1880).
—— "Second Report of the Committee of Investigation, Relative to the New Electric Generator of Professor Elihu Thomson" (New Britain, Connecticut, April 27, 1880).
Reports of the Annual and Semi-Annual Meetings of the Association of Edison Companies (1888–1890).
Thomson-Houston Electric Company, "Report of the Meeting of the Standardizing Bureau" (Lynn, Massachusetts, February 24–27, 1891).

c. Recollections

Reminiscences of the following former employees of General Electric (and its predecessor companies): W. S. Andrews, W. S. Clark, J. W. Howell, J. R. McKee, S. B. Paine, A. L. Roher.

d. Miscellaneous material

Annual reports; bulletins, circular letters, pamphlets, and so forth; corporate charters; correspondence and memoranda of various company officials; data on costs, prices, production, sales, shipments, purchases, inventories, payrolls, and so forth; minutes of various management committee meetings.

2. HISTORICAL FILES OF THE WESTINGHOUSE ELECTRIC CORPORATION, EAST PITTSBURGH, PENNSYLVANIA

a. Contracts and agreements

Galileo Ferraris of Turin, Italy, and Guido Pantaleoni of Pittsburgh, Pennsylvania, July 16, 1888.
Tesla Electric Company and Westinghouse Electric Company, July 7, 1888.
Westinghouse Electric Company and equipment purchasers, 1888.

Westinghouse Electric Company and Thomson-Houston Electric Company, December 1887 and December 29, 1890.
Westinghouse Electric and Manufacturing Company and the Missouri Electric Light and Power Company of St. Louis, February 20, 1892.
Westinghouse Electric and Manufacturing Company, lamp license, 1897.
Westinghouse, George, Jr., and William Stanley, March 5, 1884, and December 24, 1885.

b. Reports

Aspinwall, L. M., "Experience with Surface Contact Systems."
"Report on Mining Locomotives."

c. Recollections

Reminiscences of the following former employees of Westinghouse (and its predecessor companies): L. M. Aspinwall, L. M. Cargo, R. N. Ehrhart, E. H. Heinrichs, Francis Hodgkinson, E. E. Keller, B. G. Lamme, P. A. Lang, P. M. Lincoln, O. S. Lyford, Guido Pantaleoni, J. S. Peck, W. R. Pinckard, B. P. Rowe, C. E. Skinner, G. M. Verity.

d. Miscellaneous material

Annual reports; bulletins, circular letters, pamphlets, and so forth; correspondence and memoranda of various company officials; data on costs, prices, production, sales, shipments, and so forth.

II. LIBRARIES AND COLLECTIONS

(containing material relevant to the early history of the electrical manufacturing industry in the United States)

Baker Library, Harvard Business School, Boston, Massachusetts.
Frank Sprague Papers, in the Engineering Societies Library, New York City, and the New York Public Library, New York City.
Henry Villard Papers, in Houghton Library, Harvard University, Cambridge, Massachusetts.

III. BOOKS

A. AUTOBIOGRAPHIES AND BIOGRAPHIES

Bryan, G. S., *Edison: The Man and His Work* (New York, 1926).
Dyer, F. L., T. C. Martin, and W. H. Meadowcroft, *Edison: His Life and Inventions*, 2 vols. (New York, 1929).
Flint, C. R., *Memories of an Active Life* (New York, 1923).
Lamme, B. G., *Electrical Engineer: An Autobiography* (New York, 1926).
Leup, F. E., *George Westinghouse* (Boston, 1918).
Maxim, H. S., *My Life* (London, 1915).
Mottelay, P. F., *The Life and Work of Hiram Maxim* (New York, 1920).
O'Neill, J. J., *Prodigal Genius: The Life of Nikola Tesla* (New York: Ives Washburn, 1944).

Prout, H. G., *A Life of George Westinghouse* (New York, 1922).
Satterlee, H. L., *J. Pierpont Morgan* (New York: Macmillan, 1939).
Villard, Henry, *Memoirs*, 2 vols. (Boston, 1904).
Woodbury, D. O., *Beloved Scientist: Elihu Thomson* (New York: McGraw-Hill, 1944).
—— *A Measure for Greatness: A Short Biography of Edward Weston* (New York: McGraw-Hill, 1949).

B. TECHNICAL AND INDUSTRIAL HISTORY

Adams, E. D., *Niagara Power*, 2 vols. (Niagara Falls, New York, 1927).
American Electrical Directory (Fort Wayne, Indiana, 1885, 1886).
Bright, A. A., Jr., *The Electric-Lamp Industry* (New York: Macmillan, 1949).
Broderick, J. T., *Forty Years with General Electric* (Albany, New York, 1929).
Brown's Directory of American Gas Companies (New York, 1900).
Chantler, Philip, *The British Gas Industry* (Manchester, England: Manchester University Press, 1938).
A Chronological History of Electrical Development (New York: National Electrical Manufacturers Association, 1946).
Collins, F. L., *Consolidated Gas Company of New York* (New York: Consolidated Gas Company, 1934).
Cortelyou, G. B., *The Gas Industry* (New York, 1933).
Edisonia (New York, 1904).
Fleming, J. A., *Fifty Years of Electricity* (London, 1921).
Foote, A. R., *Economic Value of Electric Light and Power* (Cincinnati, Ohio, 1889).
Hammond, J. W., *Men and Volts: The Story of General Electric* (Philadelphia: J. B. Lippincott, 1941).
Howell, J. W., and Henry Schroeder, *History of the Incandescent Lamp* (Schenectady, New York, 1927).
Insull, Samuel, *Central Station Electric Service* (Chicago, 1915).
Jehl, Francis, *Menlo Park Reminiscences*, 3 vols. (Dearborn, Michigan: The Edison Institute, 1937, 1938, and 1941).
Jones, Payson, *A Power History of the Consolidated Edison System: 1878–1900* (New York: Consolidated Edison Company of New York, 1940).
Kottke, F. J., *Electric Technology and the Public Interest* (Washington, D. C.: American Council on Public Affairs, 1944).
Lewis, F. A., *The Incandescent Light* (West Orange, New Jersey: The Thomas Alva Edison Foundation, 1949).
MacLaren, Malcolm, *The Rise of the Electrical Industry during the Nineteenth Century* (Princeton, New Jersey: Princeton University Press, 1943).
Maclaurin, R. W., and R. J. Harman, *Invention and Innovation in the Radio Industry* (New York: Macmillan, 1949).
Martin, T. C., *Forty Years of Edison Service* (New York, 1922).
Martin, T. C., and S. L. Coles, *The Story of Electricity*, 2 vols. (New York, 1919).
Mason, E. S., *The Street Railway in Massachusetts* (Cambridge, Massachusetts, 1932).
Miller, J. A., *Fares Please!* (New York: Appleton-Century, 1941).
Parsons, R. H., *The Early Days of the Power Station Industry* (Cambridge, England: Cambridge University Press, 1940).
Reeves, W. F., *The First Elevated Railroads in Manhattan and the Bronx in the City of New York* (New York: New York Historical Society, 1936).

Scoville, W. C., *Revolution in Glassmaking: Entrepreneurship and Technological Change in the American Industry, 1880–1920* (Cambridge, Massachusetts: Harvard University Press, 1948).
Sprague, Harriet, *Frank J. Sprague and the Edison Myth* (New York: William Frederick Press, 1947).
Stotz, Louis, and Alexander Jamison, *History of the Gas Industry* (1938).
Terry, C. A., *Early History of the Westinghouse Electric and Manufacturing Company* (East Pittsburgh, Pennsylvania, 1925).
Thompson, R. L., *Wiring a Continent: The History of the Telegraph Industry in the United States, 1832–1866* (Princeton, New Jersey: Princeton University Press, 1947).
Usher, A. P., *A History of Mechanical Inventions* (New York, 1929).
Walker, J. B., *Fifty Years of Rapid Transit* (New York, 1918).

C. THEORY AND METHOD IN ECONOMICS, ECONOMIC HISTORY, AND ENTREPRENEURIAL HISTORY

Brems, Hans, *Product Equilibrium under Monopolistic Competition* (Cambridge, Massachusetts: Harvard University Press, 1951).
Chamberlin, E. H., *The Theory of Monopolistic Competition: A Re-orientation of the Theory of Value* (5th ed.; Cambridge, Massachusetts: Harvard University Press, 1946).
Fellner, William, *Competition among the Few: Oligopoly and Similar Market Structures* (New York: Alfred A. Knopf, 1949).
Kirkland, E. C., *A History of American Economic Life* (3d ed.; New York: Appleton-Century-Crofts, 1951).
Research Center in Entrepreneurial History, Harvard University, *Change and the Entrepreneur: Postulates and Patterns for Entrepreneurial History* (Cambridge, Massachusetts: Harvard University Press, 1949).
Schumpeter, J. A., *Business Cycles: A Theoretical, Historical, and Statistical Analysis of the Capitalist Process*, 2 vols. (New York: McGraw-Hill, 1939).
—— *Capitalism, Socialism, and Democracy* (New York: Harper, 1942).
—— *The Theory of Economic Development: An Inquiry into Profits, Capital, Credit, Interest, and the Business Cycle* (Cambridge, Massachusetts: Harvard University Press, 1949).
Triffin, Robert, *Monopolistic Competition and General Equilibrium Theory* (Cambridge, Massachusetts: Harvard University Press, 1940).
Wallace, D. H., *Market Control in the Aluminum Industry* (Cambridge, Massachusetts: Harvard University Press, 1937).
Williamson, H. F., *The Growth of the American Economy* (New York: Prentice-Hall, 1946).

D. TECHNOLOGY

Brown, H. P., *A Test of the Efficiency of a Westinghouse Alternating Current Electric Lighting Plant* (New York, 1890).
Christie, C. V., *Electrical Engineering: The Theory and Characteristics of Electrical Circuits and Machinery* (3d ed.; New York, 1925).
Fowle, F. F., *Standard Handbook for Electrical Engineers* (4th ed.; New York, 1915).

Grant, E. L., *Principles of Engineering Economy* (New York, 1930).
Higgs, Paget, *The Electric Light* (London, 1879).
Lamme, B. G., *Electrical Engineering Papers* (East Pittsburgh, Pennsylvania, 1919).
Pender, Harold, W. A. DelMar, and Knox McIlwain, *Electrical Engineers' Handbook: Electric Power* (3d ed.; New York: John Wiley, 1936).
Steinmetz, C. P., *General Lectures on Electrical Engineering* (Schenectady, New York, 1908).

IV. ARTICLES

A. BIOGRAPHICAL

Compton, K. T., "Elihu Thomson: 1853–1937," in National Academy of Sciences, *Biographical Memoirs*, XXI (Washington, D. C.: National Academy of Sciences, 1941), 143.
Jackson, D. C., "Frank Julian Sprague, 1857–1934," *Scientific Monthly*, LVII (November 1943), 431.

B. TECHNICAL AND INDUSTRIAL HISTORY

Adams, A. A., "The First Electric Light Plant in Boston," *Electrical World*, XXXIV (December 22, 1900), 954.
Beane, J. W., "The History of Electric Lighting," *Electrical World*, VII (February 20, 1886), 80.
Bentley, E. M., "First Electric Streetcar in America," *Electrical World*, XLII (March 5, 1904), 439.
Brush, C. F., "Some Reminiscences of Early Electric Lighting," *Journal of the Franklin Institute*, CCVI (July 1928), 3.
Chesney, C. C., "Some Contributions to the Electrical Industry," *Journal of the American Institute of Electrical Engineers*, LIII (May 1934), 726.
Chesney, C. C., and C. F. Scott, "Early History of the AC System in America," *Journal of the American Institute of Electrical Engineers*, LV (March 1936), 228.
Clark, W. J., "Electric Railways in America," *Cassier's Magazine*, XVI (August 1899), 518.
Cope, H. W., "A Half Century of Engineering Progress," *Electric Journal*, XXXIII (January 1936), 3.
Dodd, S. T., "Development of Railway Motor Design," *Street Railway Journal*, XXIV (October 8, 1904), 551.
—— "Evolution of the Electric Railway Motor," *Street Railway Journal*, XXII (December 26, 1903), 1092.
"Electric Railway Work in America Prior to 1888," *Street Railway Journal*, XXIV (October 8, 1904), 559.
Foster, E. C., "Early Electric Railroading in New England," *Street Railway Journal*, XXIV (October 8, 1904), 526.
Greene, S. D., "Distribution of the Electrical Energy from Niagara Falls," *Cassier's Magazine*, VIII (July 1895), 333.
Griffin, Eugene, "The Beginnings of the Electric Railway Motor," *Street Railway Journal*, XXIV (October 8, 1904), 575.
Hamill, S. M., "Beginning and Future of the Arc Lamp," *Engineering Magazine*, VII (August 1894), 700.

Hutchinson, C. T., "The Development of the Modern Electric Railway Motor," *Cassier's Magazine*, XVI (August 1899), 337.
Jenks, W. J., "Six Years' Practical Experience with the Edison Meter," *Transactions of the American Institute of Electrical Engineers*, VI (1889), 26.
Lamme, B. G., "Development of the Street Railway Motor in America," *Electric Journal*, XV, 408 (October 1918), and 454 (November 1918).
—— "Pioneer Electric Railway Work of the Westinghouse Company," *Street Railway Journal*, XXIV (October 8, 1904), 542.
—— "The Story of the Induction Motor," *Journal of the American Institute of Electrical Engineers*, XL (March 1921), 203.
—— "The Technical Story of the Frequencies," *Transactions of the American Institute of Electrical Engineers*, XXXVII (1918), 65.
Lincoln, P. M., "Some Reminiscences of Niagara," *Journal of the American Institute of Electrical Engineers*, LIII (May 1934), 720.
Martin, T. C., "The Electric Industry in America in 1887," *Electrical World*, IX (January 29, 1887), 50.
—— "Electric Streetcars," *Transactions of the American Institute of Electrical Engineers*, IV (1887), 26.
Miles, B. F., "Arc Light Carbons," *Electrical World*, XXV (January 5, 1895), 8.
Passer, H. C., "E. H. Goff: An Entrepreneur Who Failed," *Explorations in Entrepreneurial History* (Research Center in Entrepreneurial History, Harvard University), I (May 1949), 17.
—— "The Electric Light and the Gas Light: Innovation and Continuity in Economic History," *Explorations in Entrepreneurial History* (Research Center in Entrepreneurial History, Harvard University), I (March 1949), 1.
—— "Electrical Science and the Early Development of the Electrical Manufacturing Industry in the United States," *Annals of Science* (London), VII (December 1951), 382.
—— "Frank Julian Sprague: Father of Electric Traction," chapter viii in *Men In Business*, ed. William Miller (Cambridge, Massachusetts: Harvard University Press, 1952).
Reid, Thorburn, "Some Early Traction History," *Cassier's Magazine*, XVI (August 1899), 357.
Ryan, Harris J., "Developments in Electric Power Transmission," *Journal of the American Institute of Electrical Engineers*, LIII (May 1934), 712.
Sergeant, C. S., "Early Experiments in Boston," *Street Railway Journal*, XXIV (October 8, 1904), 534.
Sprague, F. J., "Digging in the Mines of the Motors," *Journal of the American Institute of Electrical Engineers*, LIII (May 1934), 695.
—— "The Electric Railway," *Century Magazine*, LXX, 434 (July 1905), and 512 (August 1905).
—— "Electric Railway Not Creation of One Man," *New York Times*, September 23, 1928, p. IX–9.
—— "Lessons of the Richmond Electric Railway," *Engineering Magazine*, VII (September 1894), 787.
—— "The Multiple Unit System for Electric Railways," *Cassier's Magazine*, XVI (August 1899), 439.
—— "Some Personal Experiences," *Street Railway Journal*, XXIV (October 8, 1904), 566.
—— "Some Personal Notes on Electric Railways," *Electrical Review*, XL (February 15, 1902), 226.

Stanley, William, "Alternating Current Development in America," *Journal of the Franklin Institute*, CLXXIII (June 1912), 561.
—— "The Beginnings of Alternating Current Engineering," *Electrical Review*, XL (February 15, 1902), 223.
Stetson, F. L., "The Use of Niagara Water Power," *Cassier's Magazine*, VIII (July 1895), 173.
Stillwell, L. B., "Alternating Current Versus Direct Current," *Journal of the American Institute of Electrical Engineers*, LIII (May 1934), 708.
Thomson, Elihu, "The Pioneer Investigations on Dynamo Machines Fifty Years Ago," *Journal of the Franklin Institute*, CCVI (July 1928), 17.
—— "Some High Lights of Electrical History," *Journal of the American Institute of Electrical Engineers*, LIII (May 1934), 758.

C. THEORY AND METHOD IN ECONOMICS, ECONOMIC HISTORY, AND ENTREPRENEURIAL HISTORY

Cochran, T. C., "Economics in a Business History," supplement to the *Journal of Economic History*, V (1945), 54.
—— "The Legend of the Robber Barons," *Explorations in Entrepreneurial History* (Research Center in Entrepreneurial History, Harvard University), I (May 1949), 1.
Cole, A. H., "An Approach to the Study of Entrepreneurship: A Tribute to Edwin F. Gay," supplement to the *Journal of Economic History*, VI (1946), 1.
—— "Business History and Economic History," supplement to the *Journal of Economic History*, V (1945), 45.
Jenks, L. H., "Approaches to Entrepreneurial Personality," *Explorations in Entrepreneurial History* (Research Center in Entrepreneurial History, Harvard University), II (January 15, 1950), 91.
Papandreou, A. G., "Market Structure and Monopoly Power," *American Economic Review*, XXXIX (September 1949), 883.
Passer, H. C., "Entrepreneurial History and Economics," *Explorations in Entrepreneurial History* (Research Center in Entrepreneurial History, Harvard University), I (January 1949), 21.
Schumpeter, J. A., "The Creative Response in Economic History," *Journal of Economic History*, VII (November 1947), 149.
Stigler, G. J., "The Division of Labor is Limited by the Extent of the Market," *Journal of Political Economy*, LIX (June 1951), 185.

D. TECHNOLOGY

Brown, H. P., "The New Instrument of Execution," *North American Review*, CXLIX (November 1889), 586.
Crocker, F. B., "The Electric Distribution of Power in Workshops," *Journal of the Franklin Institute*, CLI (January 1901), 1.
Crosby, O. T., "Practical Points in Electric Car Service," *Electrical World*, XIV (December 21, 1889), 405.
Edison, T. A., "The Dangers of Electric Lighting," *North American Review*, CXLIX (November 1889), 625.
Houston, E. J., and Elihu Thomson, "The Investigations of the Sub-Committee on Electrical Measurements," *Journal of the Franklin Institute*, CV (June 1878), 361.

Howell, J. W., "The Maximum Efficiency of Incandescent Lamps," *Transactions of the American Institute of Electrical Engineers,* V (1888), 237.
Jehl, Francis, "Electric Lighting at Brünn," *Electrician* (London), X (November 25, 1882), 38.
Lamme, B. G., "The Polyphase Induction Motor," *Electric Journal,* I, 431 (September 1904), 503 (October 1904), and 597 (November 1904).
Pearson, F. S., "The Latest Developments in Electric Conduit Railways," *Cassier's Magazine,* XVI (August 1899), 257.
Preece, W. H., "Electric Lighting in America," *Electrical World,* IV (December 27, 1884), 265.
"Report of the Committee on Dynamo-Electric Machines," *Journal of the Franklin Institute,* CV (May 1878), 289.
"Report on the Efficiency and Duration of Incandescent Lamps," supplement to the *Journal of the Franklin Institute,* CXX (September 1885).
Sprague, F. J., "Application of Electricity to the Propulsion of Elevated Railroads," *Electrical World,* VII, 27 (January 16, 1886), 36 (January 23, 1886), and 118 (March 13, 1886).
Steinmetz, C. P., "On the Use of Polyphase Motors on Electric Railroads," *Electrical World,* XXXI (January 1, 1898), 20.
Thomson, Sir William, "Electric Lighting and Public Safety," *North American Review,* CL (February 1890), 189.
Westinghouse, George, "A Reply to Mr. Edison," *North American Review,* CXLIX (December 1889), 653.
—— "Sir Wm. Thomson and Electric Lighting," *North American Review,* CL (March 1890), 321.

V. UNITED STATES GOVERNMENT DOCUMENTS

A. REPORTS OF THE CENSUS BUREAU

Abstract of the Census of Manufactures: 1914 (1917).
Abstract of the Twelfth Census (1904).
Compendium of the Tenth Census (1883).
Electrical Industries: 1902 (1906).
Historical Statistics of the United States (1949).
Manufactures: Twelfth Census, vols. VII–X (1902).
Manufacturing Industry in the United States: Eleventh Census, vol. VI (1895).
Manufactures of the United States: Tenth Census, vol. II (1883).
Transportation Business in the United States: Eleventh Census, vol. XIV, part I: Transportation by Land (1895).
Transportation in the United States: Tenth Census, vol. IV (1883).

B. REPORTS OF OTHER AGENCIES

Federal Electric Railways Commission, *Proceedings,* 3 vols. (1920).
Federal Trade Commission, *Electric-Power Industry: Supply of Electrical Equipment and Competitive Conditions* (1928).
Tariff Commission, *Incandescent Electric Lamps* (1939).

Index

Adams, Edward Dean, 174, 285, 291
Addison, Dr. T. H., 309
Air brake, Westinghouse invention, 129–130
Allegheny City, Pa., Bentley-Knight railway contract, 227–229, 232, 249
Alternating current, 132–133, 135, 138, 338–339; advantages over direct current, 139, 140, 164, 165, 191, 327; requested by Edison stations, 167; used for electrocution, 169; opposed by Edison, 171–175, 223; recommended by Sprague, 172; and electric traction, 256–258; at Niagara Falls, 286–287, 294; opposed by Lord Kelvin, 287; patents, 325; technical changes, 361
Alternating-current commutating motor, 280–281, 288, 336
Alternating current — direct current generators, compared, 312–313
Alternator, Siemens, 132, 135, 137; Stanley, 137–138
Aluminum industry, oligopoly in, 353–354
American Electric and Illuminating Company, 34–40
American Electric Company, 24, 25, 26, 34
American Electric Manufacturing Company, 36–40, 52, 54
American Electrical Directory, 115
American Institute of Electrical Engineers, 277
American Street Railway Association, Committee on Electricity as Motive Power, 225–226, 229
American (Wood) system, 38
Ames, F. L., 57, 322, 323
Ampère, André Marie, 211
Ansonia, Conn., Van Depoele installation, 232
Appleton, Wis., Van Depoele installation, 232
Arc carbons, improved by Brush, 17, 18; copper-plated, 18, 33; prices, 18, 59, 60, 61, 62, 67; producers, 58–59; consumption figures, 65
Arc light, invented by Davy, 11; improvements required, 13; double-carbon light invented, 18; Brush patent invalid, 42; double-carbon patent upheld, 42–43; use in street lighting, 50–51; enclosed arc light invented, 64–65; defects, 64, 75–76; prices, 67; Edison not interested in, 79, 80; requested by Edison stations, 123
Arc-lighting system, market for, 12–13; competition, 43, 349–351; local companies, 47–51, 70; marketed by Westinghouse, 145, 147; marketed by Thomson, 192; marketed by Edison General Electric Co., 374n. *See also* Central Stations
Armature, definition, 12; laminated, 33, 64; heat losses in, 204; surface wound, 257–258, 386n; drum and ring, 260–261
Armington engine, 116
Arnoux and Hochhausen Electrical Company, 41
Association of Edison Illuminating Companies, 122, 157, 166, 167, 174
Automatic current regulator, Brush, 18, 44; Thomson-Houston, 25, 27, 39–40, 42, 43, 44, 57

Baggley, Ralph, 130
Baltimore, Md., first gas company (1816), 12
Banker, James H., 84
Barton, Silas, 26
Batchelor, Charles, 93, 96, 101, 102
Battery, primary, current source for arc light, 11; current source for incandescent light, 75; current source for motor, 212
Battery, secondary, invented by Brush, 21; use in incandescent lighting, 164, 183, 184; use in streetcars, 216, 223–224

Belfield, Reginald, 135, 136
Belmont, August, 292
Bentley, Edward M., 225–230
Bentley-Knight Electric Railway Company, 225–228
Bentley-Knight system of electric railways, 225–230, 235–236, 240, 247–250, 252, 329
Bergmann, S. J., 94, 190
Bergmann and Company, 94, 100, 102–104
Berlin Deutsche Bank, 103, 104
Binghamton, N. Y., Van Depoele installation, 232
Boehm, Ludwig, 189
Boston, Mass., Brush central station, 19; Edison central station, 121; Julien battery car, 223; West End Street Railway Company electrification, 228, 247
Boston Edison Company, 239
Boston Elevated Railway, Sprague electrification, 274
Boulton Carbon Company, 36
Bowdoin, George S., 85, 291
Bracken, William, 223
Brackett, Professor Cyrus Fogg, 148
Bradley, C. S., 300
Bright, A. A., Jr., 359
Brockton, Mass., three-wire central station, 238
Brookline (Mass.) Gas Company, furnished electricity, 199
Brooklyn, N. Y., Edison central station, 121
Brooklyn Elevated Railway, Sprague electrification, 274
Brooklyn Heights Railroad, General Electric electrification, 275
Brooklyn Rapid Transit Company, tests on motors, 270
Brown, Harold P., 167–170
Brown and Sharpe, Providence, R. I., 244, 246
Brown Brothers and Company, 284
Brush, Charles Francis, education and early work, 14–15, 357; sells first arc-lighting systems, 16; promotes first central station, 19; begins production of arc carbons, 58; pioneer innovator in arc lighting, 67–68
Brush Electric Company, 14–21; development of dynamo, 15–16, 45–46; contracts with local arc-lighting companies, 19, 28; adds new products, 20, 21; system compared with Weston's, 32–33; Thomson-Houston acquires control, 53–55; arc-carbon production, 58–59; importance of patents, 206, 325; entrepreneurship, 356–359; economic growth, 363
Brush Electric Company of Baltimore, 140
Brush Electric Light, 20
Brush Electric Light Company of New York, 20; census data on, 31–32
Brushes, carbon replaces copper, 204, 245, 251; wear, 217, 227–228; adjustment, 234
Brussels, Belgium, Julien battery car, 223
Buckeye lamp, 161
Buffalo, N. Y., plans for Niagara power, 284–287, 292–294
Bulletins, Edison Electric Light Company, 115
Bunsen, R. W., 196
Bunsen burner, 197–198
Button system, Westinghouse, 258
Byllesby, H. M., 277–279

Cable system for street cars, 214, 226, 247, 342–343
California Electric Light Company of San Francisco, 19
Canal, surface, at Niagara Falls, 282–283, 293–294
Canandaigua, N. Y., patent infringement, 330–331
Capital good, arc-lighting equipment, 43, 44; electrical equipment, 351–352, 354
Carborundum Company, Niagara Falls, 293
Cataract Construction Company, formed, 284; purchases Niagara Power Company, 284; begins tunnel construction, 286; financial ties, 291–292; pioneer innovation, 292–295, 338
Census of manufacturers (1880) on electric-lights industry, 370n–372n
Centennial Exhibition, Philadelphia (1876), 357
Central stations, arc lighting, 19, 28, 35–37, 64; incandescent lighting, 89–92, 99, 118–121, 138, 140, 186–187; at Niagara Falls, 286; electric power, 311, 343–344
Chamberlin, Professor E. H., on oligopoly, 353
Chesney, Cummings C., 309, 338
Chicago, Ill., Thomson-Houston demonstration, 29; Edison central station, 121
Chicago Industrial Exposition (1883), 231
Chicago Railway Exposition (1883), 220
Chicago World's Fair (1893), Westinghouse lighting contract, 142–143, 281–282, 287, 290, 296; General Electric elevated system, 270
Churchill, Frederick H., 22, 23, 24, 26
Cincinnati, Ohio, Industrial Exposition (1883), 27, 111

Cincinnati Water Works, gas cost, 383n
Cities, growth of, 4
Clark, W. J., 249, 266, 267, 273, 322, 323
Cleveland, Ohio, Brush street-lighting, 18–19; Bentley-Knight installation, 225–226
Coffin, Charles A., in syndicate to buy American Electric, 26; head of Thomson-Houston, 27; initiates merger policy, 52; an aggressive leader, 57; as entrepreneur, 68, 69, 338; views on electric lighting, 249; head of General Electric, 322–324, 326–327
Columbia, S. C., textile mill electrification, 303–305, 340
Columbia Incandescent Lamp Company, St. Louis, 160
Columbia (steamship), Edison lighting plant on, 86, 96, 112, 148
Combination, arc lighting, 41, 51–52; arc carbons, 59–62
Commonwealth Edison Company, Chicago, General Electric turbogenerator installation, 311
Commutation, explanation of, 12, 217; air as insulator, 25, 27, 57, 373n; in railway motors, 261
Commutators, 204, 245, 256, 302
Comparative cost of electric railways, Edison's Menlo Park railway, 219; Edison's low-voltage railway, 221, 384n; Julien's battery system, 224; Bentley-Knight railway, 226, 227, 229, 247; Van Depoele railway, 232–233; Sprague railway, 246; Griffin's study, 253–254
Competition, incandescent-lamp industry, 155–157, 160–161, 349–351; railway motors, 258–270; effect of patent agreements, 332–334; equipment producers, 349, 351–355; determinants of, 350
Compressed air, in railroad brakes and signal devices, 129, 130; in Westinghouse control system for elevated railways, 274, 329; recommended by Westinghouse for Niagara Falls, 284; at Niagara Falls, 286, 287, 290
Condenser, use in Stanley motor, 306, 314
Condit, Hanson, and Van Winkle, 15
Conductors, problem in electric railways of, 216
Consolidated Electric Light Company, 144, 146, 152–153
Consolidated Electric Light Company (Portland, Me.), 38
Constant-current dynamo, in arc lighting, 13, 17, 25, 64, 360; in incandescent lighting, 206; not suitable for electric railway, 225
Constant-current transformer, 65–66
Constant-speed characteristic, 301–303, 336, 388n
Constants of polyphase a.c. power, standardization of, 313–316
Continental Clothing House, Boston, 16, 18
Converter, definition, 379n
Coolidge, T. Jefferson, 57, 322, 323
Copper cost, 17, 178, 369n
Cost data, street railways, 254
Cost guarantees, electric traction, 343
Cost reduction, Edison's quest for, 176–181, 186
Coster, C. H., 85, 101, 103, 291, 323
Cotton Manufacturers Association, Atlanta, 298
Cowles Electric Smelting and Aluminum Company, 21
Crescent Beach, Mass., Thomson-Houston electric railway, 249, 250
Crosby, O. T., 245, 322, 323
Crowell, Eugene, 101
Crystal Palace Electrical Exhibition, London (1882), 100, 237, 238
Current-supply problem, electric traction, 223, 235, 246
Curtis, C. G., 311

Davenport, Thomas, 211
Davidson, Robert, 211–212
Davy, Sir Humphrey, 11, 75
Dayton, Ohio, Van Depoele installation, 232
Dead-man's switch, 336
Demand, for street lighting, 12; for arc carbon, 59; for incandescent light, 76, 77; for Edison light, 91, 121, 122, 184; for electric motors, 213–215
Depressions, effects on electrical manufacturing industry, 7–8
Detroit, Mich., Edison central station, 121; Van Depoele installation, 232
Diehl, Phillip, 137
Direct current, advantages of, 139, 164–167; work of Sprague in, 276; original plans at Niagara, 286–287; innovations in, 338. *See also* Alternating current
Direct-current constant-speed motor, 256–257, 301–302, 336, 388n
Direct-current patents, importance in General Electric formation, 325
Distribution network, 178
District of Columbia, Board of Commissioners of, 253–254
Double-reduction gearing, reason for, 227,

335; at Richmond, 245–246; in Westinghouse motor, 257, 258; problems, 259
Drake, E. L., 195
Drexel, Morgan, and Company, 85, 90, 284
Duopoly, 264, 318, 322, 352, 355, 364
Dynamo, early development, 11–12, 44–45, 64, 76; tested by Franklin Institute, 15, 16; Gramme patent invalid, 41; prices, 67; efficiency, 76; "jumbo," 90–91; manufactured by Edison, 94; developed by Edison, 177, 223; similarity to motor, 211, 212; technical change in railway dynamos, 265; made by Wallace and Sons, 370n

East Cleveland Street Railway Company, 225–226
East Newark, N. J., lamp factory, 93, 97
East Pittsburgh, Pa., Westinghouse plant, 8
Eaton, S. B., 101
Economic growth, in manufacturing, 3–7; in electrical manufacturing, 7–8, 362–364; in arc lighting, 70–71; in gas industry, 200–203; in incandescent lighting, 206–207; in electric streetcars, 254–255, 341–343; in electric power, 343–345
Edison, Thomas Alva, etheric force theory, 21; early life and inventions, 78, 79; economic orientation of his work, 83, 84, 176, 177, 180, 181; invents incandescent electric light, 88; his chief assistants, 96, 97; takes control of Edison company, 100; retires from electrical industry, 102, 104; views on alternating current, 170, 173, 174; antipathy to Westinghouse, 174; work in electric traction, 218–223, 235–236, 384n; advises on Niagara power, 284; views on formation of General Electric, 321–322, 326; entrepreneurship, 356, 357, 359
Edison, Thomas A., Construction Department, 99
Edison Company for Isolated Lighting, 37, 97, 99, 115–116
Edison Electric Light Company, 27–28, 37–38; incorporated 1878, 84–85; purpose, 86; financial data, 86–88; major policy, 98; management changes, 99–103; lamp policy, 109; *Bulletins*, 115; relationship with licensees, 118–119, 123; infringement suits, 151–154; monopoly attempt, 155–161; in a.c. competition, 166–170, 174; policy of secrecy, 188–189; purchase of Sprague patents, 238, 239, 241, 248; economic growth, 364
Edison General Electric Company, formation (1889), 94, 102–104; sales organization, 124; competitors, 150; mergers, 221, 248, 321–329
Edison Illuminating Companies, Association of, 122, 174
Edison Illuminating Company of New York, 182, 185, 291; incorporated, 89–90; Pearl Street station, 91–92; contract with, 118–119; patent dispute, 332
Edison isolated-lighting plant installations, 112, 114, 117
Edison lamp, comparison with Thomson-Houston lamp, 29; at exhibitions, 110; high-resistance filament, 177
Edison Lamp Company, formation, 93–94; cost and revenue data, 95; consolidation, 102–104
Edison Lamp Works, marketing policies, 108–109, 111, 122
Edison licensees, insistence on protection, 155, 157–161, 332
Edison lighting system, compared with Westinghouse's, 138; cost-reducing components, 177–179; compared with gas lighting, 181–182, 185–186
Edison Machine Works, formation, 94–96; consolidation, 102–104; manufacturing activity, 115, 238, 240
Edison patents, 142, 324–325, 329
Edison Telephone Company, 100
Edison United Manufacturing Company, 122
Edson, Tracy R., 85
Efficiency, of Weston arc-lighting system, 33; in dynamo, 43, 76, 177; of arc light and incandescent light, 80; of incandescent lamps, 106, 107, 204; guaranteed by Edison, 116; of d.c. system, 164; in a.c. and d.c. dynamos, 165; of a.c. system, 166, 167; of induction motors, 299; at Columbia, S. C., installation, 304
Electric-lights industry (1880 census), 370n–372n
Electric locomotive, Edison's experiments on, 219
Electric motor, principles of operation, 211, 212, 213; uses, 211, 212, 276, 296–298, 344–345; Edison's work on, 218; Sprague's development of, 238–240, 244–246, 248; characteristics, 336. *See also* Motors
Electric power, in Edison lamp factory, 92, 93, 218; recognized by Edison, 218; selected at Niagara Falls, 287; growth of, 340; in industry, 344
Electric-power equipment, potential market,

213–214; technical change, 335–337; entrepreneurship in, 338–340
Electric Railway Company of the United States, 220–221
Electric traction, basic problems, 216–218, 235–236, 241; growth of, 254–255, 340–343; technical changes, 335–336; Edison cost estimates, 384n
"Electric Trust," 355
Electrical manufacturing industry, definition, ix; favorable conditions for growth, 3–8; business firms as chief customers, 7, 12–13, 70, 76–77, 112–114, 207, 214, 239, 338–339; creates markets, 19, 28, 35, 70, 118, 140, 207; early attempt to form "trust," 51, 52; identity of interest with light and power companies, 61, 122, 127, 128, 207, 351; comparison of leading firms, 150; use of own innovations, 340; use of electric power, 344; determinants of competition in, 350; growth of, 362–364; suggestions for public policy, 364–365
Electrical Testing Bureau (Johns Hopkins), 167
Electrical Tube Company, 95, 96
Electrical World, 38, 51, 59, 135, 251
Electrochemical industry, use of Brush dynamos, 21; Weston electroplating dynamos, 31, 32; at Niagara Falls, 293
Electro-Magnetic Traction Company, 258
Elevated railways, electrical experiments by Field, 220; electrical experiments by Sprague, 240–242; advantages of electrical power in, 241; locomotive use in, 270, 271; electrification of, 270–275
Emmons, G. E., 323
Engineer-entrepreneur, 1, 192–194, 249, 356, 357, 359, 360
English Edison Electric Light Company, 100
Equitable Life Assurance Company, 147
Escher, Wyss and Company (Zurich), 292
Espionage, industrial, 292, 318–319
Etheric force, 21
Evershed, Thomas, plan for Niagara power, 283, 284, 285–286, 294
Excelsior Electric Company, 53, 55

Fabbri, Egisto P., 85, 101
Faesch and Piccard (Geneva), 292
Faraday, Michael, 12, 211
Farmer, Moses, 32, 148
Feeder-main system, 178, 200, 205, 223, 324, 360, 382n
Fellner, Professor William, on oligopoly, 354
Ferrario, Galileo, 277, 278
Field, S. D., 220–221
Field, revolving, 307–308, 311
Field coils, 245, 302
Field poles, 12, 257–259
Filament, high-resistance, 105–107
Financial backing, for manufacturing, 5; for Brush, 14, 15; for Thomson-Houston, 22–25, 26, 29, 55–57; for Goff, 35; for Maxim, 32; for Sawyer, 32; for Edison, 84–88, 101–104, 189; for Westinghouse, 129–130, 136; for Stanley, 131, 136, 308; for Bentley-Knight, 225; for Van Depoele, 230; for Sprague, 238; for Niagara Falls power, 294–295
Finney, Joseph, 256
Fish, F. P., 322, 323, 324
Flashing-process patents, 325
Fleming, J. A., 187
Flicker in incandescent lamps, 313, 382n, 389n
Flint, Charles, 32, 51–52, 148
Flynn, Maurice B., 242–243, 247
Forbes, Professor George, 288–291
Fort Wayne (Ind.) Electric Company, 53–56
Franklin Institute of Philadelphia, tests arc-lighting dynamos and lamps, 15, 16, 21, 22; tests incandescent lamps, 110, 111
Frequency, comparison of low and high, 278, 280, 289, 313, 314; at Niagara Falls, 288, 290, 294, 313; standardization, 294, 313, 315–316, 337
Friction wheels, Bentley-Knight system, 225
Fuller-Wood Company, Wood system of arc lighting, 36, 41, 374n
Fulton Street line, New York City, Bentley-Knight contract, 227
Future-delivery contracts, incandescent lamps, 109

Ganz and Company, 132, 135, 136, 172
Garfield, E. I., 323
Garrett, George S., 22, 23
Gas companies, first ones in America, 12; use of electric-lighting apparatus, 37, 199, 200; their market, 76; basis for marketing policy of Edison, 118; views on electric lighting, 173; switch to heating, 198; imitate Edison system, 200
Gas illumination, for streets, 12, 48–51; incandescent, 64; studied by Edison, 82; basis for price of electric light, 91, 120, 181, 184; Westinghouse work in, 130, 131; guide to Edison, 181–186; technical change in, 195–199; inaccuracy of meter, 184, 383n

Gaulard and Gibbs system, 132–133, 163, 191
Gearing problem, railway motors, 259
General Electric Company, policy on lamp quality, 111, 112; price policies, 125–128, 161; patent agreement, 128, 161, 164, 329–334; patent policy, 155–160; electrifies elevated railways, 270, 275; buys Sprague multiple-unit-system patent, 275; plan for Niagara Falls, 287–288, 355; monocyclic system, 297; induction motors, 297–300; textile electrification, 302–305; polyphase generators, 307–308; turboalternators, 310–311; formation of company (1892), 321–329; innovations by, 338, 340, 359; economic growth, 364
General Electric motors, railway, 259–263, 268, 273; induction, 296–305
Generators, technological changes, 265, 310–313; for Niagara Falls, 288–294; "exciting," 388n
Goddard, Calvin, 101
Goebel, Henry, 160
Goff, E. H., early sales activities, 28, 34, 35, 37; organizes local arc-lighting companies, 28, 35, 37, 48, 69; becomes manufacturer, 36–37; relation with Edison companies, 37, 38; advertising and publicity activities, 38; death, 40
Gramme, Z. T., 212
Gramme armature, 260
Gramme dynamo, 15, 76, 213
Gramme Electrical Company, 41
Grand Rapids Electric Company, 124
Great Barrington, Mass., Stanley installation, 133, 136–137
Green, Dr. Norvin, 84, 101
Greene, S. D., 108, 109, 157–158, 245, 322, 323
Griffin, Eugene, 124, 253–254, 255, 266, 268, 322, 323

Hamlin, George S., 84
Harrisburg, Pa., Van Depoele installation, 232
Hartford, Conn., turbogenerator installation, 311
Hartford Electric Light Company, 37
Hastings, F. S., 322, 323
Hawks, E. C., 60, 61
Hazard, Roland R., 225
Henry, Professor Joseph, 211
Higginson, Henry L., 57, 322, 323
High-resistance filament, reason for use by Edison, 83, 189, 190; not understood by Upton, 89; size of the resistance, 105, 106; patented by Edison, 142, 154; in Consolidated lamp, 144; in Maxim lamp, 148, 189
High-speed prime mover, problem of, 310–313
Hinds, Ketchum, and Company, 112
Holborn Viaduct, London, testing station, 186, 187
Hopkinson, J., 187
Houston, Edwin J., 21–25
Howell, W. S., 110, 160
Hydraulic power, study by International Niagara Commission of, 285

Ignis fatuus, 83, 174, 175
Impulse turbine, 389n
Incandescent electric light, Maxim's, 32; Davy's experiments on, 75; advantages, 77, 113, 184; Edison starts work on, 79; discounted by Thomson and Siemens, 80; views of English scientists, 82, 83, 376n; invented by Edison, 88; technical changes in, 94, 107, 108, 204, 206, 360–361; voltage variation in manufacture, 107, 108; provided to central-station customers, 121, 122; Stanley patents, 131; Westinghouse a.c. developments, 137–138, 164; leading firms, 150; basic Edison patent upheld, 155; basic Edison patent expires, 161; price agreement, 161–163; effect on gas industry, 195–198; growth, 206–207; competition, 349–351
Incandescent gas lamp, invention of, 64
Indianapolis Jenney Company, 53, 55, 56
Induction motor, unsuited to electric traction, 256–257; invention of, 277; patents purchased by Westinghouse, 277–278; not usable as originally made, 278–279; single-phase, 279–280; speed of, 280, 316, 317; application, 296–305, 336; made by Stanley, 306; definition, 387n
Inductor alternator, 306–308
Innovation, and invention, 2, 13; and price level, 7; commercial and technical, 66, 83; main ones of Edison, 176; at Niagara Falls, 294–295; at Columbia, South Carolina, 304–305; importance of publicity, 339; and activities of a firm, 356–357; and new firms, 358–360; public policy on, 364
Insull, Samuel, 98
Inter-industry competition, arc lighting and gas lighting, 20, 48–51, 64, 65, 196; incandescent lighting and gas lighting, 184, 185, 196; gas lighting and kerosene, 195

International Electrical Exhibition (Paris, 1881), 96, 110
International Niagara Commission, established in London, 285; recommendations, 286
Inventions Exhibition (London, 1885), 27, 132
Isolated lighting plants, not emphasized by Thomson-Houston, 28; early revenue source for Edison, 97; emphasized by Edison, 99; marketed by Edison, 112–118
Ives, Brayton, 292

Jacobi, Professor H. M., 211
Jamaica, Long Island, Van Depoele installation, 232
Jamestown (N. Y.) Electric Light and Power Company, 28
Jehl, Francis, 189
Johnson, E. H., 93–94, 100–102, 104, 172, 174, 238–239, 326
Julien, E., 223–224; battery streetcar, 235–236
Julien Electric Company, 223
Jumbo dynamos, 90, 91, 94, 186, 187

Kelley, John F., 309, 338
Kelvin, William Thomson, Lord, 194, 285, 287
Kennedy, Rankin, 133, 136
Kirkland, Professor E. C., 3
Knight, Walter H., 225–230, 269
Knowledge problem, in price and product competition, 318–320
Kruesi, John, 97, 102, 322, 323
Kuhn, Loeb, and Company, 104

Labor unions, 6
Laissez faire, 6
Lamme, Benjamin Carver, 264, 290, 298, 301
Lane-Fox lamp (English), 110, 190
Lanier, Charles, 291
Laval, C. G. P. de, 310
Lightning arrester, invented by Thomson, 25; hard to compute value of, 44, 57; in Thomson-Houston system, 47; on streetcars, 246
Lima, Ohio, Van Depoele installation, 232
Lockport, N. Y., first Edison municipal installation, 206
Locomotive principle, 231, 271, 275, 359, 384n
London, England, Edison central-station system, 90–91, 100
London Inventions Exhibition (1885), 27, 132
Lorain Steel Company, 334, 340
Lovejoy, J. R., 320, 323
Lowrey, Grosvenor P., 84–85, 101, 189
Lundy, A. D., 272
Lynn, Mass., development of Thomson-Houston, 26; formation of General Electric, 322, 324

McKee, J. R., 305, 309, 323
Maclaurin, Professor W. R., on entrepreneurship, 359
Magnetic field, 211
Man, Albon, 144
Manhattan Elevated Railway Company, Sprague experiments on line of, 241–242; General Electric electrification, 275; Westinghouse alternators, 312
Manufacturing, expansion of, 4–8; growth of electric power for, 343–344
Market share, in arc lighting, 20, 34, 39, 56–57; in arc carbons, 60, 62; in incandescent lighting, 100, 115, 126, 150, 206; in incandescent lamps, 161, 162; versus market control, 163, 351; in electric traction, 248, 254–255, 340; in railway motors, 270; at Niagara Falls, 292; in textile electrification, 305; in polyphase generators, 307
Marks, L. S., 64–65
Mascart, Professor Elie, 285
Mather Electric Company, 156–157
Maxim, Hiram, 189–192; incandescent lamp, 32, 110, 147–148
Mechanics Fair, Boston (1878), 16
Menlo Park, Edison's laboratory, 79, 87–88, 91; public demonstration, 88, 90, 95–96, 97; lamp factory at, 92–93; trial central stations, 186–190; power experiments, 218; traction experiments, 219–221
Mergers and consolidations, Thomson-Houston, 52–57, 62, 145, 233, 250; among carbon producers, 62; Edison, 102–104, 248, 275, 300, 333, 334; Westinghouse, 146–150, 333–334, 379n
Meter, in Edison's lighting system, 82, 88, 94, 180, 182, 186; used by Edison central stations, 122; Edison's chemical meter, 138, 182–183; Shallenberger's a.c. meter, 139; used in Westinghouse stations, 141, 142; technical change in, 205; made by Stanley, 319–320; not needed in arc lighting, 360
Metropolitan Elevated Railway, Chicago,

General Electric electrification of, 270, 272; Sprague test train on, 273
Mills, Darius O., 291, 322, 323
Minneapolis, Minn., Van Depoele electric locomotive, 231
Monocyclic system, 297, 314
Monopoly, absence in formation of General Electric, 326–327; public policy regarding, 365
Morgan, J. Pierpont, interest in Edison's work, 85, 90, 101–102, 104; Niagara interests, 284, 291, 294; General Electric interests, 322, 323, 326, 328
Morrill Act of 1862, 5
Morton, Henry, 284–285
Motor controller, invented by Sprague, 246; patents on, 329, 332; technical changes, 335–336
Motor-axle power transmission, 217, 235
Motors, speed regulation, 388n; "surface-wound," 386n. *See also* Electric motor
Multiple-unit system of control, 271–275, 336
Municipal lighting systems, development of, 205

National Electric Light Association, 61
Natural gas, Westinghouse work in, 130–131
Neon lighting, entrepreneurship, 359
New Britain businessmen, reports on Thomson-Houston dynamo, 22–24
New Orleans Exposition (1885), 231
New York, Brush central station, 19; Edison central station, 121; Julien battery streetcars, 223–224; Bentley-Knight contract, 227
New York Brush Electric Light Company, 46
New York City elevated railroads, Edison experiments, 220; Sprague development work, 240–242
New York State Niagara Reservation, 283
Niagara Falls, advantages as power site, 282; Evershed plan for, 283
Niagara Falls, City of, 285, 293
Niagara Falls Hydraulic Power and Manufacturing Company, 293
Niagara Falls Power Company, formed 1886, 284; first customers, 293; total investment, 294; use of alternating current, 296, 338–339
Niagara International Commission, 338
Niagara River, characteristics of, 282
Niagara River Hydraulic Tunnel, Power and Sewer Company, 284
North American Review, Edison article on alternating current, 170, 173, 174; Westinghouse reply, 171

Oersted, Hans, 211
Ohm's Law, 83, 89
Oligopoly, 2, 62, 319, 351, 353, 354, 355, 365
Overhead Conductor Electric Railway Company, 256
Overrunning trolley, used by Bentley-Knight, 227; used by Van Depoele, 232, 234

Pacinotti, Antonio, 212
Page, C. G., 212
Paine, Sidney B., textile mill electrification, 302–305; entrepreneurship, 338, 359, 378n
Pantaleoni, Guido, 132, 136, 269, 277, 278
Parallel transformers, 136
Paris Electrical Exhibition (1881), 237
Parsons, C. A., 310, 311
Patent license, for Brush central stations, 19; for Thomson-Houston central stations, 28, 29; for arc-lighting central stations, 47; for Edison central stations, 118, 119, 123, 128; for Westinghouse central stations, 140, 332; for Thomson-Houston to use Westinghouse patents and apparatus, 145, 166; General Electric–Westinghouse cross license, 331
Patents, Thomson-Houston automatic-current-regulator patent, 42; Brush double-carbon arc-lamp patent, 42; and industrial development, 42, 43, 45; and competition in arc lighting, 47; and Thomson-Houston acquisitions, 54; in arc-carbon industry, 62; not enforced by Edison, 99, 100, 151; suits begun by Edison, 101, 152; on incandescent lamp, 142, 143, 144, 163; on underground conduit, 228; on streetcars, 233; on induction motor, 277–278, 297, 306, 330, 333; as cause in formation of General Electric, 324–326; influence on competition, 352
Peach, B. F., 323
Pearl Street Station (New York City), 90–91, 119–121, 178, 184, 186–188, 190
Pelzer, S. C., textile mill electrification, 305
Perkins Electric Lamp Company, 157
Pevear, Henry, 26
Phase, standardization of, 337
Philadelphia, Pa., Brush central station, 19; Edison central station, 121
Philadelphia Company, 130

Philadelphia Electric Exhibition (1884), 131
Pittsburgh, Pa., Westinghouse a.c. system tested at, 137–138
Pittsburgh Reduction Company (later Alcoa), 293
Pixii, Hippolyte, 12
Polyphase apparatus, applications of, 296–305; marketing policies in, 301, 305, 336; patents, 330
Polyphase voltages, need for in induction motor, 279; choice of two or three phases, 281, 313–315; at Niagara Falls, 288, 294
Pomona, Calif., Westinghouse hydroelectric installation, 287
Pope, Franklin L., 133, 136
Population, relation to increase in electric traction, 4–5, 342
Port Huron, Mich., Van Depoele installation, 232
Preece, Sir William, 33, 51, 82–83, 182
Price competition, not significant in arc-lighting equipment, 44; in arc carbons, 59, 350–351; in incandescent lamps, 161, 163, 350–351; stimulated by product competition, 264, 266, 354; in induction motors, 300; compared to product competition, 317–319
Price-fixing, none in arc-lighting equipment, 45; in arc carbons, 59–62; in incandescent lamps, 161, 162, 164, 351, 375n
Price level, decline of, 7
Product competition, 2, 352, 354; in arc-lighting equipment, 44, 45; leads to mergers and consolidations, 52; in railway motors, 258–265; in induction motors, 296–300; in polyphase generators, 306–308; and knowledge, 316–320
Profits, guide to Edison, 176, 177; retained in business by Thomson-Houston, 30, 56; in arc-carbon industry, 59, 60; of Edison Electric Light Company, 102; of Edison manufacturing companies, 104; of Edison Illuminating Company of New York, 121; of United States Electric Lighting Company, 148; of Sprague, 246; of General Electric, 328

Railway motors, technical changes in, 335
Rankine, W. B., 284, 291
Reaction turbine, 389n
Revolving-field generators, 307–308
Rhode Island Locomotive Works, 226, 227
Rice, E. W., 290, 322, 323
Richmond, Va., Sprague electric-railway installation, 232–233, 242–247, 251, 274, 339
Richmond City Railway Company, purchase and electrification, 247
Risks of innovation, Edison's minimizing by tests of, 184–189
Roher, A. L., 250, 338
Rotary converter, 172, 175, 186, 296, 300–301, 315, 337
Rowland, Henry, 285, 288
Rush Street Bridge, Chicago, Thomson-Houston lighting of, 29

St. Louis, Mo., Julien battery car tested, 223
St. Paul, Minn., Edison central station, 121
Sales, electric-power equipment, problems of, 267–269, 344–345; growth of, 362
Sawyer, William E., 32, 144–145, 189
Sawyer-Man Electric Company, patents, 144–146, 153; established, 145; injunction against, 157, 292
Schenectady, N. Y., General Electric factory, 324
Schmid, Albert, 290
Schumpeter, Professor J. A., 7
Schuyler Electric Company, 52, 54, 55
Scott, C. F., 315
Scranton, Pa., Van Depoele installation, 232
Second Avenue Elevated, New York City, 271
"Secondary generators," 132, 133
Sellers, Coleman, 285, 288, 289
Series direct-current motor, 388n
Series-parallel controller, 246, 274, 324, 325
Shallenberger, O. B., 139, 141, 277
Sherman Antitrust Act (1890), 6
Shunt motor, 301–302, 388n
Siemens, Werner, views on incandescent light, 80; views on alternating current, 132, 135, 137; work on dynamo, 212
Siemens and Halske Company, Chicago plant, x; competition with General Electric, 126, 127; advises on alternating current, 132; bids by, 272, 303, 304; purchased by General Electric, 334
Siemens Brothers (London), 15
Sims engine, 116
Single-phase motor and power system, 279–280
Single-reduction gearing, tried at Richmond, 245–246; in Westinghouse motors, 257, 259; in railway motors, 259, 335
Soren, George W., 84
South Bend, Ind., Van Depoele installation, 231

South Side Elevated Railway, Chicago, Sprague electrification, 272–274
Southern Exposition, Louisville, Ky. (1884), 111
Sparking problem, a.c. motors, 302, 303
Speed regulation of a motor, 388n
Sprague, Frank Julian, report on alternating current, 172; Richmond installation, 232, 242–247, 251–255, 339; refuses to buy Bentley-Knight, 233; pioneer innovator in electric traction, 233–234, 236, 275, 276, 338, 340; early life, 237–238, 357–358; works for Edison, 238; develops industrial motor, 238–240; resigns from Edison General Electric, 248; develops multiple-unit system of control, 271, 272; electrifies Chicago elevated, 272–274, 329, 334; advises on Niagara power, 284
Sprague Electric Company, General Electric purchase of, 275
Sprague Electric Elevator Company, 271
Sprague Electric Railway and Motor Company, formed 1884, 238; purchased by Edison General Electric, 248; loses engineers to Westinghouse, 257; importance of patents, 324, 325
Sprague motors, industrial, 238–240; railway, 248–249, 259
Sprengel, Herman, 76
Standard Carbon Company, 62
Standard Oil Company, 17
Standardization, among Thomson-Houston affiliates, 53; in direct current, 89, 110, 186; in electric railways, 245–246; in alternating current, 313–316; in electric circuits, 337, 362
Stanley, William, becomes associated with Westinghouse, 131; establishes laboratory at Great Barrington, 136; designs alternator, 137–138; forms own firm, 296, 306; high-voltage work, 309, 338; early life and work, 358
Stanley Electric Manufacturing Company, formed 1891, 296, 306; manufacturing activities, 306–310, 314–315, 379n; bought by General Electric, 333
Stanley lamp, 131, 138
Stanley Meter Company, 333
Stanley motor, 306
Steam engines, 87, 91, 92–93, 115–116, 120, 122, 131, 187–188, 213, 214, 280, 296, 310, 312–313
Steam-turbine development, 310–313, 337, 389n
Steinmetz, Charles P., 290, 309, 310, 314
Stetson, F. L., 284, 291
Stiles, Aaron K., 230, 233, 250
Stillwell, Lewis B., 285, 290
Stockley, George W., 14, 26
Stone, Charles F., 84
Stopper lamp, 143, 160, 161
Streetcars, use of animal power, 214, 226; cable system, 214, 226
Street lighting, early methods, 12; Brush system, 17, 18, 19, 20; gas versus arc light, 48–51, 63, 64, 196; by incandescent lamp, 122; use of series circuit, 80, 360; Edison system for, 205, 206; use of alternating current, 206
Street railways, cost data, 254; growth, 340–343; motive power, 342. *See also* Electric traction
Substitution, effect on economic growth of the industry, 362–363
Sunbury, Pa., central station, 99, 238
Surface-contact system, 257–258, 386n
Swan Incandescent Electric Light Company, 131
Swan lamp (English), 110, 151, 190, 380n
Swiss firms, Niagara plans, 285, 286, 287
Synchronous condenser, 316
Synchronous motor, 387n

Technical knowledge, in arc lighting, 13, 46, 68; in railway motors, 267–270; of electricity, 361
Telegraph, apparatus made by Cleveland firm, 14; basis of early Edison inventions, 78; relation to Edison's activities, 79, 85, 100
Telegraph Supply Company of Cleveland, 14, 15; name changed to Brush Electric Company, 20
Telluride, Colo., Westinghouse single-phase power system, 279–280, 287, 339
Tesla, Nikola, 277
Tesla alternating-current motor, 256–257, 277–279, 281, 297, 306, 314, 315, 329, 331, 333, 387n. *See also* Induction motor
Tesla Electric Company, 277–278
Textile industry, 302–305, 338
Third Avenue Street Railway Company, New York City, 247
Thompson, Professor Sylvanus, 82
Thomson, Elihu, education and early work, 21, 22, 357; arc-lighting system, 22, 25, 33, 57; invents lightning arrester, 25; invents constant-current transformer, 65–66; as entrepreneur, 67–68, 192, 194, 338, 356, 357, 358; views on incandescent light, 80, 143; perfects a.c. transformer, 145

Thomson-Houston Electric Company, formation and growth of, 26–31; plant in Lynn, Mass., 26, 55; central-station business, 28, 157; Goff as sales agent, 34; patent licenses, 47; acquires numerous companies, 52, 53, 55–56; as carbon producer, 61, 62; agreements with Westinghouse, 145–146, 166; policy on a.c.-d.c. controversy, 175; supplies motors to Bentley-Knight, 227, 228; acquires Van Depoele patents, 233, 250; enters electric traction, 249–251; contract with West End Railway, 252–253, 343; purchased by General Electric, 321–329; innovations, 338, 359; economic growth, 363–364
Three-wire system, 99, 123, 167, 178, 205, 223, 238, 324, 360
Toronto Exhibition (1884), 231
Torque, of induction motor, 257, 297; of d.c. motor, 336
Transformer, constant-current for arc lighting, 65, 66; ordered from London by Westinghouse, 132; developed by Westinghouse, 135; made safe by Thomson, 145; at Niagara Falls, 288, 292; invention of two-phase–three-phase, 294, 315; made by Stanley, 306; early name "converter," 379n
Transmission voltage, of Westinghouse system, 138; of Edison system, 138; too low in d.c. power systems, 276; in German installation, 287; at Niagara Falls, 288, 289, 290; pioneer work of Stanley, 309–310; high-voltage, 337
Transportation, application of electric motor to, 211–212
Trolley patents, 325
Trolley wires, Edison's aversion to, 222
Tunnels, Niagara Falls, 282–283, 286
Turbines, steam, 310–313, 337, 389n
Turbines, water, at Niagara Falls, 286–288, 292; at Columbia, South Carolina, 303, 304
Turboalternator, 311–313, 337
Turrettini, Lieutenant-Colonel Theodore, 285
Twombley, Harrison M., 291, 322, 323

Underground conductors, in Edison system, 89, 90, 95, 96, 182
Underground conduits, 216, 225, 227–230, 252
Underrunning trolley, used by Van Depoele, 231; used by Sprague, 238, 245; patent on, 330, 331, 333, 334
Union Passenger Railway Company, 246–247
Union Switch and Signal Company, 130, 131, 136, 137–138
United Edison Manufacturing Company, 102
United Electric Light and Power Company, 140, 332
United Gas Improvement Company of Philadelphia, 196–197
United States Circuit Court (Massachusetts), patent decision, 39
United States Circuit Court (New York City), injunction against American Company, 40
United States Company, 41, 111, 164, 206
United States Electric Lighting Company, arc-lighting system, 26–27; development of local companies, 28; purchase of Weston, 32; effort to form "trust," 51–52; factory sold to Bergmann, 94; development work, 110, 147; incandescent system, 148; integrated with Westinghouse, 149; Edison Company patent suits, 152, 153; General Electric injunction against, 157
United States Rubber Company, 52
Unwin, Professor W. C., 285
Upton, Francis R., Edison associate, 89, 93, 96, 101, 102, 110, 123; General Electric official, 322, 323
Urban transportation, streetcars in operation (1880), 214
Urbanization, 4, 7

Vacuum pump, 76, 93
Van Depoele, Charles J., 53, 54; arc-lighting manufacturer, 230; electric-railway work, 230–234, 248; trolley patents, 325, 329, 331, 334, 390n; entrepreneurship, 338, 359
Van Depoele Electric Light Company, Chicago, arc-lighting manufacturing, 230; experiments in electric traction, 230–231; installations, 231–232, 339; purchased by Thomson-Houston, 233
Van Depoele Electric Manufacturing Company, purchased by Thomson-Houston, 53, 55–56, 250
Vanderbilt, W. K., 284
Villard, Henry, 101, 189; Edison associate, 85–86, 102–104, 219–220, 221, 248; in formation of General Electric, 321–322
Voltage variations, problem of, 106–108, 302
Voltages, technical changes, 309, 336, 337

Wabash Appliance Corporation, 359
Waddell-Entz, incandescent-lighting equipment, 127

Waldorf Hotel (New York City), Sprague elevators, 272
Walker Manufacturing Company, Cleveland, 262, 333–334, 340, 386n
Wallace, Professor D. H., on oligopoly, 353–354
Wallace and Sons, Ansonia, Conn., 15–16, 375n
Wallace-Farmer dynamo, 15, 16
Wanamaker, John, 16
Washington, D. C., Thomson-Houston electric railway contract, 251, 253–254
Water gas, process and advantages, 195–196
Water power, Niagara Falls, 282–295
Water turbines, Niagara power development, 286, 288, 292
Waterhouse Electric and Manufacturing Company, 147
Waters, E. G., 318–319
Welsbach, Carl Auer von, 196, 200
Wenstrom Company, 259
West End Street Railway Company, Boston, 228, 247, 252, 253, 267, 343
Western Electric Company, 126
Western Union Telegraph Company, 79, 84–85
Westinghouse, George, early life and inventions, 129, 130, 193–194; enters electrical industry, 131; develops a.c. lighting system, 132–139; initiates patent suit, 145; anger over a.c.-d.c. controversy, 171; views on alternating current, 171; pioneer innovator, 191; advises on Niagara power, 284; refuses to submit plan on Niagara, 285, 289; on frequency problem, 315; leadership of, 327; on patent agreements, 331
Westinghouse, H. H., 131
Westinghouse Air Brake Company, 130, 311, 340
Westinghouse Electric and Manufacturing Company, 311
Westinghouse Electric Company, 8, 38; patent agreement with General Electric, 128, 161, 164, 321, 329–334; formed 1886, 136–138; pricing policy, 140; central stations, 140–141; World's Fair contract, 142, 143; mergers, 146–149; enters arc lighting, 147; stopper lamp, 160; enters electric traction, 257, 272–274; develops induction motor, 278–280; develops a.c. power system, 281–282; polyphase apparatus at Chicago World's Fair, 281–282; secures Niagara Falls contract, 287–292; induction motors, 297–300; polyphase generators, 307–308; turboalternators, 310–311; duopoly, 318; innovations, 338, 340, 357, 359; economic growth, 364
Westinghouse Machine Company, 311
Westinghouse motors, railway, 257–262, 274; induction, 270–282, 297–299
Weston, Edward, work in electroplating, 31, 32; work in arc lighting, 31–34, 66–67; efficiency of arc-lighting system, 33; begins production of arc carbons, 58–59; imitative entrepreneur, 191–192
Weston dynamo, 15
Weston Dynamo Electric Machine Company, 31
Weston Electric Light Company, 31–34, 56, 57, 370n–372n
Weston Electrical Instrument Company, 32
Wheelbarrow suspension, Sprague development, 245, 324
Whitney, Henry M., 247, 252–253, 339
Wickes, E. A., 284, 291
Windsor, Ont., Van Depoele installation, 232
Winslow, Lanier, and Company, 284, 285
Wood, James J., 40, 52, 54
Wood patents, purchased by Thomson-Houston, 40, 54–56
Woonsocket, R. I., Bentley-Knight street railway contract, 227, 229, 249
Wright, J. Hood, 85, 101

Zipernowsky-Beri-Blathy alternating current system, 172

Bei Fragen zur Produktsicherheit wenden Sie sich bitte an:
If you have any questions regarding product safety,
please contact:

Walter de Gruyter GmbH
Genthiner Straße 13
10785 Berlin
productsafety@degruyterbrill.com